MEET THE PHILOSOPHERS OF ANCIENT GREECE

Dedicated to the memory of Panagiotis,
a humble man, who found pleasure when reading
about the philosophers of Ancient Greece

Meet the Philosophers
of Ancient Greece

Everything you always wanted to know
about Ancient Greek philosophy
but didn't know who to ask

Edited by

PATRICIA F. O'GRADY
Flinders University of South Australia

ASHGATE

Published by
Ashgate Publishing Limited
Gower House
Croft Road
Aldershot
Hampshire GU11 3HR
England

Ashgate Publishing Company
Suite 420
101 Cherry Street
Burlington, VT 05401-4405
USA

Ashgate website: http://www.ashgate.com

British Library Cataloguing in Publication Data
Meet the philosophers of ancient Greece : everything you always wanted to know about
   ancient Greek philosophy but didn't know who to ask
   1. Philosophy, Ancient 2. Philosophers – Greece 3. Greece – Intellectual life –
   To 146 B.C.
   I. O'Grady, Patricia F.
   180

Library of Congress Cataloging-in-Publication Data
Meet the philosophers of ancient Greece : everything you always wanted to know about
ancient Greek philosophy but didn't know who to ask / Patricia F. O'Grady, editor.
      p. cm.
   Includes bibliographical references and index.
   ISBN 0-7546-5131-2 (hardcover : alk. paper) – ISBN 0-7546-5132-0 (pbk. : alk. paper)
1. Philosophy, Ancient. I. O'Grady, Patricia F.

   B171.M44 2005
   180—dc22

                                                                              2004021055
ISBN 0 7546 5131 2 (hb)
ISBN 0 7546 5132 0 (ppk)

Printed and bound in Great Britain by MPG Books Ltd, Bodmin, Cornwall

Contents

PART VI: THE ROMAN PERIOD

PART VII: ARCHAEOLOGICAL SITES

List of Contributors

Dr George Arabatzis
Research Centre for Greek
Philosophy
of the Academy of Athens,
Anagnostopoulou 14
106 73 Athens-Greece
arabatzi@academyofathens.gr

Dr Dirk Baltzly
Monash University
Melbourne, Australia

Professor Linos G. Benakis,
PhD, PhD hc.
Research Fellow of the Academy of
Athens
Former Director of the Research
Centre of Greek Philosophy
Sina Str. 58, GR – 106 72 Athens
benakis@hol.gr

Dr G.S. Bowe
Program in Cultures Civilizations
and Ideas
And Department of Philosophy
Bilkent University, Ankara, Turkey
geoff.bowe@gmail.com

Alan Chalmers
Senior Research Fellow
Flinders University of South
Australia

Christina Clark, PhD
Assistant Professor
Classical and Near Eastern Studies
Creighton University
caclark@creighton.edu

Gabriele Cornelli, PhD
Ancient Philosophy Professor
Methodist University of
São Paulo, Brazil
gabrielec@uol.com.br

Dr Dirk L. Couprie
Independent Researcher
Maastricht, the Netherlands
dirkcouprie@dirkcouprie.nl

Dr Trevor Curnow
Senior Lecturer
Division of Religion and Philosophy
St Martin's College, Lancaster,
England.
t.curnow@ucsm.ac.uk

Sabatino DiBernardo, PhD
Instructor of Religion, Philosophy
and Humanities
University of Central Florida-
Brevard
sdiberna@pegasus.cc.ucf.edu
phone: (321) 632-111 ext. 65508

Aude Engel, PhD
University of Toulouse
Le Mirail, France

Dr Christine Farmer
Freelance lecturer and writer
Birmingham, UK
clfarmer@btinternet.com

Anne Farrell, PhD
Visiting Instructor
Georgia State University
afarrell@gsu.edu

Kevin T. Glowacki, PhD
Assistant Professor of Classical
Studies
Indiana University-Bloomington,
USA
kglowack@indiana.edu

Dr Andrew Gregory
Senior Lecturer in History of
Science
University College London
andrew.gregory@ucl.ac.uk

Leo Groarke
Dean of the Brantford Campus
Wilfrid Laurier University
lgroarke@wlu.ca

Dr Louis Groarke
Philosophy Department
York University
Antigonish, Nova Scotia
Canada B2G 2W5
lgroarke@yahoo.com

Virginia Haddad, MA
Adjunct Professor of Humanities
Imperial Valley College, California
VirginiaHaddad@mac.com

Dr Ian Hunt
Associate Professor of Philosophy
Head, Dept of Philosophy
School of Humanities,
Director, Centre for Applied
Philosophy,
Flinders University of South
Australia.
Ian.Hunt@flinders.edu.au

Antonia Kakavelaki
PhD student
Ecole Pratique des Hautes Etudes,
Paris
pahomios@hotmail.com

Dr Doukas Kapantaïs
Research Centre for Greek
Philosophy
At the Academy of Athens
Anagnostopoulou 14
106 73 Athens-Greece
keef@academyofathens.gr

Thomas Kiefer
University of Nebraska
tkiefer@msn.com

Hye-Kyung Kim, PhD
Assistant Professor of Philosophy
Department of Philosophy
University of Wisconsin-Green Bay
Green Bay, Wisconsin 54311 USA
Kimh@uwgb.edu

Dr Jonathan Lavery
Wilfrid Laurier University-Brantford
73 George St
Brantford, ON
N3T 2Y3 Canada
jlavery@wlu.ca

Bruce J. MacLennan, PhD
Associate Professor
University of Tennessee
Knoxville
maclennan@cs.utk.edu

James M. Magrini
Graduate Philosophy Student
DePaul University, Chicago

Dr Hope May
Assistant Professor of Philosophy
Central Michigan University.
mayhopee@msu.edu

Phillip Meade
Freelance writer
Fenton, Michigan

Melanie B. Mineo
Dowling College
Oakdale, New York
mmineo@optonline.net

Marjolein Oele
Department of Philosophy
Loyola University Chicago
Chicago, IL, USA
moele@luc.edu

Dr Patricia F. O'Grady
Adjunct Research Associate
Flinders University of South
Australia
patricia.ogrady@flinders.edu.au

Tim O'Keefe
Assistant Professor of Philosophy
Georgia State University
tokeefe@gsu.edu

Kartika Panwar
Freelance Writer
Canberra, Australia
kartika_panwar@optusnet.com.au

Deborah Nash Peterson, MA Phil
Department of Philosophy
Marquette University
Milwaukee, WI 53210
deborah.peterson@marquette.edu

Dr Robert Phiddian
Senior Lecturer in English
Flinders University
South Australia

Professor Heleen J. Pott
Erasmus University, Rotterdam
Department of Philosophy
pott@philosophy.unimaas.nl

Dr Maria Protopapas-Marneli
Research Centre for Greek
Philosophy
At the Academy of Athens
Anagnostopoulou 14
106 73 Athens-Greece
marproto@academyofathens.gr

Allan F. Randall
Dept. of Philosophy
York University
Toronto, Ontario, Canada
parmenides@elea.org

Glenn Rawson
Visiting Scholar in Classics
Brown University
Providence, Rhode Island

Dr Steven R. Robinson
Associate Professor
Brandon University
Manitoba, Canada
robinsons@brandonu.ca

Suzanne Roux, MA
Flinders University of
South Australia
Suzanne.roux@flinders.edu.au

Gerasimos Santas
Professor of Philosophy
University of California, Irvine

Professor Keith Seddon
Warnborough University
Canterbury, UK
k.h.s@btinternet.com

Daniel Silvermintz
Instructor of Humanities
University of Houston-Clear Lake
silvermintz@cl.uh.edu

Peter Sommer
TV Producer and
Archaeological tour leader
London, UK
petersommer@hotmail.com

Evanthia Speliotis
Associate Professor, Philosophy
Bellarmine University
Louisville, KY
espeliotis@bellarmine.edu

Dr William O. Stephens
Associate Professor Philosophy
and Classical and Near Eastern
Studies
Creighton University, Ohama, NE

Irene Svitzou
Attached Researcher
Research Centre for Greek
Philosophy
At the Academy of Athens
Anagnostopoulou 14
106 73 Athens-Greece
svitzou15ire@yahoo.gr

Seamus Sweeney, MB BCh BAO
Dublin University Postgraduate
Training Scheme in Psychiatry
Seamus.sweeney@campus.ie

Matthew Usher
Flinders University of South
Australia

Dave Yount, PhD
Professor and Chair of Philosophy
and Religious Studies
Mesa Community College
yount@mail.mc.maricopa.edu

Acknowledgements

Many people have played a role in crafting this book, and I wish to thank them all. My thanks go to the 50 contributors who recognized the purpose of the book—to relate the philosophy of the Ancient Greeks in terms that are attractive to general readers—and engaged in the project with enthusiasm and patience, and who offered wise advice. I am grateful to the members of the Department of Philosophy at Flinders University: Rodney Allen, Lynda Burns, Allan Chalmers, George Couvalis, Ian Hunt and Suzanne Roux who offered encouragement and willingly gave time and support when it was needed. My thanks to the staff of the Department of Modern Greek, Michael Tsianikas, George Frazis, and Maria Palaktsoglou for their support and enthusiasm, and special thanks to Mary Skaltsas for her love and attention.

Sincere thanks to Keith Seddon for creating beautiful maps, to Andrew Gregory for the unique Time Line, and to Glenn Rawson for agreeing to compile the Glossary. Thank you Trevor Curnow, Glenn Rawson, Kevin Glowacki, Charlie Blacklock, Tom Hines (who, by some minor miracle, was in Selcuk photographing the nearby ancient sites, Miletus, Priene, Didyma and Ephesus, when I first contacted him for a photo of Miletus) and Anne Thompson: all willingly offered images for inclusion in the book. Thank you to the generous anonymous benefactor who donated the cost of the exciting image of Pythagoras from Raphael's painting, *The School of Athens*.

My loving thanks to Suzanne Roux and Graham Wolf who were always there when I needed them, and to my granddaughters, Katherine and Sarah who have been touched by the magic of Ancient Greece. Thank you, Maureen, Julie, and Anne, secretaries extraordinaire, who generously and willingly gave their skills and assistance.

Thank you to Paul Coulam and Ann Newell of Ashgate Publishing for prompt and patient advice, and Emma McBriarty for meticulous editing.

Not least, my thanks go to Flinders University of South Australia for my appointment as Adjunct Research Associate and for providing the amenities to enable me to pursue my passion for Ancient Greek philosophy.

Thank you, *Every One. You* made the dream come true.

Foreword

Some time ago, I met a mature-age second-year student, let us call her Jenny, who said she was interested in philosophy but was intimidated by the word itself. She was uneasy about 'philosophy': she found the idea forbidding, without knowing what it meant or involved.

Philosophy is a Greek creation or discovery and philosophy is a Greek word: philos, lover, and sophia, wisdom—philosophy, then, is the love of wisdom and philosophers are the lovers, or seekers, of wisdom and knowledge.

Meet the Philosophers of Ancient Greece is intended for all the Jennys and Jacks who have an interest in the history of ideas, and who would like to know what philosophy is and how they can delve into it with confidence.

Because the philosophy of Ancient Greece lies at the foundation of western civilization, it seems sensible and wise to ensure that the ideas, theories, innovations and discoveries of the ancient philosophers are explained in an enticing style, so that everyone can read the good news about philosophy.

This book is a collection of 70 essays, written by men and women who are experts in their chosen area of philosophy. It requires a special set of skills for academics to explain in simple uncomplicated terms the theories of the Ancient Greeks, and the contributors to this collection have managed to bring to the reader theories that are often complex. Some of the ideas are still not fully understood—that is why philosophers continue to seek answers and understanding—but all are intriguing and engaging.

The essays in *Meet the Philosophers* cover the major themes, theories and arguments of the most prominent ancient philosophers. You meet other significant figures such as historians and playwrights, and experience the glories of ancient archaeological sites. You make the acquaintance of bold, imaginative, sometimes foolish people, and recognize their human qualities and their idiosyncrasies as well as their exceptional abilities, insight and courage.

This book is not meant, specifically, for philosophers—it is for everyone. In about 300 BC, Epicurus wrote to his friend Menoeceus:

> Let no one be slow to seek wisdom when he is young, nor weary in the search thereof when he is grown old. No age is too early or too late ... and to say that the season for studying philosophy has not yet come, or that it is past and gone, is like saying that the season for happiness is not yet or that it is no more. (Diogenes Laertius, *Lives of Eminent Philosophers* Bk. 10. 122)

Philosophy is a pursuit and activity that rewards effort and enriches lives. To all the Jennys and Jacks, the young, the old and those in between, this book is intended to inform and delight.

Patricia O'Grady, Editor. Adelaide, South Australia 2004.

List of Maps and Plates

The Greco-Roman theatre at Miletus, Turkey
    ©Thomas Hines, Professor of Theatre, Whitman College

Didyma: The last few hundred metres of the Sacred Way, the Processional
    Way, which connected the temples at Miletus and Didyma
    ©Trevor Curnow

List of Figures

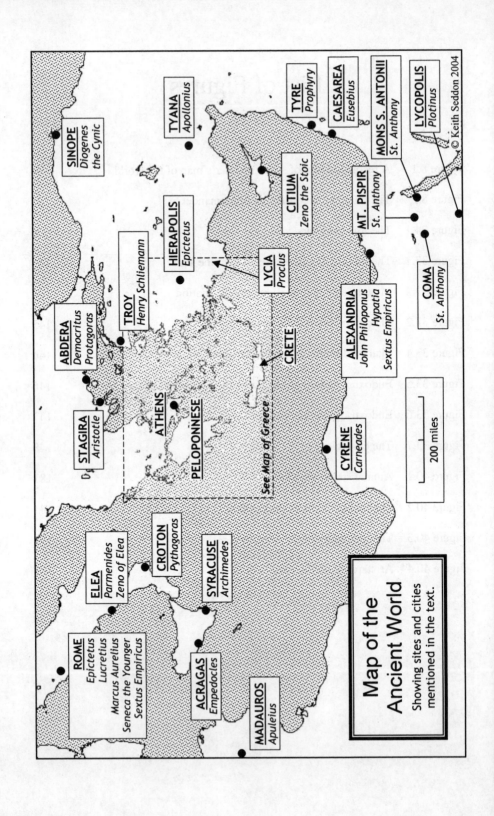

Map of the Ancient World

Showing sites and cities mentioned in the text.

© Keith Seddon 2004

SINOPE
Diogenes the Cynic

TYANA
Apollonius

TYRE
Prophyry

CAESAREA
Eusebius

MONS S. ANTONII
St. Anthony

LYCOPOLIS
Plotinus

CITIUM
Zeno the Stoic

MT. PISPIR
St. Anthony

HIERAPOLIS
Epictetus

TROY
Henry Schliemann

LYCIA
Proclus

ABDERA
Democritus Protagoras

CRETE

ALEXANDRIA
John Philoponus Hypatia Sextus Empiricus

COMA
St. Anthony

STAGIRA
Aristotle

ATHENS

PELOPONNESE

CYRENE
Carneades

See Map of Greece

200 miles

ELEA
Parmenides Zeno of Elea

CROTON
Pythagoras

SYRACUSE
Archimedes

ROME
Epictetus Lucretius Marcus Aurelius Seneca the Younger Sextus Empiricus

ACRAGAS
Empedocles

MADAUROS
Apuleius

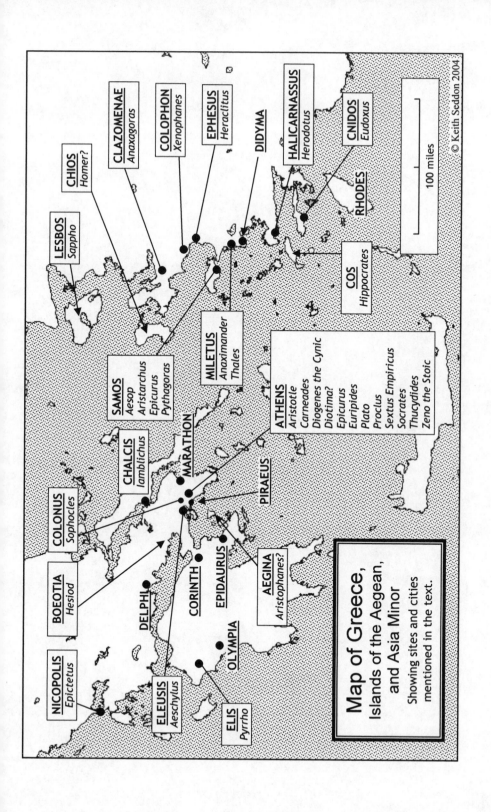

**Map of Greece,
Islands of the Aegean,
and Asia Minor**

Showing sites and cities
mentioned in the text.

© Keith Seddon 2004

100 miles

CHIOS
Homer?

CLAZOMENAE
Anaxagoras

COLOPHON
Xenophanes

EPHESUS
Heraclitus

DIDYMA

HALICARNASSUS
Herodotus

CNIDOS
Eudoxus

RHODES

COS
Hippocrates

LESBOS
Sappho

SAMOS
*Aesop
Aristarchus
Epicurus
Pythagoras*

MILETUS
*Anaximander
Thales*

ATHENS
*Aristotle
Carneades
Diogenes the Cynic
Diotima?
Epicurus
Euripides
Plato
Proclus
Sextus Empiricus
Socrates
Thucydides
Zeno the Stoic*

CHALCIS
Iamblichus

MARATHON

PIRAEUS

COLONUS
Sophocles

BOEOTIA
Hesiod

NICOPOLIS
Epictetus

DELPHI

CORINTH

EPIDAURUS

AEGINA
Aristophanes?

ELEUSIS
Aeschylus

OLYMPIA

ELIS
Pyrrho

PART I
INTRODUCTORY ESSAYS

Chapter 1

Introduction

Alan Chalmers

What is the nature of being? Is change possible? These seem extraordinary questions, the first because the degree of abstraction involved makes it difficult to get a grip on what is being asked, the second because the answer seems so obviously to be 'yes'. Extraordinary as these questions may seem to be, it was precisely the formulation and attempts to answer these and others like them that were the preoccupation of those who first introduced philosophy into the world, in Ionia in Greece in the sixth century before the Christian era. Thales answered the first question by asserting that everything is made of water, and answered the second by understanding change as the transition from one form of water to another. Anaximander proposed 'the unlimited' as the foundation of all being, a substance with no analogues in the world of our experience. He understood change as the constant conflict of opposites, the hot and the cold, the wet and the dry, which separate out from the unlimited. Heraclitus chose fire as the foundation of being to capture the idea that everything is forever in flux, as illustrated in his famous declaration that one cannot step into the same river twice.

If these views do not seem strange enough, consider how Italian philosophers responded to such attempts to capture the fundamental nature of being in the late sixth and early fifth centuries. Pythagoras insisted that it is number that lies at the basis of all things, whilst Parmenides had arguments to the effect that change is impossible, concluding that the universe is a homogeneous unchanging sphere. The apparent strangeness and degree of abstraction of these deliberations should not lead us to dismiss them as unreasonable because it is precisely reason that led these first philosophers to pose the questions that they did and propose the kinds of answers that they came up with. Imagine a particular green leaf turning brown in autumn. The appearance of the leaf changes, but it is still the same leaf, is it not? But does that not mean that the nature of the leaf, what it is that makes that one leaf what it is, is something other than its appearances? By pushing this kind of reasoning to its limits we soon find ourselves in the kind of deliberation that preoccupied the first philosophers. My example of the leaf also raises a fundamental issue about the respective roles of reason and the evidence of the senses in answering questions about the nature of the world. That is a fundamental issue that the Greek philosophers grappled with and to which they offered various answers, and it remains a central issue in philosophy today.

In the previous paragraph I talk of reason, that is, reasoned, logical thought, a notion that we take for granted. But it was Thales and the early Greek and Italian philosophers who first introduced such a notion and made it a key tool in philosophy. Previously, the nature of the world was understood in anthropomorphic terms involving myths about the actions of gods of various kinds, as evidenced in the writings of Homer, and especially Hesiod. The early philosophers struggled to give a rational account of the world that did not resort to myths involving personal gods possessing super-human powers. The sophistication of the logical machinery that the philosophers developed is very evident in their mathematics. Thales proved that a diagonal bisects a circle and developed a geometry that enabled him to estimate the height of a pyramid from the length of its shadow, whilst Pythagoras not only proved the theorem that bears his name but used it to prove that if the side of a square can be represented as made up of a whole number of units, however small, then its diagonal cannot. That is, he discovered what we now call irrational numbers. Anyone that has struggled to find a definitive answer to Zeno's paradoxes (how can you overtake the tortoise if as soon as you get to where it was it has moved further ahead) should begin to get the feel for the kind of enterprise that the first philosophy involved.

Part 3 of this collection gives an account of the pioneers of philosophy over a couple of centuries up to and including Socrates. Part 2 gives a taste of the Greek writings that preceded their work by way of contrast.

A major problem with a reconstruction of the work of many of the philosophers of Ancient Greece is the lack of access to their writings, most of which have not come down to us. Deducing what their philosophy involved from various fragments attributed to them can be little more than guesswork. It is typically the case that to interpret a quotation from the writings of a philosopher we need to put that quotation in the context that gives meaning to it. Descartes (born in France in 1596 AD, a mathematician, natural scientist and philosopher of the modern era, who brought about the rebirth of ancient philosophy and is often considered to be the father of modern philosophy) once ridiculed Aristotle for defining motion as 'the functioning of potential as potential', claiming the phrase to be unintelligible. On the face of it, Aristotle's definition gives some substance to the famous caricature of philosophers as those who discuss what everyone understands using language that no-one understands. But once we understand the context in which that definition occurs, it is not unintelligible at all. Aristotle was tackling the problem that some of the earlier philosophers had had with change by proposing that there are two kinds of being, actual being and potential being. So, for example, an important part of what makes an olive seed what it is, in addition to its state as a seed, its actual being, is its capacity to grow into an olive tree, its potential being. In the process of growing, the seed has not yet fulfilled its capacity to become an olive tree but is in the process of doing so. So the growing is the functioning of potential, the capacity to become an oak tree, as potential, because it has not yet fulfilled that potential.

Because of the need to understand the context, in order to make sense of the utterances of philosophers, our understanding of the early philosophers will always be speculative to a considerable degree because the texts that would give us that context have been lost. This, fortunately, is not the case with the major philosophers of the classical period, Plato and Aristotle. Abundant textual material on their systems of philosophy has come down to us either directly or indirectly, and our task is to try to make consistent and coherent sense of it. Accounts of the Platonic and Aristotelian frameworks, as well as of some of the contemporaries of Plato and Aristotle are given in Part 4.

Part 5 contains accounts of philosophers writing in the Hellenistic period, that is the period that stretches for about three hundred years from the date of the death of Alexander the Great, himself a pupil of Aristotle, in 323 BC, to the foundation of the Roman Empire. Three new philosophical systems emerged in that time, namely, Stoicism, Epicureanism, and Skepticism. All of these systems tended to focus on individual human beings as such and to ask how they might best fulfill themselves, this perhaps being a response to the uncertainty of the times that was experiencing the disintegration of the Alexandrian empire. The three systems gave quite different answers to the question. The Epicureans focused on providing an account of the nature of the Universe that focused on our use of reason to eliminate fears based on falsehoods, such as fear of an afterlife or attributing thunderstorms to the wrath of a God. The Stoics stressed the need to understand nature in order that we reconcile ourselves to things over which we have no control, whilst the Skeptics sought solace in the idea that we do not have the means to definitively understand anything, recommending that we become reconciled to this and stop worrying and arguing. The philosophers of the Hellenistic era still tended to congregate in Athens. However, in other centers during this period, such as Alexandria, there were developments in more specific areas of knowledge such as science, geography and astronomy as opposed to the construction of philosophical systems. Archimedes' work on the balance and flotation, and the astronomy of Aristarchus are examples.

The philosophy of the Roman period, the concern of Part 6, was eclectic, no one system gaining dominance. Stoicism had some notable Roman followers, such as Marcus Aurelius, and Platonism also had an impact in the period, especially in religious contexts. But, in general, intellectual activity was diverse. There were, nevertheless, extensive commentaries on Greek philosophy by such as Cicero and Simplicius whilst Sextus Empiricus was an able expositor of Skepticism.

With the collapse of the Roman Empire it was in the Byzantine world that the development of Greek philosophy was continued. It was not until the eleventh or twelfth centuries of the modern era that interest was resumed in the western world.

Part 7 contains descriptions of Greek Archeological sites. It helps to remind us that the Greek philosophers were real people living in specific material and social conditions. Thales made a fortune by cornering the market in olive oil, Aristotle lived in the city-state of Athens and took slavery for granted, although he himself did not qualify as a citizen of Athens because he was not born there. Epicurus lived in an Athenian house with a large garden frequented by a group of individuals, including women and even slaves, who practised as well as discussed the Epicurean philosophy.

The achievements of the Greek philosophers stand in various relations to knowledge of today. Their achievements in logic and mathematics can be recognized as such and find a place in contemporary knowledge. Pythagoras's theorem still forms a part of Euclidean geometry and the Pythagorian proof of it remains a proof, whilst it appears that Archimedes anticipated the infinitesimal calculus. The syllogism as formulated by Aristotle remains a valid form of logical deduction, whilst logicians still struggle to give the definitive answer to Zeno's paradoxes. Some of Greek science that was linked fairly directly with observation, such as Archimedes' account of the lever and of floating bodies, lives on in contemporary physics whilst the detail recorded in Aristotle's biology, such as his perceptive observations on the behavior of bees, served as a valuable basis for future work. Ancient Greek philosophy stands up least from a modern point of view in those areas where they clearly lacked the resources to answer the questions they posed but which are now available through the advances of science. Debates about whether matter is atomic or continuous come into this category. The underlying mechanisms conjured up by the early philosophers as attempts to explain such things as the operation of the senses or the origins of the earth come across as implausible and wild guesses to a modern eye. By contrast, the attempts by the Greeks to grapple with ethics and basic issues about how our lives should be organized still speak to us, perhaps because this is an area that has not been taken over by science.

Chapter 2

What is Philosophy?

Trevor Curnow

Let us accept that world of mist as the material out of which to make a life that is more Complete. (José Ortega y Gasset, *What is Philosophy?*)

Some ancient schools of philosophy divided their subject into three areas, which they called physics, logic and ethics. Each addressed a fundamental question. What is the world like? How is knowledge possible? How should we live? While this particular way of structuring the subject was never universal, these three questions seem to me to go to the heart of what philosophy is. They are questions that never go away.

Of course, over the centuries philosophers have come up with different answers to them, and had different views concerning their relative importance. Some have constructed blueprints for the cosmos. Some have doubted whether knowledge is possible. Some have denied that it is the business of philosophy to deal with practical matters. Times have their fashions and individuals have their idiosyncrasies.

Some would argue that it is for science to tell us what the world is like, or for religion to tell us how to live. But how do we judge whether science or religion has got things right? Philosophy is critical as well as creative, and for this reason there are such subjects as the philosophy of science and the philosophy of religion. And we should not be too distracted by labels. Much of theoretical physics and theology, for example, is simply philosophy by another name. Both deal with the fundamental questions.

Unfortunately, those who deal with fundamental questions are likely to have fundamental disagreements, and this is certainly true of philosophy. Students are often surprised to find that different 'introductions' to philosophy can appear to be introductions to quite different subjects! In philosophy, nothing is beyond dispute, not even the nature of the subject itself.

Naturally, this can be very confusing. However, as I have been trying to reassure students for years, confusion is an important part of the philosophical experience. In order to see the point of tackling a problem, it is necessary to see that there really is a problem. In this context, confusion is positive rather than negative. Confusion motivates us to try and discover what the problem is, and then to try and find a solution to it.

However, finding a solution is easier said than done. For a subject that has been systematically practised for well over two thousand years, philosophy is surprisingly short on solutions to the problems it identifies. While it would be wrong to say there has been no progress, it is hard to say exactly what that progress consists in. Certainly advances have been made in areas such as logic, but it is difficult to avoid the conclusion that the history of philosophy seems to be characterized more by failure than by success. Yet failure can be valuable and instructive. Closing off a blind alley may not tell us which way to go, but it can at least reduce our chances of going the wrong way.

Philosophy is often associated with the use of argument. While argument is scarcely unique to philosophy, it is a key element of it. We want to know not only *that* a particular direction is a blind alley, but also *why*. If the reasons are not convincing, then we may rightly doubt whether it is a blind alley at all.

But argument has to end somewhere, or, to look at it another way, begin somewhere. If I agree that something is true, then I may agree that a whole range of other things are also true. The problem is with that original something. If I can prove it, then it rests on something else. If I cannot prove it, and cannot disprove it, then I have to choose whether to assume it or not. One of the strengths of philosophy is that by persistent questioning it leads us to fundamental assumptions, and duly reveals them to be assumptions. And assumptions are always precarious. This is why many people find philosophy uncomfortable. The search for certainty tends to lead to its opposite.

If that is the case, what is the gain? The gain is a deepening of understanding and an increase in awareness, no small achievements. (And some do claim to find certainty, although their claims are rarely left undisputed.) To ask the fundamental questions and to come up with the best answers to them that we can, that, to my mind, is philosophy.

Chapter 3

What Greek Philosophy
Means to Us Today

Ian Hunt

Reflection on childhood can be both charming and troubling: while we might enjoy looking back on its promise and hope, we are also capable of sorrow for its lost freshness. These same feelings are evoked by the childhood of our intellectual civilization, born with such great wealth of insight and promise in Ancient Greek Science and Philosophy. But reflection on beginnings is more than a form of nostalgia: we can learn from it—even gain some renewal from it.

Ancient Greek Philosophy began with natural philosophy. From Thales to Parmenides and Zeno, early Greek Philosophers debated the ultimate nature of the world, striving for general principles by which to account for nature similar to those developed by mathematicians to explain geometrical relationships. The first philosopher, Thales, claimed that transformations from solid to liquid states held the key to natural change, and speculated that liquids were the ultimate substance of all things. Although we now see this as a first step of child-like simplicity toward natural science, Thales' ingenious use of general principles to solve practical problems can prompt a gasp of awe even today. Thus he is justly still celebrated for proposing that he could measure the height of the great pyramid at Giza by measuring the length of its shadow at the time of day when the length of his own shadow equalled his height.

Early Greek Philosophy developed into the great achievements of the Classical period, dominated by two schools of thought: the school of Plato, who thought that things could be explained by their relationship to ideas; and the school of Aristotle, who thought that nature could be explained by the four principles that we can use to account for the nature of artifacts, although natural things are self-made rather than made by another (see essay, *Aristotle*). Plato and Aristotle also introduced important ideas concerning the nature of the good life. In later Greek Philosophy, Stoics and Epicureans debated the use of Philosophy as a guide to life.

From these periods, two achievements stand out as highly significant. The Philosophers of Ancient Greece discovered powerful reasoning strategies, which they employed to make fundamental foundational discoveries in philosophy, mathematics and logic; while their contributions to social Philosophy have been of such lasting significance that they must still be included in philosophical discussion today.

Self-conscious use of rational reasoning to raise and solve challenging problems is, perhaps, the source of the great achievement of the Classical period of Greek Philosophy, in which Aristotle's Logic codified reasoning from general principles. This logic, along with the insight of the Stoics, remained definitive until the twentieth century. Ancient Greek reflection on rational reasoning not only included the development of formal logic but the more informal study of debating technique, which has its definitive expression in Plato's Socratic dialogues. In his *Parmenides*, Plato uses the dramatic form of a dialogue to reflect on one of the most celebrated and powerful reasoning strategies, first employed extensively in ancient Greek philosophy, in which an assumption is refuted by showing that an absurdity or, more strictly, a contradiction follows logically from it.

Greek mathematicians used this method of argument with devastating effect for the Pythagorean School of Philosophy, who believed that whole numbers and their ratios captured the essence of all things. According to the theorem known after the Head of this School, Pythagoras himself, the square on the hypotenuse of a right-angled triangle has an area equal to the sum of the squares on the other two sides. One member of the School then asked: does the length of the hypotenuse of a triangle whose sides are both one foot long have a proper measure by a whole number, or ratio of whole numbers? According to Pythagoras' theorem, the square of its length must be 2 square feet and its length, therefore, must be the square root of that. By supposing that this measure has a Pythagorean essence, a contradiction can then be deduced. The problem is that the square root of 2, $\sqrt{2}$, cannot be expressed as a ratio because, in decimal notation, $\sqrt{2} = 1.4142135$ only approximately, and, although we can get a closer approximation, we can never get an exact equality, no matter how many decimal places we add. So this triangle—otherwise an impeccable example of right angled triangles—cannot have a numerical essence, as Pythagorean philosophy supposed.

Though Pythagoras' fanciful philosophy of numerology ultimately survived this argument, it reputedly had a more fatal effect on its discoverer, who is said to have been drowned by other members of the Pythagorean School in an attempt to suppress the embarrassing discovery. Today the argument is more memorable for the discovery of the new realm of 'irrational' numbers, whose numerical representation as a decimal goes on endlessly after the decimal point. The most famous of these numbers is the number π, the ratio of the circumference of a circle to its diameter, which we approximate with the fraction 22 divided by 7, or the following ratio in decimal form: 3.14285; we can never get an exact expression for it, no matter how many numbers we add after the decimal point.

Equally memorable, and still intellectually disturbing, is the use of the method by the early Greek philosopher, Zeno of Elea, to demonstrate that contradictions flow from accepting the reality of visible things that are indefinitely divisible into many parts. We encounter a report of Socrates' discussion with Zeno and Parmenides in Plato's *Parmenides* dialogue, where Plato imagines a young Socrates trying to refute Zeno by proposing a distinction between a thing and its qualities. According to Socrates, significant qualities of things are archetypes, for which Plato uses the term 'Forms'. A square thing is square because it is like the archetype of all square things, the quality of squareness itself, or the 'Form' of squareness. The quality of squareness is one thing and indivisible, while things that are square are many and divisible. Socrates argues that his theory of Forms answers Zeno's claim that it is a contradiction to say that anything is both one and many—as one must seem to say if one allows that the world contains many distinct things which are also one in some respect, such as shape. Socrates proposes that many square things are one in sharing a likeness to the Form of squareness, which is consistent with their remaining many by occupying different places.

The *Parmenides* dialogue is an especially interesting demonstration of the sophistication of Greek reasoning, because Plato does not merely present the case of Socrates, with which he sympathizes, but allows Parmenides to challenge Socrates' solution to Zeno by arguing that any distinction between a thing and its qualities will raise a further problem for the relationship of likeness between the thing and its qualities.

Apart from immense advances in the art of reasoning, ancient Greek philosophy has raised issues that remain part of the currency of important philosophical debate today. Take the wonderful perception Aristotle displays, when he identifies the crucial character of a human community. According to Aristotle, human communities are distinctive in that they rest on the power of speech, which enables humans to arrive at a reasoned, shared view of what is good and bad, just and unjust. Human speech is distinct from the 'voice' some animals possess, which enables them to express parts of their experience, such as pain or pleasure, but not to share a conception of justice, as members of human communities do.

In contemporary philosophy, John Rawls has taken this conception of the foundation of human communities to identify a shared understanding of what is just and unjust that ideally would be shared by members of societies who are committed to equality of persons and respect for each other's pursuit of conceptions of what makes for a good life. He bestows the same foundational role to a shared sense of what is just and unjust as does Aristotle, and addresses the specific sense of justice, concerned with a fair share of the burdens and benefits of social cooperation, which Aristotle over two thousand years ago distinguished from an umbrella notion of justice as compliance with good laws.

Rawls takes Aristotle's views on justice and their role in constituting human communities as the starting point for his own theory of justice and engages with them as though they still had contemporary force. In particular, he repudiates Aristotle's view that justice in both senses calls for social arrangements that enable humans to function well in accordance with human nature, just as maintenance in good working order enables a machine to function well as a loom or water pump.

To engage with the works of ancient Greek philosophers like Plato or Aristotle is a double delight: they open a window on our intellectual past; and we find, sometimes to our surprise, that they confront us with issues and views of lasting significance.

PART II
THE PRECURSORS OF PHILOSOPHY

Chapter 4

Homer

Dates unknown, the Homeric poems were probably written between 725–625 BC

Seamus Sweeney

> Stay at home or fight your hardest—your share will be the same. Coward and hero are
> honoured alike. Death does not distinguish do-nothing and do-all. And it has done me
> no profit to have suffered all that pain in fighting on ceaselessly with my life at
> constant risk. (*Iliad*, Book 9 Lines 317-322, translated Martin Hammond)

It is difficult, if not impossible, to overstate the influence of the *Iliad* and the
Odyssey on Western thought, art and culture. A near-cliché of Classics is that
the *Iliad* was the template for Greek tragedy, the *Odyssey* for comedy—and given
the pervasive influence of these models on our own culture, it could be said that
Homer created it.

Whether or not Homer actually existed is a moot point, although modern
scholarship and improved knowledge of the oral poetry tradition supports the idea
that the *Iliad* and *Odyssey* were created by the same person. Naturally traditions
sprang up to fill the biographical void; Homer was said to be a blind, illiterate
singer from the island of Chios in Asia Minor (south of Troy). There is much
evidence that the *Odyssey* is of a later period in Ionian culture, but it is perfectly
conceivable that both could have been the creations of a single lifetime.

The Homeric corpus rapidly became part of the common cultural legacy of all
Greeks, although ironically Homer never used the word 'Greeks' in his work, using
instead Argives, Danaans or Achaians. Professional singers of Homeric epic—the
rhapsodes—continued to flourish alongside the emergent Athenian tragedians. In
the Socratic dialogue *Ion*, Socrates (or rather Plato via Socrates) ridicules the
rhapsode Ion, who is lead by Socrates from boasts of his skill in performing
Homer into obvious absurdities, such as asserting that a good *rhapsode* is also a
good general. Fragments of Homer are extant in manuscripts from the sixth century
BC, but it was in Alexandria from the third century BC onwards that scholars, most
famously Aristarchus of Samothrace (c.216–144 BC), created the text that we still
possess.

It is entirely possible to read the two poems purely for entertainment, as
wonderful stories in their own right. The focus of the *Iliad* is primarily on Achilles,
while that of the *Odyssey* is on Odysseus (depending on which translation you
read, there are various renderings of the names of Greek characters. The character
usually known as Achilles is often translated as Akhilleus or Achilleus—in this

essay I will use the 'traditional' names, those most often used in English) but both contain a host of memorable supporting characters.

The action of the *Iliad* is concentrated into a four-day period in the ten year war. The roots of the Trojan War lay in the abduction of Helen, wife of Menelaus of Sparta, by Paris of Troy. Menelaus and his brother Agamemnon, King of Mycenae, raised an army from all Greece. When the *Iliad* begins, the war has already lasted nearly ten years—the Greeks have had marginally the better of the battle due to the superior martial skill of Achilles, their leading fighter, to anyone on the Trojan side. The poem opens:

> Sing, O goddess, the anger of Achilles son of Peleus, that brought countless ills upon the Achaeans. (Translation by Samuel Butler, lines 1-3)

This wrath of Achilles, which is the driving force of the poem, is caused by an argument between Agamemnon and Achilles. After Agamemnon treats Chryses, the Trojan Priest of Apollo who comes to the camp seeking the release of his daughter Chrysëis, with casual disdain, Apollo inflicts plague on the Greek camp. In the council called to consider this Agamemnon—who emerges from the early part of the *Iliad* as a capricious tyrant—rounds on the augur who correctly traces the plague to the anger of Apollo, and urges the release of Chrysëis, who has been taken as a concubine by Agamemnon. Agamemnon agrees to her release only if he takes possession of Brisëis, Achilles' woman. Angered, Achilles calls on his mother, Thetis the sea-nymph. The scenes between the divine Thetis and the human Achilles are among the most touching in the *Iliad*. Thetis is aware of her son's mortal nature and all too brief predicted span of life. In the course of the poem, Thetis is agonized by the fact that her actions aimed to increase Achilles' honour and glory are inevitably hastening his death. In this case, Thetis tells Achilles to withdraw from fighting, and Zeus will ensure Trojan success which will highlight Achilles' quality.

The gods are divided on the matter of the war. Thetis aside, 'the gods who live in their ease' (Book 6, line 138), have a frivolous, carefree attitude to the affairs of men. Like Sophocles, Homer portrays humanity as insignificant yet capable of a nobility in suffering denied the gods. Over the next eight books—eight books filled with brutal battle scenes, with the famous 'Catalogue of the Ships' itemizing the Greek fighting force—of the poem, the Trojans are victorious and it becomes obvious that for the Greeks to prevail, Achilles must be persuaded to return to the fighting. In Book 9, in a masterpiece of sustained argument in which Achilles seems to question the whole heroic ideal which has underpinned his life, Achilles resists the arguments of Odysseus, his friend Ajax and his former tutor Phoinix to return to the fighting. He concedes that he will return to the fray only when Hector, the Trojan champion, reaches the ships and huts of his own troops, the Myrmidons. Now it is Achilles who is stubborn and unreasonable.

Over the next few books the fighting increases in intensity, and ultimately Achilles allows another concession—his great friend, the gentle Patroclus, is to enter battle wearing Achilles' armour to boost Greek morale. After killing the Trojan warrior Sarpedon, Patroclus is himself killed by Hector. Enraged with grief and remorse at his wrath that has led to the death of so many, Achilles demands that Thetis help him kill Hector, even though, as Thetis tells him, this will lead to his own death.

With new armour forged by Hephaistos, the blacksmith god, Achilles re-enters the combat with ferocity. Killing Hector after a long exciting pursuit, he then drags his body three times each day around Patroclus' tomb—a desecration abominable in his times. In the final scene, Priam, king of Troy, meets Achilles on the field to beg for the return of his son's body. Achilles accedes—Priam's grief reminds him of his own for Patroclus, and his own father. The *Iliad* ends with Hector's burial, and with Achilles' doom hanging heavily over the reader.

The *Odyssey*, with its adventurous story, redemptive ending and series of exotic settings and events, is often easier for modern readers than the *Iliad*, with its stern immersal in the pity of war. The *Odyssey* has become the basis for a children's cartoon series and, of course, James Joyce's *Ulysses* (Ulysses being the Latinization of 'Odysseus'). Yet suffering is never far in the *Odyssey*—indeed the word 'suffering' occurs not only in line 2 of the *Iliad* but also line 8 of the *Odyssey*. It begins:

> Sing in me, Muse, and through me tell the story
> Of that man, skilled in all ways of contending,
> The wanderer, harried for years on end,
> After he plundered the stronghold,
> Of the proud height of Troy. (trans. Robert Fitzgerald, lines 1-5)

What follows is the story of Odysseus, the man 'skilled in all ways of contending', and his return home to Ithaca. The poem opens with Odysseus held captive by the enchantress Calypso on her island. During his absence, Odysseus' wife Penelope has been besieged by dissolute, money-grabbing and increasingly insolent suitors, and their island home, Ithaca, has suffered neglect and decline.

Since the end of the war, Odysseus and his crew have had many adventures in a world of enchantment and surprise—outwitting the one-eyed Cyclops Polyphemus by blinding him and escaping from his cave under his sheep (which has the unfortunate effect of incurring the wrath of Polyphemus' father, Poseidon, with obvious repercussions for a naval voyage); rowing past the Sirens, sea nymphs whose beautiful singing lured sailors to their doom—the crew stopped their ears with beeswax while Odysseus tied himself to the mast; the twin threats of the monster Scylla and the whirlpool Charybdis in the straits of Messina; the temptation of the Island of the Lotus-eaters, who feed on flowers that banish earthly cares; and many other lively adventures that have entered the collective treasury of world literature. Odysseus' crew is gradually decimated by all this, as well as the violent storms sent by Poseidon; they also manage to let loose the bag containing the winds which Aeolus, lord of the winds, gave to Odysseus and later kill the sacred cattle of the sun-god Helios, leading to their destruction along with their ship by a thunderbolt from Zeus. These incidents are recounted by Odysseus at a later stage in the poem, when, after being released by Calypso by Zeus' orders, he is blown off course yet again by a Poseidon-sent storm and is cast up on the shores of the land of Scheria and is a guest of the King.

A Scherian ship takes Odysseus back to Ithaca (in a final fit of divine petulance, Poseidon turns the vessel into a rock on its return to Scheria). Penelope has remained faithful throughout Odysseus' absence, promising to choose another husband when she has finished a shroud for Odysseus' father Laertes, and undoing the day's work on this garment each night. This stratagem has been discovered and she is forced into choosing a husband from the unattractive array of suitors.

For his own safety, the goddess Athena disguises Odysseus as an old beggar. In a touching recognition scene he reveals his identity to his son, Telemachus. Returning to his house, still in disguise, Odysseus in beaten by two of the more noxious suitors. Penelope announces her decision to marry the man capable of stringing Odysseus' bow and shooting an arrow through a line of twelve axe-heads. All the suitors attempt this with no success, until Odysseus, still in beggar's disguise, succeeds and, aided by Telemachus and his former steward, kills the remaining suitors. Finally Odysseus convinces Penelope of his true identity by means of his detailed knowledge of their bedstead. The hero has come home and restored his house and the fortunes of Ithaca.

As the culmination of the oral poetry tradition, both epics feature its conventions; Homer uses 'epithets', adjectives which generally describe a noun when it appears in the work—'glorious Achilles fleet of foot', 'crafty Odysseus', 'rose-fingered dawn'. It never becomes a stale convention, as Homer varies his stock of epithets (for example, in both poems there is a total of over seventy words used to describe ships) and uses them to enhance our awareness of the individual characters of the vast work. Certain lines and phrases are repeated; of the approximately 28,000 lines of both poems, 2,000 different lines recur once or more, and with their recurrence make a total of 5,500 lines. Again this is part of the distinctive epic style, and the use of typical scenes, known as 'themes', recurrently, is part of the oral tradition that helps create an effect of timelessness, of an underpinning in ritual and tradition.

M.M. Willcock's description of the Homeric epics as 'the earliest and greatest works of Greek literature' is entirely justified. An equal claim could be made for their status in world literature. Only the Bible surpasses the two epic poems attributed to Homer for the range of incidents and characters seared deep into our cultural consciousness. A summary of the epics can only give a pale impression of both works. Readers are strongly advised to read them for themselves.

References and Suggestions for Further Reading

Translations of all the Homeric works are available online at
http://classics.mit.edu/Browse/index.html

Camps, W.A. *An Introduction to Homer*. Oxford: Oxford University Press, 1980.
Finley, M.I. *The World of Odysseus*. Available in New York Review Books Classics, New York. First published 1956, revised edition 1979.

Fitzgerald, Robert. *The Odyssey*. London: William Heinemann, 1961.

Griffin, Jasper. *Homer on Life and Death*. Oxford: Oxford University Press, 1980.

Hammond, Martin. Introduction to *The Iliad*. Harmondsworth: Penguin, 1987.

Willcock, M.M. '*Homer*' in *Who's Who in the Classical World*. Oxford: Oxford University Press, 2000.

Chapter 5

Hesiod

8th–7th Century BC

Aude Engel

> Shepherds of the wilderness, wretched things of shame, mere bellies, we know how to speak many false things as though they were true; but we know, when we will, to utter true things. (Hesiod, *Theogony*, 26-29)

In such a way the Muses address Hesiod, teacher of all Greeks, whose poetry in ancient times was almost as famous and revered as Homer's. This is how Hesiod introduces himself: not as a poet, not as a thinker, but as a mere farmer who happened to receive a divine revelation. This divine inspiration came to Hesiod on a mountain in Boeotia, near Hesiod's home town, 'a miserable hamlet, Ascra, which is bad in winter, sultry in summer, and good at no time' (Hesiod, *Works and Days*, 640).

There were nine Muses, lovable personifications of all aspects of knowledge and the arts, who sang and danced at the festivities of the Olympian gods. At later times, these most influential of the Greek gods were attributed with responsibility for one of the arts: Clio presided over history; Euterpe over music; Thalia over comedy; Melpomene over tragedy; Terpsichore over dance; Erato over elegy; Polyhymnia over lyric poetry; Urania over astronomy; and Calliope over eloquence. These daughters of Mnemosyne (Memory) and of the great Zeus, appear veiled in a coat of Night, to deliver words of Light, and thus transform Hesiod, a peasant, into a king, bearer of truth and interpreter of Zeus' Justice.

The new world-order, which is to replace the ancient aristocratic ideals portrayed in Homer's *Iliad*, is all about order and justice. In his *Theogony*, Hesiod writes what the muses reveal to him—he organizes in genealogies the numerous gods and goddesses from various local pantheons, in order to present the foundations of a Greek panhellenic religion, in which the figure of Zeus already announces monotheism. In his second major poem, *Works and Days*, Hesiod explains how Zeus's justice is to be transposed in everyday human life, and how one must lead one's life. So cosmic and theological developments naturally induce a moral doctrine.

As in modern physics, the Hesiodic world evolves from Chaos to some form of order. But it is modern physics that borrows a word from Hesiod's poetry: the word Chaos, a creation dating back to verses from the 8th or 7th century BC! Fond of etymologies, Hesiod uses the root of the Greek word *chasma* (the ancestor of our modern 'chasm'), and creates Chaos, a God which he places at the origins of all things:

> Verily at the first Chaos came to be, but next wide-bosomed Earth, the ever-sure foundation of all the deathless ones who hold the peaks of snowy Olympus, and dim Tartarus in the depth of the wide-pathed Earth, and Eros (Love), fairest among the deathless gods. (*Th*.115-120)

Several problems are posed in these few lines. Where does Chaos come from? What decided on the moment of its birth? What exactly is Chaos? The first question induced the famous Epicurus to embrace philosophy. Sextus Empiricus transmits the anecdote (*Adv. Math*, X, 19): when being read the *Theogony* by his teacher, Epicurus interrupted to ask what stood before Chaos, and the teacher answered that the question should be asked of philosophers. The second question must be turned around: it is because of the birth of Chaos that time exists. If there is no space, there can be no time. Finally, the last question may have induced a series of answers about the basic material which Aristotle names the 'arche' of the pre-Socratic philosophers, a substance which is the origin, and the stuff of which the universe is made.

Thales chose water, a stuff that, in the Hesiodic division of the universe, represents the source and limits of the worlds of the humans. Anaximander invented a neutral-gender word 'Apeiron', the Unlimited or Undefined, characterized, like Chaos, by its very absence of definition. Heraclitus, although believing in the eternity of the world, chose fire as the paradigm of matter. And fire, in Hesiod's description of wars among the gods, represents at once Zeus' arm of justice and a menace of total destruction and return to the original Chaos. In the epic poetry of Parmenides, Being and non-Being are revealed in a mythical encounter between a human and some goddesses, in the context of going from Night to Day or perhaps from Day to the underground House of Day and Night, where opposites meet, as in Hesiod's Tartarus. Non-Being, the forbidden way, strangely reminds us of the mythical Chaos, locked as far as possible beyond the limits of human investigations:

> as far beneath the earth as heaven is above earth; for so far is it from earth to Tartarus. For a brazen anvil falling down from heaven nine nights and days would reach the earth upon the tenth: then again, a brazen anvil falling from earth nine nights and days would reach Tartarus upon the tenth. (*Th*.721-725)

Parmenides, who was writing some two hundred years after Hesiod, is the first western philosopher to propose an ontology (a description concerned with the essence or basis of things or Being, or existing, in the abstract). His philosophy shares much with Hesiod's primordial (existing from the beginning) Earth, the mother, in godly generations, of all that 'is', leaving aside the catalogue of abstract negative divinities, like Blame or Deceit, that are the offspring of Chaos and Night. Last in the cosmology of Empedocles, two opposite forces lead the traditional four elements (air, earth, fire, water) which were, by his time, acknowledged as the four original elements in an eternal cycle: Love, a principle of union, and Hate, a principle of separation. One is here reminded of the original Hesiodic triad (Chaos, Eros, and Earth) in which the space concept of Chaos separates that which Eros, god of love, unites, all matter being embodied in the figure of mother Earth.

True, Hesiod is only partially responsible for the ulterior developments of the pre-Socratic philosophers. But did he not stimulate their imagination, with his mysterious Chaos? Hesiod does present the first outlined cosmogony in Western culture, and his works, along with Homer's, formed the basis of Greek education throughout antiquity. It is therefore not surprising to acknowledge his influence on first philosophy and science.

Leaving aside the abstract realm of the Gods, let us turn to more down to earth questions, like the shape of our world or the history of mankind. The symmetry of the sky and of Tartarus relative to the surface of the Earth (respectively the domain of the best of Gods—the Olympians, and the prison of their enemies) gives the idea of a circular structure of the cosmos. On the surface of the Earth dwell the human beings. In an important myth, Hesiod recalls the Golden Age of mankind, when humans were sitting at the table of the Gods, under the rule of Cronos, Zeus' father. Then he mentions four successive 'races' of human beings: the race of silver, of bronze, the heroes, and we mortals, the race of iron. Hesiod's pessimism thus concerns not only his hometown, but also his birth time: would that I were not among the men of the fifth generation, but either had died before or been born afterwards (*Th.*174-175).

Here again, questions arise. Why is there a non-metallic race, the race of heroes, interrupting the degradation scheme of the whole? What is going to happen after our time, which is bound to be better than the present? What happened in the first place that caused the fall from the golden times? The answer lies in the history of the Gods. Before Zeus, the god that governed was his father Cronos, who had, himself, overthrown his father Ouranos (Sky) in an act of castration. Zeus cleverly manages to gain power without actually raising his hand against his father: he enlists three hundred-armed allies to help him fight the Titans, Cronos and his brothers. Thus does he become the king of gods, without committing patricide, the worst crime for the Greeks. At this moment however, another clever god challenges Zeus: Prometheus. In both of Hesiod's poems, the story is told of how Prometheus divided the meat of a bull in two parts, one good and the other containing only bones, and tried to fool Zeus into choosing the undesirable part. But Zeus cannot be fooled: the good part was not what Prometheus thought, because consuming meat actually means becoming mortal. As a punishment, Zeus decides to withhold the power of fire, which was usually obtained from his thunderbolts. Prometheus again intervenes in favour of human beings, and steals the fire. But Zeus cannot be fooled! 'Forthwith he made an evil thing for men as the price of fire' (*Th.*570): he created the first woman.

This corresponds to the fall of mankind, the end of the Golden Age, the beginning of the childhood of humanity in its real sense, a humanity set apart from the sphere of the divine. The first human race capable of reproduction is called the 'race of silver', because silver is the colour of the primordial waters. What will happen when men will have lost all respect for the Gods? We can only guess that there will be destruction and a return to the origin of the cycle: a deluge like the biblical one, and a return of the race of silver, but not of the race of gold. For the Golden Age of Cronos is lost forever, since there will be no going back in the history of the gods. Cronos lies deep in Tartarus, with the original Chaos, and Zeus remains supreme, to reign forever.

The moral of the story is to worship Zeus, and this is attained by acting in a just way, because Justice is Zeus' favourite child. But it is not a Justice for the weak. In Zeus' world-order, Strife is also a fundamental goddess, for Zeus sets her 'at the roots of the earth' (*W and D*, 19). For example, Strife can be a form of justice, when it leads one to try to improve: 'This Strife is wholesome for men' (*W and D*, 24).

When speaking of two goddesses, both bearing the same name of Eris (Strife), Hesiod presents a dialectic vision of theology: both good and evil, both truth and lies are part of the realm of the gods. Hesiod is far, very far, from blind obedience to oracles. Life has a meaning, which lies deep in the comprehension of a divine structure. Knowing the structure allows us to learn from the past, to understand the present, and to anticipate the future. Such is the new meaning given to an old divination formula:

> Come thou, let us begin with the Muses who gladden the great spirit of their father Zeus in Olympus with their songs, telling of things that are and that shall be and that were aforetime with consenting voice (*Th*.36-40).

References and Suggestions for Further Reading

Cornford, Francis M. *From Religion to Philosophy*. Princeton: Princeton University Press, 1912 (1991).

Hesiod, Homeric Hymns. Epic Cycle. Homerica. With an English translation by Hugh G. Evelyn-White. Loeb Classical Library. Cambridge, Mass.: Harvard University Press, 1914 (2002).

Jaeger, Werner. *The Theology of the Early Greek Philosophers*. Oxford: Oxford University Press, 1947 (1967).

Snell, Bruno. *The Discovery of the Mind*. New York: Dover, 1953 (1982).

West, Martin L. *Hesiod. Theogony*. Edited with prolegomena and commentary. Oxford: Oxford University Press, 1966 (1978).

Chapter 6

Aesop

Early 6th century BC–c. 564 BC

Leo Groarke

Aesop, the most famous fabulist of all time, is a figure shrouded in mystery. Because it is unlikely that early remarks in authors like Herodotus, Aristophanes and Plato have no foundation in reality, it can cautiously be said that Aesop was a slave in the 6th century BC, that he came from Phrygia and lived in Samos, and that he was known for his ability to craft 'fables' (logoi). The story that Aesop met his end at Delphi, where he was sentenced to death and pushed off a cliff because he insulted the Delphians, is already current in the 5th century BC.

Today, everyone assumes that Aesop is a teller of fables who teaches morals to our children. This Aesop is a modern invention who is the end product of thousands of years of development. At best, he is very distantly related to the original Aesop. One might compare him to a literary figure like Mother Goose, who has become the person to whom we ascribe all nursery rhymes, even though the experts debate the identity of the real Mother Goose, and we know that these rhymes have a variety of disparate origins.

In ancient times, fables do not originate as moral tales for children. Some are versions of famous fables we all know: *The Tortoise and the Hare; The Ant and the Grasshopper; The Boy Who Called Wolf; The Lion's Share*, etc., but ancient fables may have no moral intent and simply function as a witty story, or a way to tell a witty remark. In *The Snails*, it is a witty comment made by a farm boy roasting snails which begin to pop and whistle as they cook. 'Why you miserable creatures,' he says, 'how can you make music while your houses burn?' (Daly, No. 54). In *The Boy Who Lost His Guts*, it is the response of a mother to a sick boy who, after eating the entrails from a sacrifice, reports: 'I'm going to heave my guts.' 'No,' she says, 'you're going to heave the ones you ate' (Daly, No. 47).

Often ancient fables are stories that revel in a hard nosed realism which is at odds with the view of the world that contemporary authors put in the mouth of Aesop. In *The Lions and the Rabbits* the lions respond to an erudite speech the rabbits make at an assembly in the forest, explaining why all animals should get an equal share of everything. 'A nice speech,' the lions reply, 'too bad you don't have the teeth and claws that we have' (Daly, No. 450). Here, condensed into a single sentence, is the modern doctrine we call *realpolitik*.

When Socrates turns Aesop into verse as he is awaiting execution, he seems attracted by their earthy wisdom. But the ancient thinkers who are most attracted to the fable are more interested in their ability to use them as rhetorical devices which can be used in persuading a public audience of some point of view. In keeping with this, the most important collector of ancient Aesopia is the philosopher Demetrius of Phalerum, who studied with Aristotle and became both the ruler of Athens, the librarian at the Great Alexandrian library, and an important proponent of Aristotelean rhetoric.

Though the real Aesop is obscure and inaccessible, we still have an ancient account of him in a *Life of Aesop* which bears, in its earliest version, the title *The Book of Xanthus the Philosopher and His Slave Aesop*. According to this *Life*, Aesop was born an ugly mute slave, but was granted the power to speak and craft fables in return for his generosity to one of the attendants of the goddess Isis. Having gained a knack for logoi, he engineered his way to Samos, where he became the slave of a philosopher called Xanthus. In the course of recounting Aesop's life with Xanthus, the *Life* implicates Aesop in a series of wild adventures, witty fables and obscene episodes which demonstrate, above all else, that he can outwit and out-philosophize the philosopher who owns him.

Taken as a whole, the *Life* has a flavour reminiscent of Roman satire. This has tried the patience of many authors, whose exasperation is reflected in George Fyler Townsend's 19th century remark that 'This life ... contains ... so small an amount of truth, and is so full of absurd pictures of the grotesque deformity of Aesop, of wondrous apocryphal stories, of lying legends, and gross anachronisms, that it is now universally condemned as false, puerile, and unauthentic. It is given up in the present day and unworthy of the slightest credit.' It is telling that such sentiments do not stop Townsend from including a version of the *Life* within his own popular collection of Aesop's fables.

References and Suggestions for Further Reading

Daly, Lloyd. *Aesop Without Morals*. New York: Thomas Yoseloff, 1961.
Townsend, George Fyler. *Three Hundred Aesop's Fables*. London: George Routledge & Sons, 1867.

PART III
THE PRE-SOCRATICS
AND SOCRATES

Chapter 7

Thales of Miletus

c. 625 BC–c. 546 BC

Patricia F. O'Grady

Hieronymus says that he [Thales] actually measured the pyramids by their shadow, having observed the time when our own shadow is equal to our height. (Diogenes Laertius, *Lives of Eminent Philosophers*, I, 27)

Thales was born in the Greek city of Miletus in Ionia, which is now Turkish. The ancient sources describe him as a Greek speaker of Phoenician ancestry. Cadmus and Agenor are included among his ancestors, and he is also attributed a divine genealogy, being said to descend from Zeus.

Thales of Miletus was the originator of scientific thought. In *Metaphysics* (lines 983 b6-984 a2), Aristotle analysed Thales' theories from a scientific viewpoint and, because he considered that Thales was the first person to investigate the nature of matter, he declared Thales to be the first philosopher. Thales believed that the workings of the universe were governed by laws of nature which *could* be understood by mere mortals. He was, therefore, prepared to question the old traditions and to challenge the constraints of the long-held religious understandings of the composition and organization of the universe which Homer and Hesiod had described in the 8th century BC, and which assigned authority over the entire cosmos as well as the affairs of man to the gods and goddesses who dwelt on Mount Olympus.

Thales asked a new, bold, challenging question: 'What is the basic material of all things?' Let us picture him sitting on the banks of the Maeander River, pondering and wrestling with the questions: 'What is this World about? If the gods are not the all-powerful beings most people believe them to be, what is it that brings about change, and what is the universe made of?' And as he sat pondering these questions, a ship, heavy in the water, berthed in the port. How could fully laden ships, heavier than water, remain afloat, and could that phenomenon be related to the earth floating on water?

In *Metaphysics* (983 b20-b25) Aristotle reported Thales' answers to these questions: 'Thales says ... that the primary principle is water, and for this reason declared that the earth rests on water. His supposition may have arisen from the observation that the nurture of all creatures is moist, and that warmth itself is generated by moisture and lives by it, and that from which all things come to be is their first principle.' Thales declared water to be the substance from which all things derive, which is present in all things and to which they ultimately return in a recurring and continuous cycle of apparent change. Thales arrived at this decision empirically—through his repeated observations of events and objects occurring in the world around him—and he described a recurring cyclic theory through which water could be seen to change its state into the myriad diverse things which make up the universe; the heavenly bodies, the earth upon which he walked, the sandals he wore, the food he ate, the ship upon which he travelled.

Thales accounted for this apparent change in water when he identified the force in amber and the lodestone. He believed this power, which was present in all things, to be the causal factor.

Thales was interested and involved in almost everything. We may envisage him gazing at the planets and the stars, and recording the unusual events, for he ultimately recognized a circularity and regularity in heavenly phenomena. The ancient references credit him with a number of astronomical discoveries, and it is believed that his penetrating analyses enabled him successfully to predict the total solar eclipse which occurred on 28 May, 585 BC. It was probably because of this success that, in about 582 BC, he was named as the first of the Wise Men of Ancient Greece.

Thales performed the difficult feat of determining the solstices, and was correct within a few days, perhaps assisted by astronomical records compiled by the Babylonians. Although there is only a slight possibility that he travelled to Babylonia, there is reliable testimony that he visited Egypt.

In Egypt he would have been amazed and intrigued by the wonders of that ancient land, with its monuments and temples, its strange north-flowing River Nile with its regular inundation, the role and status of the priests, and the practical art of land measurement in which its surveyors had become expert. He calculated the height of the great pyramid by measuring the shadow it cast at the time when his shadow equalled his own height. He studied Egyptian geometry which he then introduced to the Greeks, and devised five theorems which were later clarified and extended by Euclid.

He proposed a non-mythological theory of causation to explain earthquakes, denying the role of the mighty god Poseidon, and stripping him of his supernatural authority.

But Thales was no dreamer. He was neither a mystic nor an eccentric, but a practical man. Not only was he the originator of scientific investigation, but he applied his theories in practical ways to protect the Milesians, and for his own benefit. It is recorded that he assisted Croesus in taking his army across the Halys River by diverting its flow. He gave astronomical advice of economic importance on navigation by suggesting that sailors steer by the constellation Ursa Minor as a more accurate method of navigation than Ursa Major. He offered sensible political advice to his city when he advised the citizens how to overcome the danger of the Mede who threatened from the East. Unfortunately his wisdom was ignored at the critical times.

In *Politics* (1259-a6-23) Aristotle related an interesting anecdote: 'There is the story of Thales the Milesian and his financial scheme, which involves a principle of universal application but is attributed to him on account of his reputation for wisdom. He was reproached for his poverty, which is supposed to show that philosophy was of no use. According to the story, he knew by his skill in the stars while it was still winter that there would be great harvest of olives in the coming year; so, having a little money he gave deposits for the use of all the olive presses in Chios and Miletus, which he hired at a low price because no one bid against him. When the harvest time came and many presses were wanted all at once, he let them out at any rate that he pleased, and made a quantity of money.'

Thales' speculations inspired the natural philosophers who succeeded him; Anaximander, Anaximenes, Heraclitus, Pythagoras, Anaxagoras and others, and ultimately laid the foundation for the scientific discoveries of Copernicus, Galileo, Newton, and Einstein.

When Thales questioned tradition and stepped outside the constraints of religion, the beginnings of science were announced to the world. Although Thales' answers were wrong, the procedure he instigated was the beginning of a new and exciting mode of inquiry, the scientific method which almost certainly originated in Miletus with Thales who, with his disciples and associates, Anaximander and Anaximenes, analysed, debated, and tested their hypotheses for rationality and scientific content. Today, physicists still seek the answer to the question he first posed: 'What is the basic material of the Universe?'

References and Suggestions for Further Reading

Barnes, Jonathan. *The Presocratic Philosophers*. London: Routledge and Kegan Paul, 1982.

Guthrie, W.K.C. *A History of Greek Philosophy*. Vol. I. Cambridge: At the University Press, 1971.

O'Grady, Patricia F. *Thales of Miletus: The Beginnings of Western Science and Philosophy*. Aldershot, England: Ashgate, 2002.

Chapter 8

Anaximander of Miletus

610 BC–547 BC

Dirk L. Couprie and Heleen J. Pott

Only one fragment of Anaximander, consisting of a few lines, has come down to us. These lines are some of the most famous phrases in the history of philosophy:

> Whence things have their origin,
> Thence also their destruction happens,
> As is the order of things;
> For they execute the sentence upon one another
> —The condemnation for the crime—
> In conformity with the ordinance of Time.

We will return to the interpretation of this text in a later section of this essay. Everything else we know of Anaximander has come to us from the reports of later authors, the so-called doxographers (from Greek: *doxa* = opinion, and *graphein* = to write). Most of the doxography has been translated into English, e.g. by Guthrie or Kahn (see: References). Usually, the doxography on the Presocratics is quoted according to the collection of Diels/Kranz (see: References), who distinguish between doxographical reports (A) and authentic texts (B). As Anaximander is no.12 in their collection, an indication such as 'DK 12A10' means: the 10th doxographical report on Anaximander. The fragment, given above, is known as DK 12B1.

Our knowledge of Anaximander is as truncated as the heavily damaged and headless statue, found at the market-place of Miletus, that bears his name. Nevertheless, when we read the sources carefully, he emerges as one of the first great speculative thinkers. His introduction of 'the Boundless' as the principle of all things initiated the Western tradition of metaphysical thinking, and with his cosmological speculations he anticipated the Western conception of the universe.

It is said that Anaximander displayed solemn manners and that he used to dress in pompous clothes (DK 12A8), which might indicate that he was convinced of the importance of what he had to tell. At Anaximander's time, Miletus was an important trading centre and had lively contacts with Mesopotamia and Egypt. The Milesians were known as intrepid sailors and Anaximander was no exception. He led a mission that founded a colony called Apollonia on the Black Sea coast (DK 12A3). It was probably Anaximander who introduced the gnomon (a perpendicular sun-dial) from Babylonia (DK 12A2 and 4). It is also reported that he visited Sparta in order to erect a gnomon there (DK 12A1), and perhaps on that occasion he showed the king his map of the world.

Anaximander was the first Greek to draw a map of the entire earth (DK 12A1 and 6). From Herodotus' description of ancient Greek maps (Herodotus IV, 36), we may guess that Anaximander's map showed a circular earth, surrounded by the river Ocean. The map was divided into two halves by a line that ran through Delphi, which was considered to be the navel of the world. The northern half was called 'Europe', the southern half 'Asia'. The habitable world consisted of the lands around the Mediterranean Sea. The lands to the north were too cold for civilized people to inhabit. The lands to the south were too hot. The unfortunate people who lived there were burnt black by the sun (Fig. 8.1.)

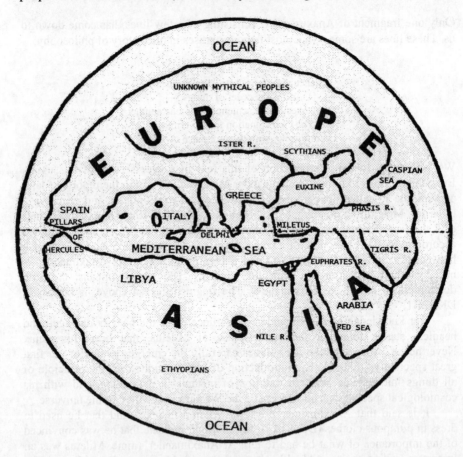

Figure 8.1   A reconstruction of Anaximander's map of the world

The first Greek philosophers were looking for the 'origin' or the 'principle' (Greek: *arche*) of all things. Anaximander is said to have identified it with 'the Boundless' or 'the Unlimited' (Greek: *apeiron*) (DK 12A9). He argued as follows: 'The origin must be boundless, in order that becoming might not stop' (DK 12A14 and 15). Thus, the Boundless seems to be associated with an inexhaustible source that guarantees the ongoing of the process of becoming.

Anaximander is also credited with writing the first book in prose (DK 12A7). Unfortunately, this treatise is lost. Aristotle, however, and his pupil, Theophrastus, could have been acquainted with it, and it is even said that Apollodorus of Athens, in the 2nd century BC, stumbled upon a copy of it (DK 12 A1), perhaps in the famous library of Alexandria in Egypt. Recent excavations reveal that the book was still part of the collection of the library of the gymnasium at Taormina in Sicily in the 2nd century AD.

At the beginning of this essay, we quoted the one remaining fragment of Anaximander's book, which has been preserved for us by Simplicius (DK 12B1). Many interpretations exist of this text, which sounds like an incantation. Our translation of the fragment tries to mirror its 'rather poetical words' (as Simplicius calls them, DK 12A9) by using such poetic devices as assonance and alliteration. Especially, we have avoided the usual inelegant translations such as 'for they pay penalty and recompense to each other for their injustice'. The most natural reading of the fragment is that it refers to the Boundless as the origin of all finite things. The German philosopher Friedrich Nietzsche read the fragment as an expression of the sinful emancipation of all finite things from the eternal Being (the Boundless) which has to be paid for by death (Nietzsche, Ch. 4). Some scholars, however, have argued that the first two lines do not refer to the Boundless at all, but to the finite things themselves. They read the fragment as a rendering of the eternal battle of give and take between things, which constitutes the everlasting circle of becoming and decay.

The Boundless is said to have played a role in Anaximander's speculations about the origin of the cosmos as well. He is reported to have stated that 'all the heavens and the worlds within them' have originated from 'some boundless nature' (DK 12A9). This process is described in evocative language: 'a germ, pregnant with hot and cold, was separated off from the eternal, whereupon out of this germ a sphere of fire grew around the vapor that surrounds the earth, like a bark around a tree' (DK 12A10). This sphere of fire is said to have fallen apart into the rings of the celestial bodies (DK 12A10). This has sometimes been read as a kind of foreshadowing of the Kant-Laplace theory of the origin of the solar system. Some sources even mention innumerable worlds (in time and/or in space), which looks like a plausible consequence of the Boundless (DK 12A 10, 14, and 17).

According to Anaximander, life originated from the moist that covered the earth before it was dried up by the sun (DK 12A11). The first animals were a kind of fish with a thorny skin (DK 12A30). Originally, men were generated from fishes and were fed in the manner of a viviparous shark (DK 12A30). Some authors have seen in these statements a proto-evolutionist theory.

A relatively large number of the reports on Anaximander are concerned with astronomical ideas. In the archaic conception of the universe, before Anaximander, the flat earth was conceived of as covered with the dome of the firmament, onto which the celestial bodies are glued. We meet this conception, e.g., in Homer, when he speaks of the bronze or iron heaven (Homer, *Iliad* XVII 425, *Odyssey* III 2, XV 329, and XVII 565), which is apparently conceived of as something solid, being supported by the mythical giant, Atlas, or by pillars (Homer, *Odyssey* I 52-54).

According to Anaximander, the celestial bodies are huge rings, turning around the earth (DK 12A11). He compares them with chariot-wheels (DK 12A21 and 22). These celestial wheels are made of compressed air which hides the fire within (DK 12 A11, 18, and 21). We cannot see the wheels themselves because they are made of the same substance as the air in which they revolve. Through a hole in the wheel we can see the fire inside, and this is what we know as the sun, the moon, or a star (DK 12A18, 21, and 22). The celestial rings incorporate, so to speak, the new awareness that the celestial bodies do not stop at the horizon but go underneath the earth as well.

The idea that the celestial bodies make full circles implies that the earth floats free in the center of the universe, unsupported by water, pillars, or whatever (DK 12A1 and 2). More than 2500 years later, astronauts provided the ultimate confirmation of Anaximander's conception when they really *saw* the unsupported earth floating in space. The obvious question, however, was why the earth does not fall. Aristotle tells us how Anaximander answered that question: 'The earth stays where it is because of symmetry. For that which is situated in the center, at equal distances from the extremes, has no inclination whatsoever to move up rather than down or sideways; so it necessarily stays where it is' (DK 12A26, see also DK 12A11). Anaximander considered the shape of the earth as a cylindrical disk, like a column-drum, its diameter being three times its height DK 12A10, 11, and 25).

According to Anaximander, the celestial bodies are at different distances from the earth (DK 12A19). He placed them, however, in the wrong order: the stars nearest to the earth, then the moon, and the sun farthest away (DK 12A11 and 18). Anaximander's order of the celestial bodies is clearly that of increasing brightness. The deeper reason for this we can only guess. The important thing, however, is that Anaximander realized that the celestial bodies were behind one another, and not all at the same distance on the firmament as in the archaic conception.

A reconstruction results in numbers for the distances of the celestial bodies (DK 12A11, 21, and 22), expressed in multiples of the diameter of the earth. The star-wheel is at 9, the moon-wheel at 18, and the sun-wheel at 27 earth-diameters distance from the earth. The thickness of each wheel is 1 earth-diameter. The numbers can easily be understood as instructions for making a map of the universe (Fig. 8.2).

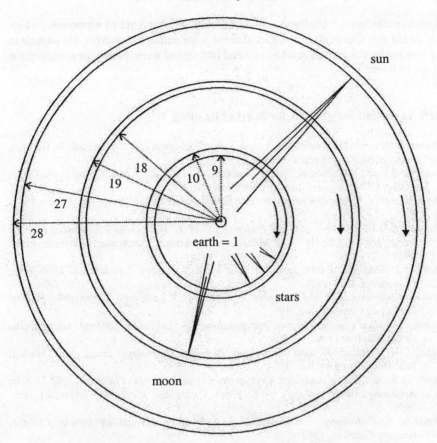

Figure 8.2   The universe according to Anaximander

In the Greek counting system, the number 9 also meant 'very big', or 'a very long time'. Thus, Troy was besieged for nine years and conquered in the tenth year. Odysseus wandered across the seas for nine years before reaching his homeland in the tenth year. An even closer parallel is in Hesiod's *Theogony*, where he says that 'a bronze anvil falling from heaven would fall nine days and nights and on the tenth hit the earth' (Hesiod, *Theogony* 722-725). We may infer that Anaximander with his number 9 for the stars was simply trying to say that the stars are very far away. The numbers 18 and 27 can also easily be interpreted as 'farther' (for the moon) and 'farthest' (for the sun).

Archaic astronomers were also astrologers, who could foretell which days were auspicious and which were inauspicious for all kinds of activities. They were concerned with the observation and description of the movements of the celestial bodies on the screen of the firmament. Records of observations, especially those of the Babylonian astronomers, have survived on numerous cuneiform tablets.

Anaximander, on the contrary, introduced quite another kind of astronomy, which we would call speculative. His speculations were extremely fruitful, for with them he broke with the archaic world-view and introduced a completely new conception of the universe.

References and Suggestions for Further Reading

'Anaximander'. In: *The Internet Encyclopedia of Philosophy*, eds. J. Fieser and B. Dowden, http://www.utm.edu/research/iep.

Couprie, D.L., R. Hahn, and G. Naddaf. *Anaximander in Context. New Studies in the Origin of Greek Philosophy*. Albany: SUNY Press, 2003.

Diels, H. and W. Kranz. *Die Fragmente der Vorsokratiker*. 6th ed. Berlin: Weidmann, 1951-52.

Guthrie, W.K.C. *A History of Greek Philosophy*. Vol. I. *The Earlier Presocratics and the Pythagoreans*. Ch. III: 'The Milesians'. Cambridge: Cambridge University Press, 1985.

Herodotus, *Histories*. Edited and translated by A.D. Godley. London and New York: Heinemann, 1921-1924.

Hesiod. *Works and Days and Theogony*. Translated by S. Lombardo. Indianapolis: Hackett Publishing Company Inc., 1993.

Homer. *The Iliad and the Odyssey* Translated by R.A. Lattimore. Chicago: Encyclopedia Britannica, Ind, 1996.

Kahn, C.H. *Anaximander and the Origins of Greek Cosmology*. Indianapolis: Hackett Publishing Company Inc., 1994.

Long, A.A. ed. *The Cambridge Companion to Early Greek Philosophy*. Ch.3: 'The Beginnings of Cosmology', by K. Algra. Cambridge: Cambridge University Press 1999.

Nietzsche F. *Philosophy in the Tragic Age of the Greeks*. Trans. M. Cowan. Chicago: Regnery-Gateway, 1962.

Chapter 9

Sappho of Lesbos

c. 600 BC

Christina A. Clark

Violet-haired, holy, sweetly smiling Sappho. (Alcaeus fr. 384)

One of the most famous poets of antiquity, Sappho was born on the Ionian island of Lesbos (just off the coast of Lydia, modern day Turkey) and lived in the city of Mytilene during the late 7th and 6th centuries BC. Admired for the sound of her poetry as well as her technical skill, Sappho was so talented that later Greeks named her the 'tenth Muse' (*Palatine Anthology* 9.506). Part of an aristocratic world, Sappho composed poetry set to the lyre. Nine papyrus rolls of her songs existed in antiquity; sadly, today only one song survives complete—the rest are fragmentary, or lost altogether. Still, we can see glimpses of Sappho's genius and versatility in the remaining fragments, which include songs for public occasions such as religious rituals as well as songs for private occasions.

We are not sure who sang Sappho's songs. Perhaps choruses of girls performed her songs for religious and public rituals, while solo performers sang the songs for private occasions. To us, Sappho is important not just because of the outstanding technical and aesthetic quality of her poetry, but also because she was a woman. While we have much literary evidence concerning women in antiquity, the majority is male-authored. Some fragments of poetry remain of other female poets such as Corinna, but Sappho is our main female voice from ancient Greece. Her songs provide us a window into the world women inhabited in Greece's largely sex-segregated society. Men spent most of their time outdoors, participating in politics and business: women spent most of their time indoors, performing domestic tasks and raising children. What makes Sappho's poetry so different from that of the male poets of her time is her portrayal of women in love. Sappho's lovers are active subjects, rather than passive objects. They pursue their beloveds, as Sappho illustrates in fragment 16, in which she uses the famous Helen of Troy as an example of the power of erotic love. While most male authors blamed Helen for the war, they also depicted her as an object of desire. Sappho shows us an actively desiring Helen, who abandons her husband, parents and daughter to be with her beloved Paris.

Some say a host of horses, some say an army of infantry, and some say an army of ships is the most beautiful thing on the black earth. But I say it is whatever one loves. (1-4)

Easy to make this entirely understood by all. For Helen, who surpassed mortals by far in beauty, left her noble husband and went sailing to Troy, nor did she remember at all her child or her dear parents, but [led her astray ...] for lightly ... reminded me of Anaktoria, who isn't here. (5-16)

I would rather see her sexy walk and the shining sparkle of her face than Lydian chariots or armed infantry. (17-20)

Sappho gives her name to the speaker in poem 1, our only complete poem, which she shapes into the form of a prayer invoking the aid of Aphrodite, goddess of erotic love. 'Sappho's' beloved spurns her love, so she begs the goddess to prevent further heartbreak by forcing her beloved to return her feelings. This is one of many homoerotic poems Sappho composed, which have led many to rediscover the poet in the last thirty years as women's and gender studies have proliferated. One of Sappho's most famous poems, 31, illustrates two main features of Sappho's style: an evocation of sensory experiences and the portrayal of strong emotions:

He seems to me to be equal to the gods, that man, whoever sits opposite you and listens to you speaking so sweetly and close to him, and hears too your tempting laughter. Truly that makes the heart in my breast pound, for when for a moment I look at you, I cannot speak at all; my tongue breaks, and a subtle flame runs immediately beneath my skin. My eyes see nothing at all and a roaring fills my ears. Sweat pours down me, and shaking seizes me all, paler than grass I am, and little short of dead I seem to me. But all must be endured since. (fr. 31)

Here Sappho selects, combines, and exaggerates bodily reactions to sexual desire, yet she leaves the speaker's intellectual capacity intact and unaffected, whereas in other poems the lover's intellect is shattered or otherwise rendered ineffective. She does this, perhaps, to mock gently the gender stereotypes of her time—that women were sexually insatiable and uncontrollable, a stereotype that both explains and justifies women's confinement to the domestic and exclusion from the political sphere.

In terms of Sappho's technical brilliance, scholars have analyzed her poetry's incantatory effect, which she creates using alliteration, assonance, rhythm and word repetition. Anne Carson incorporates some such effects in her translation of fr. 112 addressed to a bridegroom:

Blest bridegroom, your marriage just as you prayed
has been accomplished
and you have the bride for whom you prayed
gracious your form and your eyes
as honey: desire is poured upon your lovely face
Aphrodite has honored you exceedingly. (fr. 112)

Sappho's songs entice us into a world of religious ritual and domestic space. We read of incense burning, flowers blooming, cool water running. We feel the wind and enjoy the sight of leaves shivering as it blows in fr. 2, a song that invokes Aphrodite:

(Come) here to me from Crete to this holy temple,
where is your charming grove of apple-trees, and altars
smoking with frankincense, and in it cold water sounds
through apple branches, and the whole land is shadowed
by roses, and from shimmering leaves sleep drops down;
in it a meadow grazed by horses blooms with spring flowers,
and the winds blow gently. There you, Kypris, having taken
up gold cups delicately pour nectar, mingled with festivities. (fr. 2)

Sappho evokes aesthetics that trigger desire, such as the charming laughter of young women (fr. 31), the sight of a dress swirling around a girl's ankles (fr. 22), and a girl's sexy walk (fr. 16). She also describes the violent effects of desire itself:

Eros shook my mind like wind falling on oaks down the mountain. (fr. 47)

You came, and I was mad for you. But you cooled my heart, burning with desire. (fr. 48)

These songs seem spontaneous and of the moment. They use traditional forms (such as prayer formulas and epic conventions), but rework them in subtle and clever ways. Perhaps fragment 168B can hint at Sappho's aesthetic and emotional power as translated by poet and classicist Anne Carson:

The moon has set, and Pleiades: middle night, the hour goes by, and I sleep alone.

References and Suggestions for Further Reading

Carson, Anne. *If not, Winter: Fragments of Sappho*. New York: Alfred A. Knopf, 2002.
Clark, Christina. 'The Body of Desire: Nonverbal Communication in Sappho 31V.' *Syllecta Classica* 12 (2001): 1-29.
Greene, E. Ed. *Reading Sappho: Contemporary Approaches*. Berkeley: University of California Press, 1996.
Williamson, Margaret. *Sappho's Immortal Daughters*. Cambridge, MA.: Harvard University Press, 1995.

Chapter 10

Pythagoras

c. 560 BC–c. 480 BC

Thomas Kiefer

Life is like the Olympic Games: Some come to them as competitors in a struggle, others to buy and sell, but really the ones who are the best are those who come to watch. So too in life, some are born hunters for fame and gain, others as slaves, but those who are philosophers seek the truth. Pythagoras, cited in Diogenes Laertius VIII.8. (translation by Thomas Kiefer)

The influence of Pythagoras on the history of culture and ideas is incalculable, ranging from the entirety of ancient Greek philosophy, to the Jewish Essenes, the alchemy of early Arab scientists, and the geometry of today with the theorem that bears his name. Those journeying by ferry between Greece and Turkey are likely to make a stop at Pythagoreio, on the island of Samos. Those travelling through southern Italy too can encounter his presence, near Metaponto, in Basilicata, the instep of Italy's boot. There, the ruins of a temple to Hera can be found, one which purportedly incorporated Pythagoras' home and school when it was built.

This influence is one more of inspiration rather than a clear philosophical doctrine, for the information on Pythagoras, even in the day of Plato and Aristotle, is full of legend and contradiction, and the followers of Pythagoras themselves developed his ideas in individual and innovative ways. Thus, the ancient sources about Pythagoras must be taken with a degree of caution. However, one can piece together a fairly accurate, although general, picture of his life and ideas.

Pythagoras was born on Samos in the eastern Aegean. His father, Mnesarchus, was a gem-cutter. In his youth he is reputed to have studied with the philosopher Pherecydes of Syros (c. 550 BC). Thereafter he travelled to Egypt—perhaps in some sort of official capacity for the newly ensconced tyrant of Samos, Polycrates—and probably to other areas in the eastern Mediterranean as well. Sometime after this journey, but before 522 BC, Pythagoras left Samos for Croton (in the toe of Italy, now Crotone, in Calabria), where he and his followers established a new political order. This activity shows that Pythagoras was a political leader of some kind, and so hints that he either fled, or was exiled from, Samos due to a conflict with Polycrates.

This Pythagorean order spread to other cities in southern Italy and lasted for a couple of generations. Some ancients called this order a true aristocracy—rule by the best citizens—whereas others called it tyranny. Evidence for the former view is that, around the time of Pythagoras' death, Croton reached a zenith under their rule that lasted until about 450 BC. Evidence for the latter view is that this order suffered at least one, but more likely two, catastrophic rebellions. One was a revolt that seems to have led to Pythagoras moving to Metapontum (now Metaponto). The other, which apparently happened later, resulted in the incineration of the Pythagorean headquarters in Croton, killing all but a handful of Pythagoreans. Similar revolts—or to some, religious pogroms—seem to have spread to other cities as well. These survivors, for example Philolaus and Lysis (both c. 470–390 BC), then left for Greece as refugees. Pythagoras himself died in Metapontum, although the cause of his death is unclear: some sources say in political violence, others say during a fast.

The order that Pythagoras founded and led was spiritual and philosophical as well as political, with moral precepts, sacred rituals and doctrine explaining the nature of life and the universe. Many miracles and mystical events are attributed to him. For example, while crossing the river Casas, the river greeted him by name. He had the gift of bilocation, being seen at the same hour on the same day in two different cities. He was hailed as Hyperborean Apollo, Apollo from Beyond the North. He had auspicious encounters with animals. The name 'Pythagoras' was treated with reverence, and his teachings were simply and famously preceded by '*Autos epha*' or 'Ipse dixit', i.e., 'He spoke'. While attending the Olympic Games, he revealed his thigh of gold, a sign that he had survived a journey to the underworld. Legend has it that a former slave of Pythagoras, Zalmoxis, whom he set free while still living in Samos, was worshipped as a deity by the Getae (a tribe of Greeks living in the Black Sea region). The Neoplatonists of the Roman era held that the history of Greek philosophy was an unfolding process of divine revelation, one that began with Pythagoras and culminated with Plato. Pythagoras, his teachings and followers are also interconnected with the Orphic mystery cults. If Pythagoras had written anything, it probably would have been poetry like other Presocratics; some sources who held he did write report that he signed his poems with the name 'Orpheus', and not his own.

Anyone wishing to become a member of Pythagoras' order, which was open equally to both women and men, had to undergo an initiation that lasted for up to five years. Any member who broke the precepts—especially the oath never to reveal Pythagoras' teachings to outsiders—was treated as dead, and a gravestone was then erected with their name. (This oath provides evidence that Pythagoras never directly publicized his philosophy, through writing or otherwise, even though he often spoke in public. In fact, until the writings of Philolaus (born c. 470 BC), which Plato was eager to obtain, it was impossible for the uninitiated to attain knowledge of Pythagoras' doctrine.) He and his followers were often recognizable by their dress code, strict monogamy, vows of long periods of silence, dietary restrictions—most notably, vegetarianism—and the sharing of their property in common. Since these ways appeared odd to the Greeks, comedians often made Pythagoreans the butt of jokes in their plays—a sign however of how well-known they were.

This order's most distinguishing idea, which Pythagoras was almost certainly the first to introduce to the Greek world, was that of the immortality of the psyche, spirit or soul, through reincarnation. The oldest surviving evidence we have about Pythagoras is a fragment of a poem by Xenophanes about this:

> ...And once, upon passing someone beating a puppy
> He spoke, full of compassion—this portent was uttered:
> 'Stop! Do not strike, for of a man who was my friend is
> Its soul, whose crying I recognized upon it reaching my ear.
> (Diogenes Laertius, VIII. 36. Translation by Thomas Kiefer)

Their vegetarianism, as well as their other dietary restrictions, was probably based on this belief in reincarnation: the meat one is eating could have been the flesh that 'clothed', as the Pythagoreans put it, the soul of a friend. Pythagoras himself could recall his past lives, and he enjoined his followers to ask themselves three times, before falling asleep.

> Where have I been? What have I done? What ought I to do that was not accomplished? (*Golden Verses*, pp. 96, 163-167; D .L. VIII.22)

This practice is not only a means of self-examination and training one's memory, as the ancients report, but also a way in which to attain the ability to recall one's past lives: it is very similar to a practice Buddhists use for this purpose.

Pythagoras concealed his moral precepts, and his spiritual and philosophical teachings, in the form of passwords ('*sumbola*', whence we get the word 'symbol'; after Aristotle they were called '*akousmata*', 'things heard'). These passwords were a means by which members of his order could detect genuine initiates from impostors and political opponents. After the Pythagoreans' catastrophe, these passwords eventually became public, and immediately the debate began as to whether these were literal rules or riddles holding a deeper meaning. Some passwords were surely lost, others for various reasons were added later. (All the passwords below, are adapted from Burkert (170ff.) and Diogenes Laertius (VIII.17ff. *et al.*) Many of the passwords survive only as simple declarative sentences; these I have changed back into their question and answer form where the corresponding question is clear. I also have retranslated many terms and phrases where appropriate.)

These passwords can be classified, as Aristotle apparently did in his lost work on the Pythagoreans, into three different kinds: What is? What is foremost? What ought one to do? Some surviving examples of the first are as follows: Who is Pythagoras? The Hyperborean Apollo. What are the hands of Rhea? The Big Dipper and Little Dipper. What are the planets? The dogs of Persephone. What is the ringing in your ears? Voices of the Superior Powers. What is the rainbow? The reflected glory of the sun. What is friendship? Equality. What is shared? Things between friends. What is health? The retaining of form. What is disease? The degenerating of form.

Examples of 'what is foremost' are: What is most just? To sacrifice. What is most wise? Number. What is most strong? Mind. What is most beautiful?

Harmony. What is most desired? Happiness. What is most true? Human beings are evil.

Examples of 'what one ought to do' are: One ought to have children. One should never pursue one's wife. One should never give advice except with the best intent. One must only help another to load, never to unload. One must not eat beans. One must never cross a bean field. One ought to respect plants and animals that do not harm humans. One should never break bread. One must not look at oneself in a mirror by means of a flame. Upon getting out of bed, one ought to eliminate the signs of one's presence. Upon leaving on a journey, one must not look back homewards. One should not travel on main thoroughfares.

Arguably, the password which has had the greatest effect on the history of philosophy and science is this:

What is the Oracle of Delphi? The Tetraktus: This very thing is the harmony in which the Sirens sing.

The Tetraktus is the following figure, the 'perfect triangle':

Since the Tetraktus was called 'the Oracle of Delphi'—the place where Greeks went for advice, divination and communication with the spiritual world—Pythagoras probably created and used the Tetraktus as a means of divination, of understanding the universe, the spiritual and the unknown. (The use of the Tetraktus then parallels the use of the bars —— and —— in the Chinese *I Ching*.) Moreover, since the Tetraktus was applied in this way, and is also based on number, it became the means by which the Greeks first began to examine and to understand the natural world through number—that is, through mathematics. Finally, since it is also 'the harmony in which the Sirens sing', the Tetraktus became the basis for musical theory, a theory which was the first in the Greek world to posit that the relation between the octave, fourth and fifth correspond to the ratios 2:1, 3:2, and 4:3.

After Pythagoras' death and their political catastrophes, the Pythagorean order split into two factions: the 'Learned' or the 'Scholars', those who worked more with the Tetraktus; and the 'Hearkened' or the 'Password-Keepers', those who focused on his moral and spiritual teachings. The Scholars recognized the Password-Keepers as legitimate Pythagoreans, but the latter did not recognize the former as such: Arguably, the reason for this is that the Scholars were the ones who first began to make Pythagoras' philosophy public, thereby violating, in the view of the Password-Keepers, the oath of secrecy. The political power of both factions eventually waned, dying out around the time of Alexander (356–323 BC). In contrast, Pythagoras' philosophy survived and developed, coming to influence not only the greats of Greek philosophy, medicine and science, but the world's culture up to the present day.

References and Suggestions for Further Reading

Burkert, Walter. *Lore and Science in Ancient Pythagoreanism*. Translated by E.L. Minar Jr. Cambridge, MA.: Harvard University Press, 1972.

Diogenes Laertius. *Lives of Eminent Philosophers*. Vol. II. Loeb Classical Library 185. Trans. R.D. Hicks. Cambridge MA.: Harvard University Press, 1991.

Huffman, Carl A. *Philolaus of Croton: Pythagorean and Presocratic*. Cambridge: Cambridge University Press, 1993.

Kahn, Charles H. *Pythagoras and Pythagoreans: A Brief History*. Indianapolis/Cambridge: Hackett Publishing Co., 2001.

Kingsley, Peter. *Ancient Philosophy, Mystery and Magic: Empedocles and the Pythagorean Tradition*. Oxford: Clarendon Press, 1995.

Thom, Johan C. *The Pythagorean 'Golden Verses'*. With Introduction and Commentary. Leiden: E.J. Brill, 1995.

Pythagoras: Detail from Raphael's School of Athens ©Photo SCALA, Florence
Courtesy of an anonymous donor
Pythagoras is shown working on Harmonics, watched by admirers of his
own and later times. To identify the characters see the clickable image at
www.newbanner.com/AboutPic?SOA.html

Marble bust of Socrates 3rd century AD: ©Ephesus Museum, Selcuk, Turkey

Aristotle: ©Anne Thompson. Drawn from photographs taken in Thessaloniki by Glenn Rawson

Coins of the period: c. 500 BC–565 AD ©George Couvalis
¹/₁₂ silver stater, Miletus (?), c. 500 BC

silver tetradrachm, Athens, 449–413 BC

silver tetradrachm, depicting Apollo, Myrina, north-west Asia Minor, c. 160 BC

bronze nummus, Roman Emperor Justinian, 527–565 AD

The Ancient Athenian Agora: The reconstructed Stoa of Attalos, with the Acropolis in the background ©Kevin Glowacki

The Athenian Agora: Looking along the length of the Colonnade of the reconstructed Stoa of Attalos ©Kevin Glowacki

Delphi: The Temple to Apollo, with the theatre in the foreground ©Kevin Glowacki

Chapter 11

Xenophanes

c. 570 BC–c. 470 BC

Hye-Kyung Kim

But if horses or lions had hands or could draw with their hands and accomplish such works as men, horses would draw the figures of the gods as similar to horses, and the oxen as similar to oxen, and they would make the bodies of the sort which each of them had. (fr. 15)

Xenophanes began his long life in the Ionian city of Colophon which was then Greek and is now Turkish. When Colophon fell to Persian invaders in 546 BC, Xenophanes, like many other Greeks of the time, became a political exile. The invasion was a disaster for the Ionians. We can see its long-lasting effects in one of Xenophanes' poems:

One ought to say such things as these, beside a fire in wintertime,
Lying fully fed on a soft couch,
Drinking sweet wine and eating chick-peas for dessert:
'Who among men are you and what family are you from?'
'How old are you, good sir?'
And 'What age were you when the Mede came?' (fr. 22)

Xenophanes' words indicate that the coming of the Mede (Persians) marked a momentous date in the history of the Greeks. Lives were changed. Xenophanes, now a refugee, travelled to a number of cities, and lived in Sicily and on the mainland of Italy. We learn much of the life of Xenophanes from his poetry: In fragment 8, he tells us of his long life as a refugee.

Already there are seven and sixty years
Tossing about my counsel throughout the land of Greece,
And from my birth up till then there were twenty and five to add to these,
If I know how to speak truly concerning these things. (fr. 8)

Despite his wanderings as a refugee, Xenophanes was a renowned poet and theologian as well as a social critic and philosopher. His thoughts on the nature of god exerted an especially powerful influence on the subsequent flourishing of civilization on the Greek mainland. In fragment 1, for example, a banquet scene, with food and drink, song and festive spirit, is described in detail, but Xenophanes also calls for piety to 'hymn the god with reverent words and pure speech', and for moderation in drinking. This is not merely an enchanting poem, but is a brilliant account of Xenophanes' ideals. It is charged with emotion, and displays his sensitivity as well as his wisdom.

> For now the floor is clean as are the cups and hands of all.
> One puts on the woven garlands;
> Another passes along a fragrant ointment in a bowl.
> The mixing bowl stands full of cheer
> And another wine, flower fragrant in the jars, is at hand—
> Which says it never will give out.
> In the midst frankincense gives forth its sacred scent,
> And there is cold water, sweet and pure.
> Golden loaves lie near at hand and the noble table
> Is loaded down with cheese and rich honey.
> An altar in the center is covered all about with flowers
> While song and festive spirit enfold the house.
> But first glad-hearted men must hymn the god
> with reverent words and pure speech.
> And having poured a libation and prayed to be able to do
> What is right—for these are obvious—
> It is not wrong to drink as much as allows any but an aged man
> To reach his home without a servant's aid.
> Praise the man who when he has taken drink brings noble deeds to light,
> As memory and a striving for virtue bring to him.
> He deals neither with the battles of Titans or Giants
> Nor Centaurs, fictions of old,
> Nor furious conflict—for there is no use in these.
> But it is good always to hold the gods in high regard. (fr.1)

What is novel in Xenophanes' idea of piety in this poem is the prayer for the power for right conduct. The traditional, conventional piety and respect for the gods involved prayer for divine intervention for personal success or victory in battle, not for the power to do what is right. But for Xenophanes, it is the power to do what is right that is most important, and the gods' help is needed to acquire such power.

Xenophanes also asks his audience to praise the person who, enabled by memory and striving for virtue, tells a story to bring noble deeds to light while avoiding old stories about the warfare of the gods. In effect, Xenophanes is criticizing conventional stories about divine warfare, stories which Homer and Hesiod had collected and incorporated into their writings. Homer and Hesiod, Xenophanes thought, had 'attributed to the gods all sorts of things which are matters of reproach and censure among men: theft, adultery, and mutual deceit.' (fr. 11) That is especially deplorable, 'since from the beginning all have learned according to Homer' (fr.10).

Why did Xenophanes feel so strongly about such stories? His stated reason is that 'there is no use in' them, and Xenophanes was very concerned with what is useful. Stories of conflicts between and battles among the gods are unhelpful to the

city, and may even undermine it. A concern with usefulness for the city is also
evident in Xenophanes' criticism of excessive rewards for and public adulation of
athletic achievement:

> But if by swiftness of foot one were to gain a victory
> Or in the pentathlon, there by Pisa's stream in Olympia in
> The sacred grove of Zeus,
> Or again the painful art of boxing
> Or the fearsome sport they call pankration,
> He would appear more glorious to his townsmen
> And win the front-row seat of honour at games.
> And there would be food from the city's public stores
> And a keepsake gift for him.
> And even if he were to win with horses he would get all these,
> Not being as worthy of them as I.
> For our expertise is better than the strength of men and horses….(fr.2)

Xenophanes thinks that his expertise—the expertise of the poet and pious
man—is worthy of the honor and glory heaped on winners of athletic competitions.
Victories at the athletic contests should not be the cause of great joy, for it is
expertise on moral and religious matters that brings harmony and unity to the city
and is useful to the city.

Another reason why Xenophanes is unhappy with the old stories of divine
warfare is that they are simply wrong. Such stories arise from a projection of
ourselves. We wrongly suppose, Xenophanes says, 'that gods are born, wear their
own clothes and have a voice and body' (fr. 14). It is natural for us to try to
understand the gods in terms which are anthropocentric—that is, in terms of human
traits and human experiences—but it is unwarranted to do so. We have no reason
to believe that the gods live on Mt. Olympus and have the same tendencies that we
do, or bodies that resemble ours. Xenophanes was thus disenchanted with
traditional Greek religion. He clearly had a concept of the gods that differed in
fundamental respects from that found in Homer and Hesiod.

'One god is greatest among gods and men,' he says, and 'not like mortals in
body or in thought' (fr. 23). Xenophanes' main focus is on this greatest of all gods.
This god does not have the sort of body we have and does not think the way we do.
He does not have separate sense-organs for sense-experience, or separate faculties
for thought and understanding. 'Whole he sees, whole he thinks, and whole he
hears' (fr. 24). In addition, he always 'abides in the same place, not moving at all,
nor is it seemly for him to travel to different places at different times' (fr. 26). He
'completely without toil shakes all things by the thought of his mind' (fr. 25). The
greatest god also seems to be a rational being, for although the fact that he moves
all things 'by the thought of his mind' can mean merely that he moves things
without having to exert himself, the phrase strongly suggests that such movement
is guided by his thought, and is rational.

It is for these reasons that, in fragment 1, Xenophanes expresses his
dissatisfaction with older, more anthropomorphic stories of divine warfare. Praise
should be reserved for those who bring the noble deeds of the gods to light. To do

so is to hold the gods in the high regard they deserve, and to do so is always good. Cheerful, sensuous verse is combined with serious theological intent in Xenophanes, and in both his poetry and his theology he made major contributions to Greek culture.

But Xenophanes was more than an inspiring poet and an innovative theologian. He was also a philosopher of nature who believed that all the things we see around us are composed of two ultimate elements, either separately or in combination. 'All things which come into being and grow,' he says, 'are earth and water' (fr. 29). The belief that all the objects of our everyday experience are composed of two ultimate elements is known as dualism, and Xenophanes is unique among pre-Socratic philosophers in being a dualist. He applied his philosophy of nature to explain the events of nature, such as rainbows. A rainbow, according to him, is merely 'a cloud, purple, red and greenish-yellow to behold' (fr. 32). Since the sea is 'the begetter of clouds', (fr. 30) a rainbow is water.

Xenophanes was a subtle and enjoyable poet, a reformer in spiritual and moral matters, and an imaginative philosopher. He was intent on creating beauty, serious about piety, proper religious belief, the civic good, and right conduct, and interested in the ultimate nature and explanation of the world around him. His views were both innovative and radical. He was the first outspoken critic of Homeric religion, the first thinker to criticize our anthropocentric view of the gods, and the first theologian who argued that the greatest god is an unchanging and rational being who is the moving force behind the natural world. His views about the gods influenced the philosophies of Parmenides, Anaxagoras, Socrates, Plato, and Aristotle. Xenophanes' theology and critical spirit are more than enough to rank him as one of the great pre-Socratic thinkers.

References and Suggestions for Further Reading

Barnes, J. *The Presocratic Philosophers.* 2 vols, London: Routledge and Kegan Paul, 1979.
Burnet, J. *Early Greek Philosophy.* 4th ed. London: Adam and Charles Black, 1930.
Guthrie, W.K.C. *Orpheus and Greek Religion.* London: Methuen, 1953.
Guthrie, W.K.C. *A History of Ancient Philosophy.* Vol. I. Cambridge: Cambridge University Press, 1962.
Lesher, J.H. *Xenophanes of Colophon.* Toronto: University of Toronto Press, 1992.
Sandywell, Barry. *Presocratic Reflexivity: The Construction of Philosophical Discourse c. 600–450 BC.* New York: Routledge, 1996.

Note Lescher's translation and the numbering of the fragments are used throughout this article.

Chapter 12

Aeschylus

c. 525 BC–c. 456 BC

Seamus Sweeney

> Zeus it is that has made man's road;
> he it is who has laid down the rule
> that understanding comes through suffering. (*Aeschylus,* 'Agamemnon' lines 176-78,
> translated by David Grene and Wendy Doniger O'Flaherty)

Like many Classical figures, details of Aeschylus' life are sketchy, and of his seventy to ninety plays only seven survive. Born in about 525 BC of a noble family, Aeschylus fought in the Persian Wars. He took part in the battle of Marathon, at least according to his (allegedly self-penned) epitaph, and may have also been at the decisive naval battle of Salamis. At some stage he was initiated into the Eleusian Mysteries—secrets which he was later prosecuted for revealing. The charge, which was probably politically motivated, was unsuccessful. According to Pliny the Elder, he died after an eagle dropped a tortoise on his bald head, mistaking it for a rock. Two of his sons also wrote plays, and some attribute *Prometheus Bound* to one of them.

Aeschylus' major innovations in drama might strike contemporary readers as almost childishly simple, but in the context of the deep ritual underpinnings of Greek drama they were truly revolutionary. Before the time of Aeschylus, plays consisted of a chorus—a group of actors standing aside from the main action of the play (although interacting with the characters) and commenting on events—and a single actor; the single actor had been introduced by the playwright, Thepsis, only thirty years previously. Aeschylus introduced first a second actor and then (along with Sophocles) a third and even more actors. In his earlier plays there are only two characters, who largely interact with the chorus rather than each other. Over the course of his *Oresteia* trilogy, Aeschylus' drama evolved to involve actors interacting with each other, and the final play in the series would incorporate changes in scene and what, to the modern ear, is much more recognizable as natural dialogue between characters.

The *Oresteia* trilogy—*Agamemnon*, *The Libation Bearers* and *The Eumenides*—is the most famous of Aeschylus' work. It begins with the return of Agamemnon, the leader of the Greek force at Troy, to Mycenae. His wife Clytemnestra murders him once he re-enters the threshold of his house; before their departure to the Trojan War, Agamemnon had decided to sacrifice their daughter Iphigenia to obtain favourable winds. As the Chorus ask:

> Who shall expel from the house the brood of curses?
> The whole race is welded to destruction. *(Agamemnon,* lines 1577-1578)

The Libation Bearers, the next play in the trilogy, begins with Clytemnestra and her lover Ægisthus seizing the throne of Mycenae. Agamemnon's daughter, Electra, beseeches Apollo to recall her absent brother Orestes to avenge their father. In due course Orestes returns and, impelled by Apollo, murders his mother. The play ends with Orestes, unsurprisingly, fleeing in madness.

The 'Eumenides' of the third Oresteia play are the Furies, three vengeful female figures, of a race of gods older than the Olympian deities, who haunted the guilty and are pursuing Orestes. The play begins at the Oracle in Delphi—Orestes has fled there, pursued by the Furies. The shrine of the Oracle is protected by Apollo, who induces sleep in the Furies allowing Orestes to make his escape. They wake to find the ghost of Clytemnestra taunting them, and berate Apollo for hindering their torment of the godless matricide Orestes. Apollo replies that there may have been justice in Orestes' action, since Clytemnestra had abused the holy bonds of marriage by killing Agamemnon:

> In your argument, Aphrodite is discounted utterly—
> Yet from her the very dearest things come to human kind;
> For man and woman, the bed,
> When justly kept, their fated bed,
> Is greater than any oath that can be sown. *(Eumenides,* lines 215-219)

The whole sorry affair should be judged by the goddess Pallas Athena (goddess of Athens). The action shifts to the temple of Pallas Athena, where the goddess judges the case and acquits Orestes. The Furies respond with fury; Athena calmly hears them out and gently persuades them to accept the verdict. Athena's eloquence changes the Furies and they accept the title 'Eumenides'—'The Kindly Ones'. The play ends with a redemptive ritual: a procession sings:

> Now, now, sing in songs of praise
> Peace be forever on the houses and citizens of Athens. *(Eumenides,* lines 1040-1042)

Prometheus Bound is the middle play of a trilogy. In Greek mythology, Prometheus was a Titan, a race begotten by the Primitive, pre-Olympian Gods but of the Earth. Unlike other Titans, Prometheus was endowed with rationality, cunning and a love of freedom and justice. The human race had been created by this stage, but was generally felt to be a botched experiment and kept in subservience. Prometheus helped Zeus defeat his father Cronos and thus begins the reign of the Olympian gods. Zeus planned to eliminate the human race; being of the Earth, Prometheus pitied them and stole fire from heaven to give to them.

The gods decide to punish Prometheus. This was portrayed in *Prometheus the Fire-Bringer*, the now-lost opening play in the trilogy.

Prometheus Bound begins with Prometheus being manacled to a rock by two gods, Strength and Violence. After bemoaning his fate for some time, and proudly repulsing the offer of his relative, Oceanus, to intercede with Zeus, a talking cow appears and bemoans her fate with Prometheus. This was not an early example of surrealism; the talking cow is Io, daughter of the King of Argos and unfortunate enough, like most attractive young maidens, to arouse the lust of Zeus. Zeus' wife Hera transforms Io into a cow, which does nothing to cool Zeus' ardour. Hera sent a gadfly to madden Io, which drives her into various wanderings, culminating in Egypt where Hera's power does not work and Zeus and Io (in cow form throughout) consummate their love. In *Prometheus Unbound* Io is only partly through this wandering and after delivering a travelogue describing her progress so far, the gadfly stings again and sends her on her way. Finally Hermes, the messenger of the gods (or 'the underling of gods', as he is dubbed by Prometheus) appears and exchanges some bitter banter with Prometheus. *Prometheus Unbound*, now lost, completed the trilogy, and presumably portrayed a redemptive conclusion to events.

The story of Io is background to *The Suppliants*; Io bears Zeus a son, Epaphos, and three generations later the family consists of two brothers, Aegyptus and Danaus, who each had fifty sons and fifty daughters. The sons of Aegyptus decided *en masse* to marry their cousins, who fled to Argos from whence Io had begun her bovine wanderings. *The Suppliants* ends at this point, with the Argives defying the Egyptians (as the sons of Aegyptus become) by offering sanctuary to the Danae. In the legend, Danaus then agrees to marry his daughters to the Egyptians, but plots with his daughters to slaughter them on the wedding night. Only one daughter, Hypermestra, finds love for her husband stronger than family loyalty and refuses. Hypermestra's fate in the legend is unclear, but surviving fragments of Aeschylus' subsequent plays in the trilogy seem to involve Aphrodite, the goddess of love, defending Hypermestra and persuading the other daughters, who had slaughtered their husbands as planned, to marry. Surprisingly enough, they found husbands willing to brave the possibility of being murdered on their wedding night.

Seven Against Thebes is the final play of a trilogy, following two plays portraying the legend of Oedipus, who killed his father Laius, became King of Thebes and married his mother. The play opens after the death of Oedipus; his sons, Eteocles and Polyneices, initially agreed to share power but Eteocles seized sole power and Polyneices has joined forces with seven other kings to attack Thebes. A messenger describes the six kings who attack six of Thebes' seven gates; Eteocles dispatches various champions to each gate, until, inevitably, Polyneices turns up at the remaining gate, Eteocles fights him and both, inevitably, die. Thus the curse—originally placed on Oedipus' father Laius—is resolved.

The Persians is unique among Aeschylus' surviving works in dealing with events within living memory. *The Persians* is essentially a commentary on the triumph of the Athenians over the Greeks at the Battle of Salamis in 472 BC, in which Aeschylus may have fought. The play was first performed eight years later.

It portrays the reception of the news of the battle received in the court of Xerxes, the defeated Persian King. With its catalogue of exotic Persian names and litany of action, it is supposed that it was to accompany a sort of pageant of the recent war.

Aeschylus' influence on modern drama and literature is tremendous. The *Oresteia* in particular, with its labyrinthine family dynamics and cycle of bloodshed spawning bloodshed with a final redemption, has continued to resonate with writers and artists; Eugene O'Neill, T.S. Eliot, Jean-Paul Sartre, William Faulkner and sundry others bear the influence of Aeschylus. The word 'Cassandra', Agamemnon's Trojan concubine in the *Oresteia* whose unfortunate destiny was to predict the truth and yet be ignored, has entered the English language as a term for any ignored prophet.

Philosophically, Aeschylus' works portray tremendous human suffering, but nevertheless depict the gods as fundamentally just. Suffering in Aeschylus is due to some human action, and the consequence of action spreads from the individual to their family and to the community. The *Oresteia*, the only complete trilogy, shows a resolution to this spreading misery with the measured judgement of Athena. The Gods become more 'humane' over the course of the trilogy—in *Agamemnon* and *The Libation Bearers* they are stern, implacable figures, while, by *Eumenides*, they take a more tender interest in human affairs, as demonstrated by Apollo's and Athena's actions. It is reasonable to suppose that his other trilogies followed a similar pattern.

The elements of the word 'democracy' first appear as *demou kratousa cheir*—'the sovereign hand of the people'—in *The Suppliants*. Aeschylus was known as a strong supporter of the recently established Athenian democracy, which probably inspired the prosecution for revealing the Eleusian mysteries: and all his works have political overtones; *Seven Against Thebes* portrayed the stout defence of a walled city and was interpreted as supporting the bolstering of Athens' defences, the *Oresteia* shows the importance of judicial resolution of disputes rather than retaliatory murder, and setting the peaceful resolution of the trilogy in the domain of Pallas Athena, goddess of Athens, asserts the city's primacy in Greece.

References and Suggestions for Further Reading

All of Aeschylus' works are available online at http://classics.mit.edu/Browse/browse-Aeschylus.html translations by E.D.A. Moreshead.

Quotations from the Oresteia are from Grene and Doniger O'Flaherty's translation cited below.

Bloom, Harold. *Aeschylus: Comprehensive Research and Study Guide*. Philadelphia: Chelsea House Publishing, 2001.

Goward, Barbra. *Telling Tragedy: Narrative Technique in Aeschylus, Sophocles and Euripides*. London: Duckworth Press, 1999.

Grene, David and Wendy Doniger O'Flaherty. *The Oresteia by Aeschylus: A new translation for the theatre*. Chicago: University of Chicago Press, 1989.

Herrington, John. *Aeschylus*. New Haven: Yale University Press, 1986.

Sommerstein, Alan Herbert. 'Aeschylus', entry in *Who's Who in the Classical World*. Oxford: University University Press, 2000.

Vellacott, Philip. Introduction to *'Prometheus Bound and Other Plays'*. Harmondsworth: Penguin, 1961.

Chapter 13

Anaxagoras of Clazomenae

c. 500 BC–428 BC

Patricia F. O'Grady

'Don't you care about your homeland?' he was once asked.
'Very much I care, indeed', he said and he pointed to the heavens. (Diogenes Laertius, *Lives of Eminent Philosophers*, II. 7.)

Anaxagoras of Clazomenae was born into a noble and wealthy family but he renounced his inheritance in order to devote his life to the study of philosophy. He was influenced by the natural philosophy of the Milesians, especially by the theories of Anaximenes.

There is little about Anaxagoras' life and teaching that is not the subject of rigorous debate. It is said that he was aged twenty when Xerxes (the Persian king) invaded Greece, that he then began to study philosophy at Athens, still aged twenty, during the archonship (archon, a magistrate, a position held for a year) of Callias, and that he lived in Athens for thirty years (D.L. II.7). There is considerable acceptance that Anaxagoras was a member of the invading force of Xerxes, and that he remained in Athens after the Greek defeat of the Persians. As Callias was archon in 456 BC, it is probable that Calliades, who was archon in 480, is intended: the name Calliades was commonly shortened to Callias (Guthrie, 322; O'Grady, 4). A difficulty arises with this chronology: Anaxagoras lived in Athens for thirty years, but they may not have been consecutive years.

Anaxagoras is credited with introducing philosophy to Athens, where he continued his study of natural philosophy. We may be sure that the young Anaxagoras, bursting with innovative ideas and speculating about the events of nature, soon began to discuss the new philosophy with his associates, and commenced his teaching.

The ancient sources tell us that Pericles was tutored by Anaxagoras (Plutarch, *Pericles*, IV.1-2), and this is also recorded by Isocrates (Isocrates, 235), but dates are unknown. Pericles, who was about five years younger than Anaxagoras, was born into a politically prominent, noble family. Certainly there was a strong friendship between them, and Pericles was influenced by Anaxagoras' views.

Over the following years, Anaxagoras continued his research and teaching, and developed his explanations of natural phenomena. Anaxagoras was accepted into the intellectual circle of Pericles, the young aristocrat who was rising as a political force. There began a flowering of cultural development in Athens, brought about by the philosophy of Zeno of Elea, Parmenides and Empedocles; Protagoras, Socrates and the other Sophists; and the literature of the playwrights, Aeschylus, Sophocles, Euripides and Aristophanes. These brilliant writers delved into politics and mythology, and taught, criticized and publicized the new philosophy. It is not certain that all these philosophers spent time in Athens, but Anaxagoras almost surely associated with those who did, and both influenced and was himself influenced by them.

Diogenes Laertius informs us that Anaxagoras wrote one book (D.L I.16), *Physica,* written in 'attractive and dignified language' (D.L II.6). We are fortunate that *Physica* was still available to Simplicius in the 6th century AD, nearly one thousand years after it was written. From the opening section of *Physica* we see that his subject was the nature of matter, the primary principles, and the cause of change.

Anaxagoras was working at about the same time as Empedocles who was probably just a few years younger, and there is considerable debate about who was writing first. Let us look at the opening lines of Anaxagoras' book:

> All things were together, infinite in respect of both number and smallness; for the small too was infinite. And while all things were together, none of them were plain because of their smallness; for air and aether held all things in subjection, both of them being infinite; for these are the greatest ingredients in the mixture of all things, both in number and in size. (Fr. 1.; Guthrie, 294)

Again from Anaxagoras' book we read of

> the moist and the dry, the hot and the cold, the bright and the dark, since there was much earth in the mixture and seeds countless in number and in no respect like one another. For none of the other things either are like one to another. And since this is so, we must suppose that all things were in the whole. (Fr. 4; Guthrie, 294)

The opening sentence of Anaxagoras' *Physica* indicates that his views ran counter to those of Empedocles who declared that 'there is no birth nor death but only mixture and separation of what has been mixed' (Fr. 8; Guthrie, 271). Empedocles speaks of two causes of change, defining mixture and separation as causes, whereas Anaxagoras proposed one cause, Mind, to which we will return. Although there are further differences between the theories of these two philosophers, there is no space in this paper to discuss them. The curious reader should search for a detailed analysis in the longer works listed in the references.

We see that in the original mixture Anaxagoras envisaged an infinite number of things. He identifies these: air and aether (fire), with much earth in the mixture, and seeds, countless in number and in no respect like one another. All things are both infinitely large and so small as to be without magnitude. In addition there are the opposites, 'moist and the dry, the hot and the cold, the bright and the dark'.

We now turn to a discussion of the seeds in Anaxagoras' theory of formation and change. We commence with part of fragment 3, in which Anaxagoras wrote:

Neither is there a smallest part of what is small, but there is always a smaller (for it is impossible that what is should cease to be). Likewise there is always something larger than what is large. And it is equal in respect of number to what is small, each thing in relation to itself, being both large and small. (Fr. 3, Simplicius *in Phys.* 164, 17; Schofield, 118)

No piece of matter is absolutely large or small, because whatever size that piece is, it will be small compared with a piece, say 1000 times larger, and large compared with a piece 1000 times smaller. The possibility of the latter is guaranteed by Anaxagoras' belief that matter is infinitely divisible, that is, can be divided without end. In each composite thing there is a portion of every elemental substance, and each contains the same number of ingredients but in a different proportion. Each thing is characterized by the substance that prevails in it proportionally. The seeds are elemental substances from which the composite things of our world will be formed by means of the cosmic process of separation, which comes out of the surrounding. Anaxagoras explains that 'in everything there is a portion of everything' (Ffr. 6, 11, 12). Each thing is characterized by the substance that prevails in it proportionally, according to the principle of predominance (Fr.12). Thus, every composite thing contains the same number of ingredients but in a different proportion.

Aristotle defined a 'homoeomer' as a substance any part of which is also an instance of that substance. Water is a homoeomer because a part of it is still water, whereas cats are not because part of a cat is not a cat. For Anaxagoras, what Aristotle defined as homoeomers were indestructible and could not be changed into each other, for how is it possible, for example, for the body to change bread into flesh and water into blood. Anaxagoras solved this difficulty by assuming that soul particles, or seeds, of everything exist in everything else. Bread can be changed into flesh by rearranging the seeds in bread so that the flesh seeds become predominant whereas, before, the bread seeds were predominant.

Anaxagoras' declaration that 'there was much earth' in the mixture may be associated with the fall of a meteorite at Aegospotami, in the Goat's River district in Thrace in 467 BC. Pliny wrote that 'the stone is still shown—it is the size of a wagon-load and brown in colour.' (Pliny (II.LIX.149). The fall of the meteorite would have created a sensation, and one could expect that Anaxagoras would have visited the site to view the stone or, at the least, have sought information about it. This stone falling from the heavens would probably have cemented his theory that the heavenly bodies are earthy in nature, and not gods. 'He declared the sun to be a mass of red-hot metal and to be larger than the Peloponnese' (D.L. II.8).

Now to Mind, or Intellect, which Anaxagoras envisaged as the single motivating cause of change: 'All things were together; then came Mind and set them in order' (D.L. II.6). Anaxagoras himself described Mind:

Mind is something infinite and independent, and is mixed with no thing, but alone and by itself. ... It is the finest and purest of all things and has all judgment of everything and greatest power ... and it controlled the whole revolution to make it revolve in the beginning. (Fr. 12; Guthrie, 273)

It is seen that Anaxagoras introduces Intellect mainly as a cosmic agent, responsible for the arrangement of everything from living beings to the heavenly bodies. Anaxagoras' theory of Intellect is his main contribution to the history of ideas. It had a great influence on Plato and for Aristotle, who does not hide his admiration (mentioning Anaxagoras more than 60 times in his writings), intellect plays a very important role in his *Metaphysics* as well as in his psychology.

During the years when Anaxagoras continued to develop his philosophy, he seems to have retained his involvement with the Periclean circle. Pericles rose to prominance, and became the most powerful politician in Athens but he was not all powerful and he had enemies. His opponents dare not indict him, but they attacked him through his friends, indicting Anaxagoras, and others, on charges of impiety.

Some of the ideas in Anaxagoras' godless philosophy became a weapon for the political opponents of Pericles. A certain Diopeithes introduced a bill aimed at those who promoted false gods. Under the law Anaxagoras could be charged with impiety—he had declared the sun to be a red hot stone, and this was impious.

It must be acknowledged that Anaxagoras was guilty as charged—denying the heavenly gods was impious. He escaped to Lampsacus, a prosperous city on the southern shore of the Hellespont where he lived until 428 BC, dying at 72 years of age. He lived sufficiently long to establish an important school of philosophy, some pupils of which were later associated with Epicurus. He was so highly honoured that he was given a public burial, and a coin was struck in his honour. School children were granted an annual holiday in his honour, a custom that was still being followed more than 700 hundred years later (D.L. II.15).

Anaxagoras pursued interests in astronomy and meteorology but his main legacies are his explanation of the nature of matter, and the theory of Mind which influenced later thought and the whole of modern philosophy.

Anaxagoras was one of the most innovative of the early philosophers, shining out even amongst many other outstanding philosophers of the ancient period. Much more should be written about his philosophy—the interested reader would be well rewarded by further investigating the work of this remarkable man.

References and Suggestions for Further Reading

Guthrie, W.K.C. *A History of Philosophy*. Vol. II. Cambridge: Cambridge U. Press, 1965.

Mansfeld, J. 'The chronology of Anaxagoras' Athenian Period and the Date of his Trial' In *Mnemosyne* Part I, vol. 32 1979: 39-69; Part II, vol. 33, 1980: 17-95.

O'Grady, Patricia F. 'Anaxagoras and Athenian Politics: Towards a Chronology.' Chap. in *Greek Studies in Australia*. Eds. Close, Elizabeth, Michael Tsianikas and George Frazis. Adelaide: The Flinders University of South Australia, 2001: 1-27.

Schofield, M. *An Essay on Anaxagoras*. Cambridge: Cambridge University Press, 1980.

Strang, Colin. 'The Physical Theory of Anaxagoras.' Chapter in Allen, R.E. and David J. Furley. *Studies in Presocratic Philosophy*. Vol. II. London: Routledge & Kegan Paul, 1975.

Chapter 14

Heraclitus

c. 544 BC–484 BC

G.S. Bowe

The way up and the way down is one and the same. (Heraclitus, Fragment 60, Kahn, p. 75)

An unapparent connection is stronger than an apparent one. (Heraclitus, Fragment 54, Kahn, p. 65)

Heraclitus was from Ephesus, near the modern port town of Kuşadasi (Bird Island), Turkey, north of Miletus and an hour's ferry ride to Samos, the Greek island where Pythagoras was born. After the destruction of Miletus by the Persians in 494 BC, Ephesus became the most powerful city in Asia Minor. Today, among other ruins on the site there stands the remains of the beautiful Roman Library of Celsus (a late 2nd century AD Platonist and opponent of Christianity) and the temple of the goddess Artemis, which was built in emulation of the temple of Hera on Samos. Heraclitus is said to have dedicated his book to this Temple of Artemis. Given his geographical location, it is not surprising that Heraclitus seems to have a good knowledge of the Milesian philosophers, Thales, Anaximander and Anaximenes, and Pythagoras. As Ephesus rivalled Miletus and Samos, and her architects challenged their temples, Heraclitus challenged their philosophers.

There are several apocryphal stories about Heraclitus' death. I give the most extended version here, because the account, while itself quite fantastic, provides a very interesting way of speaking about Heraclitus' thought.

Heraclitus contracted a condition (edema, dropsy) that caused excessive water retention and also caused him to stumble around blindly seeking help (see Fr. 117, Kahn, p. 77. See Note at the end of this paper). Dropsy is a condition whereby the failure of the body properly to drain lymphatic fluid causes swelling in the feet, and other parts of the body, including stomach and head. Heraclitus, who hated doctors and was prone to speaking in riddles, could not communicate his problem to them. The doctors could not understand Heraclitus' complaints, so walking away in disgust, he buried himself in cow manure, in the hope that the warm, moist substance would draw the water out of his system. Coated thus, he was eaten by wild dogs and died (Diogenes Laertius, IX 3-4).

Heraclitus says that it is death for souls to become water (Fr. 36, Kahn, p. 75), that a dry soul is wisest and best (Fr. 118, Kahn, p.77), and that it is delight, not death for souls to become moist (Fr. 77, Kahn, p. 77). 'Moist' here seems like drunkenness. Heraclitus also says that doctors poke and prod and charge a fee which they should not get (Fr. 58, Kahn, p. 63), and that 'dogs bark at those they do not recognize' (Fr. 97, Kahn, p. 57). Indeed the doctors did not help him and the dogs that devoured him did not recognize him. Another of his statements is that corpses deserve more to be thrown out than manure (Fr. 96, Kahn, p. 69). In short the elements of the strange story of Heraclitus' death look like a humorous collection of his obscure ideas into a series of misadventures that ironically recall his own words, possibly by detractors of his cryptic style.

The difficulty with Heraclitus' book is that it is written rather darkly, and that all we have today are indirect reports and quotations of writings which were obscure in the original. Indeed he earned himself the epithet *ho skoteinos* (obscure or dark) because of his writing style or his personality, or both. The style however, certainly made an impact: it has been suggested that Euripides recommended it to Socrates. Socrates' own opinion of the work is reported by Diogenes Laertius 'What I understand of it is good, as is I suspect the part I don't understand, but it would take a diver from Delos to get to the bottom of it' (D. L. II, 22).

Despite the obscurity, it is possible to piece together some of the ideas of Heraclitus from the fragments of his work that remain. In the rest of this essay I will try to point out some central ideas in the thought of Heraclitus, those of *fire*, *flux*, *strife* and *logos*, all of which will be discussed below.

For Heraclitus, the order of the cosmos is represented by fire:

> This ordering, the same for all, no god nor man has made, but it ever was and is and will be fire everliving, kindled in measures and in measures going out. (Fr. 30, Kahn, p. 45)

The ancient Stoics took Heraclitus' account of fire to mean that the world constantly underwent cycles of conflagration. Continuous condensation and rarefaction of the fiery element meant that the cosmos would contract, explode and expand again and again over long periods of time.

One might think that Heraclitus resembles the reductionism of the Milesian philosophers (who suggest that everything can ultimately be reduced to one thing, such as water, or the air of Anaximenes or the boundless of Anaximander). Heraclitus appears to say that all is fire. But fire is also identified with the divine *cosmos* (order) and also the soul. The fire that kindles and goes out in life and death is connected, in structure and substance, with the fire that kindles and goes out in the universe. There is something highly symbolic, and not quite so literal in the discussion of fire. While the physical sense of fire may serve as an illustration of Heraclitus' insight, the depth and form of his words suggest that his account is not limited merely to physics, but to the structures large (*macrocosmoi*) and small (*microcosmoi*) in the universe.

The idea that everything is in flux (*panta rhei*—literally all things flow), is attributed to Heraclitus by Plato in his dialogue the *Cratylus*, a dialogue named for Heraclitus' follower. Aristotle claims that Plato had known and been interested in Heraclitus' ideas of flux in his youth, and held to them in later years, combining these ideas with the Socratic search for definitions and turning that search into a search for stable Ideas that ground the physical world of flux and our knowledge of them (Aristotle, *Metaphysics*, 987 a-b). This notion of flux is consistent with the idea of the continuously changing universe, a fire kindling in measures and going out in measures, but is perhaps most famously captured in the idea that man cannot step twice into the same river (Frs. 12, 91, Kahn, p. 53). The idea may be interpreted either physically, that because the water is flowing it is different water that you step into, or in terms of perspective—the river you step into the second time is the river you have stepped into before, and hence not the same as the river you first stepped into when it was the river previously un-entered. In both cases, when extended to the universe, it seems that Heraclitus is suggesting that the world and even apparently stable parts of it are constantly in motion, even though, like the river we refer to them as fixed things.

Heraclitus, a man of noble birth, seems to have shown a great disdain for many of his contemporaries and his philosophical predecessors. He was unimpressed by reputation, nobility and position; he is reported to have refused the hereditary priesthood of Demeter, a goddess of the Eleusinian mysteries, as well as refusing, in a rather ungracious fashion, the invitation of the Persian King Darius' invitation to give instruction at the royal court. In his writings, those whom he insults include Homer, Hesiod, Pythagoras, and Xenophanes (Frs. 40, 57, 106, 42, 81, Kahn, pp. 37 and 41). Perhaps the most interesting polemic is his statement that when Homer wished that strife be banished from the world (in *Iliad,* 18.107) he was asking for the end of the world. (Fr. A22, Kahn, p. 67). Strife is necessary for the structure of the universe—strife and opposition in fact make the universe work:

The God: day and night, winter and summer, war and peace, satiety and hunger. It alters as when mingled with perfumes, it gets named according to the pleasures of each one. (Fr. 67, Kahn, p. 85)

One must realize that war is shared and Conflict is Justice and that all things come to pass ... in accordance with conflict. (Fr. 80, Kahn, p. 67)

The universe is the result of a unity of opposites or unity in opposition. To take a simple analogy, if you imagine a very simple pup tent, what is required to make it stand is the force of the two ropes that you pull in opposite directions to right the poles and make the tent stand. If there were not this opposition, there would be no structure to the universe. All of the opposites are really unified by strife in the larger structure of the *cosmos*, and distinguishable only as the fire kindles in measures and goes out in measures.

It is important to see that this order or structure is rational. The unity of opposites that through strife is given a structure is spoken of as a kind of hidden 'word' or *logos*. Heraclitus says: 'It is wise, listening not to me but to the [*logos*] to agree that all things are one' (Fr. 50, Kahn, p. 45).

Although this [*logos*] holds forever, men ever fail to comprehend, both before hearing it and once they have heard. Although things come to pass in accordance with this [*logos*], men are like the untried when they try such words and works as I set forth, distinguishing each according to its nature and telling how it is. But other men are oblivious of what they do awake, just as they are forgetful of what they do asleep. (Fr. 1, Kahn, p. 29)

Just as the meaning of Heraclitus' own words (*logoi*) this divine, hidden rational order is not obvious to most people, who believe in their own 'private' conceptions of things, without realizing that they exemplify the *logos* on a small scale and are part of the *logos* on the 'macrocosmic' scale. Just as the sun god only gives a sign (Fr. 93, Kahn, p. 43), and the Sibyl raves with the voice of a god in her (Fr. 92, Kahn, p. 45), nature's structure, which loves to hide (Fr. 123, Kahn, p. 33), often passes unappreciated by most men. But the *logos* is common to all; people 'hear' it everywhere, although they act as if they do not understand its language.

It would of course take a book to go into all of the ideas introduced here. Heraclitus has left us with many fragments that are evocative, comical and deeply profound, and there are many ways to make connections among them. The best introduction to the thought of Heraclitus is the fragments themselves, and there are several good editions.

References and Suggestions for Further Reading

Barnes J. *Early Greek Philosophy*. NY.: Penguin, 1987.
Burnet, J. *Early Greek Philosophy*. 3rd ed. Cleveland and New York: 1930.
Diogenes Laertius. *Lives of Eminent Philosophers*. Heinemann: 1994.
Kahn, C.H. *The Art and Thought of Heraclitus*. Cambridge, 1979.
Kirk, G.S., J.E. Raven and M. Schofield. *The Presocratic Philosophers*. 2nd ed. Cambridge, 1983.
Zeller, E. *Outlines of the History of Greek Philosophy*. 13th edition. New York, NY.: Dover, 1980.

Note 'Fr.' followed by a number refers to the standard ordering of the fragments by the two German scholars, Hermann Diels and Walther Kranz. So, for example, in 'Fr. 117, Kahn, p. 77' 'Fr. 117' refers to Diels and Kranz, and p. 77 refers to the translations and page numbers of Charles Kahn's book, *The Art and Thought of Heraclitus*. At the back of Kahn's book is a 'concordance' of his presentation of the fragments and that of Diels and Kranz. For a further explanation of Diels and Kranz, refer to the essay on Anaximander.

Chapter 15

Parmenides

c. 515 BC–c. 450 BC

Allan F. Randall

> Whatever can be thought of or spoken of necessarily is, since it is possible for it to be, but it is not possible for nothing to be. (Parmenides of Elea, *On Nature* (Diels-Kranz 28 B6 = Barnes, 158. See references))

The oldest surviving work in the Western philosophical tradition is the metaphysical poem *On Nature* by Parmenides of Elea. Written in the epic hexameter verse of Homer and Hesiod, the poem has not survived in its entirety, although we have significant fragments of it. It represents the first known rigorous and sustained logical argument. Because it attempted to logically prove ultimate truths about the universe, its author is widely considered to be the father of both metaphysics (the study of ultimate reality) and philosophical rationalism (the assumption that reason is the primary means of coming to know reality).

Parmenides was known in his day as a scientist, philosopher, physician and lawmaker. He wrote the legal code for the city of Elea, which may well have been in force for many hundreds of years. The ancient city no longer stands, but recent decades have witnessed an impressive archaeological excavation of the ruins (called by its Latin name 'Velia'), which has unearthed many fascinating artifacts, including a bust of Parmenides himself.

Parmenides' poem argues for a fundamental distinction between belief (that which *seems* to be) and truth (that which actually *is*). According to Parmenides, all the 'things-that-seem' that we perceive around us (such as trees, rocks, rivers and cats) are not, in themselves, the true reality. There is a greater reality of which the world of our everyday perceptions is but a part.

The poem opens with the philosopher himself carried off to an ethereal realm of an omniscient Goddess, whose words form the rest of the poem (DK 28 B1 = Barnes, 156). The Goddess, representing the point of view of logic, explains that there are three ways of knowing: the 'Unthinkable Way', the 'Way of Truth' and the 'Way of Belief', each of which yields a different approach to metaphysics.

The essence of metaphysics is summed up in every child's question, 'Why is there something, rather than nothing?' The 'Unthinkable Way' expresses the second option: that there might have existed nothing at all. But what would this 'nothing' be, and what could we mean by saying it 'exists' if we cannot even conceive of it? For if nothing exists, then surely the very word 'exists' is meaningless. So Parmenides asks us to agree that we must allow that *something* exists. Yet, the moment we allow Parmenides this one assumption—that 'nothingness' is meaningless—he will use this to push us, by force of logic, into a very counter-intuitive conclusion.

Once we have granted that *something* exists, Parmenides gives us another choice: do all *possible* things exist, or are there some possibilities that exist and some that do not? The 'Way of Truth' argues that anything conceived of purely through reason (as opposed to mere perception) *must* exist. In some sense, by clearly conceptualizing it, we have already admitted some sort of existence for it.

What Parmenides thinks these rationally conceivable things actually are is not entirely clear, but we can guess that logical proofs and mathematical equations would certainly count. Rocks and trees and rivers and cats probably are not rationally conceivable *by us*, but the omniscient Goddess should be able to conceive of them. But if the Goddess could conceive of the natural order around us, then she surely could conceive of *other* ways the world *could have been* instead (like a world without a moon, or a world with unicorns). But from the Goddess's viewpoint (that of logic), why should *this* world—the one we live in—exist, while another possible world does not? From a logical perspective, all possible worlds that are logically conceivable are equally possible and hence equally real.

Parmenides' 'Way of Truth' was the beginning of philosophical rationalism: conceivable things just *are*, by virtue of their being conceivable:

> Whatever can be spoken or thought of necessarily *is*, since it is possible for it to be, but it is not possible for nothing to be. (DK 28 B6 = Barnes, 158)

> It is the same thing, to think of something and to think that it *is*. (DK 28 B8 = Barnes, 157)

The Goddess nonetheless acknowledges the importance of understanding the empirical world of the senses. She tells Parmenides:

> And it is right that you should learn all things, both the unshaken heart of persuasive Truth, and the beliefs of mortals, in which there is no true trust. But you shall learn these too: how, for you who are passing through them, these things-that-seem must 'really exist', being—for you—all there is. (DK 28 B1 = Barnes, 156)

In fact, the bulk of the poem was originally the section that put forth a comprehensive physics and cosmology—the 'Way of Belief' (although not much of this section has survived). As with our common everyday beliefs, empirical scientific theories—both those of Parmenides and of modern science—generally assume that there is only one possible world that actually exists—our world. Yet there is nothing we can rationally say about any one logical possibility that could mean it exists, while others do not. When we say that the others 'do not exist', we are saying that they are 'nothing'. Yet, we already agreed that the idea of 'nothing' was nonsensical, when we rejected the 'Unthinkable Way', and so we are trapped in a contradiction.

From the Goddess's point of view, our perceptual world is real enough, but so are all the other possible ways the world could be. The 'Way of Truth' combines together all these possible ways of being into a new conception of reality, which we will call the 'One Reality'. Because the One Reality contains all possibility, it must be a homogenous, undifferentiated whole. To see why this is so, consider a block of marble from which Michelangelo is about to carve the statue David. The block of marble will represent, for us, the totality of logical possibility—it already implicitly contains all possible sculptures. To create David, Michelangelo need only remove the bits that are not part of what he has in mind. Once some bits are removed, certain sculptures are then eliminated from the marble forever. But if all possible sculptures are included, no bits can be removed and the block remains continuous, undifferentiated and homogeneous. David, then, existed *inside the marble* before Michelangelo took chisel to hand. He merely discovered David, by chipping away the non-David bits to reveal what was already there.

To the Goddess, as to Michelangelo, the One Reality is a marble that already contains all possible 'sculptures', of which the world of our senses is but one. Of course, it is only the omniscient Goddess, standing *outside the marble*, who can conceive of all possibilities. We, who are living *inside the marble*, perceive the particular sculpture that makes up our environment as the one and only 'true reality'.

Thus, if unicorns are as logically conceivable as horses, then unicorns must exist in the One Reality every bit as much as horses. Trapped in our 'Way of Belief', we mere mortals see horses, but no unicorns, in our corner of reality. But the Goddess sees both, or else none at all (but then, that would be the 'Unthinkable Way').

The One Reality cannot even exist within the flow of time, or within the extent of space. For how could it exist 'here' or 'at this time'?—that would imply that there is some other place or time outside of it. The universe itself must somehow be timeless and placeless:

> What-is, never having come-to-be, is ... whole, of a single kind, immovable and complete. ... For what kind of coming-to-be will you seek for it? How and from where did it grow? I shall not permit you to say or to think that it grew from what-is-not, for it is not to be said or thought that *it is not*. What necessity could have impelled it to grow later rather than sooner, if it began from nothing? Thus it must either fully be, or be not at all. (DK 28 B8 = Barnes, 178)

Some have dismissed Parmenides as a dreamer who saw the physical world as mere illusion, but this is a serious misreading. Parmenides clearly saw empirical science as important—it originally formed the bulk of his poem. His own scientific theories—put forward in the 'Way of Belief'—were not themselves especially influential, but his overall approach set the example for the rest of ancient Greek science. If we cannot describe the world of our perceptions as one homogeneous thing, Parmenides reasoned, then we can at least strive for logical simplicity, and keep our theories as compatible with the homogeneous One Reality as possible.

Parmenides himself theorized that the natural world could be explained in terms of just *two* basic categories: light and night.

While earlier philosophers had certainly grasped the basic requirement of simplicity (Thales of Miletus had tried to reduce everything in the universe to water), not until after Parmenides did theories deal in the highly abstract form of logical simplicity that is so characteristic of post-Eleatic Greek science. Empedocles of Acragas reduced everything to Earth, Air, Fire and Water, driven by the forces of Love and Strife. Leucippus of Miletus and Democritus of Abdera reduced the universe to a swarm of uniform, unchanging, indivisible atoms separated by empty space. Each atom was a 'little One', with some of the rationally elegant features of the One Reality. In fact, every major Greek philosopher after Parmenides made answering the Eleatic challenge a central concern.

Today, we continue to push our conception of the universe closer and closer to the 'One' of Parmenides. Some cosmologists have even taken a kind of Eleatic view of the universe by suggesting that the total mass-energy of the universe, on a global scale, might be zero—our universe of nonzero mass and energy being only a local phenomenon ('within the marble', so to speak). There is even a very popular theory amongst cosmologists, supported by the paradoxes of quantum mechanics, that the universe as a whole is really a 'multiverse' of all possible universes— another echo of Parmenides.

Parmenides would be well pleased to see this latter-day revival of Eleaticism, for as scientists race to discover the Unified Theory of Everything, ancient Eleatic ideas are arguably being taken more seriously now than they have been for more than two thousand years.

References and Suggestions for Further Reading

Barnes, Jonathan. *The Presocratic Philosophers*. Revised Ed. London: Routledge, 1982.

Diels-Kranz. For an explanation of this form of referencing, please turn to the first page of the essay on Anaximander, Chapter 8.

Gallop, David. *Parmenides of Elea: fragments*. Toronto: U. of Toronto Press, 1984. (For serious students who want to interpret Parmenides for themselves.)

Herbert, Nick. *Quantum Realities*, New York: Anchor Press/Doubleday, 1985. (Easy-to-understand introduction to the 'Eleatic' qualities of modern physics.)

Kirk, G.S., J.E. Raven and M. Schofield. *The Presocratic Philosophers*. 2nd. Ed. Cambridge: Cambridge U. Press, 1983.

McKirahan, Richard D. Jr. *Philosophy before Socrates*. Indianapolis: Hackett Pub., 1994.

Parmenides of Elea. *On Nature*. A.F. Randall (Ed.). http://www.elea.org/Parmenides/ (For the nonspecialist; all quotations in this chapter are from this translation.)

I would like to thank Vee Ledson and Brian Blair for their invaluable assistance.

Chapter 16

Empedocles

c. 493 BC – c. 433 BC

James M. Magrini

But, O gods, turn the madness of these men from my tongue,
And from holy mouths channel forth a pure spring.
And you. Muse of long memory, white-armed maiden,
I beseech: what it is right for mortals to hear,
Send to me, driving the well-reined chariot of piety.
She will not compel you to accept the flowers of reputation and honour
From mortals on condition that you say more than is holy
With temerity. And then indeed do you sit on the summit of wisdom.
(Empedocles: Sextus Empiricus, *Against the Mathematicians*, VII, 122-123)

Dressed in regal purple, with a gold crown and matching slippers, the pre-Socratic philosopher Empedocles must have raised more than a few eyebrows as he walked through the streets of ancient Acragas. Adored by men and women alike, the eccentric Empedocles was sought out for prophecy, healing, and advice in all matters.

Apocryphal lore depicted Empedocles as a miracle-worker who performed many superhuman deeds, such as curing the plague and raising the dead. Although these entertaining tales reveal an endearing human personality behind the philosophy, one must not allow such colourful accounts to surpass the importance of his philosophy.

Empedocles was born on the island of Sicily, in the city of Acragas (now Agrigento). Drawn to the noble, humanist way of the philosopher, he shunned the wealth and power of his aristocratic lineage by refusing a kingship within the oligarchy. In 474 BC, when the citizens of Acragas ousted the ruler, Thrasydaeus, in an attempt to establish a democracy, Empedocles played a pivotal role in assuring the success of their new government.

A philosopher and poet of exceptional merit, Empedocles was blessed with a gift for creative expression and put forth his views in two epic poems, *On Nature* and *Purifications*. In these works, Empedocles reconciled the methods of Ionian philosophy with the Eleatic thought of Parmenides, attempting to give a reasoned account of the world. This account relied on observation, sensory perception, and rational explanation.

Within the poem, *On Nature*, Empedocles outlined his natural philosophy, or 'physics,' as follows: First, he attempted to identify the basic material, or 'stuff' of the universe. Second, he attempted to provide a rational explanation of motion and change within the world. Finally, he sought to identify a controlling principle of order within the world, or abstract law of change.

Unlike Thales, Anaximenes, and Heraclitus, who identified a single substance as the original cause, or starting point of life, Empedocles envisioned the world as a plurality of the four basic, immutable, and eternal elements: fire, air, water, and earth. Empedocles believed that each of the 'four roots' possessed the necessary attributes to be considered 'real' in the Parmenidean sense; each was complete and unchanging:

> For these [the four elements] are equal and of the same age,
> But each rules in its own province and possesses its own individual character,
> But they dominate in time as time revolves.
> And nothing is added to them, nor do they leave off,
> For if they were perishing continuously, they would no longer be.
> (Simplicius, *Commentary on Aristotle's Physics*, 158.1-159.4 = 31B17)

While Parmenides denied the reality of motion and change, Empedocles saw change as a legitimate aspect of existence. He suggested that change occurred as the four imperishable elements were arranged and rearranged in varying ratios. Although Empedocles believed that the universe was infused with life, he followed Parmenides's lead and denied that motion was an attribute of 'true' Being. Thus, change, which required a sufficient cause, had to be explained by an external mover or agent that would give impetus to motion.

To support this position, Empedocles identified Love and Strife, as being immaterial 'motive' forces that elicited motion and change within the universe. Based on the actions of Love and Strife, the elements were attracted, broken apart, and reconfigured to create the great variety of things in existence.

> For from these [i.e., the elements] come all things that were and are and will be in the future.
> Trees have sprouted and men and women,
> and beasts and birds and fishes nurtured in water,
> and long-lived gods highest in honors.
> For there are just these things, and running through one another
> They come to have different appearances, for mixture changes them.
> (Simplicius, *Commentary on Aristotle's Physics*, 159.13-26 = 31B21)

When Love controlled the universe, harmony and order existed, as Love united the unlike elements through 'attraction'. When Strife gained ascendency, there was a movement towards discord and chaos. Through 'repulsion' Strife separated the unlike elements that Love had gathered and caused the like elements to band together. Under the relative supremacy of Love and Strife, world development continually alternated between the extremes of unity and diversity and proceeded in four phases within an eternal cycle.

The process begins with a homogeneous fusion of the elements under Love's rule. During the second phase, Strife begins to act on the universe and the elements begin to separate out like to like. In the third phase, under Strife's complete dominance, the elements separate into four individual bodies of matter. In the fourth and final phase, Love begins to gain over Strife and the elements, once again, blend or attach unlike to unlike. Finally, the universe returns to phase one, where a perfect blending of the elements is achieved under Love's rule.

Empedocles believed that the universe underwent a 'double creation': First, as the cycle progressed from Love's harmonious rule to that of Strife's discordant ascendancy, and again, as the cycle reversed, from separation to fusion.

Empedocles's work seems to suggest the existence of an eternal law of 'fate,' or Necessity, which directly controlled the world cycle, standing above the elements and the motive forces of Love and Strife. When analysing Empedocles's thought, philosopher and classicist Helle Lambridis observed: 'Although they [Love and Strife] predominate in turn, they don't seem to have the power of extending or shortening their reign. What presides over their alternate supremacy is an eternal and ineluctable law.' One may ascertain that these motive forces acted as 'representatives' of a higher cosmic law, which directed their actions in accordance with some universal design. This line of thought is expressed within *On Nature,* as Empedocles speaks of Love and Strife:

In turn they get the upper hand in the revolving cycle, and perish into one another and increase in the turn as appointed by Fate. (DK 31, fr. 26)

On Nature also contains speculations on biology, physiology, psychology, and the immortality of the human soul. When examining human physiology for example, Empedocles hypothesized that blood was a harmonious blending of all the elements, while bones contained a mixture of only fire, water, and earth in varying ratios. Empedocles advanced a general theory of respiration, which he connected to the circulation of the blood. He compared the process of breathing to the action of the *clepsydra* (water pipe), which works by means of air pressure to retain and release liquids. As Professor M.R. Wright observes, 'The *clepsydra* is used in a simile in which the movement of air into and out of the openings of the body (pores) in respiration is compared to that of water into and out of the perforated base of the clepsydra.'

Empedocles's physiology was intimately linked with his psychology and he believed that the blood pumping around the heart was the organ of human cognition:

The heart, nurtured in the seas of rebounding blood,
where most especially is what is called thought by humans,
for the blood round the heart in humans is thought.
(Porphyry, in Stobaeus, *Selections* I.49.53 = 31B105)

Empedocles's final work, *Purifications*, written in the form of a myth, outlined the fall of humanity from a glorious Golden Age when Love ruled the cosmos. Empedocles identified humanity's Original Sin as the first

Promethean-like sacrifice, i.e., the consumption of animal flesh. Polluted by this act, the human's body and soul endured a series of incarnations, which eventually cleansed and purified the individual, bringing her back to a perfected state of godly bliss. This cycle of 'sin and redemption' along with the idea of the souls' transmigration strongly resembled the beliefs found in the religious teachings of the enigmatic philosopher, Pythagoras of Samos.

> There is an oracle of Necessity, an ancient decree of the gods, eternal, sealed fast with broad oaths, that when one of the divine spirits whose portion is long life sinfully strains his own limbs with bloodshed, and following Hate has sworn a false oath – these must wander for thrice ten thousand seasons far from the company of the blessed, being born throughout the period into all kinds of mortal shapes, which exchange one hard way of life for another. For the mighty air chases them into the Sea, and the Sea spews them forth on to the dry land, and the Earth (*drives them*) towards the rays of the blazing Sun; and the Sun hurls them into the eddies of Aether. One (*element*) receives them from the other, and all loathe them. Of this number am I too now, a fugitive from heaven and a wanderer, because I trusted in raging Hate. (DK 31, fr. 115)

Because of the kinship he enjoyed with all of the earth's creatures and his views on reincarnation, Empedocles vehemently opposed all forms of the ancient blood-ritual, which were part of the religious practices of his day. Empedocles equated religious sacrifice with murder! This being so, since the animal to be sacrificed may in fact be a human in a lower transitionary form of existence. Here, in what is perhaps his most recognized verse, Empedocles poetizes his varied past lives:

> For by now I have been born a boy, girl, plant, bird, and dumb sea-fish. (DK, 31 fr. 117.)

In 1997, Alain Martin discovered that a papyrus fragment, stored at the University of Strasbourg since 1904, contained 70 lines of Empedocles' text. After analysis of the 'Strasbourg papyrus,' it is now believed that verses previously traced to *Purifications*, may instead be from his earlier poem, *On Nature*. This fact suggests a blurring of the lines between Empedocles' views on natural science and theology. Although scholars disagree on this matter, perhaps there is a legitimate interconnection between the works, a reconciliation in which the science, as outlined in *On Nature*, is only to be understood in its totality when analysed within the religious content of Empedocles' later poem, *Purifications,* and *vice versa*.

It is said that Empedocles died peacefully, after exile from Acragas, somewhere in the Peloponnese. Given his character however, such a placid ending seems unfitting. Perhaps we would rather believe the story of Empedocles's demise related by Diogenes Laertius, which accentuates the 'endearing' personal element behind the philosophy. Longing to return to his beloved gods, with a soul purified through a life of doing philosophy, it was said that Empedocles leaped into a crater from the heights of Mount Aetna.

Sharing the hearth of the other immortals, sharing the same table, freed from the lot of human griefs, indestructible. (DK, 31 fr. 147)

References and Suggestions for Further Reading

Barnes, Jonathan. *The Presocratic Philosophers*. London: Routledge and Kegan Paul, 1979.

Cohen, Mark, S., Patricia Curd and C.D.C. Reeve, editors. *Readings in Ancient Greek Philosophy*. Indiana: Hacket, 1985.

Empedocles, *Empedocles: The Extant Fragments*. Trans. M.R. Wright. New Haven: Yale University Press, 1981.

The Poem of Empedocles: A Text and Translation with an Introduction. Trans. B. Inwood. Toronto: University of Toronto Press, 1992.

Kirk, G.S and J.E. Raven, *Pre-Socratic Philosophers*. United Kingdom: Cambridge Press, 1962.

Lambridis, Helle. *Empedocles: A Philosophical Examination*. Alabama: University of Alabama Press, 1976.

Chapter 17

Protagoras of Abdera

Born c. 490–480 BC

and Plato's *Protagoras*

Jonathan Lavery

> Socrates ... I have debated against many men in my time; and if I had argued by the rules of debate laid down by my opponent, as you demand, I should have proved no better than the next man, and the name of Protagoras would not be celebrated throughout Greece. (Plato, *Protagoras*, 335a)

Even Plato, who seems to have taken issue with Protagoras on virtually every front, had to acknowledge the sophist's fame and accomplishments. Few intellectuals ever have enjoyed the reputation and influence of Protagoras in his prime. He was the first and most successful sophist (see Sophists), he was an intimate acquaintance of Pericles (the leader of Athenian democracy in its golden age), he set the constitution for the Athenian colony of Thurii, he wrote on a wide range of subjects (morality, linguistics, the afterlife, mathematics, argumentation, and wrestling), and, as Plato attests, he was a renowned public speaker and debater.

Reports about Protagoras' life are sketchy, but about some details we may be confident. He was born in Abdera, Thrace, and he had some association with the island of Teos. He lived at least 70 years, during which time he travelled much, visiting Athens more than once. He had a long and successful career as a professional teacher, which was the basis of his considerable fame. Beyond this, the details are less certain, for our biographical sources are inconsistent, and many come from several hundred years after Protagoras' death.

Philostratus reports that Protagoras' father was one of the wealthiest men in Thrace, whose connections were so powerful that Protagoras was permitted to study with the Zoroastrian priests by special order of Xerxes, the Persian king. Another source, Athenaeus, suggests that his origins must have been humbler than this, since he was at one point employed as a porter. Both of these stories are questionable, although the porter story may be derived from a reliable report that Protagoras invented a special shoulder-strap for carrying wood. There is also some controversy over the state of Protagoras' fortunes at the time of his death. Plato (who was born during Protagoras' lifetime [c. 429 BC) reports that the sophist's career spanned 40 years, and that he died with his reputation intact. Later biographers report that his books were publicly burned for promoting irreligion. In response to this charge Protagoras is supposed to have fled Athens, only to die in a shipwreck.

Few passages remain of Protagoras' writings, but what we have suggests that he would fit quite comfortably in a humanities department at most modern universities. The extant fragments form a fairly coherent set of doctrines, despite being from separate works. In religion, Protagoras was agnostic. One book began:

> About the gods, I am not able to know whether they exist or do not exist, nor what they are like in form; for the factors preventing knowledge are many: the obscurity of the subject, and the shortness of human life.

His agnosticism ties in with what, today, we might call secular humanism. This position is further suggested by the most famous of the surviving fragments, which is the opening sentence of another book, *Truth*:

> Of all things the measure is Man, of things that are, that they are, and of things that are not, that they are not.

This principle, the Man-measure doctrine, may be referring to 'man' (*anthropos*) as the community, or to the subjective judgment of individuals. If 'man' is understood as a community, then Protagoras may be saying that when a group of people collectively agrees to call something cold that agreement makes it correct to call it cold. This interpretation would make Protagoras a cultural relativist. If 'man' is understood in a subjective sense, then he may be saying that something which appears cold to me is cold for me, while at the same time if it appears hot to you it is hot for you. This interpretation would make Protagoras a subjectivist. In any case, Protagoras' views of God and humanity seem to anticipate perfectly the 18th century English poet, Alexander Pope: 'presume not god to scan, the proper study of mankind is man'.

On scientific matters, Protagoras maintained that all things are in flux, and that the nature of any phenomenon is nothing other than the sum of its appearances. Because we cannot get beyond the appearances of natural phenomena in order to grasp their essences, Protagoras—as with other sophists—was skeptical about the prospects of scientific research. Protagoras believed that, there being no objective state of affairs to validate or invalidate a claim, one could argue with equal force for or against any proposition. For this reason, his program of education probably concentrated on rhetoric and oratory, with the final fragment suggesting that he understood education to have a moral purpose:

> Teaching needs natural endowment and practice. Learning must begin in youth.

> Education does not take root in the soul unless it goes deep.

> Skill without concern, and concern without skill, are equally worthless.

The wealth Protagoras amassed from teaching was extraordinary, and his method of charging students seems to have been calculated to demonstrate how highly they valued his instruction. Reportedly, a student had to pay Protagoras only after receiving instruction and only as much as the student deemed the instruction to be worth. Apparently Protagoras made a special arrangement with one student, Euathlus, for instruction in forensic oratory. Euathlus would need to pay his fees only if he won his first case. After completing his studies, Euathlus declined to put his skills to the test, in this way avoiding both the disgrace of losing a case and the obligation to pay Protagoras. When Protagoras realized what Euathlus was up to, he sued for payment. Protagoras' argument was simple:

> If I win the case you [Euathlus] must pay me according to the decision of the judges, and if you win you must pay me according to the terms of our agreement; thus win or lose you are equally condemned.

Evidently Euathlus was an apt pupil, for he turned the argument against his former teacher:

> Whatever the outcome of the suit, I am freed of having to pay what you demand. For either I win the case and thus am cleared by the court's decree, or I am beaten and thus am cleared by the terms of our original bargain.

It is a sign of Protagoras' prestige that Plato turned the spotlight on him in two major dialogues. In the *Theaetetus* the Man-measure doctrine is introduced as part of an account of knowledge as perception. Protagoras was, in fact, dead by the time of the dialogue, but Socrates asks everyone to imagine him popping his head out of the ground in order to defend his most famous doctrine. (The doctrine is also discussed briefly in the *Cratylus* and in the *Euthydemus*.)

In the *Protagoras* (written in the 4th century BC), however, the whole man appears and, although the Man-measure doctrine is never discussed, he is given ample room to speak at length. The dialogue pits Protagoras, the leading sophist of the era at the height of his powers, against Socrates, Plato's own intellectual inspiration. They discuss the nature and value of Protagoras' programme of education, and at times Protagoras gets the better of Socrates. At the outset of their discussion Protagoras describes his program of higher education as instruction in political virtue and good judgment. While other sophists teach technical subjects, Protagoras promises to prepare students for political careers that will bring them influence and fame. In a litigious, democratic city such as Athens, this preparation would consist in training for public speaking in the law courts and the assembly. When Socrates expresses doubts that political virtue can be taught, Protagoras responds with a tour-de-force speech that includes a mythical account about the origin of humanity, an illuminating picture of conventional primary education, law and morality, and an innovative penology.

The myth about the origin of humanity that is related in the *Protagoras* is one of our few ancient sources for the Prometheus myth. Protagoras' version appears to be a variation of the story as it is found in Hesiod's *Theogony* (510-616) and *Works and Days* (42-106). Epimetheus, Prometheus's brother, created all the animal species, equipping each with a set of physiological defenses and behavioural habits designed to help it survive—fur, talons, speed, prodigious breeding, and so on. Human beings were equipped last, but because nothing remained in Epimetheus' stockpile, we were left entirely defenseless. Prometheus then sought to save human beings by stealing fire and technical know-how from the gods, and giving these to humanity. Still, people were vulnerable to predation because they lacked the social skills to live in groups and protect each other. At this point, Zeus intervened to instill in everyone reverence and respect, the virtues required for social harmony.

Protagoras' subsequent account of punishment corroborates his point that everyone believes political virtue to be teachable. When a person is deprived of natural qualities, such as good looks, other people pity them for their deficiencies and do not attempt to censure them. But when someone behaves unjustly the person is punished, for the purpose of punishment is moral correction. Only because people believe political virtue to be teachable do they correct others with an eye to the future. Moreover, every person in a community participates in the moral development of every other citizen, and all education from the beginning has such guidance in mind. Protagoras claims only that he is a little better than others in providing guidance, and since his teachings apply to more advanced social interactions in the courts and assembly his lessons are only for the most promising citizens.

References and Suggestions for Further Reading

Ancient Textual and Biographical Sources

Diogenes Laertius. *Lives of Eminent Philosophers*. Vol. II. Translated by R.D. Hicks. Cambridge, MA.: Loeb Classical Library, 1925.
Philostratus *Lives of the Sophists*. Translated by Wilmer Cave Wright. Cambridge, MA.: Loeb Classical Library, 1961.
Plato. *Protagoras*. Translated with notes by S. Lombardo and K. Bell. Indianapolis: Hackett Publishing Company, 1992.
Plato. *Theaetetus*. Translated with notes by M.J. Levett, revisions by M. Burnyeat. Indianapolis: Hackett Publishing Company, 1992.

Contemporary Sources and Commentaries

Guthrie, W.K.C. *The Sophists*. Cambridge: Cambridge University Press, 1971.
Kerferd, G.B. *The Sophistic Movement*. Cambridge: Cambridge University Press, 1981.
McKirahan, Richard D. *Philosophy Before Socrates*. Indianapolis: Hackett Publishing Company, 1994.
Waterfield, Robin. *The First Philosophers: the presocratics and the sophists*. Oxford University Press, 2000.
Wheelwright, Philip. *The Presocratics*. Chapter 8. New York, Macmillan Publisher: 1964, reprinted 1985.

Chapter 18

The Sophists

5th Century BC

Jonathan Lavery

One of the most exciting developments of the 5th century BC was the transformation of Greek intellectual culture by a motley, controversial set of figures known as the Sophists. Unlike the Pythagoreans who appeared before them or the Platonists and Peripatetics who emerged after them, the Sophists did not exhibit the cohesion of a school subscribing to a common creed or owing allegiance to a single founder (e.g., Pythagoras, Plato or Aristotle). Nevertheless, the individual Sophists had enough in common to justify collecting them under the same label—even if much of the movement's vitality was due to some fierce internal rivalries. They shared an orientation that was practical rather than a theoretical, and the subjects of their thought were humanistic rather than scientific or metaphysical. Most importantly, the Sophists earned their living by teaching, which makes them the first professionals working in higher education in western history. In fact, it is for this distinction that they remain significant. We should think of the first generation of Sophists as leading members of the 5th century intelligentsia and pioneers in the field of higher education.

The most prominent figures were Protagoras of Abdera, Gorgias of Leontini, Hippias of Elis, Prodicus of Ceos, and Thrasymachus of Chalcedon. Protagoras, the first and most renowned Sophist, offered a program of instruction that promised to improve a student's persuasive powers in oratory and his moral judgment (see Protagoras). Gorgias concentrated on rhetoric (persuasive speech or writing), disavowing any claim to improve his students morally. Hippias was famed for his powers of memory, his versatility and his polymathy (great and varied learning). Prodicus' reputation was based on an analytic ability to draw fine, semantic (verbal) distinctions between synonymous terms. Thrasymachus taught rhetoric and, if Plato's unforgettable portrayal of him in *Republic I* is authentic, he had a cynical view of morality.

Only titles, fragments and a few short examples of the Sophists' written work have survived to the present, but what we have indicates that they made contributions in the study of rhetoric, linguistics, literary theory, anthropology, psychology, social theory, ethics and a number of related fields. In this regard, the Sophists were early forerunners of humanities and social science professors today. What most clearly set them apart from the scientists-philosophers who preceded them is their general indifference to speculative, metaphysical questions about the basic constituents of material entities, the principles governing natural change, the shape of the cosmos, and so on. Instead, the Sophists concentrated on issues of social and political significance: the distinctive features of human nature, the origins of human law, the obligation of a citizen to obey the law, the functions of language, the principles of argumentation, and other questions of this sort. The issue that appears to have attracted the most interest amongst the Sophists is a controversy over whether standards of human conduct should be derived from nature (*physis*) or from law or custom (*nomos*). All the major Sophists staked a position on this question, which we now refer to as the *nomo-physis* debate.

Many Sophists were famous for argumentative innovation. One stock claim was that a Sophist could defend any position on any question, and, moreover, he could teach others the skill to do this too. This oratorical facility went beyond speech-making, for several Sophists also devised techniques for answering briefly any question put to him. The argumentative method used to defend any and all sides of a debate has come to be known as *antilogy*, and facility with this method is lampooned in the debate between the Stronger *Logos* and the Weaker *Logos* in Aristophanes' *Clouds*. We have one unattributed text, *Dissoi Logoi* (Opposing Arguments), that illustrates the antilogical technique of pairing contrary theses. Herein lies a clue as to why the Sophists concentrated on practical matters rather than scientific research: If no given proposition is more defensible than its contrary, then it is not possible to assert either proposition as true in the scientific sense that one of them uniquely corresponds to a mind-independent state of affairs. For this reason, it was believed that debates hinged not on one side establishing the truth of their fundamental claim, but, rather, on one side swaying the audience through oratorical virtuosity, clever wordplay, and any rhetorical means at the speaker's disposal. On the issues that fascinated the Sophists and their student-patrons the decisive factor was not how the world is structured in itself, but how people conceive it to be structured. In this regard, the Sophists would have endorsed the famous remark in Wittgenstein's *Tractatus Logico-Philosophicus*: 'The limits of my language mean the limits of my world.'

The Sophists thrived in what is now acknowledged to be a golden era of Greek culture, and their accomplishments were in keeping with the times. Arguably, they were more intimately connected to the zeitgeist, the spirit of their times, than any other group of intellectuals since. If general prosperity and comparative peace were fertile conditions for spawning the cosmological and metaphysical speculations of the Pre-Socratic scientists in the 6th century, greater prosperity and unbounded political ambition proved to be equally fertile for a humanist turn in the middle of the 5th century. The Greek city-states—led by Athens and Sparta—had repelled Persian invasions in 490 and 480 BC, Aeschylus and Sophocles brought drama to full maturity by 431, the silver mines of Laurion (south-east of Athens, at the tip of the Attic peninsula) fuelled an economic boom, and bold leaders such as Pericles channelled political willpower into grand civic projects (e.g., the Parthenon). Athens, especially, was a cauldron of creative and intellectual energy, with the period from 480 to 431 being marked by a verve and buoyancy that has rarely been approached anywhere since.

Because the Sophists taught practical argumentation, rhetoric and oratory, it was natural that they gravitated to Athens, where such skills were in demand. Theoretically, every male citizen had an opportunity to participate in the political life of history's most famous democracy. Indeed, a male was *expected* to take an active role in public life, be that in commerce, the assembly, or the law courts. As innovative teachers, the Sophists had an indirect influence on the character of the city, even though, as foreigners, they could not participate directly in official political affairs.

When the golden age came crashing to an end with the long, divisive Peloponnesian War between Athens and Sparta (431–404 BC), the conditions in which the earliest Sophists flourished disappeared, and the movement lost much of its initial vitality. This misfortune, combined with a long-standing distrust of their new education by traditional aristocrats and Plato's influential criticism of sophistry (both of individual figures and of the movement as a whole), blighted their reputation for most of the next 2500 years. The label 'Sophist' soon became a pejorative term in most circles, synonymous with 'charlatan'. Aristotle's work on fallacious reasoning is emblematic of the antipathy directed towards the Sophists a century after their finest hour. The title of this work is *Sophistical Refutations*, and in it Aristotle defines sophistical reasoning as bad reasoning that, through deception, passes for sound argumentation (164b25-165a19). This abuse of the Sophists at the hands of Plato and Aristotle had a lasting affect on their legacy, for few of their own writings survived to correct any misrepresentations or exaggerations by Plato or Aristotle. The spirit of sophistry was revived during the Second Sophistic in the 2nd century AD, but by the time Flavius Philostratus wrote *Lives of the Sophists* in the 3rd century AD very few works of the early figures were available still for him to consult.

References and Suggestions for Further Reading

Ancient Textual and Biographical Sources

Aristophanes. *Clouds*. Translated with notes by Peter Meineck, with an introduction by Ian C. Storey. Indianapolis, IN.: Hackett Publishing Company, 2000.
Athenaeus. *Deipnosophists*. 7 volumes. Translation by Charles Burton Gulick. Cambridge, MA.: Loeb Classical Library, 1955-61.
Diogenes Laertius. *Lives of Eminent Philosophers*. Translated by R.D. Hicks. Cambridge, MA.: Loeb Classical Library, 1925).
Philostratus. *Lives of the Sophists*. Translated by Wilmer Cave Wright. Cambridge, MA.: Loeb Classical Library, 1961.
Plato. *Complete Works*. Edited by John M. Cooper. Indianapolis, IN.: Hackett Publishing Company, 1997. See, especially, the following dialogues: *Protagoras, Gorgias, Hippias Minor, Hippias Major, Apology, Meno, Euthydemus, Cratylus, Republic, Theaetetus* and *Sophist*.

Contemporary Sources and Commentaries

Grote, George. *Plato, and the other companions of Sokrates.* London: J Murray, 1867.
Guthrie, W.K.C. *The Sophists.* Cambridge: Cambridge University Press, 1971).
Kerferd, G.B. *The Sophistic Movement.* Cambridge: Cambridge University Press, 1981.
Richard D. McKirahan, Richard D. *Philosophy before Socrates.* Indianapolis: Hackett Publishing Company, 1994.
Romilly, Jacqueline de. *The great Sophists in Periclean Athens.* Translated by Janet Lloyd. Oxford: Oxford University Press, 1992.
Waterfield, Robin. *The First Philosophers: the presocratics and the Sophists.* Oxford: Oxford University Press, 2000.
Wheelwright, Philip. *The Presocratics.* Chapter 8. New York: Macmillan Publisher, 1964, reprinted 1985.

Chapter 19

Zeno of Elea

c. 490 BC–??

Doukas Kapantaïs

The debate has lasted these several thousand years.
Most likely, it will last several thousand more. (Paul Benacerraf on questions raised by Zeno's puzzles in Salmon, see bibliography, pp. 103-104)

Born in Elea, South Italy, Zeno was a pupil and follower of Parmenides. In around 450 he travels with his mentor to Athens where they undertake a philosophical discussion with Socrates, who was then under the age of twenty. This is how Plato reports the meeting:

Parmenides was then about 65 years old, very white with age but looking good. Zeno was about 40, tall and handsome. When he was younger rumors are that he was the lover of Parmenides. [...] (Parmenides and Zeno) lodged with Pythodorus in the Ceramicus, outside the wall, where the very young Socrates came to see them. [...] (they) wanted to hear the treatise of Zeno, which had been brought to Athens for the first time on the occasion of their visit. (Plato, *Parmenides*, 127A-B)

Later in the dialogue Zeno said that he wrote the treatise when very young, and in order to defend Parmenides. As tradition has it, the book contained forty arguments, all directed against the hypothesis that there are many things; a hypothesis going against the teaching of his master that there is only the 'One'. More precisely, Zeno's defense of Parmenides was directed against those who were presenting Parmenides' theory as a counterintuitive, if not ridiculous, doctrine. Who exactly these people were is not clear, and, in any event, not necessary in order for us to see the purpose of Zeno's book. What Zeno was trying to do was to present their own beliefs as even more absurd. In other words, he was trying to extract absurdities out of the innocent and seemingly self-evident premise that there is a plurality of things. The forty paradoxes were the way he approached it. They all commenced with an assumption based upon the thesis that there are many things, and concluding with a sentence which defies belief by any person of common sense.

Only a dozen of the paradoxes have survived to our times, and some of them are possibly inauthentic. The paradox of the millet seed is not the most elegant, but it is quite impressive. Zeno addresses the following question to Protagoras, the famous sophist:

> 'Tell me, Protagoras', he said, 'does a single millet seed make a sound when it falls? Or the ten-thousandth part of a seed?' Protagoras said that it didn't. 'What about a bushel of millet seed', he said, 'does that make a sound when it falls or not?' He said that the bushel did make a sound. 'Well', said Zeno, 'isn't there a ratio between the bushel and the single seed, or the ten-thousandth part of a single seed?' He agreed. 'Well then', said Zeno, 'won't the sounds too stand in the same ratios to one another? For as the sounders are, so are the sounds. And if that's so, then if the bushel makes a sound, the single seed and the ten-thousandth part of a seed will make a sound too.' (Simplicius, *Comments on Aristotle's Physics*, 1108, 18)

The technical points of the argument and the exact details about how they might negate the fact that there are many things are rather complicated (the reader is invited to consult Barnes, in the bibliography). In any case, one cannot fail to admire the acuteness of its presentation. There is a certain ratio between every magnitude and any of its parts. Nevertheless, the same ratio does not hold between the sound it makes, when it falls to the ground, and the sound its parts are making. If the part is too small, the sound is annihilated—it makes no sound at all. The whole argument is not to be counted among Zeno's best. One could object that the sound a very small part makes is just inaudible to human ears. Does this mean that it makes no sound at all?

Among the arguments which survive, four stand out: the paradoxes of motion. They have haunted such brilliant intellects as Aristotle's and Kant's, and even today there is no unanimous agreement upon how they are to be solved—*if* there is a way to solve them! Consider the first. It is called the *Dichotomy*:

> There is no motion, for what is travelling must reach the midpoint before the end (Aristotle, *Physics* VI. 8. 239b11).

Do you believe that any distance (however small it might be), has a midpoint? If yes, you have a paradox on your hands. Consider the distance to be from point A to point B. The traveller who begins from A has, in order to reach B, to arrive first at the mid-point of the AB distance. Call this point C. Now, the same traveller has, in order to reach C, to arrive first at the mid-point of the AC distance. Call that point D. The same argument can go on infinitely. But, then again, it must be agreed that one cannot perform an infinite number of travels, within a finite period of time; can one?

A possible objection to the paradox is that the distance AB is not infinitely divisible: there might be some indivisible minimal distances. In that case you have to solve the second paradox of motion, the *Flying Arrow*:

> If everything is always at rest when it occupies a space equal to itself, and if what is moving is always 'at a now,' the moving arrow is motionless (Aristotle, *Physics* VI. 9. 239b5-7).

You are watching the flight of an arrow on your video screen. Using the remote control you freeze the picture. Consider this to be a 'now' within the arrow's travel. One cannot help but agree that the arrow is looking both motionless *and* occupying a space equal to itself. But one also has to admit that he can freeze the screen whenever he likes. How many times can that be? Well, since there are minimal distances, it might not be an infinite number of times. Therefore, the arrow's flight is made out of a certain finite number of 'now-s' during which it does not move. But, then again, how has the arrow moved in the first place? Has it been jumping from each minimal distance to the next in no time? Many 'no times' when taken together make no time. Did the arrow travel in no time at all?

'This is a plain sophism!' one might object. Well, the objector has to think again: notable physicists of the 20th century, although convinced that there has to be a fallacy in the argument, have been unable to spot it. And, until now, no one has ever proposed a definite solution.

Another striking paradox, combining notions of both space-time and motion, is the *Achilles*. Achilles, the Homeric hero, is exceedingly swift. Suppose he is trying to catch a tortoise. Will he do it? Well, according to Zeno, if the tortoise continues to move in the same direction, he never will:

> …the slow will never be caught in running by the fastest. For the pursuer must first get to where the pursued started from, so it is necessary that the slower should always be some distance ahead. (Aristotle, *Physics* VI. 9. 239b14)

Even in the case that the faster is as quick as swift Achilles, and the slower as slow as the tortoise, he will never catch him. If Achilles starts from point A at the time that the tortoise has reached point B, Achilles has to arrive at B before catching the tortoise. But the tortoise is moving in the same direction, and so, by the time Achilles reaches B, the tortoise is at C. Now Achilles has to reach C before catching the tortoise. By the time he does, the tortoise is at D. And this goes on forever …

The fourth argument against motion is both complicated and unclear. It is called the *Stadium* or the *Moving Rows* and, because there is no space to pursue this paradox, the reader who seeks further exhilaration in attempting to unravel it, should refer to Aristotle's *Physics,* 239b33-240a18, or to the reference list.

Now, how did these arguments defend Parmenides against his critics? Was there an internal structural plan within the book? Was the book a collection of forty independent puzzles? Scholars have long debated these questions, without reaching a definite answer.

Zeno's paradoxes reveal insoluble mathematical problems. In reality Aristotle proposed solutions to some of them. What he did was based upon the distinction between 'potential' and the 'actual'. In modern times, many mathematicians have tried to exploit the tools of the infinitesimal calculus, but, in any event, it is very unlikely that the final word has been pronounced for any one among the four paradoxes of motion.

Some people owe posterity to their lives. Others owe it to their work. Zeno certainly belongs in the latter category. But the fact which is so utterly surprising about him is that his work, as we now know it, is but a bunch of fascinating puzzles, which continue to captivate philosophers and mathematicians who still strive, and still fail, to attain the answer. And, still we wonder how, and in what way they unexpectedly attack our common notions of place, time and motion.

References and Suggestions for Further Reading

Aristotle. *Physics*. The revised Oxford translation. Princeton, 1984.

Barnes, J. *The Presocratic Philosophers*. London: 1979; vol. 1, pp. 231-295. (For a study and evaluation of Zeno's work.)

Kirk, G.S., J.E. Raven and M. Schofield. *The Presocratic Philosophers*. Cambridge: Cambridge University Press, 1983. (Provides English translations and brief commentaries of the fragments.)

McKirahan, R. Jr. Zeno, in A.A. Long (ed). *Early Greek Philosophy*. Cambridge UP, 1999. (A recent study.)

Plato. *Parmenides*. Loeb Classical Library. London: Heinemann, 1963.

Salmon, Wesley C. Ed. *Zeno's Paradoxes*. Indianapolis and New York: Bobbs-Merrill, 1970. (A glimpse into the impact Zeno still has upon modern scientists and philosophers.)

Chapter 20

Sophocles

c. 490 BC–c. 401 BC

James M. Magrini

You that live in my ancestral Thebes, behold this Oedipus,—
him who knew the famous riddles and was a man most masterful;
not a citizen who did not look with envy on his lot—
see him now and see the breakers of misfortune swallow him!
Look upon that last day always. Count no mortal happy till
he has passed the final limit of his life secure from pain.
(*Oedipus the King*, 1525-1530)

As Oedipus, the once proud king of Thebes walked in exile, a blind and broken man, the chorus proclaimed, 'Call no one happy who is of mortal race, until they have crossed life's border, free from pain.' Unlike the characters in such plays as *Oedipus Rex*, who experienced tragic reversals of fortune, Sophocles, the greatest of the Greek tragedians, enjoyed a remarkably long, prosperous, and happy life.

Sophocles was born in Colonus, near Athens in approximately 490 BC and his final tragedy, *Oedipus at Colonus*, served as an encomium to the land of his birth. His vivid descriptions of the green, fertile land, majestic wild horses, crocuses blooming with golden beams, and nightingales singing amid groves of olive and fruit trees, expressed the heartfelt adoration he held for Colonus.

From early on, Sophocles received training in the arts. As a youth, he earned a coveted position within the dancing chorus, celebrating the Greeks' sea victory over the Persian fleet at Salamis. While both singing and dancing fascinated the young Sophocles, his mind was set on successful playwriting. In 468 BC, he submitted three tragic plays for the city's annual drama competition, being held in conjunction with the festival of Dionysus. There, he was awarded his first victory. How self-assured Sophocles must have been when he defeated, at his inaugural outing as a poet, the older, reigning king of Greek tragedy, Aeschylus.

Sophocles, 'The Attic Bee,' so nicknamed for the ability to extract 'honey' from words, was the most successful of the Greek playwrights, recording an astounding twenty-four first place finishes, thereby exceeding the accomplishments of both Aeschylus and Euripides. For competition, Sophocles composed his plays as 'tetralogies', or, more specifically, three tragic dramas and a comic farce or *Satyr* play. It is likely that Sophocles composed over 120 plays during his life. Unfortunately, only seven of these remain intact. Yet, because of his unparalleled record of victories, one can safely assume that his lost works were every bit as powerful as those that have survived.

With his technical and dramatic innovations, Sophocles explicitly shaped the development of the Athenian theater in three ways. First, he introduced a technique of scene painting on large backdrops. Next, he increased the size of the chorus from twelve to fifteen members. No longer in the background, the chorus emerged as a main character and directly participated in the action. Finally, and most importantly, he increased the number of actors from two to three. This change substantially increased the number of speaking parts, allowing the playwright to illuminate the chief character from several points of view.

Archaic mythology served as Sophocles' subject matter. He loved stories about the Trojan War as well as those concerned with the fortunes of Thebes and its royal family (The Theban Cycle). Sophocles attempted to understand human suffering by: (1) reassessing traditions and ideals from the past, (2) questioning the public and private responsibility of the individual, and (3) exploring profound issues of justice and morality. While Aeschylus struggled with the gods, and Euripides strove for psychological realism, Sophocles focused on the human 'divinity' of the uncompromising hero or heroine as they battled the unseen forces of fate.

Characters such as Ajax, Antigone, and Oedipus raised the standards by which ordinary humanity was judged. They were wiser and stronger than others, always more pious and courageous than the rest, yet flawed. For in addition to their 'god-like' qualities, they also possessed human weaknesses, such as a great capacity for suffering. Thus their imperfections were inseparable from the qualities that defined them as 'tragic' heroes.

For example, Ajax, the archaic Greek warrior, was portrayed as violent, arrogant, and self-serving. His Old World values were out of place in the democratic era of Sophocles, where forgiveness, compassion, and compromise ruled the day. Ajax could not bring himself to accept that the 'warrior's code', while once honored, had no place within a changing world. While his imperfections were significant, he was nonetheless the only Greek brave enough, strong enough, and skillful enough to have engaged Hector in battle.

Antigone too suffered because of the heroic dichotomy present to all of Sophocles' greatest characters. The girl, 'who feared to cast away the fear of heaven', could not have sacrificed love and life were she not on some level cursed with a greater than human obsession for moral justice. Although her defiant attitude ultimately leads to destruction, her courageous actions succeed in illustrating that not even a king holds entitlement to trample on a person's fundamental natural rights.

Finally, we see Oedipus, the man who eventually discovered, through unyielding probing, that the abhorrent crimes of patricide and incest were in fact his own. Admittedly, he was overly self-righteous and quick-tempered, 'exciting his soul overmuch with all manner of alarms'. However, were it not for these traits, he could never have continued on in his quest to rid Thebes of its curse. Sophocles is telling us that only a virtuous man would pursue the truth, even if it resulted in his own downfall.

Sophocles played a substantial role in the Athenian government prior to and during the Peloponnesian Wars (431 BC–404 BC). In 439 BC he acted as treasurer to the Delian league, an office of considerable prestige. In this capacity, he was in charge of collecting taxes from the member states of the Athenian Empire. Sophocles also served as a military general under the command of Pericles during the famous Athenian siege of the Island of Samos in 441 BC.

During the year 415 BC, at the advanced age of 83, and following many years of dedicated civil service, Sophocles was appointed to a special executive post within the government. At this time, Sophocles was twice married with two sons, one of whom, Iophon, went on to enjoy a thriving career as a tragic poet, presumably benefiting from his father's mentoring. Between his political and artistic commitments, the altruistic Sophocles found time to help those afflicted with illness and was a dedicated priest in the religious cult of *Asclepius*, the god of healing and medicine.

Sophocles' final play *Oedipus at Colonus*, completed in 400 BC, a year before his death, centred on the final days of Oedipus. After years of wandering in exile, Oedipus arrives in Colonus and at last finds sanctuary with the legendary Athenian king Theseus. We might imagine Sophocles, at the end of his days, like Oedipus, led by Antigone and Ismene to the place where he will depart the land of the living. As the messenger describes the death of Oedipus, he may well have referred to Sophocles:

> It was no fiery thunderbolt of god
> That made away with him, nor a sea hurricane rising;
> no, it was some messenger
> sent by the gods, or some power of the dead
> split open the fundament of earth, with good will,
> to give him painless entry. He was sent on his way
> with no accompaniment of tears, no pain of sickness;
> if any man ended miraculously,
> this man did.
> (*Oedipus at Colonus*, 1659-1667)

Aristotle in *Poetics*, praised Sophocles and singled out *Oedipus Rex* as the paragon of Greek tragedy. Sophocles expressed a profound understanding of the human situation and his plays continue to furnish consummate and eternal models for artistic and moral emulation. As tribute to his protracted genius, the works of Sophocles regularly appear in new translations and are frequently adapted for both the modern stage (*Antigone*, Jean Anouilh, 1944) as well as the screen (*Oedipus Rex*, Pier Paolo Pasolini, 1967).

References and Suggestions for Further Reading

Aristotle. *Aristotle Poetics*. Trans. Malcolm Heath. Harmondsworth: Penguin Group, 1996.
Kitto, H.D.F. *Greek Tragedy*. London: Methuen, 1961.

Knox, Bernard. *The Heroic Temper: Studies in Sophoclean Tragedy.* Berkeley: University of California Press, 1964.

Sophocles. *The Complete Greek Tragedies: Sophocles.* Trans. David Grene and Richard Lattimore. Chicago: University of Chicago Press, 1957.

Sophocles. *The Complete Plays of Sophocles.* Trans. Sir Richard Claverhouse Jebb. Ed. Moses Hadas. New York: Bantam, 1982.

Woodward, Thomas, editor. *Sophocles: A Collection of Critical Essays.* New Jersey: Prentice-Hall, 1966.

Chapter 21

Euripides

c. 484 BC–c. 407 BC

Seamus Sweeney

> To be rich and powerful brings no blessing;
> Only more utterly
> Is the prosperous house destroyed, when the gods are angry. *(Medea*, lines 127-129,
> translated Philip Vellacott)

Of the 'big three' Athenian tragedians, Aeschylus, Sophocles, and Euripides, Euripides was the least regarded in his own lifetime. Perhaps for that very reason, he chimes well with modern sensibilities; a pacifist who portrayed sympathetically the suffering of believable female characters, whose drama challenged the Athenian self-image, he is among the most performed and adapted ancient dramatists.

Trojan Women and *Medea* in particular are regularly revived. *Trojan Women* (made into a movie, in 1971, with Katherine Hepburn and Vanessa Redgrave) focuses on the immediate aftermath of the sack of Troy—with the menfolk murdered and the city in flames, the women of defeated Troy bemoan their fate (and hurl abuse at Helen, whose beauty triggered the conflict) as they wait to be taken off to Greece as slaves. A contemporary Athenian audience would have seen the parallels with the Athenian sack of the city of Melos, and the subsequent slaughter of the inhabitants which had occurred a few years earlier. This refusal to flatter Athenian sensibilities contributed to his unpopularity—little wonder he is supposed to have isolated himself with his library on the island of Salamis.

Euripides won the Great Dionysia, the supreme festival of Athenian drama, only five times compared with Aeschylus' thirteen and Sophocles' eighteen. In his dialogue, *Poetics*, Aristotle alludes to a saying attributed to Sophocles: he (Sophocles) portrayed men as they ought to be, while Euripides portrayed them as they are. Born into an aristocratic family, Euripides was early exposed to the philosophical and social ideas current in Athens at the time—the philosopher Anaxagoras, who insisted on the physical reality of, for example, the Sun (which he declared to be a red-hot stone as opposed to it being a divine phenomenon), was a particular influence. He was also early involved in the religion of Athens, which he would subsequently question—as a child he served as cup bearer to the dancers of the Guild of Apollo.

In later life Euripides was much satirized by Aristophanes and other comic poets as a subversive influence and a near-unintelligible dramatic innovator. As intolerance and militarism swept Athens, friends and associates of Euripides were executed—Euripides escaped death only because it was his characters who voiced impiety, not him. Tradition has it—though modern scholarship casts doubt upon the belief—that he left or was exiled from Athens, a disappointed, disillusioned man. In any case, he went to live at the court of King Archelaus of Macedonia. A year and a half later, he was (again according to tradition) accidentally torn to pieces by the King's hounds.

Like Sophocles and Aeschylus, Euripides was a great innovator within the framework of Athenian drama. His later plays are seen as marking the decline of the importance of the Chorus in Greek drama, its role being increasingly limited to poetic decoration rather than relating to the action of the play. Euripides uses a more everyday, less elevated style than Sophocles or Aeschylus. Along with this tendency towards naturalism, Euripides increasingly used song for dramatic purposes in near-operatic fashion.

Medea, like *Trojan Women*, is oft revived, and is seen as one of the great female roles in the theatre of any age. Medea helped Jason and his Argonauts win the Golden Fleece, in the process betraying her father, the King of Colchis. As the play opens she has returned to Corinth with Jason, and as her nurse tells us:

> But now her world has turned to enmity, and wounds her
> Where her affection's deepest. Jason has betrayed
> His own sons, and my mistress, for a royal bed,
> For alliance with the King of Corinth. He has married
> Glauce, Creon's daughter. (*Medea*, lines 15-19)

Creon plans to send Medea and her sons into exile. Medea gives a magnificently defiant speech, and then manages to persuade Creon to give her a day to prepare for exile. He might have done better to heed his own earlier words that:

> A woman of quick temper—and a man the same—
> Is a less dangerous enemy than one quiet and clever. (*Medea*, lines 319-320)

After pleading with Jason, Creon is persuaded to spare Medea's two sons by Jason from exile. Medea then begins to conceive a truly horrifying act—the murder of her own children. Medea's agonizing about this is genuinely moving, and the psychological realism of Euripides' approach gives the play its great power. Medea kills her children, and for good measure uses her magical arts to bring a horrible death to Glauce. Creon dies on seeing his daughter dead, and in a final *coup de theatre*, Medea appears with the bodies of her two children on the top of the stage in a chariot drawn by dragons, hurling invective at Jason. As the Chorus ends the play:

> Many matters the gods bring to surprising ends.
> The things we thought would happen do not happen;

The unexpected God makes possible;
And such is the conclusion of this story.

Electra concerns the house of Atreus, material covered by Aeschylus in the *Oresteia* (see the entry on Aeschylus for a summary of the plot), and specifically the events leading to the killing of Clytemnestra by her son, Orestes, with the aid of her daughter, Electra. With his very different attitude to the piety of the Athenians, Euripides portrays the revenge as a product of fear and weakness, as opposed to Aeschylus' ultimate vindication of Orestes. Euripides emphasizes the sacrilegious, taboo aspects of the killing. Violence in Euripides is never heroic, or redemptive.

The Bacchae and *Iphigenia at Aulis* were both written in Macedonia and had not been performed when Euripides died. Focusing on the cult of Dionysus, *The Bacchae* is sometimes seen as a return to the worship of the gods by the freethinking Euripides, yet it is more likely to be an exploration of the consequences of denying the physical, 'Dionysian' side of human nature—as Philip Vellacott writes: 'when the civilised becomes arrogant and masterful, it is betrayed from within by the bestial'. The king of Thebes, Pentheus, has excluded Dionysus from public rites. The god takes human form and travels to Thebes, and practises his rites with his followers, the Bacchae. Pentheus orders Dionysus' arrest, yet in long dialogues (an example of Euripides' naturalism) the god-in-human-form persuades Pentheus to disguise himself as a woman and witness the rites of the Bacchae, Dionysus' followers. The Bacchae tear Pentheus limb from limb—his own mother, Agauë, tears his head off believing it to be a young lion's, and thus the ultimate price is paid for denying the physical side of life. After a heartbreaking recognition scene where she realizes she has killed her own son, Agauë and the other Bacchae go into exile.

Iphigenia at Aulis explores cowardice and cruelty practised in the name of religion. Iphigenia, daughter of Agamemnon, was brought with the Greek army campaigning against Troy in the expectation that she would be married to Achilles; instead she was sacrificed to gain favourable winds.

Twenty of Euripides' tragedies survive, more than either Sophocles or Aeschylus. Ironically the only surviving complete 'satyr-play'—a sort of broad farce that would conclude an Athenian theatrical performance, after a tragic trilogy—is Euripides' The *Cyclops*.

References and Suggestions for Further Reading

All of Euripides' works are available online at http://classics.mit.edu/Browse/index.html

Quotations are from Philip Vellacott's translations cited below.

Bates, W.N. *Euripides: Student of Human Nature.* New York: University of Pennsylvania Press, 1930—reprinted 1969.
Decharme, Paul. *Euripides and the Spirit of His Dramas.* Translated by James Loeb. New York: Kennicat Press, 1968.

Gould, John P.A. Entry on Euripides in *Who's Who in the Classical* World. Oxford: Oxford University Press, 2000.

Goward, Barbra, *Telling Tragedy: Narrative Technique in Aeschylus, Sophocles and Euripides*. London: Duckworth Press, 1999.

Vellacott, Philip. Introduction to *'Medea and Other Plays'*. Harmondsworth: Penguin, 1963.

Vellacott, Philip. Introduction to *'The Bacchae and Other Plays'*. Harmondsworth: Penguin, 1973.

Chapter 22

Herodotus

c. 490–425/420 BC

Christine Farmer

It is always the great buildings and the tall trees which are struck by lightning. It is God's way to bring the lofty low. Often a great army is destroyed by a little one, when God in his envy puts fear into the men's hearts, or sends a thunderstorm, and they are cut to pieces in a way they do not deserve. For God tolerates pride in none but Himself. (*Histories*, VII. 10e-f)

In *The Histories*, Herodotus traces the cause and direction of the Persian Wars, in which the poor, independent city-states of Greece acted in concert to defeat invasion by a mighty eastern empire. He saw the origins of the conflict in a series of mythological abductions and counter-abductions between East and West, amongst them Helen of Troy. Retribution (*tisis*) then motivated each act of the war itself: 'Grant, O God, that I may punish the Athenians,' exclaimed Darius upon learning they had burnt the Persian provincial capital of Sardis (*Histories*, V. 105). Athens herself was to burn in retribution.

Herodotus' stated aim was to record and give fame to great human acts, and he painted a lively picture of the Persian kings Cyrus, Darius and Xerxes, and the Greek leaders Leonidas and Themistocles. Yet we know little of Herodotus' own life. He tells us that he was born in the Persian dependency of Halicarnassus, in south-west Asia Minor, and tradition suggests he died in Thurii, Italy. He described travelling south to the first cataract of the Nile (*Histories*, II. 29), and north to the Black Sea (*Histories*, IV. 76-81), and it is probable he spent some time in Athens. His dates are approximated from events mentioned in his work.

The word '*historia*' meant 'investigations', and Herodotus studied in disciplines that today are called anthropology, religious studies, natural history and geography. He described the peoples involved in the invasions, notably the Egyptians and the Scythians. Indeed his treatment of the latter remains the most important ancient source on this culture. While he had precursors in many areas of investigation, Herodotus was unique in bringing together such a wide variety of information to answer a question he was the first to ask: Why do wars happen? He believed that environment and custom played as great a part in human events as personal motivation, the divine and Fate. Herodotus wove these themes together to create a readable and fascinating account of the conflict, and a document of his own beliefs and thoughts.

Soft countries ... breed soft men. It is not the property of any one soil to produce fine fruits and good soldiers too. (*Histories*, IX. 122)

For Herodotus, the Persian Wars were within living memory, and he interviewed priests, record-keepers and veterans, visited cities and temples, and inspected the heaped bones of the fallen on battlefields (*Histories*, III. 12). Much of Herodotus' data was oral evidence from peoples with conflicting views of the past. Rather than choose between them, Herodotus often recorded two or more versions of events, reminding his audience:

My business is to record what people say, but I am by no means bound to believe it. (*Histories*, VII. 152)

It is thought that Herodotus originally read aloud his work in private and public performances. It was therefore necessary that his work was informative, entertaining and stimulating. From him we learn the main theories of the Nile's inundations (*Histories*, II. 19-27), the erection of the pyramids (*Histories*, II. 124 ff.), the process of mummification (*Histories*, II. 86-88), and how to catch a crocodile (*Histories*, II. 70).

Herodotus often presented events and themes in the form of conversations and speeches that he himself scripted. This allowed him to suggest the thoughts and motivations of his protagonists in much the same way as a speech in a play, or the *Dialogues* of Plato. In one such example, the Lydian king Croesus attempts to persuade the wise Athenian Solon to admit that his vast wealth and power made him the happiest man alive. Solon responded that until a man is dead he could not be called happy, simply 'lucky':

Look to the end, no matter what it is you are considering. Often enough, god gives a man a glimpse of happiness, and then utterly ruins him. (*Histories*, I. 32)

With these words, we are forewarned of Croesus' demise, and that of the Persians. According to Herodotus, Croesus could have called himself happy had he simply enjoyed 'the blessings of a sound body, health, freedom from trouble, fine children, and good looks' (*Histories*, I. 32). Herodotus stressed the mutability of all things; great cities, empires and kings eventually fall, and small things become great, for: 'Human prosperity never abides long in the same place' (*Histories*, I. 5).

Herodotus was writing at a time when the Greek city-states that had acted in unison to defeat the Persians, had embarked upon internecine conflict that was to last for twenty-seven years: The Peloponnesian War (431 – 404 BC). The *Histories* can be read in part as a warning against this conflict, and in particular against Athens' imperialism. Herodotus demonstrated that the Persian's failure was due to the overweening pride (*hybris*) of leaders who transgressed nature to extend their empire. By constructing a bridge across the Hellespont, they joined Asia and Europe, and in the words of Xerxes intended to:

... so extend the empire of Persia that its boundaries will be God's own sky, so that the sun will not look down upon any land beyond the boundaries of what is ours. (*Histories*, VII. 8c)

This theme of pride and inevitable downfall is familiar to readers of Greek plays and epic poetry. The Persians met their *nemesis* after fighting a number of now famous battles on land and sea. Before the battles of Thermopylae, Marathon and Salamis, Herodotus had Persian leaders ask how the independent Greeks could prevail against massed numbers under a single king. Xerxes:

If, like ours, their troops were subject to the control of a single man, then possibly for fear of him, in spite of the disparity in numbers, they might show some sort of factitious courage, or let themselves be whipped into battle; but, as every man is free to follow his fancy, it is not conceivable that they should do either. (*Histories*, VII. 103)

But the Persians did not understand that the Greeks were not completely free, but obeyed the rule of Law, and:

Whatever this master commands, they do; and his command never varies: it is never to retreat in battle, however great the odds, but always to remain in formation, and to conquer or die. (*Histories*, VII. 104)

Ultimately, the self-discipline of the Greeks proved superior to slavish obedience to sometimes arbitrarily cruel Persian kings. Yet Herodotus did not seek to mock the Persians. He had great respect for foreign cultures, and often refused to record details of religious beliefs for fear of misinterpretation, since he did 'not think that any one nation knows much more about such things than any other' (*Histories*, II. 3).

In the end, while the events of his life remain unknown, Herodotus' skill as a storyteller, his intelligence, humanity and piety become clear to us through his work:

If all mankind agreed to meet, and everyone brought his own sufferings along with him for the purpose of exchanging them for somebody else's, there is not a man who, after taking a good look at his neighbour's sufferings, would not be only too happy to return home with his own. (*Histories*, VII. 152)

References and Suggestions for Further Reading

Gould, John. *Herodotus: Historians on Historians*. Bristol Classical Press, 2000.

Herodotus. *The Histories*. Trans. Aubrey de Sélincourt. Penguin Classics, revised edition 1972.

Romm, James. *Herodotus*. Yale University Press, 1999.

Thomas, Rosalind. *Herodotus in Context: Ethnography, Science and the Art of Persuasion*. Cambridge: Cambridge University Press, 2000.

Chapter 23

Diotima of Mantineia

c. 470 BC–c. 410 BC

Melanie B. Mineo

> And now I will take my leave of you, and rehearse the tale of love which I heard once upon a time from Diotima of Mantineia, who was a wise woman ... and my instructress in the art of love. (Socrates (Plato, *Symposium* 201D)

Ever the social commentator and reactionary, it should come as no surprise that the Platonic Socrates had a *female* teacher of notoriety: Diotima of Mantineia, the legendary subject of our inquiry.

Situated on a flat marshy plain, surrounded on all sides by mountains, Mantineia was an ancient city in the central district of the Peloponnesian peninsula known as Arcadia. The founding of Mantineia was attributed to Mantineus, a grandson of Pelasgus, the mythical first king of Arcadia, and one of the reputed fifty, impious sons of the infamous Lycaon. Lycosoura, the oldest city, the oldest cult, and the first civilization of Arcadia are all attributed to Lycaon who, myth has it, entertained the disguised Zeus with a dish of human flesh: a child sacrificed on the altar to the new God. It was here, in a wild mountainous region of southwestern Arcadia, that Lycaon is said to have founded and practised the ritual of his Zeus Lycaeus—formally an old Pelasgian or non-Hellenic god—on Mt. Lycaeus, upon whose summit no shadow ever fell (Pausanias, *Description of Greece*: 8.38.1-7).

Zeus Lycaeus was associated with wolves, but ancient legend has it that Mt. Lycaeus received the first and last light from the sun, hence this Zeus was also a radiant God of Light. He-wolves were said to have been kept at Zeus Lycaeus' sanctuary as sacred animals; human sacrifices were offered there, and many of his images were dressed in wolf skins. The cult of Lycaon was eventually absorbed by the Hellenic Zeus, a new deity to whom the practice of human sacrifice and cannibal feasts as forms of worship were forbidden, and thus abandoned. A heap of ashes and a retaining wall—the ruins of the temple complex—are all that remain on the slopes of Mt. Lycaeus (Cook, 1914). It was here, however, to the west of her native city of Mantineia, on a remote mountain on the Peloponnesian peninsula that this bloody cult of Zeus Lycaeus once flourished. Moreover, Diotima, whose name means 'she who is honored by Zeus', was thought, by later Greek writers, to be none other than a priestess and philosopher of the Lycaean Zeus in Arcadia (Dindorf, *Schol. Aristeid.* III, 468, 15f).

The character of Diotima is found only in Plato's *Symposium*, represented by Socrates as a woman wise in diverse types of knowledge, and the source of the Platonic doctrine of *eros*. That Diotima was introduced by Socrates as one who could shift the outbreak of epidemic diseases, as in the case of the Athenian plague (201D), indicates that she was considered the type of seer-healer whom, like Empedocles or Epimenides, advised cities in crisis situations. She is depicted as an extraordinary and singular figure, for rather than using oracles or prophecy as a priestess might to convey her points, Diotima uses what, for a woman, would be highly unusual means of instruction: reason, proof, and argument. Though it cannot be said for certain that Plato is crediting Diotima with the invention of the Socratic, or dialectic method of question and answer (201C), she is offered as having used it with considerable skill prior to the central discussion of *eros* as found in the *Symposium* (201DE).

Diotima was not Athenian, a literary facet which uniquely reflects the ambivalence of Socrates' social position, that of *atopos*, or outsider. Socrates, according to Plato, seems to learn only from women teachers, whereas men who try to instruct him are portrayed as failing under his scathing and ironic cross-examinations (Blair 1996). Moreover, in contrast to the overarching maleness of Athenian Greek culture, several characteristics (decidedly feminine) and the Platonic use of female imagery, such as pregnancy and *maiuetique*—or midwifery—to convey the philosophical art (*Theaetetus* 148-152; *Symposium* 206BE), also contribute significantly to Socrates' *atopia* (Trudeau 1999, 84). With the integration of the courageous masculine (Socrates as military man) and the caring feminine (Socrates as midwife), the *Symposium* offers, of standard social conventions, a new model of development for the ideal Greek male: *the philosopher*—the androgynous, self-sufficient, divinely-inspired man for whom the final revelation of love is Feminine in nature (De Vita 2001).

Diotima's theory, as found in the *Symposium* (210A-212A), centered on *eros* defined as 'love engendered by beauty', and as such, it was the medium by which 'to beget and bear offspring', whether of the body or of the mind (206E), out of a 'desire for immortality' (208B). Diotima posits that there are those whose erotic impulse was mental or spiritual, whose contained *eros* made them 'pregnant of soul'—more psychically creative than physically so. These 'pregnant of soul' bore offspring of the mind, producing 'what you would expect the mind to conceive and produce': *phronêsis* and *aretê*, thoughtfulness and virtue in general (209A). Moreover, if the soul was 'so far divine' that it was 'made pregnant with these from youth', on attaining physical maturity, it would immediately have a 'strong urge to give birth, or beget', and would go about seeking union with a beautiful object as a medium within which it could do this begetting (209AB).

According to Plato, *eros* could be diverted by philosophy (inclusive of mathematical, ethical, and ascetical training), rather than dissipated in sexuality, for the purpose of using erotic energy as a vehicle for the transformation of consciousness, and union with the Divine. This philosophical path as outlined by Diotima, is 'a ladder of love', a progression from a love of particular examples of beauty to an appreciation of beauty in general—beauty in all its forms. All beauty is related, says Diotima, from physical beauty to the beauty that can be found in the right qualities of human behavior, mind, custom, and institution (210BC). It was an evolutionary process intended to purify the soul, and free one from enslavement to physical pleasure. A step-by-step spiritualizing of love, it was movement out of a self-indulgent enjoyment of physical beauty to an altruistic, intellectual love of the one Beauty in all things. In the transformation from gratified sexual lust to continent erotic devotion, the heart center is opened and united with intellect. The philosopher becomes *theophilés*, 'loved of God'. He or she can love selflessly and impersonally, appreciating the 'limitless ocean of beauty' (210D) in all things without attachment, possession, or need for physical expression—a key step not only toward psychological maturity but toward a mystical sharing in the life Divine. Though there are no guarantees, if a person is diligent and devoted in this study, Beauty's final revelation is sudden, a beatific vision—the evidence of things unseen—and worth all the effort that has been put into this education in love. It is eternal, existing for all time, by itself and with itself, unique (211B).

> Such is the experience of the man who approaches, or is guided towards, love in the right way, beginning with the particular examples of beauty, but always returning from them to the search for that one beauty. He uses them like a ladder, climbing from the love of one person to love of two; from two to love of all physical beauty; from physical beauty to beauty of human behavior; thence to beauty in subjects of study; from them he arrives finally at that branch of knowledge which studies nothing but ultimate beauty. Then at last he understands what true beauty is (211BC) (Plato 1989).

While existing evidence, ranging from written testimony to bas-relief bronzes, cannot with certainty prove the historicity of Diotima, never, since Plato's writing of the *Symposium* (c. 388 BC), has it been suggested that Diotima of Mantineia was anything but a 'long-deceased philosopher-priestess' and the revered teacher of Socrates. To be pointed, her present status in philosophical circles as a Platonic literary fiction can be traced to a misogynistic remark made in 1485 by the Renaissance humanist, Marsilio Ficino, in his *Oratio Septima* II. Thus, despite nineteen hundred years of being considered an historical person, and in contrast to Plato's revolutionary view that women could indeed philosophize and be valued guardians of the Republic, 'Ficino's remark on the absurdity of thinking a woman a philosopher achieved and retained the status of received doctrine for the next 500 years' (Waithe 1987, 106).

References and Suggestions for Further Reading

Blair, E. 'Women: The Unrecognized Teachers of the Platonic Socrates.' *Ancient Philosophy* 16 (Fall 1996), 333-50.

Cook, A.B. *Zeus: A Study in Ancient Religion*. Vol. I. UK: Cambridge, 1914.

Plato, *Symposium of Plato*. Reproduction of Libanus edition 1986. Trans. Tom Griffith. Berkeley/Los Angeles: University of California Press, 1989.

Trudeau, D. 'Socrates' Women.' *South Atlantic Quarterly* 98: 1/2 (Winter/Spring 99), 83-93.

Vita, A B. De. 'Selfless Love: Reading the Woman in Plato's Symposium's Ideal Man.' *English Language Notes* 39/2 (Dec 2001), 1-10.

Waithe, M.E. 'Diotima of Mantinea' in *A History of Women Philosophers: Vol. 1, Ancient Women Philosophers, 600 B.C.-500 A.D.* Ed. M.E. Waithe. Dordrecht: Martinus Nijhoff, 1987.

Chapter 24

Hippocrates of Cos

c. 460 BC–c. 370 BC

Andrew Gregory

> Each disease has its own nature and power and there is nothing in any disease which is
> unmanageable or inexplicable. (Hippocratic writer, *On the Sacred Disease*, XXI 8-10)

Beyond his fame as a doctor, not a great deal is known about the life of
Hippocrates of Cos. We do not know whether he himself wrote any of the works
that are now known as the Hippocratic corpus, the written works. It is possible that
he wrote some (though we do not know which) and others are the works of his
colleagues, students and later followers. This is an extensive collection of works,
covering case histories, treatises on surgery, the treatment of trauma and disease,
the nature of disease and the human body, medical ethics and the effect of the
environment on disease. Many of these works have come down to us whole and
they provide us with a fascinating insight into the origins of ancient medicine.

The great importance of Hippocrates and the Hippocratics is that they founded
medical science and the profession of medicine. They did this in competition with
many other sorts of ancient healers, such as herbalists, spiritualists, faith healers
and excorcists. They needed to assert some important philosophical points, as well
as lay the basis for medical ethics and the application of scientific method to
healing.

Prior to the Hippocratics, disease was commonly thought to be the result of
divine intervention. The first task of the healers was often to diagnose the sin which
had offended the Gods and to recommend rituals to appease the Gods before
proceeding to any treatment. The approach of the Hippocratics was radical and
straightforward. According to them, all diseases had a natural cause. They took on
the hardest case which was epilepsy, known to the ancients as the 'sacred disease'.
It was here that it seemed most evident that a person was afflicted by the Gods in
their irregular fits. Yet a Hippocratic writer stated that:

> This so-called sacred disease is due to the same causes as all other diseases ... whoever
> has the knowledge of how to produce by means of regimen dryness and moisture, cold
> and heat in the human body, could cure this disease too ... He would not need to resort
> to purifications and magic and all that kind of charlatanism. (Hippocratic writer, *On
> the Sacred Disease*, XXI 1-26)

One remarkable aspect of this passage is the quite general attack on magic and magicians. Prior to the Hippocratics, one can find criticism of incompetent individual magicians, but not attacks on magic as a whole. We need to place this in the context of early Greek philosophy. The Milesian thinkers rejected mythopoeic thought (explanation in terms of myths or poems) in favour of theories which they could philosophize about. Thus they sought purely natural, physical explanations for physical phenomena. So too they considered the cosmos to be an orderly and intelligible place. Like the early philosophers, the actual theories of the Hippocratics may seem a little crude to the modern eye, but at least they were theories as opposed to appeals to the Gods, or myths and poems.

The Hippocratic conception of the body and disease is a case in point. We can find in the Hippocratic corpus the origins of the idea that there are four humours which are critical to health: blood, black bile, yellow bile and phlegm. If a proper balance of these humours is maintained, then a person is healthy. If not they are ill, and an appropriate treatment needed to be prescribed.

In the diagram below observe the following:

- The four humours and their associated character types
- The combinations of the four basic contraries associated with the four humours
- Then compare these with Aristotle's theory of the elements

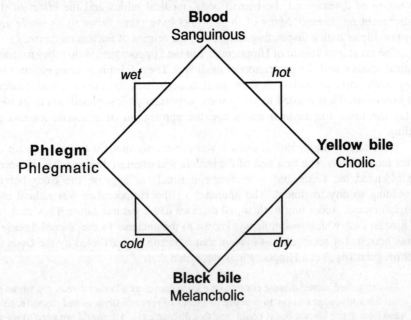

Figure 24.1 The four humours

This conception gave an entirely natural and physical rationale for treatment, in attempting to balance the humours by increasing or decreasing hotness, coldness, wetness or dryness in the body. In the absence of effective medications, this would be attempted by a regime of diet and exercise. This conception of health and disease was dominant in the Greek and Roman world and lasted in the West up to the scientific revolution of the 17th century.

In the absence of any effective treatment for many diseases, diagnosis and prognosis were critical to a Hippocratic doctor's practice, in order to gain a patient's confidence. It was critical that a doctor was able to give a full description of the symptoms from the patient's account of his own history, and be able to tell them the likely course of the disease.

Here the Hippocratic doctors could draw on the marvelous case studies of the Hippocratic corpus. While detailed observations can be found in other ancient societies (notably the Egyptian and Babylonian) there are some distinctive features of the Hippocratics. Their candour about the patient's symptoms and the effects of their treatments is remarkable, and they record cases where the patient died. This was unprecedented and indeed in the whole of ancient science it is very rare for anyone to mention negative results from experiments or observations.

The Hippocratics produced a series of practical treatises on the treatment of various diseases and traumas. Doubtless here they drew on the experience and practice of their predecessors and contemporaries, but there is much that is new as well. Ancient medicine was rather better at the treatment of trauma than disease. Treating trauma is in many ways easier and of course they had a great deal of practical experience, not least from warfare. The Hippocratics were also the first to investigate the effects of the environment on the nature and occurrence of disease. This would have been particularly useful for itinerant doctors, who travelled around Greece seeking employment, as they would have at least some knowledge of what diseases to expect in certain areas and cities.

The Hippocratics also laid a moral basis for medicine, and indeed the Hippocratic oath is one of their most enduring legacies, laying down principles for professional conduct. Many of these principles, such as always helping and never harming the sick, not abusing their professional position and client confidentiality have informed medical practice right down to the current day. Others such as the refusal to suggest or help in euthanasia and refusal to give women the means to produce an abortion have been highly influential and remain a matter of debate even now.

References and Suggestions for Further Reading

Gillispie, C.C. ed. The Dictionary of Scientific Biography. New York: 1971. S.v. 'Hippocrates of Cos'.
Jouanna, J. *Hippocrates*. Baltimore, MD.: Johns Hopkins University Press, 1999.
Lloyd, G.E.R. *Early Greek Science: Thales to Aristotle*. London: Chatto and Windus, 1970.
Lloyd, G.E.R. *Hippocratic Writings*. London: Penguin, 1978.

Lloyd, G.E.R. 'The Hippocratic Question'. *Classical Quarterly* 25, 1975, pp. 171-192.

Note The Hippocratic writings, with English translation and short commentaries are available in full in the Loeb Classical Library series.

Chapter 25

Socrates

469 BC–399 BC

Hope May

> It is the greatest good for an individual to discuss virtue every day ... for the unexamined life is not worth living. (Plato, *Apology*, 38a)

Imagine looking out of your window one morning and seeing a throng of reporters and news crews at your front door. Confused and still half asleep, you walk downstairs to the front door and open it. You are bombarded with a cacophony of questions and finally are able to discern a single voice. It asks 'so tell me, how does if feel to be named the wisest person in the universe?' Another reporter asks 'would you consider doing a reality show?' Of course, you are stunned upon hearing this. You ask yourself, 'Am I dreaming?' But you are not. It is real. The Committee of Sages has just released its pronouncement of the wise, which it does every thousand years. This time, they have announced that *you* are the wisest.

What would you do if you were told that you were the wisest person in the Universe? Would you say 'it's about time that someone recognized the greatness of my intellect!' Would you shrug it off and ignore it? Would you be disturbed? Would you begin to do research on the Committee of Sages? Would you doubt its authority? Approximately two thousand years ago, Socrates was told that he was the wisest of all mortals. This greatly disturbed him, and caused him to investigate the meaning of such a pronouncement. Ultimately, Socrates' desire to understand the message caused him to be put on trial and sentenced to death by his fellow Athenians. In 399 BC, when he was seventy years old, Socrates died by drinking a concoction made with the poisonous plant, hemlock.

Socrates was born in Athens, Greece. Since we have no writings by Socrates, we are forced to learn about him from those who knew him. Three of Socrates' contemporaries wrote about him: Plato, Socrates' student and friend; Aristophanes, a comic playwright; and Xenophon, an historian. Many people find Plato's writings to be the best source on Socrates. Plato wrote in a dialogue form and Socrates appears as a character in practically all of Plato's writings. Plato's *Apology* (which here means 'defence' rather than 'a saying sorry') is an account of Socrates' defence at his trial.

In Plato's *Apology*, we learn that a turning point in Socrates' life was when his friend, Chaerephon, approached the shrine to the God Apollo and consulted the Pythia—a woman who was a priestess or medium through whom Apollo was believed to speak. Chaerephon asked the Pythia 'who among the mortals is wisest?' The Pythia responded 'Socrates'. Arrogance was a stranger to Socrates, and rather than saying 'of course I am wisest', he was stunned upon hearing the oracle's response. Socrates did not think he knew anything important, and so he simply could not understand why he was deemed to be the wisest. Nevertheless, Socrates believed that there must be *some* truth in the oracle's response since it was 'not right' for Apollo to lie. But what could Apollo mean? Socrates set out on a quest to find out.

In attempting to understand the meaning of the oracle, Socrates tried to find someone wiser than himself. He interviewed many people who were considered to be wise, and discovered something rather surprising. Although the people that Socrates interviewed knew *some* things, they wrongly believed that they therefore knew *everything*. Socrates' mission taught him the important lesson that his fellow citizens did not understand their limitations. Rather, the Athenians were puffed up and conceited: because they knew a little, they believed that they knew a lot. Socrates, on the other hand, understood that there were things that he did not know. Because Socrates understood his limitations when everyone else was puffed up from vanity and self-conceit, Socrates was the wiser. Socrates understood how important it was for his fellow Athenians to understand that their knowledge was limited. In fact, he interpreted the oracle's message to be a sort of command. In Socrates' mind, Apollo had commanded him to reveal to as many people as possible that their knowledge was limited. But why should people be reminded constantly that their knowledge is limited? What of the adage 'ignorance is bliss'? Can you see why Socrates believed that it was important to show others that they do not know what think they know?

Although he was trying to help, Socrates frustrated his fellow citizens by constantly revealing that their knowledge was limited. But how exactly did Socrates reveal the limitations of his fellow Athenians? Did he ask them trick questions about obscure subjects? Did he ask them to discover the largest prime number? Not at all. Actually, Socrates' questions were rather simple: he would merely ask his interlocutor to define some term—the very term about which the interlocutor was supposed to have expertise. Usually, Socrates would question people who claimed to have expertise about *moral* matters. Socrates often questioned the sophists, paid teachers who claimed to be able to teach moral virtue. Socrates would ask sophists the question 'what is virtue?' And it makes sense that Socrates would ask sophists this very question. For if someone claims to be able to teach virtue, they had better be able to say what it is! Socrates would also question holy men who claimed to know what was and was not 'righteous'. And Socrates would question politicians who claimed to know what laws were and were not just.

In focusing his questions on those who claimed to be experts on moral matters, Socrates was providing a great service to his fellow citizens, for it is indeed important to understand that one's moral knowledge is limited. If not, one will rush to judgment and make hasty and probably incorrect decisions based on emotion and passion. Furthermore, if one thinks that their moral beliefs are infallible, one will be close minded and will be unwilling to take advice and counsel from others. We all know someone who regards themselves as a 'know it all' and we all recognize that this type of person is annoying. But when moral beliefs are concerned, such a person can also be dangerous not only to themselves, but also to others. For example, one of the world's most dangerous terrorist organizations, Al Qaeda, claims to be doing the work of Allah. Osama Bin Laden, the leader of Al Qaeda, also claims and that by killing any United States citizen, the amount of evil in the world is decreased. Of course, many people disagree with Al Qaeda's conception of 'evil', not to mention their interpretation of the Koran. It is no coincidence that Al Qaeda is completely unwilling to question their moral beliefs. In fact, in one of Al Qaeda's training manuals, they explicitly mention Socrates and reject his methods! Their manual explicitly states 'the confrontation that we are calling for with the apostate regimes does not know Socratic debates ... but it knows the dialogue of bullets, the ideals of assassination, bombing, and the diplomacy of the cannon and machine gun'. In other words, Al Qaeda's ideology is not open to criticism: violence and force, rather than reason and debate, are their methods. Al Qaeda explicitly refuses to enter into a dialogue with others about what is and is not 'good' and 'right', and hence are unwilling to accept the possibility that their conceptions of 'good' and 'evil' are incorrect. Such a group is patently dangerous, as is any person who refuses to subject their moral beliefs to Socratic scrutiny.

By asking his interlocutors to define moral terms, Socrates would compel them to reflect on their moral beliefs. And although his interlocutors were ashamed when Socrates pointed out that their definitions were problematic, Socrates' refutations actually helped his interlocutors. In showing that their definitions were faulty, Socrates provided an excellent incentive for them to 'slow down', and not 'rush to judgment' when making moral decisions. If one is aware that their moral knowledge is not perfect, then one is more likely to be careful when a moral decision is to be made. Rather than acting immediately or from passion, one will hopefully reflect on one's options and seek counsel and advice from others.

One of Socrates' conversations with a prophet named 'Euthyphro' (pronounced 'youth-e-fro') illustrates how Socrates' refutations helped his interlocutor to reflect on his moral beliefs, and hence to make more prudent decisions. Socrates' conversation with Euthyphro is recorded by Plato in a dialogue by the same name. In Plato's *Euthyphro*, Socrates learns that Euthyphro is prosecuting his father for murder. It was unheard of in Athenian society to prosecute your own parents, and Socrates is appropriately surprised when he hears that Euthyphro is prosecuting his father for murder. And when Euthyphro explains what his father did, Socrates becomes even more disturbed! According to Euthyphro, his father had gagged and bound a slave who got into a drunken brawl with another slave. While Euthyphro's father was deciding what to do with the murderous slave, he put the slave in a ditch where the slave eventually died. For this reason, Euthyphro is prosecuting his father for murder!

Given Euthyphro's story, it is not at all clear that his father *murdered* the slave: murder is willful and wrongful killing. But Euthyphro's father did not *intentionally* kill the slave. It was an accident, a result of mere negligence or carelessness. Nevertheless, Euthyphro decides to prosecute his father for murder. Importantly, Euthyphro is *absolutely certain* that he is doing the right thing, and that the gods are smiling upon his decision. At one point in the conversation, Socrates asks Euthyphro 'are you sure you are doing the good and righteous thing?' Euthyphro says 'of course!' Socrates then reasonably states, 'well, if you know that this is the good and righteous thing, then you must know what "goodness" and "righteousness" are!' Euthyphro responds by saying 'of course! If I did not know what "righteousness" was, then I would not be the special person that I am!'

Socrates is pointing out that in order to be certain that what he is doing is right, Euthyphro must know what 'righteousness' is. Put differently, if one is to know that this particular action is evil, then one must know what evil is. And if one knows what evil is, then one should be able to define 'evil'. This is why Socrates focused on definitions: by showing that his interlocutor could not give a satisfactory definition, Socrates demonstrated that his interlocutor's moral knowledge was limited. Euthyphro attempted to define 'righteousness' a number of times, and each time Socrates pointed out the problems with these definitions. Through Socrates' questioning, Euthyphro learned that his knowledge of 'righteousness' is limited, and hence that he could not be sure that prosecuting his father was the right thing. One of our ancient biographers, Diogenes Laertius, tells us that after talking with Socrates, Euthyphro decided *not* to prosecute his father. Socrates helped Euthyphro to see that since he could not give an adequate definition of 'righteousness', his moral judgments could not be absolutely correct. Once Euthyphro came face to face with his own limitations, he was more cautious, and less likely to 'rush to judgment'.

We live in an age where ignorance is deemed a sin. Like Socrates' interlocutors, we are ashamed when our ignorance is exposed. But Socrates showed us that reflecting and examining our beliefs, and subsequently being reminded of our ignorance and limitations, is perhaps one of the best things for us: it keeps us open minded, it makes us more cautious in our decision making, and helps us to seek counsel from others. Given the benefits that come from examining one's own beliefs, it is understandable why Socrates said 'the unexamined life is not worth living'.

References and Suggestions for Further Reading

Brickhouse, Thomas and Nicholas Smith. *Plato's Socrates*. New York: Oxford University Press, 1995.

Brickhouse, Thomas and Nicholas Smith. *The Trial and Execution of Socrates: Sources and Controversies*. New York: Oxford: Oxford University Press, 2002.

Colaico, James. *Socrates Against Athens: Philosophy on Trial*. New York: London: Routledge, 2001.

May, Hope. *On Socrates*. Belmont, CA.: Wadsworth, 2000.

Vlastos, Gregory. *Socrates, Ironist and Moral Philosopher*. Ithaca, NY.: Cornell University Press, 1991.

Chapter 26

Thucydides

c. 460–c. 400 BC

Matthew Usher

And it may be that my history will seem less easy to read because of the absence in it of a romantic element. It will be enough for me, however, if these words of mine are judged useful by those who want to understand clearly the events which happened in the past and which (human nature being what it is) will, at some time or other and in much the same ways, be repeated in the future. My work is not a piece of writing designed to meet the taste of an immediate public, but was done to last forever. (Thucydides, *The Peloponnesian War* 1.22)

Thucydides is the author of *The Peloponnesian War*, an account he called an *historia* (inquiry) of the war between the two Greek city-states, Athens and Sparta, and their allies and subjects, that lasted from 431–404 BC. In Thucydides' *Historia* however, Athens and Sparta become more than states engaged in war; they become representations of opposite ways of looking at the world. For Thucydides, the Peloponnesian War provided an opportunity to glean insights into human nature and the morality of power.

Thucydides provides the little biographical detail that we have of his life. He was an Athenian born into a prominent aristocratic family. Sometime between 430 and 427, he contracted the plague (which possibly caused one quarter of the Athenian population to perish), but he recovered. In 424 he was elected to be one of ten generals of the Athenian military forces, and must have been at least thirty years old at this time. He was given a command in northern Greece (Thrace, and the north Aegean). In the same year there was a surprise assault by the daring Spartan general, Brasidas. Thucydides set sail at once and secured the nearby city of Eion, but he could not save Amphipolis. For this failure he was exiled. He returned to Athens after twenty years in exile but died shortly afterwards, his work unfinished and unpublished.

Thucydides grew up and, until his exile, lived in an Athens whose culture was flowering. He was alive when the Parthenon was built and in a period where arts and sciences blossomed: there existed an unprecedented level of intellectual curiosity, a questioning of superstitions and conventions, and a belief in progress. All of the arts, particularly the literary arts, oration and rhetoric, reached their zenith as the masters in the various disciplines competed for fame and honour. We may presume that Thucydides would have encountered at least some of these famous masters, such as Socrates, and great statesmen, such as Pericles. It is likely that he would have heard the visiting Sophists, Protagoras and Gorgias, and attended performances of tragedies and comedies by Sophocles, Euripides and Aristophanes.

Thucydides is himself one of these innovative masters though he was not recognized as such in his time. His contribution 'for all time' was a new presentation of old themes that avoided the abstractions of philosophers and the myths of the poets, and instead, began a new direction in the emerging discipline which we would recognize as history. Thucydides wrote not about the distant past, but about current events, selecting and presenting particulars in a way that made them universally relevant. He did this with an artistic skill that makes his commentary especially poignant. It is achieved without moralizing, his commentary pointing the reader in certain directions by what it includes and what is tacitly omits. Authorial comments are for the most part withheld, Thucydides leaving it to the reader to decide for him or herself the significance of events and the merit of the various arguments put forward by the leaders on both sides.

Thucydides' proclaimed desire for accuracy in reporting, and analysis suggests that he was impressed by the methods and goals of ancient medical science. He called his work by the same name that the followers of Hippocrates used for their 'case history', and he borrowed the methodology for analysis of symptoms, as well as diagnosis, and prognosis in his *historia*. What seems to have motivated Thucydides was his belief that just as the study of medicine may aid sufferers of disease, his history might help statesmen and citizen alike intelligently to predict the course of future events. From what he says it is evident that he upheld the view that there is a human nature, that there are some fundamental constants underpinning human action, even while human actions are determined by the individual qualities of human actors and by the conventions of the culture into which they are born. Although Thucydides acknowledges the role of luck and chance in human events, he thought that it was likely that many events of the future would resemble those of the past.

Two fundamental themes in Thucydides' work are the morality of power and human nature as they are revealed under the pressure of necessity. He wrote of Athenian diplomats justifying acts of aggression against small independent and neutral states, by arguing that their actions are in accordance with 'universal law': the strong rule and the weak yield (1.76), but we are not left thinking that there is a failure to understand the nature of powers and morality for he has Hemocrates of Sicily argue that to resist aggression is not only natural but commendable (4.61).

Thucydides declares that the war was an inevitable outcome of '... the growth of Athenian power and the fear which this caused in Sparta' (1:23). The desire for security is listed by the Athenians as one of three powerful motives for imperial ambition and war, along with honour and self-interest. What interested Thucydides was how these powerful motives, under the strain of war, plague, and hardship, led to a breakdown in conventions, lawfulness and morale. He records how the plague caused despair and anarchy so overwhelming '... that men, not knowing what would happen next to them, became indifferent to every rule of law or religion' (2:52). He observed that, faced with harsh necessities, it seemed to many people futile to behave honourably, because it was likely they might die before enjoying the fruits of a good reputation. To Thucydides, it seemed that honour and even fear and the desire for security came second to the powerful motive of self-interest.

The war has very much the same effect as the plague in causing a breakdown of ethics and morale. A terrible symptom of this breakdown that Thucydides focuses upon was the extent to which ethical and moral terms became twisted and lost or had their meaning changed. What had previously been regarded as thoughtless aggression came to be regarded as courage, while the exercising of caution came to be perceived as cowardice, and victory won by treachery became victory won by intelligence. The behaviour of people changed along with the transformed ethical and moral terminology, and actions previously regarded as dishonourable became praise worthy:

> Fanatical enthusiasm was the mark of a real man, ... Anyone who held violent opinions could always be trusted and anyone who objected to them became suspect, ... In short, it was equally praise worthy to get one's blow in first against someone who was going to do wrong, and to denounce someone who had no intention of doing any wrong at all. (3:82)

In Thucydides' *Historia* these appear as symptoms of the overall breakdown in the norms of civilized society as the pressure of war dissolved the commitment to the common good. Human nature '... showed itself proudly in its true colours, as something incapable of controlling passion, insubordinate to the demands of justice, the enemy of anything superior to itself ... ' (3:84). This phenomenon was not so observable in times of peace and prosperity because there was no pressure of necessity. However '... war is a stern teacher ...' and soon stripped away the façade of civilization revealing mankind's baser instincts as its foundation.

Thucydides was a man whose despair at the ruin brought by war was tempered by an acceptance of the nature of things and an optimism that some excesses may be avoided or diminished by a commitment to careful, rational, and scientific analysis of events and human nature. His *Historia* is not only full of profound insights: it is so artfully written that it is genuinely moving. It is a compelling and engaging narrative that challenges the reader and lives up to its author's intention.

References and Suggestions for Further Reading

Crawley, Richard, trans. *History of the Peloponnesian* War. Edited and introduced by W. Robert Connor, consultant ed. Richard Stoneman. London: Everyman, 1993.

Luce, T.J. *The Greek Historians.* London: Routledge and Kegan Paul, 1997.

Warner, Rex, trans. *The Peloponnesian War.* Edited by Betty Radice. Introduction and Notes by M.I. Finley. Harmondsworth: Penguin, 1972.

Chapter 27

Democritus

c. 460 BC–560? BC

Alan Chalmers

Fine words do not hide foul actions
nor is a good action spoilt by slanderous words. (Clement, *Pedagoge*, II, XV, 40)

If we draw selectively and uncritically on the range of commentaries and comments on Democritus by the Ancient Greeks and Romans who followed him, we can paint a picture of him as an extremely colourful, productive and important philosopher. A short version of such an account might run as follows: Democritus, born about 460 BC in Abdera, lived to be over a hundred years old, and in that time travelled widely, to Egypt, Persia, India and beyond, and encountered many of the leading philosophers of the day (although when he visited Athens no-one recognized him). He wrote extensively on many topics, especially atomism and ethics, and earned himself the nickname 'Wisdom'. The Romans referred to him as the 'the laughing philosopher'. Hippocrates was impressed with Democritus' acuity when he was able to identify the milk served to him for breakfast as coming from a black she-goat who had recently had its first kid. Democritus' character aside, the atomic theory that he constructed became one of the main schools of thought in Ancient Greece with wide-ranging implications that have reverberated down to the present day.

Getting at the truth behind such fables is not easy. Only a few disconnected fragments of Democritus' extensive body of writings have come down to us. We have to rely on reports of those Greek and Roman authors who had read Democritus' work, and some of these are inconsistent with each other.

Most of the anecdotes about Democritus' life cannot be documented and should be taken with a grain of salt. Enough can be documented, however, confidently to situate his philosophical work with respect to the problems he inherited from his predecessors. Democritus wrote at a time when Ancient Greek philosophy, characterized by an attempt to give a logical and rational, as opposed to a mythical, account of the material, social and moral world, was well into its second century. One of the key problems facing philosophers in the second half of the fifth century BC was to work out a response to the arguments of Parmenides and Zeno to the effect that change and motion are impossible. Parmenides had argued as follows. Of the two opposites, being and non-being, the latter cannot exist by its very nature. Parmenides concluded that being is unchangeable because there is nothing to separate one piece of being from another and no place for it to move. For Parmenides, the world is an unchanging, homogeneous sphere, in spite of appearances to the contrary.

In a strong sense, atomism involved the acceptance of most of the terms of the Parmenidean argument. The individual atoms in Democritus' theory are undifferentiated pieces of being. As such they are homogeneous and cannot be changed in any way. They are miniature Parmenidean worlds. The one major difference on which the atomists' solution depends lies in their insistence that the void, nothingness, can and does exist. For the atomists like Democritus, it exists as the space between atoms. Once space is allowed this minimal degree of existence, then Parmenides' argument can be defeated. Whilst the individual atoms cannot be changed, they can move and be rearranged. All change is to be traced back to the motion and rearrangement of unchanging atoms in the void. This key argument for atomism was introduced by Leucippus. Democritus developed it into a detailed system.

For Parmenides, reality was just a slab of unchanging being. The world, according to the basics of Democritean atomism, is almost as stark. It consists of atoms in the void, where the atoms themselves are pieces of bare being, each with its unchanging shape and size and some degree of motion. If this is the case, whence comes the degree of variety and change that our senses reveal? After all, the world does seem to be rather different from the collection of dust that it would seem to be on Democritus' account! How can we accommodate birds and bees and honey and trees and thunderstorms and their characteristic properties within atomism? Democritus had answers to this problem. Some aspects of the variety to be found in the world can be explained in terms of the great variety of macroscopic structures that can be made of arrangements of atoms of all sorts of shapes and sizes combined together in innumerable ways. Whilst this move introduces some variety into the world, it does not yet account for the qualitative difference between an assembly of atoms each with their characteristic shape and size, on the one hand, and objects of our experience that have a whole range of properties such as being coloured and heavy and sweet and bouncy and magnetic, on the other. Democritus dealt with this by utilizing his account of the human senses.

When Democritus declared that all that exists are atoms in the void he meant it quite literally. In particular, human beings are nothing but collections of atoms, not only their bodies but also their souls. Democritus was a thoroughgoing materialist. Thoughts and sensations that we think of as being 'in the mind' are nothing but arrangements of soul atoms. On this assumption, the sensations of colour and taste and so on that we experience when looking at birds or tasting honey or whatever correspond to arrangements of atoms in our minds. Properties such as colour and taste do not exist in the birds, honey, etcetera, as properties of them. After all, the observed items are nothing but collections of atoms. The robin looks red because characteristic streams of atoms leave the robin's breast, interact with the observer via the eyes and gives rise to an arrangement of soul atoms that correspond to redness. Democritus wrote:

By convention sweet, by convention bitter, by convention hot, by convention cold, but in reality atoms and the void. (Sextus Empiricus, *Against the Mathematicians VII*, 135)

So Democritus had an explanation of how the world as it appears to us seems to be qualitatively richer than the stark collection of featureless atoms that it really is. But how did there come to be such a world at all? According to Democritus it came about as the result of chance collisions of atoms in the void. As atoms move in space they occasionally collide, and some of them become entangled on doing so. (We can imagine a hook on one atom catching onto an eye on another.) Innumerable collisions of this kind can end up forming a world like ours. The improbability of this happening is offset by the fact that the atoms have existed and have been moving in the void for ever, so all sorts of unlikely meetings of atoms will eventuate sooner or later.

There is a difficulty with this idea that the world is formed by chance. It seems to clash with the idea, stressed by Democritus, that everything happens of necessity. This latter claim presumably captures the idea that when atoms collide, their motions after collision are completely determined by the direction and magnitudes of their motions before collision. An atom is made to move in a definite way by any atom it collides with. The world of atoms is a deterministic world. So why say that the world is formed as a result of chance? One answer is that chance is analogous to something like colour insofar as it is a feature of the world as it appears to us that does not have a correlate in the real world of atoms. It seems to us that the lightning strikes the tree by chance, but that is simply a result of our ignorance. Had we known in detail the motions of the atoms that make up the lightning and the tree we would have appreciated that the strike was destined to happen of necessity.

The status of the evidence of our senses is an issue that required a subtle answer from Democritus. In one sense, the whole purpose of atomism was to reinstate that evidence and resist the Parmenidean conclusion that it is totally illusory insofar as it reveals variety and change that does not exist. On the other hand, Democritus recognized that the senses have their limits (water appears continuous to the senses but is really atomic) and can vary from one observer to the next (what tastes sweet to one can be bitter for another). It is clear that Democritus needed a position that was intermediary between complete rejection and unconditional acceptance of the evidence of the senses, but we do not know whether he worked out the details of such a position.

There are conflicting views on the extent to which Democritus developed a systematic ethics. At one extreme we have the view that Democritus did not, and that his writings are nothing more than a collection of moral platitudes, as some of them certainly appear to be on the surface. ('Men enjoy scratching themselves— they get the same pleasure as those who are having sexual intercourse' would be fine if it possessed in profundity what it so clearly lacks in veracity.) At the other extreme is the view that Democritus constructed a system that constituted the first attempt at a naturalized ethics, that is, an ethics that is explained as a consequence of the nature of humans and the world in which they live, rather than being imposed by a higher authority such as a God. Democritus was perhaps the first philosopher explicitly to deny the existence of life after death. Both this and the rejection of God would seem to be a natural consequence of his atomism. Democritus's ethics aimed to give an account of how we should behave if we are to make the most of what we are as material beings living in a material world.

There is a basic problem with Democritus' position. It assumes that individual humans can make choices and control their actions. And yet at the atomic level everything happens of necessity. In a deterministic universe there are no options for humans to choose between. Part of an answer to the problem involves a move similar to that involved in Democritus' understanding of chance. Just as it seems to us, because of our ignorance, that there are chance events, so there seem to us to be choices available, for a similar reason. But this 'solution' will not do. If our choices are to make a difference, (and Democritean ethics does not make sense if this is not so) then the course of the world must be changed by the actions that flow from our choices. A deterministic world of atoms and the void would seem to leave no room for such a thing. This problem persists as a basic one for materialists up to this day.

In assessing the merit of Democritus' atomism, it is important that we should not allow our judgement to be coloured by the fact that we now know that there are indeed atoms. Modern atoms differ widely from what Democritus had in mind and the modern scientific case for them differs widely from the abstract arguments offered by Democritus. His atomism is least plausible when it comes to common biological processes. How is a heap of dust of a kind meant to interact with a heap of dust of like kind to produce a little baby heap of dust of the same kind? Perhaps it was difficulties such as these that explain why atomism was not generally accepted by the Ancient Greeks, and that other responses to Parmenides, such as Aristotle's, won more support.

References and Suggestions for Further Reading

English translations of most of the key Ancient sources related to Democritus, together with some commentary, appear in:

Kirk, G.S., J. E. Raven and M. Schofield. *The Presocratic Philosophers: A Critical History with a Selection of Texts.* Second Edition. Cambridge: Cambridge University Press, 1983, pp. 402-433.
Another source of extracts, containing much more on Democretian ethics, is:
Barnes, Jonathan. *Early Greek Philosophy.* London: Penguin Books, 2001, pp. 203-253.

An attempt to find a systematic ethics in Democritus is 'Ethics and Physics in Democritus' by

Vlastos, Gregory in *Studies in Presocratic Philosophy, Volume 2*, Edited by R.E. Allen and David J. Furley, Atlantic Highlands: Humanities Press, 1975, pp. 381-408.

For unsubstantiated gossip on Democritus see

Diogenes Laertius: *Lives of Eminent Philosophers, Volume 2*, Translated by R.D. Hicks, New York: Heinemann, 1925, pp. 443-463.

PART IV
THE CLASSICAL PERIOD

Chapter 28

Aristophanes

c. 449–c. 385 BC

Robert Phiddian

Strepsiades:	Look over this way. You see that nice little door and that nice little house?
Pheidippides:	Yes. What is it, actually, father?
Strepsiades:	It is a Thinkery for intellectual souls. That's where the people live who try to prove that the sky is like a baking-pot all around us, and we're the charcoal inside it. And if you pay them well, they can teach you how to win a case whether you're in the right or not.

(Aristophanes, *The Clouds*, ll. 93–99, trans. Sommerstein)

The great comic playwright, Aristophanes, belongs in a book about the philosophers of Ancient Greece for a number of reasons. One is that he provides a sceptical reality-check on the abstractions and rhetoric of fifth-century Athenian philosophy; his eleven surviving plays are the first surviving record of ridicule and parody being used extensively to test the validity of ideas. Second, he was a contemporary and friend of Socrates, part of the intellectual milieu, the social environment, of Athens, particularly during the years of the Peloponnesian War, when politics, literature, art, and ideas were thrown into dramatic conflict. Even the hyper-serious Plato includes him in the *Symposium* as more than comic relief: Aristophanes' first attempt to speak is frustrated by a violent attack of hiccups, but he recovers and returns to make a moving speech on the centrality of wholeness and reconciliation to any search for the meaning of love. These are the two main elements of the philosophical claim for the comic vision. On the one hand, comedy claims to serve truth by exposing untruth to the scourge of ridicule. On the other hand, it claims to serve human happiness by pointing towards reconciliation and celebration.

But for the philosophical tourist, the third reason that Aristophanes belongs in this book is likely to be the most vivid one. More than any other classical writer, he reminds us just how intimate, how downright personal, cultural life was, especially in Ancient Athens. Ideally, you should be reading this while standing in the Theatre of Dionysos on the Acropolis, but any other classical theatre will do almost as well; if all else fails, use your imagination. It is a big, open space with only natural light and very little stage machinery. In Aristophanes' time it seated about 14,000 spectators—a very large percentage of the free citizens of Athens, including nearly all the culturally and politically active ones—and operated only twice a year, for the festivals of the great Dionysia and the Leneia. Plays were not commercial things (there was no entertainment industry, as such), but were at the heart of the city's ritual and cultural life.

While you are imagining all this, imagine also that two comically masked characters have just stormed on stage, cursing a character called the Paphlagonian, who seems to be debauching the city's finances. One character rants: 'Oh, he's been guzzling a haul of gorgeous cakes, the bastard, confiscated from the convicts, and now he's snoring, dead drunk, lying on his back among his hides'. (Aristophanes, *The Knights*, ll. 101-103, trans. Sommerstein). But everyone in the audience knows that the real Paphlagonian is not drunk and asleep. Everyone knows that the characters are referring to Cleon, the most prominent politician in Athens at the time, and the butt of many Aristophanic jokes. And he is there, in one of the best seats, trying desperately to appear amused while these actors attack him.

When Aristophanes in a play ridicules Cleon for corruption, or Socrates for sophistry, or Euripides for absurd heroic rhetoric, or the people of Athens for their insane devotion to war, the criticism is not confined to a cult following in a specialist theatre or a pay-TV channel. It is occurring in public space—on the one-and-only channel, if you like—and nearly everyone is paying attention. The audacity of it is breathtaking, even two and a half millennia later. Or, perhaps, it is especially breathtaking for us, who live in a world of specialized audiences, independent professions, and separate intellectual disciplines. For Aristophanes and his contemporaries, philosophy, literature, politics, religion, and the rest all existed together, and the practitioners of these now-separate activities lived under each others' feet; often under each other's skins.

So Aristophanes' was a theatre of ideas and public debate, where the issues of the day were bluntly addressed, but it was also a theatre of hilarious physical comedy and riotous wordplay. The sober explanation for the prevalence of fart jokes and sexual innuendo is that comedy, like tragedy, had only fairly recently evolved from even more ancient fertility rituals sacred to Dionysos, the most riotous of the gods. Whatever the reason, recalcitrant bodily urges and functions have always been at the heart of comedy. They still make us laugh, and they also serve another purpose that may be almost as important: they provide a standing criticism of philosophy's tendency to assume that everything can be sorted out by a sound, rational argument.

We only know about the 'Old Comedy' of Athens from the eleven surviving plays of Aristophanes (he wrote about forty in all) and from fragments of other playwrights' work in accounts by classical rhetoricians. However, its main features are fairly clear, and if you are seeking a modern comparison, it would be fair to say that it was more like a Monty Python movie or a comic review than like a well-made play by Oscar Wilde. Aristophanes' plays were full of song and dance, especially from the chorus, and were never far from collapsing into a riot of topical jokes and physical humour. This has nothing to do with any lack of literary skill or sophistication—Aristophanes was a superlative poet, as anyone who can read *The Birds* in the original will tell you. The reason lies more in a deep comic hostility to the idea that more order and discipline are likely to provide the best solution to human problems. These are not undisciplined plays, but rather plays that ask whether certain forms of discipline gone mad are the real problem that faces the city.

And there were plenty of problems to address. Almost the whole of Aristophanes' career as a playwright coincided with the Peloponnesian War between Athens and Sparta, and this decades-long crisis is a constant counterpoint to the joy of his work. Scholars argue whether or not Aristophanes was opposed to all wars on principle, but there is no doubting his hostility to what he saw as the pointless and fratricidal war between fellow Greeks. In a string of plays, he exposed the stupidity of war, and railed against his fellow citizens for their willingness to be led into disaster by war-mongers.

In *Lysistrata*, for example, he has the women of Greece go on a sex strike until the men of all the warring cities make peace. Given the oppressed condition of women at the time, especially in Athens, this was meant and received as a bizarre fantasy, but the crucial point is that it was a fantasy of sanity and humanity in a world gone mad with blood-lust. Aristophanes' message is that we should trust the body and its natural desires for comfort, pleasure, and procreation. Pride and ambition guide us only into conflict, he suggests. While this is a simplistic political philosophy, it is not necessarily a bad one, and has a lot to recommend it against some more sophisticated and authoritarian approaches. As the world lunged inexorably towards the second Gulf War in Iraq during late 2002 and early 2003, there were performances of *Lysistrata* in many countries. They did not stop the war (theatre seldom does, alas) but they did ask audiences whether the goal was worth all the deaths.

Shakespeare's Falstaff famously concludes that 'the better part of valour is discretion' (*Henry IV, Part I,* V, iv, 121), and in doing so voices one of comedy's deepest messages. It is a voice we should attend to carefully every time before we set out to slaughter each other yet again. At the end of *Lysistrata*, after peace has been made and the ritual banquet held, a couple of Athenians have staggered out and are talking:

Second Athenian: Never known a party like it. The Spartans were really fun to be with, weren't they? And we kept our wits pretty well, considering how sozzled we were.

First Athenian: Not surprising, really. We couldn't be as stupid as we are when we're sober. If the Athenians took my advice they'd always get drunk when going on diplomatic missions. As it is, you see, we go to Sparta sober, and we're always looking for ways to make things more complicated. Result is, we don't hear what they do say, and we hunt for implications in what they don't say—and we bring back quite incompatible reports of what went on. *This* time, on the other hand, everything seems splendid.

(*Lysistrata*, ll. 1225-1239, trans. Sommerstein)

Perhaps the prescription is a bit radical, though it seems a shame that the Muslim proscription of alcohol rules it out as an option in intractable conflicts in the Middle East and Kashmir. Still, it is the diagnosis that remains as sharp as a knife after two and a half thousand years. We suspect Them of all sorts of cunning and malevolence, when really They are just 'fun to be with' and want much the same things that we want. If we can laugh and sing together, we should be able to sort something out.

It may not amount to a coherent moral philosophy, but there is a lot of wisdom in Aristophanes' comic vision. In 1933, the great classicist Gilbert Murray responded to the rise of totalitarianism in his world by completing a long-considered book on Aristophanes. He makes the pacifist point explicitly in his preface, and writing a book of literary criticism against Hitler is not as odd a gesture as you might imagine. Reading Aristophanes (or any other playwright) is unlikely to save the world, but if you combine it with practical political action, as Murray did in the 1930s, you can do your bit to increase the grip of sanity on public life. Comedy expresses the hope that, if we can laugh together across social, professional, and national boundaries, we are less likely to want to exploit and murder each other.

So, if you are still reading this while standing on the Acropolis or in some other classical theatre full of tourists, remember Aristophanes and start giggling. It might prove infectious, and it is the least you can do for world peace.

References and Suggestions for Further Reading

Aristophanes, *Lysistrata and Other Plays*. Trans. with an introduction by Alan H. Sommerstein. London: Penguin, 2002.

Aristophanes, *The Knights, Peace, Wealth, The Birds, The Assemblywomen*. Trans. Alan H. Sommerstein and David Barrett London: Penguin, 1978.

Cartledge, P.A. *Aristophanes and the Theatre of the Absurd*. Bristol: Bristol Classical Press, 3rd ed. 1995.

Dover, K.J. *Aristophanic Comedy*. London, 1972.

MacDowell, D.M. *Aristophanes and Athens*. Oxford: Oxford University Press, 1995.

Murray, G. *Aristophanes*. Oxford: Oxford University Press, 1933.

Plato, *The Symposium*. Trans. Walter Hamilton. London: Penguin, 1951.

Silk, M.S. *Aristophanes and the Definition of Comedy*. Oxford: Oxford University Press, 2002.

Chapter 29

Plato

427 BC–347 BC

Gerasimos Santas

Thinking is silent dialogue of the soul with itself (Plato).

Plato is generally regarded as the father of philosophy. In the middle of the twentieth century two major philosophers, Alfred Whitehead and Bertrand Russell, testified to his abiding influence. The first famously remarked that the history of philosophy is a series of footnotes to Plato, and the second suggested that philosophy can be defined as the sum total of all those inquiries that can be pursued by Plato's methods.

How did Plato accomplish these two great pioneering feats, define the subject matter of philosophy and sketch the methods by which the main questions of philosophy can be pursued?

Plato was born in Athens of an aristocratic family whose ancestors went back to Solon, the first legislator of Athenian democracy. His education included the Pre-Socratic Philosophers, the Sophists, and above all his master teacher Socrates. His early experience included the Peloponnesian Wars, bitter civil wars and tyrannies, and the trial and death of Socrates during the restored Athenian democracy in 399. Embittered by this experience, Plato did not enter Athenian politics, the usual destiny of a young aristocrat. Instead, he began to write dialogues in which Socrates questioned his fellow citizens about the dominant values of the day, their conceptions of virtue and happiness; and in the 380s Plato created the first university in Europe, Plato's Academy, which became a major intellectual centre for philosophy and the sciences for a thousand years. He continued to write dialogues, most of them with Socrates still the protagonist, but gradually he developed his own conception of philosophy and pursued issues beyond the historical Socrates.

Plato was a questioner. His philosophical hero, the 'Socrates' of his dialogues, is a master questioner. He asks deep questions of universal and abiding interest to all human beings, and he knows how to put his questions in illuminating sequences. Should we pursue power and wealth above all, or should we care more about virtue, the excellence of our souls? Does wealth bring us virtue, as Hesiod suggested, or does virtue enable us to use wealth and power well? Does wealth and power make us happy, or does happiness depend on virtue? And do we know what virtue is? Could we define piety, courage, temperance, or justice?

By asking these questions and discussing critically the dominant answers of the day Plato begun a branch of philosophy, Ethics. Ethics is about virtue and the good things that make for human happiness; these are choice-guiding concepts, virtue being mainly a social value, our good and happiness mainly individual values. If we examine these concepts critically and learn to think clearly about virtue and happiness, perhaps we can choose rightly about how to live, the most important of all questions.

When Plato's Socrates, in Plato's early dialogues, raised these questions with Athenian leaders and with sophists, he found out that they thought they knew the answers, but the answers they gave could not withstand Socrates' questions and arguments. Meno, for example, a young follower of the sophist Gorgias, defines virtue as the desire for good things and the power to get them; but he admits that one can get such good things as wealth or power unjustly, which cannot be virtuous; so his definition is not correct. Again, Euthyphro thinks he can define piety as what god(s) loves; but when Socrates asks him whether something is pious because god loves it, or god loves it because it is pious, he chooses the latter; but in that case it is not god's love that makes something pious or right, as the definition implies. God may indeed love the good and the just and the beautiful, but he loves them because they are the good and the just and the beautiful, not conversely.

This kind of thing happens again and again in Plato's early dialogues, and they end with young aristocrats, Athenian leaders, and sophists admitting that they thought they knew what virtue and good and happiness are, but they did not know. The conventional wisdoms about these value concepts were no wisdoms. Plato's Socrates confesses that he does not know the answers either, but he at least knows that he did not know them.

Two lessons emerged from Plato's earlier dialogues. One is that there must be important differences between knowledge and opinion or belief, and these are worth investigating. Young Athenian aristocrats and sophists had only opinions about virtue and happiness, but they mistook these opinions for knowledge, and as a result they made confident but often mistaken choices about how to live. By beginning to investigate the differences between knowledge, opinion, and sense perception as well, Plato began a second branch of philosophy, the theory of knowledge. One difference he found is that opinions can be true or false, but knowledge can be only of what is true; false knowledge is really an oxymoron. A second difference is that opinion need not be supported by evidence or proof, but knowledge has to be; something that Plato learned from the mathematicians of the day, such as the Pythagoreans, who would not claim to know a geometrical theorem to be true unless they could prove it. In subsequent dialogues, such as the *Republic*, the *Theaetetus*, and the *Timaeus*, Plato showed also that knowledge is not identical with sense perception, because sense perception gives us only appearance, not reality. Finally, he argued that knowledge cannot be shaken by rhetoric, the art that produces persuasion by appealing to emotions more than to reason. With Geometry and Arithmetic as his star examples, Plato thus began to hammer out the concept of science we have, as something distinct from and superior to ordinary everyday experience and opinion.

A second lesson was that if the conventional wisdoms about virtue and good and happiness were really not knowledge but more or less uncritical opinions, then these important human concepts must be investigated anew, from scratch, as it were: an effort must be made to illuminate them, reshape them if necessary, and try to put them on more secure foundations. Not only these fundamental values, but also other concepts and phenomena of permanent human concern: love, divinity and its relation to human beings; the nature of the universe and what can be known of it; human beings themselves, their bodies and souls; their city-states, their constitutions, their uses of political power; literature and the fine arts and their place in society. In his middle and late philosophical dialogues Plato launched a series of investigations which left a permanent mark in the history of thought.

In his dramatic masterpiece, the *Symposium*, Plato presents a dinner party of famous Athenians who make some remarkable speeches about Eros, the god of love, and love itself. Dramatic and comic poets, men of letters, a physician, the philosophers Diotima and Socrates, they all take turns telling us what love is, its causes and effects, its role in human affairs and in the life of the species. Here we have accounts of Greek sexual customs; Aristophanes' hilarious story of sexual love as the product of human arrogance and divine punishment, and his influential idea that every human being has an ideal other half that would complete him/her if only s/he could find her/him; a story that Goethe admired and Freud found instructive. Here we also find Plato's own theory of love, whose highest attracting objects are the good and the beautiful, and his famous ladder of love, in which love of knowledge, virtue, and beauty itself are ranked far above love of the body; a theory whose marks we can find in Dante's *Divine Comedy* and even in Shakespeare's *Romeo and Juliet*. A wild and brilliant young Athenian aristocrat, Alcibiades crashes the party and makes a glorious speech in praise of Socrates as his love.

In the *Phaedo*, whose dramatic scene is Socrates' last day in jail, Plato stages a debate about the nature of human beings and the universe in which they exist. Just before taking the hemlock Socrates argues that death is the separation of body and soul, and that the human soul continues to exist after this separation. He also tries to establish the existence of Platonic Forms, objective abstract entities, such as ideal geometrical figures, which serve to bring order into the material world. Here and in a later dialogue, the *Timaeus*, Plato postulates a divine craftsman who creates the world in the image of the ideal Platonic Forms, and suggests accordingly a teleological explanation of the nature of the physical universe: the universe, the system of heavenly bodies, for example, is the way it is because it is best for it to be that way. Just as human beings make artifacts to be the best we can make them, so the divine craftsman brought order into the physical universe so that it is the best it can be. What we call natural entities, including ourselves, are really divine artifacts. To understand the universe more completely we have to discover other explanations as well: the causes of motion and change, the structure of matter and physical objects, and the materials out of which things are composed. But the teleological explanation of the universe is the best explanation and it completes all the others. Not till the theory of evolution was there an alternative explanation to Plato's (and Aristotle's) teleology, and that theory applies only to living entities;

while the other three kinds of explanations, invented and clarified by the Greek Philosophers, still stand. Though Plato wrote that these cosmic suggestions of his are at best a likely story, rather than knowledge, he believed that the human soul has a divine element in it, reason, which is capable of understanding the universe, especially if it can be freed from the demands of the body or at least exist in a sufficiently disciplined body.

At about the time he founded the Academy Plato wrote the *Republic*, generally regarded as his masterwork, the most comprehensive and rich of all his dialogues, containing his theories on justice and the other cardinal virtues, human happiness, education, his pioneering analysis of the human soul, his daring proposal for the equality of women, the good and bad uses of wealth and power, the art of government, his reformation of the popular Greek gods, his theory of knowledge, and his metaphysics of Platonic Forms and the Form of the good. It outlines the principles of the first utopia, an ideal aristocracy of knowledge, to replace aristocracies of honour, wealth, even the Athenian demos, and certainly tyranny.

The *Republic* is the most wonderful philosophy book ever written for any reader. Plato's masterful use of informal dialogue, his easy conversational style, his use of analogies, metaphors, similes, allegories, and myths, take the reader into philosophy almost imperceptibly, leading her from the concrete to the abstract, causing her to question ideas she took for granted and to wonder about the new ideas in the book.

This has made the book enormously popular; it is taught in colleges and universities worldwide, and may be the most popular philosophy book ever written. It is difficult to find a better introduction to philosophy than Plato's dialogues, especially the early dialogues, and the *Symposium* and the *Republic*.

Plato's methods have also been extremely influential. The Socratic Method of questioning and testing our assumptions is almost universally practised in classrooms. The quest for definitions of basic concepts has also become part of philosophy; not definitions that we make up as we please, but definitions which reveal the nature of things, as the scientific definition of water as H2O reveals the essence of water, or Euclid's definition of a triangle tells us what a triangle really is. Many kinds of arguments are also exhibited and used in Plato's dialogues, such as analogies, inductive generalizations, direct and indirect deductions, the method of hypothesis, and dialectic which investigates the relations among abstract entities, the Platonic Forms. Plato believed that human reason can discover the nature of the universe. And he elaborated the philosophical methods—taking or adopting some from the Pre-Socratic philosophers, some from Socrates, some from mathematics, some inventions of his own—by which he thought human reason can accomplish this great feat.

References and Suggestions for Further Reading

Cornford, F.M. trans. *The Republic of Plato*. Oxford U.P., 1945.
Irwin, T. *Plato's Ethics*. New York: Oxford U.P., 1995.

Kraut, R. ed. *The Cambridge Companion to Plato*. Cambridge, N.Y. Cambridge U.P., 1992.

Nehamas A. and P. Woodruff, trans. *Plato: Symposium*. Indianapolis: Hackett, 1989.

Santas, G. *Goodness and Justice: Plato, Aristotle, and the Moderns*. Malden, Mass.: Blackwell, 2001.

Vlastos, G. *Platonic Studies*. Princeton, N.J.: Princeton U.P., 1981.

Chapter 30

Plato's *Symposium*

c. 380 BC

Steven R. Robinson

> I doubt whether anyone has ever seen the treasures which are revealed when Socrates
> grows serious and exposes what he keeps inside. However, I once saw them ...
> (Alcibiades in Plato's *Symposium* 216e)

Socrates and Alcibiades were lovers—after a fashion—as we learn in some detail
from the gossipy final speech in *Symposium,* a brief book full of speeches about
love, all written by Plato. But to hear it from Alcibiades, their affair has now
soured, leaving bitterness and recrimination in place of their old affection, a
testament to the hazards of this most intimate and transcendent emotion. What is
this thing we call love? Why do we give it such an important role in our lives? Is it
really worth all of its attendant risks—risks of pain, humiliation, frustration, and
loss? And what does it mean when love goes wrong? In this philosophical
'dialogue', Plato offers a fascinating variety of answers to these questions. By
putting those answers into the mouths of a group of friends and lovers, Plato also
invites us to compare the words of his speakers to their own lives. The writing style
(of which Plato is both the inventor and the undisputed master) is a type of
dramatic historical fiction; the characters are historical persons from the generation
prior to Plato's own, many of them well known to both ancient and modern
audiences.

The dramatic occasion in the dialogue is a drinking party set in the year 416
BC and hosted by Agathon, a famous writer of tragedies. Many guests are present,
including Socrates, the great philosopher (Plato's mentor); Aristophanes, the writer
of comedies who had lampooned Socrates on stage just a few years before in a play
called *Clouds*; and of course Alcibiades (mentioned above), the notorious
politician whose career was soon to be the ruin of Athens' empire. Instead of the
usual drinking and debauchery, the friends agree on this night to take turns
delivering speeches in honour of Eros, the divine personification of erotic love,
who all of them agree is great and powerful. In the speeches that follow, love is
defined alternatively as a psychological drive for personal honour; a social
institution for the training of virtuous citizens; a cosmic force that maintains
balance and harmony (in the physical world as in the social); a longing for
wholeness; an infatuation with youth and beauty; and the pursuit of immortality.
Though Plato composed all of these speeches himself, he leaves it up to his reader

to decide whether love is one, all, or none of these things. Once these speeches are finished, the party is interrupted by a gang of drunken revellers led by Alcibiades. He declines to praise Eros himself but instead delivers a speech praising Socrates—his ex-lover, now seated next to him. Here Plato gives us a remarkable glimpse into the personality of Socrates, through the eyes of one who knew him intimately. After this final speech, drinking and debauchery erupt in force and continue unabated until sunrise, at which time Socrates rises and departs for his regular day, apparently unaffected by the vast quantities of wine and lack of sleep.

The *Symposium* has always been recognized as the most dramatic and entertaining of Plato's dialogues, and is one of the cluster of great 'middle period' dialogues (along with *Republic*, *Phaedo* and *Phaedrus*) that are normally taken to express Plato's mature, positive philosophy. The centrepiece, of course, is Socrates' speech, wherein love is described as a universal force that moves all things—as far as they are able—towards peace, perfection and divinity. Accordingly, love is active at many levels and is expressed in diverse ways, from animal lust to sexual love, to friendship, to politics and community service, to the creation of art and literature. What brings all of these together under the single rubric of 'erotic love' is that they can all be understood as types of 'reproduction'. Sex can produce children that carry the trace of their parents' identities into a subsequent generation; likewise, social action and artistic expression are the 'children' of intense, but non-physical, love between creative persons. In each case these 'offspring' project into the future an imprint of the identities and potentialities of their past creators, who thereby achieve a sort of 'mortal immortality'.

Socrates does not claim to be the originator of this theory but attributes it to a 'wise woman' named Diotima, who was his 'instructress in the art of love' (201d). Diotima taught that philosophy is the highest expression of love and can be successful only after a careful progression through all of the lower stages—the famous 'ladder of love'. Though every lover pursues some manifestation of beauty, only the philosopher is positioned to perceive Beauty itself, a divine Form (or Idea) which is the ultimate cause of all physical and spiritual beauty:

> In that region alone where he sees beauty with the faculty capable of seeing it, will he be able to bring forth not mere reflected images of goodness but true goodness, because he will be in contact not with a reflection but with the truth. (Diotima, in Plato's *Symposium* 212a)

The goal of philosophy, then, is to give birth to true and lasting goodness, to the best of one's ability, within the mortal realm. And such is the greatest degree of happiness and immortality that a human can achieve.

One of the most remarkable features of the *Symposium* is the way that it tends to erase the distinctions between heterosexual and homosexual love, and this has earned it wide appreciation and even devotion from gay and lesbian readers the world over. Plato himself was likely homosexual (he never married and had no children, which was highly unusual in his time). While all of his party guests in this dialogue are male and clearly conceive of Eros mainly as the love of men for boys (part of the socially accepted Greek practice of male bisexuality), we also find here the first explicit references in Western literature to exclusively gay and lesbian couples (191e). Part of the appeal of this dialogue no doubt lies in the very generality of its concept of Eros, which makes it instantly recognizable and applicable to people of any sexual orientation.

But in fact, human love and sexuality are just the beginning of Plato's philosophy in this dialogue—the entry point, if you will, into a deep and complex treatment of the nature of reality and the ultimate meaning of life. Eros, in Diotima's doctrine, is not a god but a *daimon*, or 'spirit', which mediates between gods and humans:

> Being of an intermediate nature, a spirit bridges the gap between them, and prevents the universe from falling into two separate halves. (Diotima, in Plato's *Symposium* 202e)

Eros is thus a binding force that draws opposed elements together and unites them into a self-identical whole. As it turns out, this principle of erotic unification finds application across the whole range of theoretical analyses of relations, be it male and female, lover and beloved, rich and poor, rulers and ruled, soul and body, god and mortal, being and becoming, ritual and revelation, tragedy and comedy, or poetry and philosophy. In every case, Eros is the principle that is active in the cooperative pursuit of goodness by these opposed elements, and in all subsequent articulation of truth, beauty, and justice. As Socrates concludes, on this account, 'Human nature can find no better helper than love' (212b).

Like most of Plato's dialogues, and all of his finest, the *Symposium* puts discussions of profound and important philosophical concepts into the mouths of everyday sorts of characters that seem to step right off the page at the reader. Logically challenging, yet sometimes comical and always motivated by serious issues, the writing immediately engages the reader. It makes you feel that you too could take part in such a discussion—and it invites you to give it a try. The *Symposium* is one of the jewels of world literature. It should be enjoyed not once only, but again and again, as a gateway to self-knowledge and reflective contemplation upon matters that are important to all people, everywhere.

References and Suggestions for Further Reading

Quotations in the essay are from Plato. Symposium. Translated by Walter Hamilton. Harmondsworth: Penguin, 1951.

Bacon, Helen H. 'Socrates Crowned.' *Virginia Quarterly Review* 35 (1959) 415-430.
Dover, Kenneth J. *Greek Homosexuality*. Cambridge, Mass.: Harvard University Press, 1978.
Gould, Thomas. *Platonic Love*. New York: The Free Press of Glencoe, 1963.
Lissarrague, F. *The Aesthetics of the Greek Banquet*. Princeton: Princeton University Press, 1990.

Chapter 31

The Anonymous Iamblichi

Louis Groarke

The Greek philosopher Iamblichus includes a collection of anonymous sayings in his Protrepticus. These fragments, which derive from an older Sophist from the late 5th or early 4th century BC, have been alternatively attributed to an Athenian follower of Democritus or (implausibly) to the ancient sophist Hippias of Elis. While the precise identity of this author has been irretrievably lost, the extant text elaborates a coherent political doctrine. During an era marked by unrest and political intrigue, amidst a chorus of rhetoricians and slick persuaders, the author referred to as the Anonymous Iamblichi stands out as a sober advocate for solidarity, justice and law.

This unknown author attacks the view, as common today as then, that 'the power which is based on a consideration of one's own advantage is virtue, or that obeying the laws is cowardice'. The argument he makes in favour of morality and social restraint resembles and foreshadows the arguments of modern social contract theorists such as Thomas Hobbes, John Locke and, more recently, John Rawls. The Anonymous Iamblichi emphasizes the role of trust in a healthy society. 'An atmosphere of trust is the first result of the observation of law. It benefits all men greatly and may be classed among those important things which are called good.' In a lawless society, social harmony dissolves and relationships between citizens are marred by enmity and suspicion.

The Anonymous Iamblichi considers two patterns of social interaction. In a society that fosters morality and respect for the law, 'Those who have good fortune enjoy it in safety ... [and] those who have bad fortune receive help from those who have good fortune.' Conspiracy and political wrangling give way to the natural activities of life. The result is a peaceable kingdom. 'If [citizens] go to sleep, ... they approach it without fear and without painful anxieties; when they rise from it, they enjoy the same state of mind.'

In a lawless society based on self-interest, on the other hand, 'good fortune is not safe ... and ill fortune is not driven away but grows stronger'. Citizens 'hoard money [which] becomes scarce, even if it exists in large quantities'. Internal strife increases as men 'plot against one another', and 'external war is kindled'. Inhabitants live in dread and foreboding. 'When they awake their thoughts are not pleasant; and when they have gone to sleep, they do not find a pleasant place of refuge but one filled with fear.' This unrest leads naturally to tyranny.

The Anonymous Iamblichi argues that it is in our best interests to obey the law and care for others, for we cannot live in safety in a lawless society. Even someone blessed with superhuman abilities cannot flaunt the law. 'If he should be invulnerable, not subject to disease, free from emotion, extraordinary and hard as adamant in body and soul, perhaps someone might believe that the power based on a consideration of one's own advantage would be sufficient for such a man on the grounds that such a man is invulnerable even if he does not submit to the law.' But anyone who thinks such a man can prevail is sadly mistaken. 'All men would be in a state of hostility to a man formed of such a nature, and because of their own observance of law and numbers, they would surpass such a man in skill and force and they would get the better of him.'

The Anonymous Iamblichi is primarily an ethicist. The only goal worth pursuing is a virtuous reputation. The wise person exits from this life leaving 'everlasting and immortal fame in place of a soul that is only mortal'. Someone who wishes to achieve the 'immortal glory' of a good reputation needs to seize every opportunity and to persevere in virtue over a long period of time. Fellow citizens will then come to recognize their abiding worth.

Reference and Suggestion for Further Reading

The standard reference in English for the Anonymous Iamblich:

'The Anonymous Iamblichi.' Translated by Margaret Reesor. *The Older Sophists*. Edited by Rosamond Kent Sprague. Indianapolis, USA: Hackett, 2001: 271-278.

Chapter 32

Diogenes of Sinope

c. 413 BC–c. 323 BC

Marjolein Oele

Plato, on being asked what he thought of Diogenes, replied: 'He is a Socrates gone mad.' (Diogenes Laertius, *Lives of Eminent Philosophers*, VI.54)

Whether or not it was indeed Plato who spoke of him in this way, the image of Diogenes as a 'Socrates gone mad' remains significant and powerful. For who else can foreshadow the radical lifestyle of Diogenes the Cynic, the homeless beggar who questioned all social norms and conventions than the figure of a reflective Socrates, barefoot and wearing an old cloak? However, even the controversial figure of Socrates falls short if we try to describe the radical stance that Diogenes took towards Greek civic life. It is precisely this uncompromising attitude towards society that has earned him the title 'mad'. Simultaneously, it has made Diogenes into the most influential and leading figure of Cynicism, more so than his teacher Antisthenes.

Although some of the ancient sources are uncertain about the exact year of his birth, we can establish with certainty that Diogenes was born in Sinope, a Milesian colony on the southern coast of the Black Sea (modern Sinop, Turkey). Around 370 BC he left Sinope, allegedly because either he or his father (a banker) was accused of having defaced the Sinopean coinage. Some report that he was banished from the city, others say that he fled fearing the consequences. This biographical fact is often related to an oracular pronouncement. In Diogenes Laertius' account, Diogenes travelled to Delphi and asked the oracle what he should do to gain the greatest reputation. The answer the priestess gave was 'Adulterate the coinage'. Supposedly, Diogenes interpreted this pronouncement by the oracle as a personal call to undermine the 'currency' of his time—to challenge the social norms and conventions. Many of the remaining anecdotes about his life describe him doing exactly this: challenging the beliefs of the Athenians while he talked and wandered through the streets of Athens. Later he lived in the Greek city of Corinth, where he met Alexander the Great and where he died, allegedly in the same year that Alexander died: 323 BC.

Among the writings attributed to Diogenes are thirteen dialogues, several letters, and seven tragedies. However, none of these are extant; what remains of them are some scattered fragments. One of the most helpful sources of information about his life and his ideas is his biography written by Diogenes Laertius, a Greek writer from the 3rd century AD. That a description of his life can be as insightful as an account of his literary ideas is in great part due to the fact that for Diogenes, and for the whole school of Cynicism, philosophy did not rely merely on philosophical ideas. Philosophical discourse was limited for the Cynics, as the following anecdote illustrates. In the account of Sextus Empiricus, when a philosopher argued that motion is impossible, Diogenes 'without uttering a single word, simply got up and began to walk about, showing thereby that motion does in fact exist' (Sextus Empiricus, *Hyp. Pyrrh.*, III, 66).

This anecdote shows insightfully how the 'technical experts' of philosophical discourse annoyed Diogenes. Avoiding fancy discourse, in fact without saying anything at all, he showed how life itself can reveal truth. Thus, Diogenes thought truth and virtue are not solely a matter of speaking, but basic principles that need to be attended to in our own day-to-day life. Therefore, we can study the concrete acts and actions of his life in order to gain more understanding about his philosophical ideas.

In his choices and actions, the behaviour of animals provided specific guidelines, as this story recounted by Diogenes Laertius indicates:

> Theophrastus tells in his dialogue *The Megarian* that one time [Diogenes] saw a mouse running around, not looking for a place to sleep nor did it have a fear of the dark nor did it seek any of those things which are [commonly] desired, and in this way it discovered the remedy for its difficulties. (D.L.VI.22)

The mouse running around aimlessly, unconcerned about comfort and devoid of fear proved to be an important guide for Diogenes. The mouse indicated to him how we need to live our life as much as possible without the self-imposed goals of society, without fear, without need of a permanent residence nor having any other artificial needs. Diogenes tried to approximate this natural way of living as much as he could, living in a tub in the Metroön, a public building in Athens that both accommodated a sanctuary and the state archives:

> According to some, [Diogenes] was the first to fold his coat because he had to sleep in it as well; and he carried a knapsack in which he kept his food; he used indifferently any place for any use, for eating, for sleeping, or for conversing. ... He had written to someone to try to procure a small house for him. When this man was a long time about it, he took for his abode the tub in the Metroön. (D.L.VI.22-23)

In his view, *self-sufficiency* is one of the most desirable and valuable things in life. It makes one independent of the pressure of others and therefore allows oneself to be as free as possible. The Gods lead a life of freedom, needing nothing. The natural life of animals emulates this life of the Gods, and should therefore be held up as an example. However, not only animals, but also children come close to living their lives in a natural, self-sufficient way. As Diogenes Laertius writes, they also had a profound influence on Diogenes' way of life:

> One time seeing a child drinking out of his hands, he threw away his cup from his knapsack saying: 'A child has given me a lesson in simplicity.' He also threw away his bowl when he saw a child who had broken his bowl take the lentils in the hollow part of a piece of bread. (D.L.VI.37)

For Diogenes, one of the ways to attain freedom and happiness is through discipline. We need constantly to exercise and discipline our body and soul so as to strengthen our physical and spiritual capacities. Diogenes therefore went in search of opportunities that could strengthen him physically and spiritually—rolling over hot sand in his tub in the summer, embracing statues covered with snow in the winter. Simultaneously, we need to acquire contempt for pleasure, because pleasure is dangerous insofar as it weakens us. For example, the pleasure of buying new clothes can make us slaves of our own wallet and can thereby impinge upon our moral strength. According to Diogenes, we need to detach ourselves from such pleasures, in order to allow for complete freedom and independence.

Imitating the natural role model that animals provided, it must have been neither a surprise nor an insult to Diogenes that many of his contemporary critics came to call him and his followers 'dog' (Greek: *kuōn*). Diogenes and his followers were so much associated with this canine epithet that they came to be known as Cynics (Greek: *kunikoi*), literally meaning 'those who are or behave like a dog'. But why did his 'enemies' call him by the name of a dog and not another animal? One of the primary reasons quoted is that the Greeks thought of dogs as particularly shameless animals. Diogenes, in their view, was making a cult of *shamelessness*. Diogenes Laertius wrote that 'It was his custom to do *everything* in public, even the works of Demeter and those of Aphrodite' (D.L.VI.69). Going against the general view of decency, Diogenes thought that needs such as urination, defecation, and masturbation are merely natural and should not remain hidden. Better to understand his shamelessness, we need to regard it within the framework of pure *freedom of action*. Diogenes thought that humans are often insincere about their motives of actions or hide their physical pleasures behind veils of so-called sophistication and decency. That those veils have concealed our genuine, authentic human nature comes to the fore in the following famous account:

> He lit a lamp in broad daylight and said, as he went about, 'I am looking for a human being'. (D.L. VI. 41)

Diogenes took it upon himself to expose the true origins of human behavior through his shameless public actions. He thereby showed the artificiality of our pretentious habits and norms.

Not only did Diogenes express complete freedom in his actions, he also proclaimed that *freedom of speech* is the most beautiful thing for humans. The following excerpt from Diogenes Laertius is witness to this:

> The Stoic Dionysius says that after [the Battle of] Chaeronea he [Diogenes] was captured and taken to [king] Philip. When Philip asked him who he was, he replied: 'A witness to your insatiable greed.' For this he was admired and set free. (D.L. VI. 43)

The absolute frankness to which Diogenes submits his speech and life allows the Cynic to pierce through the superficial layers of convention. Unimpressed by the status of whomever he speaks to, either the powerful Alexander, his father

Philip, or an ordinary citizen, the Cynic says whatever he thinks in service of leading a truer way of life:

> Once while Diogenes was sunning himself in the Craneum, Alexander stood over him and said: 'Ask of me whatever you wish.' And Diogenes replied: 'Stand out of my light.' (D.L. VI.38)

Ultimately, the image often remaining of Diogenes is of someone whose uncompromising way of life set him at odds with philosophers and non-philosophers alike. The biting criticism embodied in his words and actions often diametrically opposed him to his society. This is well illustrated in one of the anecdotes, where Diogenes is described as entering a theatre when everyone was leaving it. However, the image of the radical philosopher who seeks his way counter to the powerful forces of society's norms and conventions has proven to be not only of shocking value, but more so of instructive value for future generations. It is therefore appropriate to conclude with a description of his funerary monument. This monument is said to have been a pillar, which supported a dog. It carried the following inscription:

> Even bronze grows old with time, but your fame, Diogenes, not all eternity shall take away. For you alone pointed out to mortals the lessons of self-sufficiency, and the path for the best and easiest life. (D.L. VI.78)

References and Suggestions for Further Reading

Dudley, Donald R. *A History of Cynicism: From Diogenes to the 6th Century AD*. London: Bristol Classical Press, 1937.

Sextus Empiricus, *Sextus Empiricus*. 4 volumes, translated by R.G. Bury. Cambridge, MA: Loeb Classical Library, 1967.

Diogenes Laertius, *Lives of Eminent Philosophers*. Vol. II, translated by R.D. Hicks. Cambridge, MA: Loeb Classical Library, 1961.

Navia, Luis E. *Diogenes of Sinope: The Man in the Tub*. Westport, CT: Greenwood Press, 1998.

Reale, Giovanni. 'Diogenes "The Dog" and the Development of Cynicism'. *The Systems of the Hellenistic Age*. Albany, NY: SUNY Press, 1985, pp.21–38.

Sloterdijk, Peter. 'Diogenes von Sinope—Hundmensch, Philosoph, Taugenichts'. *Kritik der Zynischen Vernunft*. Frankfurt am Main: Suhrkamp Verlag, 1983. 2 vols. Vol. 1, pp.296–319.

Chapter 33

Eudoxus of Cnidus

c. 400 BC–c. 347 BC

Andrew Gregory

> Plato offered this problem to the mathematicians: which hypotheses of regular, circular and ordered motion are capable of saving the phenomena of the planets? Firstly, Eudoxus of Cnidos produced the hypothesis of the rolling spheres. (Simplicius, *In Aristotelis De Caelo Commentaria*, 492.3)

Eudoxus of Cnidus led an immensely active life, and had many interests. He developed theories in philosophy, theology, astronomy, geography and mathematics and was also active on developing a code of laws for his own city. He travelled widely, and was an associate of Plato, though little is known of the interaction between them.

Eudoxus performed a most remarkable feat of mathematics and astronomy, and effectively established a research programme for astronomy that was to last around 2,000 years. To the Greeks, the stars moved in perfect circles around the night sky. The five planets visible to the naked eye, however, behaved oddly. They would move relative to the fixed stars in one direction, but would then sometimes come to a halt and reverse their motion, before halting once more and proceeding again. This is known as the retrograde motion of the planets. This behaviour was well known to the ancient Babylonians, who called the planets 'bibbu', sheep, and indeed our word planet derives from the Greek *planetes*, which means wanderer or vagabond.

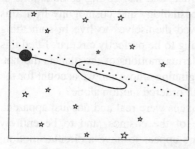

If one watches the motions of the planets relative to the stars, periodically the planets apparently stop, reverse their motion, stop again and proceed again.

Figure 33.1 The motion of a planet relative to the stars

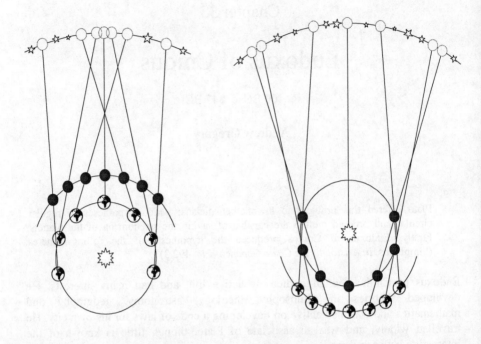

Figure 33.2   Modern explanation of retrograde motion

The modern explanation of retrograde motion is that the earth and the planets each have different sizes of orbits and different speeds of orbits. In certain arrangements the planet will appear to move backwards relative to the fixed stars due to the relative motion of earth and the planet.

The Greeks believed themselves to live in a cosmos. That is significant because the Greek *cosmeo* meant to put in order, and had strong connotations of good order. We not only derive words like cosmology and cosmogony from this root, but also cosmetic. So the Greeks believed themselves to live in something well ordered. The motions of the stars, appearing to be perfectly circular, fitted this idea well, but the apparently disorderly, wandering motions of the planets did not. Hence the challenge of the quotation at the beginning—how can we account for the motion of the planets using regular, circular and ordered motion alone?

To the Greeks, all the motions of the heavens were real and not just apparent. They believed the earth to be at the centre of the cosmos, and to be entirely unmoving. Today, we understand that the stars appear to have a circular motion, but really this is due to the daily rotation of the earth. The Greeks, believing the earth to be entirely still, treated all the motions of the heavens as real and not apparent. This meant that to the Greeks, the planets really did stop, reverse their motion, stop, and then go forwards again. The Greeks had some interesting arguments as to why the earth was central and stable, which are examined in the chapter on Aristarchus, who was the only ancient to believe the earth orbited the sun. Plato made a start on this problem by combining two circular motions together.

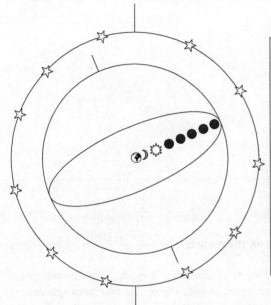

The outer sphere of the fixed stars rotates once in 24 hours. The sun, moon and planets are also carried around in 24 hours. The sun, moon and planets are also given a motion relative to the fixed stars by the motion of their own sphere on an offset axis. Each body has a specific speed around the inner sphere—for the sun a year, for the moon a month. Mercury and Venus are also a year, the outer planets have longer periods.

Figure 33.3   Plato's model of the cosmos

Plato supposed all of the fixed stars to be on one sphere, which rotated once in 24 hours. The sun, moon, and planets each had another circular motion, which moved them relative to the fixed stars. So each time the sphere carrying the stars rotated, sun, moon and planets were in a slightly different position. The sun moved around its second circle once a year, the moon once a month. The sun, moon and planets would all follow the same path relative to the fixed stars, but at different speeds. Actually, the sun follows this path (the ecliptic) but the moon and planets move in a broader band (about 12 degrees) of the sky known as the zodiac. A major drawback with Plato's model was that it could not account for the retrograde motion of the planets.

Eudoxus took this model and made it more sophisticated and much better at accounting for the motions of the planets. At first sight it looks quite complex, but each part has a logical purpose. While Plato supposed two spheres for each planet, Eudoxus supposed four.

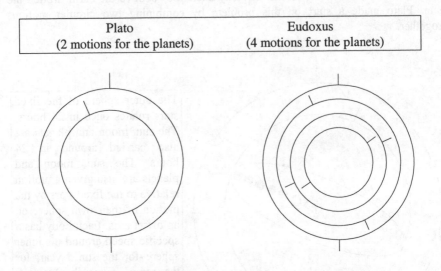

Plato (2 motions for the planets)	Eudoxus (4 motions for the planets)

Figure 33.4   Plato and Eudoxus on the planets

The outer sphere carries the fixed stars, as with Plato's model. The second sphere generates motion along the ecliptic, again as with Plato. The two inner spheres are set at such an angle that they produce a pattern known to the Greeks as a hippopede, or horse fetter.

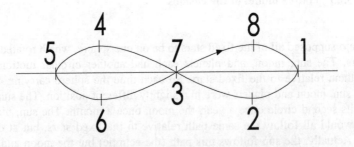

The two inner spheres are so arranged as to produce this pattern, known to the Greeks as a hippopede.

Figure 33.5   Eudoxus: pattern produced by the two inner spheres

When all four circular motions are combined, this is what happens:

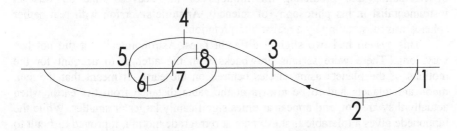

> The pattern produced by all four spheres working together, which gives an approximation to planetary retrograde motion.

Figure 33.6   Eudoxus: planetary pattern

This means that at least to a first estimation, the retrograde motion of the planets has been accounted for using perfect circular motion alone. So too the planets will move within the zodiac rather than simply along the ecliptic (here the ecliptic is represented by the horizontal line). Eudoxus also introduced three sphere models for the sun and moon to better model their motions.

This is a quite stunning achievement given Eudoxus' resources, which would have amounted to records of the positions of the planets and some crude writing instruments, like a wax tablet and a stylus. Although Eudoxus' system was not perfect, mathematically it was quite powerful. It is very likely that Eudoxus was aware of several of the drawbacks of his system. The system is best treated as a prototype, a first attempt that has flaws but gets the basic principle across, rather than as a finished article. It was however hugely influential. It seemed to show that with a cunning enough use of combinations of regular circular motion, it would be possible for all the motions of the heavens to be brought under one comprehensive system. This remained the guiding principle for astronomy right down to Johannes Kepler in the early part of the 17th century, who was the first to realize that planetary orbits are in fact ellipses about the sun.

Apart from this work on the motions of the planets, Eudoxus produced two books on the positions of the stars (The *Enoptron* (mirror) and The *Phenomena*), which although superseded by the more detailed work of Hipparchus (an important later astronomer) were an important basis for later work.

Eudoxus' model was later improved by Callippus, who directly followed Eudoxus. By adding even more spheres, he was able to account for several more phenomena. The great philosopher Aristotle accepted Callippus' mathematics, but took the step of conceiving of the spheres as made out of aether. It is unclear whether Eudoxus thought the spheres to be real and made of something (and so was a realist in his philosophy of science) or whether he thought this was merely a way of calculating and predicting the motions of the heavens (and so was an instrumentalist in his philosophy of science). Aristotle's version with real aether spheres was most definitely a realist interpretation.

This system had two slightly different fates. Astronomically, it did not last very long. There were serious drawbacks with the attempt to account for the motions of the planets using circles centred on the earth. It meant that the sun, moon and planets had to be always at the same distance from the earth, when actually they are not, and appear at times significantly larger or smaller. While the hippopede gives a tolerable first estimate at retrograde motion, it proved difficult to improve the modelling to fit all the shapes of retrograde motion. It was also difficult with Eudoxus'' system to model the changes in speed of the planets relative to the fixed stars even when they were not in retrograde motion.

So concentric sphere astronomy gave way to another type of astronomy, known as epicyclic astronomy, developed by the later astronomers, Apollonius and Hipparchus, and brought into a completed system by Ptolemy in the second century AD, who was perhaps the greatest astronomer in the ancient world. This was based on a device known as the epicycle.

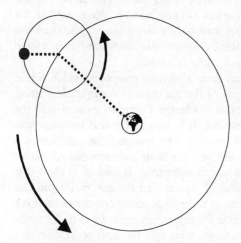

> The basic device of later Greek astronomy. The planet revolves around a point, and that point itself revolves around the earth. By a suitable choice of speeds of rotation retrograde motion can be produced. Differing types of retrograde motion can be produced, and the planets are not always held at the same distance from the earth.

Figure 33.7   The epicycle

Mathematically this was a very powerful system, as multiple epicycles could be used, in conjunction with two more sophisticated variations on the basic epicycle known as eccentrics and equants. Given sufficient complexity, one can model the motions of the heavens arbitrarily well. The basic scheme of Ptolemy was to last well over a millennium. It was improved upon both by the medieval Islamic culture and the medieval West, and was only finally rejected with the acceptance of Copernicus' work. Copernicus, the first person in the modern West to argued that the earth orbited the sun and not vice versa, first published in 1543 and was accepted in the early part of the 17th century.

In terms of cosmology, Aristotle's scheme based on Eudoxus' concentric spheres lasted much longer, indeed well into the middle ages. People thought of the heavens as an arrangement of spheres of aether, centred on the earth, all nesting together with no gaps between them. There was often a tension between this rather simple cosmological picture and a rather more sophisticated astronomy. This was only resolved with the change to heliocentrism in the 16th and 17th centuries.

Of Eudoxus' other work, his most important contribution is to the theory of numbers. His definition of a number allowed mathematicians to deal properly with irrational numbers, which had been a difficulty since their discovery by the Pythagoreans. Archimedes tells us that Eudoxus proved important theorems in geometry, and undoubtedly his work influenced Euclid and is incorporated into Euclid's geometry. In philosophy, Eudoxus held a hedonist position in ethics, claiming that pleasure is the good. It may well be this view that inspired Plato, in part, to write his work the *Philebus*, which disagrees with such a view.

References and Suggestions for Further Reading

Dreyer, J.L.E. *A History of the Planetary Systems from Thales to Kepler.* Cambridge U.P., 1906.

Gillispie, C.C. (ed.) Dictionary of Scientific Biography. s.v. *Eudoxus.* New York: Scribner, 1970.

Gregory, A.D. 'Eudoxus, Callippus and the Timaeus Astronomy.' In R.W. Sharples and A. Sheppard (eds.). *Ancient Approaches to Plato's Timaeus.* Bulletin of the Institute of Classical Studies, Supplement 76.

Lloyd, G.E.R. *Early Greek Science: Thales to Aristotle.* London: Chatto and Windus, 1970.

O'Neil, W.M. *Early Astronomy From Babylonia to Copernicus.* Sydney U.P., 1986.

Wright, M.R. *Cosmology in Antiquity.* London: Routledge, 1995.

Chapter 34

Aristotle

384 BC–322 BC

Hope May

All men by Nature desire to know. (Aristotle, *Metaphysics*, 980a)

Whereas a rattle is a suitable occupation for infant children, education serves as a rattle for young people when older. (Aristotle, *Politics*, 1340b)

Sometimes referred to as the 'Stagirite' (because he was born in Stagira, a city in Macedonia), sometimes referred to simply as 'the philosopher', Aristotle remains one of the most important thinkers of all times. Although he was a student of Plato for twenty years, Aristotle devised theories that opposed those of Plato, his mentor. For example, unlike Plato who denied that sense experience was necessary for knowledge, Aristotle held that knowledge was impossible without sense experience; unlike Plato who believed that the soul could exist independently of the body and survive death, Aristotle rejected the notion of personal immortality and held that the soul could not exist without the body; and unlike Plato who believed that matter was created by something he called the 'demiurge', Aristotle believed that matter was eternal—it has always existed and always will exist.

Aristotle's philosophy is at odds with the Christian doctrines that were to develop later: that the Universe is created by God; that the soul survives bodily death, and that man needs God in order to know. Consequently, when Aristotle's ideas were discovered by the European Christendom in the 13th century, some in the Western World found Aristotle's views threatening and dangerous. Thus, in 1277, the Bishop of Paris condemned portions of Aristotle's philosophy that contradicted the Christian worldview. If someone taught or asserted such Aristotelian propositions as 'the world is eternal' and 'man can understand nature on his own', he was excommunicated from the church. (Ironically, some medieval scholars, such as Thomas Aquinas, believed that Aristotle's ideas could be used to help illuminate Christian doctrine. These scholars united Aristotle's ideas and Christianity into a philosophical system known as Scholasticism.) If someone was a professor at a university, he was forbidden to teach these propositions.

At the time when Aristotle was born in 384 BC, Socrates had been dead for fifteen years, and Athens had already been defeated by Sparta in the twenty seven year long Peloponnesian war (431–404 BC). Because he was born in Macedonia to

Macedonian parents, and although he lived in Athens for many years, Aristotle was never a citizen of Athens. Consequently, he was unable to participate in Athenian politics.

Aristotle came to Athens when he was 17 to study with Plato at Plato's Academy, *the* university of the day. There he remained for 20 years until Plato's death in 347. Aristotle was supposedly Plato's brightest student and earned the nickname 'the reader'. After Plato's death, Aristotle left Athens to tutor the son of King Philip of Macedon, Alexander (who later became 'Alexander the Great'). After tutoring Alexander, Aristotle returned to Athens and opened his own school, the Lyceum. When Aristotle's famous pupil, Alexander the Great, died in 323, the Athenians became hostile to those with ties to Macedonia. Probably for this reason, Aristotle was charged with impiety. Rather than face the charges, Aristotle chose exile. In 320, Aristotle died a lonely man, exiled from the cultural centre of Athens and the students whom he loved.

Only a fraction of Aristotle's works have survived. Nevertheless, his extant works cover a range of topics including the biological development of living beings, logic, ethics, politics and even the nature of dreams. Aristotle was a systematic thinker—his works forming a unified whole. Aristotle's theory of the soul depends upon his ideas on nature; his theory of the human good depends upon his ideas of the human soul; and his theory of politics depends upon his idea of the human good.

One important tenet of Aristotle's philosophy is the distinction between *matter* and *form*. Matter, according to Aristotle is 'pure potentiality'. Matter is not yet a specific 'thing' that is 'individuated', that is, having its own borders and boundaries. Rather, matter is that out of which a particular thing is made. It is *form*, according to Aristotle, that transforms matter from an undefined mass to a particular 'this'. Aristotle says that the form of a thing is understood by understanding the thing's *function*.

To illustrate Aristotle's distinction between matter and form, think of a hunk of silver which is not a particular identifiable thing. Now imagine a pen-maker named Mr. Dupont who is about to make a pen from this hunk of silver. Since he is a pen-maker, Mr. Dupont has knowledge of how to transform the silver into a pen. As Mr. Dupont makes the pen, he imparts the *form* of a pen onto the silver. In other words, he is transforming the silver into something that can perform a particular function, namely *to write*. Notice that it is *knowledge* of how to make a pen that enables Mr. Dupont to impart the form of a pen into the matter.

Aristotle's distinction between matter and form is importantly connected to his doctrine of the 'four causes'. It is useful to think of this doctrine as a doctrine about the different factors or 'causes' that go into making something like a pen. In order to make a pen, one first has to find the right kind of material—one needs to be able to hold the instrument without it dissolving in one's hand. Thus, pens are not made out of water, dirt, or wax, but are made out of things like plastic or some sort of metal like silver. Aristotle refers to the material out of which a thing is made as its *material cause*.

Of course, one does not have a pen once the right kind of material is found. One then needs to manipulate that material to produce the pen—it has to be shaped, drilled, sanded, and so on—the material has to be *set in motion*. Aristotle refers to the agent that sets in motion the material the *efficient cause*. In our example above, it is Mr. Dupont that is the efficient cause of the pen. Note that Mr. Dupont does not manipulate the silver for the fun of it. Rather, Mr. Dupont manipulates the silver *for the sake of* making a pen. Every step, from the acquiring of the material, to the melting, to the shaping, and to the buffing is done for the sake of producing a pen. In other words, the production of a pen is the 'goal' or 'end' of Mr. Dupont's work. Aristotle refers to the end or goal of a process as its *final cause*. Mr. Dupont does not shape and buff simply for fun—there is a 'final cause' compelling Dupont to move his hands this way and that—namely, the production of a pen.

The fourth cause of which Aristotle speaks is the 'formal cause'. Just as the material cause of a pen refers to the matter out of which the thing is made, the formal cause refers to the pen's form. As you now know, the form of a thing is related to its function. Thus, the formal cause of a pen is what the pen is, namely, an instrument for writing.

Aristotle's doctrine of the four causes can be summed up as follows: the 'material cause' is the material or 'stuff' out of which an object is made; the 'efficient cause' is what sets the material in motion; the 'final cause' is the goal or end of a process; and the 'formal cause' is related to the product's function, and is what the final product is (i.e., what it is designed *to do*).

Importantly, Aristotle thinks that the four causes are at work not only in the production of man-made objects like pens, but also are at work in the production of *natural* objects like plants, dogs and human beings. Aristotle sees a profound similarity between craftsmen and 'nature'. Both are similar in that both are responsible for the orderly making of a thing. Just as pens do not 'pop into existence' but are a result of an orderly process that is set in motion by an agent for the sake of producing a particular object, so too, living organisms like human beings and dogs do not simply appear. Rather, they are a result of an orderly *natural* process.

Of course, there is no man like Mr. Dupont who is behind the orderly natural process that results in the production of a human being or dog. Nor does Aristotle claim that human beings and dogs are made by God. Rather, Aristotle says that the *soul* is behind the orderly natural process in which the development of a living being consists. Doubtless, Aristotle's idea that the soul is responsible for the production of living beings is at odds with our notion of 'soul'. For most of us, the word 'soul' refers to something that is different and even potentially independent of the body. Few of us think of animals as having souls, even fewer think that plants have souls. However, Aristotle claims that plants, animals and human beings all have soul. For Aristotle, anything that is living and develops has soul. In fact, 'soul' for Aristotle is the final, formal and efficient cause of the body. That is, the soul not only sets in motion the development of the body (efficient cause), but it also is the goal or end of development (final cause), and it is what the body is and *does* (formal cause).

Aristotle's ethical theory, his theory about what is good for human beings, rests upon his theory of the soul. As you now know, Aristotle thinks that both man-made objects and natural organisms have a particular form and function. Just as pens are designed to write, human beings are 'designed' by nature to perform a particular function. But what is it that human beings are designed by nature to do? According to Aristotle, one discovers a thing's function by discovering what is not only unique to that thing, but is also what is *last* in that thing's development. Aristotle says that it is reason and thinking that is not only unique to humans but also comes last in the development of a human being. Think of the development of a baby into an adult. Surely reason is not possessed in infancy, but is only fully developed in adulthood. Because reason is unique to human beings, and because it comes at the end of human development, Aristotle claims that the particular function that human beings are naturally designed to do is *to reason and to think*.

The fact that function of a human being is to reason and to think is crucial to Aristotle's ethical theory. For Aristotle, as well as for other Greek philosophers like Socrates and Plato, being ethical was not about 'following God's rules'. Rather, Aristotle believes that ethics is about achieving what the Greeks called '*eudaimonia*' (pronounced you-dime-own-eea). '*Eudaimonia*' is usually translated as 'happiness', but think of it as a deep, profound and lasting happiness and contentment, rather than the sort of happiness that can come and go.

For the Greeks, ethics was about achieving *eudaimonia*. But how does one attain deep, profound and lasting contentment? By winning the lottery? By becoming the President? Although Aristotle mentions both wealth and political honour as candidates for *eudaimonia*, he denies that they are sufficient for eudaimonia. Rather, in order to become *eudaimon*, one must perfect the human function which, according to Aristotle is reasoning and thinking. Note that while practically all adults have reason and thought, few have perfected these abilities. According to Aristotle, it is only in the perfection of reasoning and thinking whereby a human being will achieve the profound happiness and contentment of which human beings are capable. Of course, many people disagree with Aristotle's view of the human good. Nevertheless his view that a human being is 'designed' by nature to think, rather than to spend money or rule over others is a profound and provocative view of human nature .

Although he lived over two thousand years ago, Aristotle's ideas have shaped and continue to shape the Western World. His view of the natural world was the received view until Sir Isaac Newton's *Principia Mathematica* gave us yet a different way of conceiving nature. Aristotle's notion of 'biological form' is regarded as a forerunner to the notion of DNA. And his ethical theory is regarded as one of the most important works on the subject. Aristotle's influence on Western science and religion is unsurpassed.

References and Suggestions for Further Reading

Adler, Mortimer. *Aristotle for Everybody: Difficult Thought Made Easy*. New York: Simon and Schuster, 1997.

Barnes, Jonathan. *Aristotle: A Very Short Introduction*. Oxford: Oxford University Press, 2001.

Barnes, Jonathan (ed.) *The Cambridge Companion to Aristotle.* Cambridge: Cambridge University Press, 1995.

Lear, Jonathan. Aristotle: *The Desire to Understand.* Cambridge: Cambridge University Press, 1988.

Ross, W.D. *Aristotle.* New York: London: Routledge, 1995.

PART V
THE HELLENISTIC PHILOSOPHERS

Chapter 35

Theophrastus of Eresus

c. 372 BC–c. 288 BC

Irene Svitzou

...For the Earth is a common hearth for both Gods and Men and we all must ...love her affectionately...reclining on her as our nurse and our mother ... (Theophrastus, *On Piety*, quoted in Porphyry, *On Abstinence from eating animals*, 32.1-2)

Theophrastus of Eresus was born on the Greek island of Lesbos, about fifteen years after the foundation of Plato's Academy (Diogenes Laertius, *Lives* V.40.15). Diogenes also notes that his real name was Tyrtamos but, because of his eloquence, Aristotle named him Theophrastus ('theos'=God and 'phrasso'=speak: the one that speaks in a heavenly way, like God) (D.L. V.38.27-39.1). In his native city, he probably studied under Alcippus and later, in Athens, under Plato, finally forming a fruitful association with Aristotle, former teacher and friend of Alexander the Great. When Alexander died in 323 BC, Aristotle had to leave Athens for fear of his life, so he moved to Chalcis, in Euboea (D.L. V.36, 4). At that time the headship of Aristotle's school, the Lyceum, passed to Theophrastus who managed it for about 35 years until his death.

The school gained support from politicians in Athens such as Antipater and Demetrius of Phalerum. Demetrius modified an old law and made it possible for Theophrastus to acquire his own estate in Athens. Theophrastus purchased the land originally ceded to Aristotle for his school, and so became the owner of the Lyceum as well as its principal. Under the guidance of Theophrastus, the number of books in the library of the Lyceum increased considerably, new teaching rooms and conference rooms were added, the dining-room was enlarged and the number of pupils reached 2,000 (D.L. V.37, 12-13). Under the leadership of Theophrastus the School gained great renown throughout the known world. It is said that his last words to his pupils were about glory:

Life greatly wrongly depreciates many pleasures for the sake of glory, for we die the moment we begin to live ... Farewell and either forsake my teaching— for the labour is too much—or hold it in your mind—for the glory is great... (D. L. V.41, 22-27)

After his death the Lyceum (otherwise called the *Peripatetic School*) passed to the direction of Strato of Lampsacus.

Theophrastus' work was far from a simple continuation or imitation of Aristotle's theories although he continued the enterprise initiated by Aristotle of the collection and interpretation of information in every scientific field, and adopted some Aristotelian arguments. Diogenes Laertius (V.42.10-50.9) attributes 227 works to Theophrastus, which include about 440 'books' on a great variety of subjects, a detail that indicates that he was a prolific writer in many areas of scholarship.

In physics and metaphysics, Theophrastus followed his teacher's views on the definition of time. Time is perceived as a countable motion, strictly connected to the movement of the heavenly sphere and of course to the soul, as there can be no time and no numbering without soul. Yet we know that Theophrastus raised a number of objections to Aristotle's definition of place, rather interpreting place as a certain position of a part in a whole (Theophrastus, *Fragment* 49, in Fortenbaugh, Huby and Sharples eds. p. 304). He rejected the idea of fire being the primary element, because it is in constant need of fuel supply, and he seems also to have rejected the idea of Aristotle's fifth element, aether.

Theophrastus still held the idea of ensouled heavens and used the Aristotelian meaning of 'pneuma' (spirit or breath) to explain body processes but he denied the existence of the 'unmoved mover'. (The unmoved mover, or prime mover, is an immovable, eternal kind of 'being' which Aristotle may have envisioned as the cause of all movement of the heavenly bodies.) In his work, *Metaphysics*, Theophrastus tries to present the world as an organic whole and he seems to reject the majority of Aristotelian ideas and arguments concerning metaphysics. Some had already been rejected by Aristotle himself—for instance those referring to the role of purpose in nature. It has been suggested that Theophrastus probably argues more against Plato's theories than against Aristotle's. It seems that Theophrastus was probably trying to develop a method of reasoning based on questioning, debating and opposition to existing theories, rather than forming a theory of his own.

In his two major scientific works, *Enquiry into Plants (Historia Plantarum)* and *Plant Explanations (De Causis Plantarum)* Theophrastus systematically gathers information about various plant species and when speaking, for instance, about art in nature, about ends (aims, scopes) existing in the growth of plants or about differences of 'genus' between wild and cultivated varieties. In that work he was greatly advantaged by having immediate access to the notes of the scientists who followed Alexander the Great on his expeditions.

It is probably in the field of ethics that we meet Theophrastus' greatest contribution. In his work, *Characters,* he introduces a new kind of treatise in which he describes thirty human personality types through a presentation of their moral defects. In the beginning of every description a definition of each defect is given and then he quotes examples of the respective behaviour. Although short, this study became famous in antiquity and even later, during the Renaissance, and has been used in many ways and on numerous occasions (in theatre for the study of comedy, in rhetoric, in politics, in psychology).

From Cicero we learn that Theophrastus valued material goods more highly than Aristotle did, and acknowledged them as necessary for human happiness.

Yet, the point in which his opposition is expressed most strongly is his dislike of marriage which, he thinks, detracts men from their service to science. Another interesting theory in his Ethics is his belief in the existence of a relationship between all living creatures, a belief that firmly guided him to the rejection of sacrifices and of eating meat.

Theophrastus was the philosophical thinker who made scientific listing and classification indispensable and opened the way to real observation and research in natural sciences. His book, *On Senses (De Sensibus)* is of great interest because, apart from its philosophical theories, it is the only work that records the fragments of most of the pre-Socratic philosophers.

Theophrastus devoted his life to study and research and made the world of philosophy, truth and science his only family. This was perhaps one reason, amongst others, why he gained fame and recognition during his life time. Still today, almost every student of ancient Greek philosophy reads and studies Theophrastus for his important contribution to the advancement of philosophy during his life and for the influence of his work to other philosophers after his death.

References and Suggestions for Further Reading

Fortenbaugh, W.W. and D. Gutas. Eds. *Theophrastus: His Physical, Doxographical and Scientific Writings*. Rutgers University Studies in Classical Humanities. New Brunswick: Transaction Books, 1992.

Fortenbaugh, W.W., P.M. Huby, and R.W. Sharples (Greek and Latin) and D. Gutas (Arabic) eds. *Theophrastus of Eresus, Collections of fragments with English translation*. Leiden: Brill, 1992.

Fortenbaugh, W.W. and R.W. Sharples eds. *Theophrastean Studies on Natural Science, Physics, Metaphysics, Ethics, Religion and Rhetoric*. Rutgers University Studies in Classical Humanities. New Brunswick: Transaction Books, 1988.

Fortenbaugh, W. and P. Steinmez. Eds. *Cicero's knowledge of the Peripatos*. New Brunswick: Transaction Books, 1989.

Ophuisjen, J. van and M. van Raalte, eds. *Theophrastus: Reappraising the Sources*. Rutgers University Studies in Classical Humanities. New Brunswick: Transaction Books, 1998.

Raalte, M. van. *Theophrastus' Metaphysics*. With introduction, translation and commentary. Leiden; New York: E.J. Brill, 1993.

Chapter 36

Pyrrho

c. 360 BC–c. 270 BC

Leo Groarke

> O old man, O Pyrrho, how and whence did you escape the servitude to the opinions
> and theorisings of the empty sophists. How did you unloose the shackles of every
> deception and persuasion? You did not trouble to investigate what winds prevail over
> Greece, from whence all things arise and into what they pass. (Timon, fr. 822;
> Diogenes *Laertius, Lives of the Eminent Philosophers*, IX. 65)

Pyrrho was a native of Elis in the Peloponnese. He is famous for a radical
scepticism which remains a matter of great controversy. In his own time, Pyrrho
was famous as a moral figure. His goal was a life of happiness characterised by a
calm and studied peace of mind. This is a moral ideal which leaves no room for the
anxiety, impatience, anger, fear or frustration we ordinarily feel when we deal with
physical hardship, do not get what we want, or are envious of others. It is an ideal
which is tested in conditions of adversity, when difficulty, disaster, hardship and
disappointment make most of us lose our composure.

Pyrrho was famous because his life demonstrated his philosophical ideal.
According to the biography in Diogenes Laertius, he was indifferent to trials and
tribulations, endured pain without complaint, and was committed to a life of
poverty which renounced fame and fortune. He made such a strong impression on
his fellow citizens that they appointed him a high priest and on his account passed
a law exempting philosophers from taxes. His famous equanimity is celebrated by
his follower, Timon of Phlius, who wrote:

> This, O Pyrrho, my heart yearns to hear, how on earth you, though a man, act most
> easily and calmly, never taking thought and consistently undisturbed, heedless of the
> whirling motions and sweet voices of wisdom? You alone led the way for men, like
> the god who drives around the whole earth as he revolves, showing the blazing disk of
> his well-rounded sphere. (Timon, fr. 841; Diogenes Laertius, *Lives of the Eminent
> Philosophers*, IX. 65)

In later ancient and in modern times, Pyrrho is famous (and *in*famous) for the
philosophical perspective with which he was associated. According to Timon, he
held that anyone who wished to be content should ask three questions: What is the
nature of things? What should be our attitude toward them? And what will be the
consequence of such an attitude? Pyrrho answered that things are by nature

indifferent, unstable and indeterminate; that we should, therefore, adopt an agnostic attitude which refuses to assent to anything (declaring of each thing that it no more is than is not, or both is and is not, or neither is nor is not); and that the result of such an attitude will be an inclination not to make judgements (*aphasia*) followed by 'freedom from anxiety' (*ataraxia*).

The roots of this philosophy are unclear. Some have suggested that it originates in a trip to India which Pyrrho undertook in the company of Alexander the Great, where Pyrrho came in contact with the Indian 'gymnosophists' ('the naked wise men'). More simply, Pyrrho may have been influenced by earlier Greek philosophers whose competing arguments convinced him that our senses and opinions are weak, contradictory, and uncertain.

Whatever the roots of Pyrrho's views, his vaunted peace of mind is founded on a decision to adopt a sceptical attitude which refuses to endorse particular beliefs. Judging by later Pyrrhonism (and by the ethics of Democritus, which influenced Pyrrho), this sceptical attitude can help us maintain our peace of mind because it casts doubt on those opinions which are the cause of our anxieties. Even when we are faced with death, considered the worst of all calamities, it may be argued that we do not know the nature of death and that it may turn out not to be an evil, but even the greatest good. Judging by Plato, Socrates used arguments of this sort when he was faced with death. In part because of them, he was able to maintain a heroic attitude that displays no trace of fear or bitterness.

Over time, the sceptical attitude that Pyrrho advocated made him a figurehead for scepticism. One frequent, but implausible, interpretation of his philosophy (already evident in the 3rd century B.C., in the writing of Antigonus of Carystus, a somewhat unreliable collector of anecdotes about philosophers of the day) makes him a representative of a scepticism so radical that it rejects beliefs our lives depend upon (i.e. the belief that there is food or a train or a precipice in front of us).

In the history of philosophy, Pyrrho became an important figure because the adherents of 'Pyrrhonism' collect and systematize the arguments for scepticism, putting his philosophy forward as a kind of anti-philosophy which maintains that ultimate truths cannot be established, and that metaphysical philosophers cannot prove the truths which they propose as the fruit of their philosophy.

References and Suggestions for Further Reading

Bett, Richard; 'Pyrrho', *The Stanford Encyclopedia of Philosophy* Edward N. Zalta (ed.), URL = <http://plato.stanford.edu/archives/fall2002/entries/pyrrho/>.

Burnyeat, Myles and Michael Frede, eds. *The Original Sceptics: A Controversy.* Indianapolis: Hackett Publishing Inc., 1998.

Groarke, Leo; 'Ancient Skepticism,' *The Stanford Encyclopedia of Philosophy*, Edward N. Zalta (ed.), URL = http://plato.stanford.edu/archives/fall1998/entries/skepticism-ancient/

Hallie, Philip P., Sanford G. Etheridge and Donald R. Morrison. *Sextus Empiricus: Selections from the Major Writings on Scepticism, Man and God.* Indianapolis: Hackett Publishing, Co., 1985.

Long, A.A. and D.N. Sedley. *The Hellenistic Philosophers*. Vol. 1. Translations of the principal sources with philosophical commentary. Cambridge: Cambridge University Press, 1987.

Popkin, Richard H. *The High Road to Pyrrhonism*. Ed. by Richard A. Watson and James E. Force. San Diego: Austin Hill Press, 1980.

Chapter 37

Epicurus

341 BC–270 BC

Dirk Baltzly

Friendship dances around the world announcing to all of us that we must wake up to happiness. (*Vatican Sayings*, 52)

This is one of the many aphorisms that Epicurus advised his students to memorize and integrate into their daily living. It tells us much about this most unlikely Olympian of the mind—he supposed that whereas the Olympic Games require demanding training to become something that we are not yet, real happiness requires that we only awaken ourselves to the value of what we already have. A life as good as that which the gods enjoy is ours for the taking if only we can wake up to the real facts about our world and ourselves. The central facts are these: First, pleasure alone has value. Second, we—like all things in the cosmos—are simply material aggregates of atoms plunging through an endless void.

We will return to Epicurus' philosophy in a minute. What about the man? Epicurus was born on Samos in 342/1. He was nonetheless an Athenian citizen because Samos had become an Athenian colony in 405. His first exposure to philosophy was the Platonism taught by Pamphilus on Samos. When he turned eighteen he went to Athens to pass the examination required of young citizens. He did not return to Samos, but rather to Colophon where his family moved to avoid political unrest following the death of Alexander the Great. At nearby Teos he seems to have encountered the philosophical ideas of Democritus through Nausiphanes.

Though Epicurus' own philosophy resembles Democritean atomism in some ways, Epicurus seems to have been critical of many aspects of the thoughts of Democritus. He struck out on his own and founded a philosophical community at Mytilene in 311/10. This was followed by another school in Lampsacus. In 307/6 Epicurus moved at last to Athens and purchased a property near the Diplyon Gate, not far from the site of Plato's Academy. This was the Garden of Epicurus—a community of both men and women who lived in accordance with the dictates of Epicurus' philosophy. Epicurus left the property to Hermarchus of Mytilene and it endured as a community for long after. Epicurus also made provision for his birthday to be celebrated with an annual feast.

So how would an Epicurean live? Not simply by feasting—that much is sure. In spite of the modern connotations of the term 'epicure', Epicurus himself had an austere conception of pleasure. The apogee of pleasant living is the tranquility we experience in the absence of physical pain or mental anxiety. This condition of tranquility or *ataraxia* is the best that life can get. We can achieve it with very minimal physical requirements—we do not require fine wines or sumptuous meals in order not to be hungry. Indeed, many of the things that people must do in order to acquire the wealth necessary for such luxurious living are absolutely inimical to freedom from mental anxiety. Epicurus thought that a nice bottle of wine or a fine meal could *vary* the pleasure of a tranquil life, but it could in no way *improve* upon it.

How are we to achieve this tranquility? The hardest part is undoing the damage that culture does to us. We believe—falsely according to Epicurus—that the gods intervene in our affairs in this life and that they will punish us in the next. In truth, there are gods, but they do not bother with our affairs since they are blessed and happy and basically can't be bothered to care a thing about what we do. Part of the task of Epicurus' atomistic physical theory was to provide purely material and mechanical explanations of things such as lightning bolts that people incorrectly suppose to be manifestations of divine anger. It also dispensed with the idea that the universe is the product of divine creation and providence.

The gods will not punish you in the next life either: there isn't one. According to Epicurus, Plato and others who posit an immaterial and immortal soul are simply talking nonsense. The fact of interaction between mind and body shows that our minds really are just an aspect of our bodies. If he were alive today, he would doubtless identify thinking and sensing with processes in the brain and central nervous system. His own theory of mental functioning is, of course, much cruder but involves the same general idea.

Nor is the eventual fact of our utter non-existence anything that should worry us. Epicurus argued that a thing can be called genuinely bad for a person only if it is at least possible that the person should experience it. But one never experiences non-existence. So, death is not a bad thing for the person who dies.

But achieving tranquility is not simply as easy as accepting the arguments for such conclusions about the gods, death and the afterlife. Popular culture surrounds us with misleading images that we do not even see as images. It shapes the metaphors in terms of which we understand things, so that freedom from anxiety is not a question of simply changing our beliefs. It requires learning to see things differently.

For example, one thing that disturbs tranquility is insecurity. We must defend ourselves from 'them'—those who are not like us. Epicurus claims instead that we must make friends with those who are amenable to discussion. At the very least, we must not alienate people who are not so open to discussion. Friendship makes a far greater contribution to our security than walls or armies. And friendship is possible with all other humans, since in their natural state they are all just like us: mortal creatures whose sole good is the simple, pleasant life.

If we doubted this, Epicurus would surely suggest that we should gather evidence by the best means possible. This, Epicurus thought, was sense perception. To see whether 'they' really are a threat to us and our way of life, we would need to get to know them. Would the popular image of those who are a threat to our security survive an actual encounter with 'them'?

Perhaps, unfortunately, it would. People can be bad indeed. Epicurean philosophy survived the death of Epicurus and thrived for several centuries. However with the coming of the Christian era, Epicurus was reviled by writers such as Lactantius, who grossly misrepresents his ethical teachings and scorns his physics as absurd. How, ask Lactantius and other Christian critics, could anyone be so foolish as to suppose that all the world around us is the product of chance collisions among invisible, material particles. How foolish indeed ...

References and Suggestions for Further Reading

Though Epicurus was a prolific writer, his works were not cherished by the middle ages as the books of Plato and Aristotle were. As a result, we have only three complete works from him in the form of letters to friends summarizing his views. These and other fragments are translated in:

Inwood, B. and L. Gerson. Eds. *Hellenistic Philosophy: Introductory Readings* 2nd ed. Hackett: Indianapolis, 1997.
Sharples, R. W. *Stoics, Epicureans and Skeptics.* London: Routledge, 1996. A gentle introduction to the philosophy of Epicurus, as well as his contemporaries.

Chapter 38

Zeno of Citium

c. 332–262 BC

Maria Protopapas-Marneli

To the question 'Who is a friend?' his answer was, 'A second self'. (Diogenes
Laertius, *Lives of Eminent Philosophers*, VII, 23)

Zeno, the founder of the Stoic philosophy, was the son of Mnaseas (or Demeas).
He was born in Citium, Cyprus, which was a Phoenician province, having been
colonized by the Phoenicians.

His father, a rich merchant of porphyry (a rock containing feldspar)
frequently travelled from Cyprus to Greece, in order to sell his merchandise in
Athens. There, in, the cradle of philosophy and civilization, he used to buy Plato's
Dialogues for his son who was eager for learning. In his very early days, Zeno
started reading and dreaming that, one day, he would also travel to Athens, and be
able to visit the birthplace of Plato and Socrates.

The opportunity came by mere chance. After he succeeded his father in
merchant travels, he visited Athens among other places. Once, as he was
approaching the port of Piraeus, his ship foundered. Diogenes Laertius tells us that:

> He went up into Athens and sat down in a bookseller's shop, being then a man of
> thirty. As he went on reading the second book of Xenophon's *Memorabilia*, he was so
> pleased that he enquired where men like Socrates were to be found. Crates passed by
> in the nick of time, so the bookseller pointed to him and said, 'Follow that man'. (D.L.
> VII.2.)

Later, when referring to the incident, Zeno used to say, 'It is well done of
thee, Fortune, thus to drive me to philosophy' (D.L. VII, 5).

Zeno could not accept the extreme position of the Cynics and abandoned his
teacher, Crates. Zeno remained in Athens for a decade, attending classes in
different philosophical Schools. He followed the teachings of Stilpo, Xenocrates,
and Polemo, before founding his own School. Stilpo, the philosopher from Megara,
taught in Athens around 320 BC. The ethical part of his teachings agrees with
those of the Cynics. It appears that Zeno has been influenced in the shaping of his
Logic by the corresponding teachings of the philosophers of the School of Megara.
Xenocrates, Head of the Platonic Academy, taught at approximately the same

period. From Xenocrates, Zeno seems to have adopted the tri-partite division of philosophy into its Logic, Natural, and Ethical parts.

In order to emphasize the immutable nature binding those three aspects together, the Stoics resort to quite illustrative metaphors. For example, they often represent philosophy as an animal whose skeleton and sinews are Logic, while the fleshy parts are Ethics, and soul is Physics. In that tri-partite division of Stoic philosophy, no part is inferior to another. This is reflected in their teaching. They lay equal stress in the teaching of each of those parts, attributing equal significance to each one of them. They maintain that neglecting of any of those parts would result in the collapse of the whole corpus (collection of written work) of their philosophy. It is believed that Zeno learnt dialectical reasoning (the art of debating the truth of opinions) from Diodorus Cronus (of Iasos).

According to the testimony of Diogenes Laertius, when Zeno's philosophical thinking matured considerably, he attended the teaching of Polemo, the Platonist. Zeno was influenced by Polemo's philosophy regarding the theory of the supreme good as well as regarding the latter's view that the τέλος (telos, final aim) of the human being is the leading of a life in accordance with nature. Having realized that Zeno was not attending the teaching sessions out of love for his philosophy but only out of a desire to enrich his knowledge, Polemo is supposed to have said: 'I can see, Zeno, that you enter through the School's garden gate to steal my ideas and then transform them according to your Phoenician way' (D.L. VII, 25).

Zeno, having been initiated into the Greek Philosophy in its entirety and having studied Heraclitus, chose the site at which he would establish his School. The most appropriate place, in his opinion, would be the 'Stoa'—the colonnade or Portico of Pisianax which received its name from the painting of Polygnotus in its interior (D.L. VII, 5).

It was on this site that, during the period of the tyranny of the Thirty (between September 404 and the beginning of 403 BC), 1400 Athenian citizens had been put to death. This was the reason that the Athenians asked Polygnotus to paint the Stoa afterwards so that the sacrilege of the Athenians could be forgotten. This was the place that Zeno frequented and where he talked with the Athenians who in the course of time grew in such numbers that the School of Zeno was established. Initially, these were called Zenonians, renamed later to Stoics, owing to the site where the teachings were held, a name which the Athenians attributed formerly to poets who frequented the 'Stoa'.

Zeno's philosophy survived for six centuries, not only in Athens and the broader Hellenic area, but also in Rome where it flourished, and was represented by great personalities such as Seneca, Epictetus and the Emperor Marcus Aurelius. Christianity borrows basic principles of Stoicism, especially in the aspect of ethics, and incorporates them into its own principles.

From the Cynics, Zeno adopts the new division of people in two classes, the wise and the depraved (those, who being totally unable to benefit from the experiences of life, behave in such a way that their actions exhibit a kind of corruption similar to the lack of wisdom that characterizes them) and not according to origin and wealth. He distances himself, however, from them because of their excesses and because in contrast to those who believed solely in the ethical aspect of the philosophy, Zeno supports the idea that the study of natural phenomena proves useful in the progress of sciences, which finally leads to the ethical perfection of the human being. This is because he believed that only the wise man is able to make shrewd use of the experiences he collected throughout his life. He can create the art of living (*arts vitae*), in order to abide in the perfect city of gods and mortals. The Stoics perceive the world as a two-part system, resembling a city, where gods and men co-exist in harmony. This co-existence is founded on their participation in 'logos' (logic) which includes the natural law of the universe, since it imposes logical rules that necessarily form order. Thanks to the law, man creates coherence with other people by uniting himself to others through logos, in a kind of natural association. Man, through logic and, therefore through wisdom, participates in the cosmic being and makes himself equal to God, since, according to the Stoics, the wise is divine. On the contrary, the depraved, lacking wisdom, is undesirable in the cosmic city, and is exiled and city-deprived. The contrast between the wise and the depraved lies, therefore, in the fact that the depraved is unable to co-exist with Gods and the wise.

Zeno's philosophy was established in the difficult times of the post-Alexandrian period (323–146 BC) during which the city-states begin to decline, and the big kingdoms become established. The citizen loses the protection he had felt within the close limits of his city while, simultaneously, his respect towards it is waning. The citizen of the Hellenistic city is converted suddenly from a typical inhabitant of the ancient *polis* into a cosmopolitan, a world citizen. Zeno then tries to free the human being from the mental intolerance he finds himself in, due to the social-political changes. Zeno's stoicism becomes a work of conciliations of elements as he teaches a new mental, ethical and religious consciousness of a new civilization.

Zeno maintained, however, that there is only one criterion for the truth. He taught people how to proceed in their quest for happiness by granting their consent to the cosmic events to the extent that those emerge as an expression of divine will. This is because one who consents to events which happen in accordance with the natural laws is virtuous and wise. Conversely, the corrupted man, being unable to consent (deprived of the ability to comprehend) so that he can live in harmony with those laws, is unwelcome in the city of Stoics, where both gods and mortal people cohabit harmoniously, and is regarded as a defector deserving banishment.

The acceptance of cosmic events is linked to truth which, according to the Stoics, is a fruit of knowledge, while its acquisition is equal to science. Even though the corrupted man, as they claim, is capable of constructing a logical argument, this does not presuppose the conquest of truth. According to Zeno, experience is tantamount to science, which in turn consists in the facility of infallible judgement. This facility is exclusively attributed to the wise man, as in the Stoics' world the wise man alone is infallible. The Stoics claim that, when the man is born into the world, the principal part of his soul is like a *tabula rasa* (a blank slate), ready to be imprinted by external stimuli.

There are, however, two ways of imprinting. The first is in the impressions conveyed through one or more sense-organs. For instance, through vision we perceive white or black and we continue to recognize it through memory even when its image is not there any longer. Through the sense of touch, we perceive the sense of smoothness or roughness. A repeated impression is acquired because it is imprinted upon the principal part of our soul, is recorded in our memory, is reproduced by the mind so that, finally, it becomes experience. The second way of imprinting is realized through the process of thought and the ensuing impressions are thoughts which are not formed by objects but are created by sentences. This latter way of imprinting characterizes all logical beings. The Stoics, led by Zeno, hold the view that God, Logos, and Nature are similar concepts and that the human being is logical, because God has endowed him with part of his logos, the seeds of logic.

Through logos the mental image resulting from logic is imprinted onto the soul. At the time it receives the imprint of the object, the soul is immovable. It suffers, however, a certain passion because, at the moment the object or the verbal expression penetrates it, the soul must react. The first passion is involuntary. The human mind receives an abundance of stimuli. However, the reaction (the movement of the soul) of each individual, the acceptance of the stimulus or its rejection, is voluntary. The movement which shakes our soul exclusively belongs to us because ours is the decision to accept, or not accept, that impression. Zeno, in fact, warns us that we should not trust all the images, because there are fallacious ones. Here lies the ability of the wise man: his ability to distinguish between the true and the false presentations. He must give his consent only to those which are true. On this very choice human happiness depends along with the smooth current of life, the *true life*.

> The people of Athens held Zeno in high honour, as is proved by their granting him the keys of the city walls, and honouring him with a golden crown and a bronze statue. (D.L. VII 5)

So, the Athenians proclaimed him an Athenian citizen, an honour which was bestowed on only few foreigners, and on his death they would 'build him a tomb in the Ceramicus at the public cost' (D.L. VII 11).

References and Suggestions for Further Reading

The fragments of Zeno and Cleanthes Ed. and with Commentary by A. C. Pearson. London: C.J. Clay and Sons, 1973.

Diogenes Laertius. *Lives of Eminent Philosophers*. With an English translation by R.D. Hicks. Loeb Classical Library. London: Harvard University Press, 1958.

Hunt, H.A.K. *A Physical Interpretation of the Universe: The Doctrines of Zeno the Stoic*. Melbourne: Melbourne University Press, 1976.

Rist, J.M. *Stoic Philosophy*. Cambridge: Cambridge University Press, 1969.

Sandbach, F.H. *The Stoics*. London: Chatto and Windus, 1975.

Schofield, M. *The Stoic Idea of City*. Cambridge, Cambridge University Press, 1991.

Chapter 39

Archimedes

c. 287 BC–212 BC

Suzanne Roux

'Give me a place to stand on and I can move the earth.' (In *Aristotelis Physicorum Libros Commentaria*, ed H. Diels. Berlin: 1895, 1110; quoted by Dijksterhuis, 15)

This was the boast of Archimedes to King Hiero of Sicily. Such apocryphal tales and the utterings of Archimedes have survived more than two millennia and his acclaim as a mathematician, a scientist, an ingenious inventor and an engineer has been maintained through the ages. Although there is no certainty about his birth date, place of birth or parentage, it is said that he was born in Syracuse and that his father was an astronomer called Phidias who, according to Archimedes in his work *The Sand Reckoner*, estimated the diameter of the sun to be twelve times that of the moon. Archimedes spent some time in Egypt and kept in contact with scholars from Alexandria, especially the astronomer Conon of Samos, to whom he used to send his mathematical discoveries before their publication.

In Plutarch's *Life of Marcellus* it is recorded that when Archimedes made his proud boast about moving the earth, King Hiero, amazed by this claim, asked Archimedes for a practical demonstration. At the time there was a ship in the dock that could not be drawn out except with a great deal of labour by many men. The ship was fully laden with passengers and freight:

> [Archimedes] seated himself at a distance from her, and without any great effort, but quietly setting in motion with his hand a system of compound pulleys, drew her towards him smoothly and evenly, as though she were gliding through the water. (*Plutarch's Lives, 'Marcellus'* xiv. 8-9)

The king was astonished by this display, which convinced him of Archimedes' skill and genius. After this he requested that Archimedes devise and construct many machines for use in all aspects of a wartime siege, such as catapults, battering rams, and cranes. These were later used with great success in the defence of Syracuse against the Roman attack led by Marcus Claudius Marcellus.

Archimedes' boastful claim about moving the earth is related to the principle of the lever which was discussed in the first book of his work *On the Equilibrium of Planes*. This work is mainly concerned with establishing the centres of gravity of various plane figures, completely flat figures, but the law of the lever that magnitudes balance at distances from the fulcrum in inverse ratio to their weights is the reason that Archimedes is often called the founder of theoretical mechanics.

Another tale about the extraordinary talents of Archimedes begins when King Hiero commissioned a craftsman to make him a golden wreath. The king supplied the gold, but when he received the crown he suspected the craftsman of replacing some of the gold with the less expensive metal, silver. He asked Archimedes to investigate his suspicions. Whilst contemplating the problem posed by the king's wreath, Archimedes stepped into his bath which was full to the top. He became aware that as he sat in the bath the water in the tub rose higher and flowed over the edge. In fact the deeper he sat in the bath the more water flowed over the edge. He leapt from his bath and ran down the street crying 'Eureka! Eureka! [I have found it! I have found it!'] He then took gold with the same weight as the wreath and silver with the same weight as the wreath and immersed the two lumps of metal into a tub of water and measured the amount of liquid displaced. Finally he repeated the experiment with the original wreath and informed King Hiero that indeed the craftsman had deceived him.

His genius for mechanical invention is legendary. Cicero describes a construction by Archimedes representing the motion of the Sun, the Moon and the Planets. According to Cicero, the machine was so accurate it would even show the eclipses of the sun and the moon. It is said that the Roman General Marcellus took these to Rome. Archimedes constructed many war machines that delayed the capture of Syracuse by Marcus Claudius Marcellus in about 211 BC. During the sacking of the city Archimedes was killed.

There are other versions of the killing of Archimedes: two are recorded by Plutarch. Some say that he was working on a mathematical or geometrical theorem when a Roman soldier commanded him to follow him to General Marcellus. Archimedes declined to do so until he had finished his work. The soldier drew his sword and slew him. Others claim that Archimedes was bringing mathematical instruments to Marcellus when a soldier, believing him to be carrying gold, killed him. No doubt the soldier was disappointed with the sundials, spheres, quadrants and no gold.

Plutarch records that Marcellus was deeply affected by the death of Archimedes and regarded the soldier responsible as a murderer. He sought the relatives of Archimedes and bestowed them with favours and honour. Archimedes had asked 'his kinsmen and friends to place over the grave where he should be buried a cylinder enclosing a sphere, with an inscription giving the proportion by which the containing solid exceed the contained' (*Plutarch's Lives*, 'Marcellus' xvii.7). In about 75 BC, more than a century after the death of Archimedes, Cicero, who was then quaestor (an official of the state) of Sicily, discovered the tomb of Archimedes in Syracuse near the Agrigentine Gate on the road leading to Agrigento. The grave was overgrown with vines and plants and Cicero restored it with honour, such was Archimedes fame two centuries after his death.

There are nine extant treatises by Archimedes in Greek. These include two books *On the Sphere and the Cylinder*. In these it is determined that the surface area of a sphere is four times that of its greatest circle or, in modern notation, that

$S = 4\pi r^2$ and that the volume of a sphere is two-thirds that of the cylinder in which it is inscribed $V = {}^4/_3 \pi r^3$. Archimedes applied some inventive geometry and arithmetic to estimate the perimeters of two 96 sided polygons, one circumscribing a circle and the other inscribing the circle. These calculations enabled him to estimate that the value of π lies between $3^1/_7$ and $3^{10}/_{71}$. Archimedes' calculations, particularly in his works, *On the Sphere and Cylinder* and *Quadrature of the Parabola* served as a precursor to the theories of derivatives and integration by Leibniz and Newton in the 17th Century.

In another small treatise, *The Sand Reckoner*, which was written to Gelon, the son of King Hiero, Archimedes set out to remedy the inadequacy of the Greek numerical notation by demonstrating how to express large numbers, at the same time presenting his notion of the arithmetic infinite. This is explained by Sir Thomas Heath in 'A History of Greek Mathematics'. He notes as one of Archimedes' achievements the invention of a 'system of arithmetic terminology by which he could express in language any number up to that which we should write down with 1 followed by 80,000 million million ciphers' (Heath, 81). He did this by setting out to determine the number of grains of sand which the sphere of the fixed stars could hold. This led Aristarchus of Samos (c. 310–230 BC), who was about 25 years older than Archimedes, to considerations of the dimensions of the universe. He provided the most detailed description of the heliocentric system (which has the sun at the centre of the universe) and was the first of the ancient philosophers to propose this view.

Archimedes' two books *On Floating Bodies* are the first known works on hydrostatics, studying the properties and behaviour of stationary liquids. In them he establishes several principles of hydrostatics including that known as Archimedes' principle: that a body immersed in a fluid is subject to an upward force equal in magnitude to the weight of the fluid it displaces. For these works he is known as the father of hydrostatics.

In July 1907, an editorial headline in the New York Times read 'An Archimedean Find'. The article revealed that a year earlier a Danish philologist, J.L. Heiberg, had discovered, in the Convent of the Holy Grave at Constantinople (now Istanbul), a manuscript of a previously unknown work by Archimedes. This manuscript was a copy of a work called 'Method of Mechanical Theorems' and had been transcribed by a monk in about the year 900 AD. Archimedes sent 'The Method' to his friend Eratosthenes and in an introduction explained how it was easier to gain practical knowledge of some things by the mechanical method and afterwards to prove them geometrically.

Plutarch records that although Archimedes was renowned for his mechanical and engineering inventiveness it was for his mathematics and geometry that he became most esteemed. Plutarch wrote:

> [Archimedes] repudiating as sordid and ignoble the whole trade of engineering, and every sort of art that lends itself to mere use and profit, placed his whole affection and ambition in those purer speculations where there can be no reference to the vulgar needs of life. (*Plutach's Lives, 'Marcellus'* xvi. 4)

If Plutarch's records represent the truth then Archimedes would be pleased that, although he gained fame and honour throughout the ancient world because of his mechanical inventions, it is his works of a theoretical character that remain. More than 2000 years have passed since the death of Archimedes but he is still renowned as a mathematician, engineer and inventor. Extraordinary tales are told of his inventions and scientific findings and today even children hear the tale of Archimedes in the bath.

References and Suggestions for Further Reading

Allen, Pamela. Mr Archimedes' Bath. Sydney: Collins, 1980. A charming picture book for children, that is suitable for all ages.

Archimedes. *The Works of Archimedes including the Method* translated by Sir Thomas L. Heath. Encyclopaedia Britannica 30th Printing, 1988, University of Chicago. This encyclopaedia article is included because it includes Archimedes' mathematics.

Cicero. *Tusculan Disputations* and *De Republica.* With an English Translation by J.E. King. Loeb Classical Library. London: William Heinemann Ltd., 1927.

Dijksterhuis E.J. *Archimedes.* Princeton, New Jersey: Princeton University Press, 1987.

Gordon, Sydney. *Archimedes: His life, work and experiments.* Oxford: Basil Blackwell, 1971. Incorporates many diagrams, and is suitable for younger readers.

Heath, Sir Thomas. *A History of Greek Mathematics.* 2 Vols. Vol. 2. Oxford: Clarendon Press, 1921.

Plutarch. *Plutarch's Lives.* Vol. V. With an English translation by Bernadotte Perrin. Loeb Classical Library. London: William Heinemann Ltd., 1917.

Stein, Sherman. *Archimedes. What Did He Do Besides Cry Eureka?* The Mathematical Association of America, 1999.

Chapter 40

Aristarchus of Samos

c. 310 BC–c. 230 BC

Andrew Gregory

> Cleanthes thought the Greeks ought to prosecute Aristarchus of Samos, for setting in motion the hearth of the cosmos (the earth) in order to save the phenomena, as this man hypothesized that the heavens remained at rest, and that the earth moved in a circle, while at the same time spinning around on its own axis. (Plutarch, *De Facie Quae in Orbe Lunae Apparet*, (*Concerning the Face which Appears in the Orb of the Moon*) 922f-923a)

Aristarchus of Samos lived sometime between 310 and 230 BC, though his exact dates are unknown. He was a pupil of Strato, third head of Aristotle's Lyceum, but little that is reliable is known of the rest of his life. His main work was in geometry and mathematics, but he is best known for his suggestions in astronomy.

Aristarchus is famous for having been the only ancient to suggest that the earth moves around the sun, rather than the sun around the earth. Others, such as Heraclides of Pontus, had suggested that the earth rotates once a day, but only Aristarchus went as far as to say the earth changed position. His idea was universally rejected by the astronomers and cosmologists of the ancient world, and was only revived much later, in the 16th century, by Copernicus. Why was this so? It is easy to blame some form of social or religious prejudice towards a central and stable earth, and undoubtedly this is part of the answer. However, Aristarchus' hypothesis, although in one sense correct, and in many ways a brilliant insight, was also in many ways weak and its rejection illustrates some interesting points in the history and philosophy of science.

Firstly, scientific theories cannot be taken in isolation. Often they have implications for our understanding of many other phenomena. The ancient argument for a stable earth was, in outline, simple and sound. If the earth is in motion, they argued, we expect to experience the effects of that motion, but we do not experience those predicted expected effects. Therefore the earth is not in motion. What did the ancients expect to experience, if the earth moved?

If the earth rotated, the Greeks wondered why there was not a persistent wind in the opposite direction to the rotation. The error here of course is in assuming that the earth's atmosphere would not rotate with the earth. What reason did the Greeks have to suppose that it would? According to their physics the heavens had a natural circular motion, but air did not. For them, nothing would make the air rotate with the earth, and so they expected effects relative to the static air if the earth rotated.

If the earth was in motion around the sun, again the ancients wondered why there was not a wind blowing them off the surface of the earth. Their physics did not predict that the earth would carry its air with it, if it was in motion. Nor, for the ancients, would the earth be moving through empty space. Many of the ancients denied that there could be any such thing as a vacuum so, if the earth was orbiting the sun, the earth would be moving through some medium.

Imagine virtually any form of transport in the ancient world. If you are moving, then you know you are moving, even if you are moving relatively slowly. You feel a wind in your face, and your hair streams out behind you. The ancients were aware that if the earth moved, either spinning on its axis or orbiting the sun, the speeds would be much greater than those they encountered in everyday transport, yet still there seemed to be no effect from this motion.

Another problem, if the earth moved, was the Greek account of why things fall to earth and why the earth holds together. The ancient Greeks never developed a conception of gravity. They knew that objects fell, but they explained this in different ways. The dominant view was that of Aristotle. There were four known elements, earth, water, air and fire. Earth and water were heavy, and naturally moved towards the centre of the cosmos, air and fire were light and moved away from the centre of the cosmos. Objects dropped, that is moved towards the centre of the cosmos because they were predominantly earth or water. The earth held together, and was at the centre of the cosmos, because all the pieces of earth strove to be at the centre of the cosmos. Set the earth in motion though, and none of this applied, as the earth would no longer be at the centre of the cosmos. Moreover, what would keep the earth in its orbit? As pieces of earth and water move to the centre of the cosmos, the earth, if it ever were moved from the centre, would simply return to the centre again.

Finally, if the earth was in motion, why did the moon follow the earth about the cosmos? Again the modern answer of gravity is simple, but given Greek physics there was no reason why the moon would follow the earth in its motions. Aristarchus, as far as we are aware, had no way of resolving these difficulties. To convince people of the motion of the earth he needed a new physics.

There was also observational evidence against Aristarchus. If the earth orbits the sun, then the stars should appear to be in slightly different positions at each end of the orbit, an effect known as annual stellar parallax. As no ancient could detect this effect, it was assumed that the earth did not move.

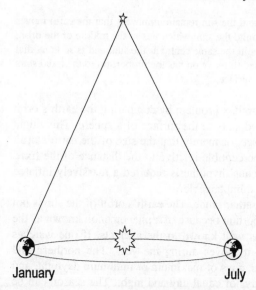

If the earth orbits the sun in one year, it will change its position slightly relative to the stars. In fact this is difficult to defect, as the amount the earth moves is very small compared to the distance of the stars, and parallax was not detected until 1838. Parallax for alpha-centauri (the nearest star, 4 light years away) = 0.75 of 1" (one second of arc), of 1/ 5,000th of one degree.

Figure 40.1 Annual stellar parallax

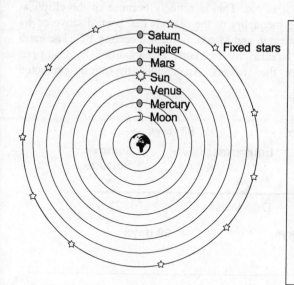

Not to scale, but note that all of the stars are equidistant (the standard ancient view) and that relative to any modern view they are quite near to the planets. With such a small cosmos (by modern standards), not detecting parallax is more significant, and satisfied with this cosmos, many ancients were unwilling to believe in the vastly larger one suggested by Aristarchus.

Figure 40.2 The ancient view of the cosmos

In his work, *The Sand Reckoner*, Archimedes, tells us that:

Aristarchus of Samos produced a book of some hypotheses, in which it follows from what is laid down that the cosmos is many times larger than is currently said. The hypotheses are that the fixed stars and the sun remain unmoved, that the earth moves on the circumference of a circle around the sun, which lies in the middle of the orbit, and the sphere of the fixed stars lies in the same centre as the sun, and is so great that the circle which the earth is supposed to move on has the proportion to the fixed stars that the centre of a sphere has to its surface.

So Aristarchus dealt with the parallax problem by comparing the earth's orbit to the centre of a sphere and the fixed stars to the surface of a sphere. This might mean that the cosmos is infinitely large, or merely that the size of the earth's orbit is incomparable, insignificant or imperceptible relative to the distance of the fixed stars. However we take this, Aristarchus' hypothesis required a massively inflated cosmos, which the ancients considered implausible.

Aristarchus' proposal was also rather crude. The earth's orbit of the sun is not a circle, but is an ellipse. That is important because of a phenomenon known as the inequality of the seasons, which was well known to the ancients. If one watches where the sun sets on the horizon, it moves during the year. The northern and southern most points are the solstices, days of maximum or minimum daylight, and the central point is the equinoxes, days of equal day and night. The season can be defined as beginning from when the sun passes these points. One might expect the time taken for the sun to progress from solstice to equinox and equinox to solstice to be equal in each case, but it is not. This is actually because of the elliptical nature of the earth's orbit. The inequality of the seasons had been discovered by two Athenian astronomers, Euctemon and Meton, in the 4th century BC. The earth centred system of astronomy created by Eudoxus, and modified by Callippus predicted different lengths for the seasons. Aristarchus' hypothesis predicted perfect equality of the seasons.

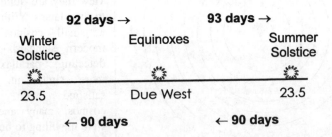

One might expect the times taken between solstice and equinox and equinox and solstice to be equal—in fact they are not—and this was recognized quite early by the Greeks.

Figure 40.3   The inequality of the seasons

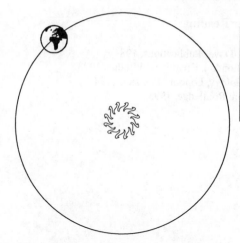

With the earth in regular circular motion around the sun there would be entirely equal seasons. The inequality of the seasons is due to the earth's elliptical orbit of the sun.

Figure 40.4   Aristarchus on the earth's orbit

Aristarchus' hypothesis, though in essence correct, was too simplistic and failed to account for some phenomena other contemporary systems could deal with.

The reason why Aristarchus was largely ignored after his death was the success of later Greek earth centred astronomy and cosmology. Apollonius and Hipparchus were instrumental in developing this system, which was brought to its highest point by Ptolemy (see here the chapter on Eudoxus). Although it was complex, mathematically it was very powerful and it was able to give a very good account of the phenomena. Not only did these astronomers come up with plausible theories, they greatly improved the accuracy of observation as well. Despite this, no evidence was found in favour of Aristarchus and the absence of annual stellar parallax became more glaring.

In the Christian era, it became even more difficult to suppose that the earth orbited the sun, as the Bible seemed to contradict this. At Joshua 10:12, God orders the sun and the moon to stand still (but not the earth) in order to lengthen the day and allow the Israelites victory in battle. Also important to Christianity was the idea that man should be at the centre of God's creation.

Aristarchus produced a brilliant and original insight. It is an error though to believe that Greek earth-centred astronomy and cosmology, although mistaken, was not sophisticated, and, for its time, very good at describing and predicting the motions of the heavens. It required much more than a simple statement of the heliocentric thesis to dislodge it. This was something Copernicus also found out many centuries later. When he revived Aristarchus' proposal, he did so in a much more sophisticated manner, but it still took the work of Galileo and Kepler, 70 years later, before it began to be accepted. They needed to create a new physics capable of dealing with a moving earth, produce observational evidence and overcome religious opposition. Aristarchus had no such able supporters.

References and Suggestions for Further Reading

Heath, T.L. *Aristarchus of Samos*. New York: Dover Publications, 1981.
Lloyd, G.E.R. *Greek Science After Aristotle*. London: Chatto and Windus, 1973.
North, J. *The History of Astronomy and Cosmology*. London: Fontana, 1994.
Wright, M.R. *Cosmology in Antiquity*. London: Routledge, 1995.

Chapter 41

Carneades

c. 214 BC–129 BC

G.S. Bowe

'Give me a draught of honeyed wine.'

Carneades was from Cyrene, a beautiful place near what is now Shahat in Libya. He was born c. 214 BC and committed suicide by drinking poison in 129 BC. The quotation above is what he is reported to have said in requesting the poison. He was apparently inspired to drink poison upon hearing that the Stoic philosopher Antipater of Tarsus, successor of Diogenes of Babylon, had done the same.

Carneades seems to have been something of a scraggly fellow, neglecting his personal appearance because of devotion to study. Perhaps because of this he declined invitations to dine out; he seems to have a love interest however, for Diogenes Laertius reports that he expelled a student from the Academy for being too close to one of his concubines. (Of course, we must always be careful in trusting Diogenes' reports because much of what he writes is more akin to gossip than to history.) While reporting very little of Carneades' philosophy, he does take the time to remark on the length of Carneades' fingernails, and the fact that he died during an eclipse of the moon. Diogenes also tells us that Carneades suffered from night blindness, wrote letters to the King of Cappadocia, and that he was a brilliant orator and debater.

Carneades continued the tradition of skepticism which Arcesilaus had introduced in the Academy of Athens. Arcesilaus (316-242 BC) of Pitane (modern day Candarli, Turkey, not far from Izmir (Smyrna)) is usually called the founder of the Middle Academy, whereas Carneades himself marks the beginning of the New Academy.

Carneades was considered the most important Greek philosopher of the 2nd century BC, and his reputation at that time was such that it is said that teachers of rhetoric in Athens would cancel their classes to go and hear him lecture. He was sent as part of an ambassadorial embassy to Rome by the Athenian government in 156/5 BC, along with the leading Stoic and Cynic Philosophers of the day (Diogenes of Babylon and Critolaus). The philosophical envoy caused quite a stir, and the Roman Forum was filled with an audience anxious to catch a glimpse of Greece's finest thinkers. Carneades gave two lectures on two different days. In the first lecture he praised justice with much pomp and circumstance. In the second he argued against the possibility of human knowledge, and refuted everything he had said about justice in the previous lecture. The point of the two lectures is not to make fun of justice but rather to show how it is possible to be wrong about it, and hence there is an exhortation to be wary of dogmatism. (The Roman Cato the Elder, concerned about the effect of Greek philosophy and literature on the youth generally, had the Greek envoy expelled from Rome as undesirable nonetheless). The concern against dogmatism extends further. Carneades argued against the Stoic conception of the gods, not because he was an atheist, but in order to show that the Stoics were dogmatic about something which they really had not established philosophically. In the same way Carneades would attack the possibility of finding what all of Hellenistic philosophy was after—the *summum bonum* or highest good. Carneades made an itinerary of all the candidates for the *summum bonum*, i.e. happiness, love, pleasure etc., and went on to refute each possibility, not out of some kind of pessimism, but to reveal the limitations of our knowledge as an antidote to dogmatism.

Carneades' most lasting impact was in the field of epistemology, or theory of knowledge. Because Carneades left nothing in writing, we have to piece together what he thought from later Latin sources, such as Cicero and Sextus Empiricus. This is at best third hand, because these authors depend on the writings of Carneades' student and successor as head of the Academy, Clitomachus, but Clitomachus is known to have confessed that he was uncertain regarding what Carneades really thought. Because Carneades used to argue both sides of an argument in order to combat a dogmatic commitment to one of two possible philosophical positions, it was not always clear what he himself believed to be the case. One is tempted to say that Carneades believed nothing, but it would be better to say that Carneades thought nothing could be known with absolute certainty, but that at the same time, we can be more or less convinced by certain things and take them to be reasonably true. Perhaps because of his approach to philosophy, and our reliance on third hand knowledge, our understanding of Carneades is somewhat unclear. Translation from Greek to Latin itself causes problems. For example, Carneades seems to have talked about whether sense impressions are convincing. Cicero translates the Greek word for convincing (*pithanon*) into Latin as *probabile* (which from *probare* should mean 'acceptable'). Unfortunately this seems to suggest that Carneades endorsed a theory of 'probabilism', the idea that we work out the probability of something being true or false. This seems inconsistent with the rest of what we know about Carneades, and is probably not what he really meant. In order to get closer to what he really did mean, it is useful to see what Carneades was reacting to.

Carneades is usually taken as reacting to Stoic epistemology and sometimes to the epistemology of the Epicureans. Here I will talk only about his reaction to the Stoics. Most Greek philosophers are wary of information that comes to us from the five senses because this information (sense impressions) can deceive us. For example, a straight stick can appear bent if half immersed in water, or a large building can look very small when far away. The Stoic epistemology suggests that we deal with the unreliable sense organs by advocating a procedure by which we make rational decisions about the sense impressions which are 'presented' to the mind. We examine, mentally, these sense impressions, and give rational assent to the ones that are true based on this examination of the sense impressions. Arcesilaus had argued that no sense impressions are reliable foundations for knowledge, which led to the more refined Stoic position of Chrysippus. It is usually to Chrysippus that Carneades is thought to be responding. Indeed Diogenes tells us that Carneades was fond of saying, 'Without Chrysippus where should I have been?' (D.L. IV.62).

Carneades reaction to Chrysippus' theory of rational assent was to suggest that for any such presentation that appears to be true, we can imagine an equally 'convincing' sense impression that is false—in other words there is always the possibility that sense expressions can deceive us regarding what they truly represent. For example, dreams can be so realistic that we mistake them for reality. No amount of examination can guarantee their falsity. Of course, if upon waking we realize that what we had dreamt could not really have happened, we can determine by examination that the dream is false, but then we have to rely on other sense impressions to determine the coherence of the dream with the rest of what is going on in our lives. But those sense expressions also require, on the Stoic account, the kind of assent that our inability to trust sense expressions calls into question in the first place, and hence the whole process of examination is flawed. The end result of this kind of reasoning is that there is never a place for rational assent in determining truth or falsity. All that we have to go on, according to Carneades, is whether or not sense impressions are convincing. The fact that they are convincing does not guarantee that they are a true depiction of reality—we can never say yes or no to them regarding whether they are true—in short there is no possibility of rational assent, only sense impressions that are more or less convincing.

Skeptics, in the broadest sense, see limitations regarding how we can know what we think we know, and argue for a suspension of judgment about what we know. At first glance this seems to raise problems for living; if I do not know that the bread in front of me is really bread, how can I eat it without fear of poisoning myself? How do I know that I do not know that the bread in front of me might not be real. And so on. Because Carneades' own approach to skepticism led him to accept certain things as convincing enough to accept, he is perhaps saved from such objections. His real interest is probably more about rejecting dogmatically held philosophical positions, and in the case of epistemology the Stoic dogmatism about how to obtain correct rational assent regarding sense impressions. Once we see this, we can also see how a convincing set of sense impressions can guide our lives without a dogmatic theory of rational assent, or a way of working out whether to give assent to sense impressions or not. In short, because Carneades thinks that rational assent is impossible, because there are no good criteria by which to judge it, he must say that we live our lives without it—convincing sense impressions are all we have to go on, but they service us quite well in most cases.

Carneades also offered opinions on Stoic and Epicurean debates about fate. The Stoics believed in a kind of determinism that depends on a belief that every event is caused by a previous event; because everything we do is caused by some preceding event, everything that we will do in the future is already determined. In order to get around this, the Epicureans introduced a theory of random 'swerving' atoms. Because these atoms were indeterminate, it was possible to suggest that the series of causes and effects generated by these atoms was also impossible to determine. This 'indeterminacy' preserves free will because not every action is the result of predetermined steps. Carneades seems to have suggested that the Epicureans did not need this strange physics, and said that while all actions require a preceding cause, we ourselves, by our free thought, can be the cause of our own actions, and hence all of our actions are not determined.

References and Suggestions for Further Reading

Algra, K., J. Barnes, J. Mansfeld and M. Schofield. *The Cambridge History of Hellenistic Philosophy*. Cambridge, UK: Cambridge University Press, 1999.

Cicero. *Academica*. Loeb Classical Library. Cambridge: Harvard University Press, 1994.

Diogenes Laertius, *Lives of Eminent Philosophers*. Loeb Classical Library. Heinemann, 1972.

Hankinson, R.J. *The Skeptics*. London: Routledge, 1995.

Plutarch. *Life of Cato the Elder* in *Lives*. Loeb Classical Library. Cambridge: Harvard University Press, 1998.

Sextus Empiricus. *Against the Mathematicians* and *Against the Academics*. Loeb Classical Library. Cambridge: Harvard University Press, 1933.

Chapter 42

Lucretius

c. 99 BC–55 BC

Tim O'Keefe

> Our terrors and our darknesses of mind
> Must be dispelled, not by the sunshine's rays,
> Not by those shining arrows of the light,
> But by insight into nature, and a scheme
> Of systematic contemplation. (*De Rerum Natura*. Book I lines 146-148, trans. here
> and elsewhere by Humphries)

Titus Lucretius Carus was an ardent disciple of Epicurus and the author of the *De Rerum Natura (On the Nature of Things)*, one of the greatest poems in Latin. Other than his approximate dates of birth and death, we have next to no reliable information about him. (St. Jerome's report, in the 4th Century AD, that Lucretius was driven insane by a love potion and composed the *De Rerum Natura* in the lucid intervals between bouts of madness has been widely repeated but is almost certainly scurrilous.) Because of his family name and his apparent familiarity with Roman upper-class mores, it is thought that Lucretius was probably a member of the aristocratic clan of the Lucretii, but this is not certain. And so any insight we wish to gain into the thought and personality of Lucretius must come from the *De Rerum Natura* itself.

Lucretius burns with devotion to the Greek philosopher Epicurus, whom he regards as the saviour of humanity. The *De Rerum Natura* is Lucretius' attempt to spread the gospel of Epicureanism. But Epicurus is a strikingly atypical messiah, and the *De Rerum Natura* a correspondingly odd bearer of good news. We are enslaved, thinks Lucretius, by the empty superstitious fears fostered by religion. Epicurus has delivered us from these fears by revealing to us, by the use of reason, that the universe is nothing more than a concatenation of atoms flying through the void, with no purpose or plan, and that death is annihilation, the permanent cessation of all consciousness. And so we do not need to worry about meddling gods or punishments in an afterlife. Instead, we are freed to concentrate on attaining tranquility here and now.

> When human life, all too conspicuous,
> Lay foully grovelling on earth, weighed down
> By grim Religion looming from the skies,
> Horribly threatening mortal men, a man,
> A Greek, first raised his mortal eyes

Bravely against this menace.
[...]
So his force,
His vital force of mind, a conqueror
Beyond the flaming ramparts of the world
Explored the vast immensities of space
With wit and wisdom, and came back to us
Triumphant, bringing news of what can be
And what cannot, limits and boundaries,
The borderline, the bench mark, set forever.
Religion, so, is trampled underfoot,
And by his victory we reach the stars. (*De Rerum Natura* I 62-79)

The *De Rerum Natura* is an epic poem, in six books, which tries to establish the truth of the Epicurean atomic hypothesis and show how it can successfully account for all natural phenomena. The scope of the poem could not be more ambitious—Lucretius seeks to determine the nature of the fundamental building-blocks of the universe and explain the origins of the earth, life, and society. But in order to fulfill these ambitions, the poem contains page after page of versified arguments concerning matters such as why Empedocles' four-element theory is false, how mirrors operate, and why foods have the tastes that they do (sweet foods are composed of smooth round atoms which caress our tongue, whereas bitter foods are composed of barbed atoms that slash at our tongue).

Lucretius explains his choice of epic poetry as the vehicle to express such arguments by comparing himself to a doctor. If a doctor has to administer some nasty-tasting medicine to a child, says Lucretius, he will smear the lip of the cup with honey in order to make the draught more palatable. The child is 'fooled, but not betrayed, but rather given health and strength'. Likewise, says Lucretius, many people find philosophical argument dry and repellant, or initially think that the Epicurean world-system is impious and harsh, and so he is clothing the healing message of Epicurus in poetry in order to make it go down more easily (*De Rerum Natura* IV 10-25).

Lucretius explicitly claims to be following in the footsteps of Epicurus, and so chances are that little of his argumentation is original. However, Lucretius' therapeutic project extends beyond simply giving rationally convincing arguments. He also wants to redirect harmful attitudes and emotions in the reader and reveal their true nature. He does this mainly in two areas—attitudes toward nature and toward death.

Lucretius' own attitudes toward nature are complex. He argues at length that the natural world is not prepared for us by any gods, because there is too much wrong with it, and the poem closes with a horrific description of the ravages of the bubonic plague on Athens. Furthermore, nature has no sentience or purpose inherent in it—it is simply the result of the blind motions, reboundings, and entanglements of atoms. At the same time, Lucretius says that having the working of nature exposed to him fills him with a sort of 'divine pleasure' and 'shuddering'. (*De Rerum Natura* III 28-30). In fact, Lucretius often describes nature in religious terms. The *De Rerum Natura* opens with a hymn of praise to nature as Venus and a request for her help. Later, he says:

We have all come from heavenly seed; we all
Have the same father, and our mother earth
Receives from him the fertilizing showers.
So pregnant, she brings forth the shining grain,
The trees that make us glad, the race of men,
The generations of wild beasts, the food
By which they feed, increase, and multiply.
She is rightly called our mother. (*De Rerum Natura* II 991-998)

But Lucretius is ambivalent about using this sort of imagery. Immediately after his most elaborate description of earth as a mother-goddess, he adds that we must be careful not to let religion infect and pollute us when using such metaphorical personifications, because the world is entirely insensate and 'acts' without purpose (*De Rerum Natura* II 594-660). Lucretius wants to show that we can retain attitudes of awe toward nature, even if we do not have the usual sorts of religious beliefs about divine providence directing nature. In addition, by skilfully evoking such an attitude in his poetry, minus any teleological underpinnings, Lucretius hopes to direct the attitude toward its proper object—the natural world itself, in all its marvelous complexity—rather than allowing it to reinforce damaging, superstitious beliefs.

Lucretius pursues a similar project against the fear of death. Again, the main weapon in his therapeutic arsenal is rational argumentation—Lucretius tries to establish that death is annihilation, and thus that there is nothing to fear in death, since in death nobody exists to be either benefited or harmed. But in a remarkable passage that is reminiscent of the German philosopher Ludwig Feuerbach, Lucretius argues that the various mythological afterlife tortures described by Homer and Hesiod are really projected versions of fears of pain in this life. One by one, he goes through the figures tormented in Hades and says that, even though no such afterlife sufferings literally exist, we can see earthly versions of them all around us:

Sisyphus, too, is here
In our own lives; we see him as the man
Bent upon power and office, who comes back
Gloomy and beaten after every vote.
To seek for power, such an empty thing,
And never gain it, suffering all the while,
Which over and over comes bouncing down again
To the flat levels where it started from. (*De Rerum Natura* III 995-1002)

Lucretius concludes his catalog by saying 'Hell does exist on earth—in the life of fools' (*De Rerum Natura* III 1023). Once we have unmasked our fears of Hades and recognize that they really are just such projections, we can stop worrying about nonexistent afterlife punishments and redirect our attention to avoiding pain and suffering in this life—the only life there is.

Lucretius is not an original philosopher, but he is still a tremendously important figure, both poetically and philosophically. Because almost all of the writings of Epicurus are lost to us, Lucretius is one of our main sources of information about Epicureanism. The rediscovery of *De Rerum Natura* in the Renaissance helped shape the birth of modern science. The *De Rerum Natura* was an inspiration for many thinkers who were forging a new, 'mechanistic' conception of nature against the dominant Aristotelianism of the medieval period.

Most of the particulars of the atomic theory that Lucretius expounds—the indivisibility of atoms, his accounts of vision and magnetism, etc.—have been subsequently disproven. Nonetheless, the basic world-view he so eloquently expresses—his rejection of an afterlife, his awe at beholding a complex world without purpose or plan, his trust that through the use of reason we can both discover the way the world works and attain blessedness—is still very much a live option today.

References and Suggestions for Further Reading

Humphries, Rolfe, trans. 1968. Lucretius. *The Way Things Are. The De Rerum Natura of Titus Lucretius Carus.* Bloomington: Indiana University Press, 1968.

There are a huge number of translations of the *De Rerum Natura*. But for those who want to experience (in English) Lucretius' poetry as poetry, Humphries' translation is best. Accessible, accurate, and powerful. (All translations of Lucretius in this entry are by Humphries.)

Johnson, W.R. 2000. *Lucretius and the Modern World.* London: Duckworth, 2000.

An introduction to the *De Rerum Natura* by an unabashed and enthusiastic apologist for Lucretius' world-view, written in an engaging and accessible style. Johnson also gives a good overview of the reception and influence Lucretius has had from the 17th century until today. A very good read.

Sedley, David. 1998. *Lucretius and the Transformation of Greek Wisdom.* Cambridge: Cambridge University Press.

A detailed study of Lucretius' poetic debt to Empedocles, his philosophical debt to Epicurus, and how he combined the two to construct the *De Rerum Natura*. For those interested in the sources for the *De Rerum Natura*, this is the book to look at, although it is aimed mainly at specialists.

Chapter 43

Seneca the Younger

c. 4 BC–65 AD

Kartika Panwar

> To live happily, my brother Gallio, is the desire of all men, but their minds are blinded
> to a clear vision of just what it is that makes life happy. (*De Vita Beata* (*On the Happy
> Life*), I.1)

Lucius Annaeus Seneca (pronounced Sen-ah-ka), 'Seneca the Younger' was a
prolific writer, philosopher, orator and statesman in imperial Rome. His dramatic
works, in particular the tragedies he wrote, influenced later Renaissance theatre
and Elizabethan England where playwrights such as Marlowe and Shakespeare
imitated parts of his style. It his however, for his philosophical works, which
continue to offer counsel and wisdom to his readers, that he is renowned.

Seneca was one of the most fascinating figures of his age. He lived during the
reign of three emperors. One, Claudius exiled him due to dubious allegations of
adultery and another, his erstwhile pupil, Nero, forced him to commit suicide for
alleged treason. The capriciousness and volatility of imperial political allegiances
and intrigues meant that day-to-day existence was uncertain and could ultimately
result in, as they did for Seneca, an early death.

Stoic philosophy then, obtained a particular importance for Seneca as he was
able to use it to help himself find comfort in such times and to help others achieve
happiness. Indeed, Seneca saw philosophy not only as concerning the intellect but
directly involved with the soul (animus). Whilst physicians cure physical ills,
philosophy was to help cure the ills of men's souls. He believed in a practical
approach and eschewed the more rigorous intellectual exercises, which sought to
arrive at conclusions of truth.

His main philosophical works were delivered in the form of letters, written in
a clear and simple style, to friends and relatives. Through these, he aimed to assist
people not just to exist but to live well by helping them to arrive at a state of
emotional equanimity and tranquillity, regardless of the external circumstances
they were facing. When they reached such a state they were living 'a life in
harmony with its own nature'.

Seneca believed that there was a divine Providence or Fortune, which
oversaw the world. In one of his many letters to his friend Lucilius, he asks the
timeless question 'Why do bad things happen to good men if the world is ruled by
a divine Providence? (*De Providentia*, *On Providence* I.1). Seneca felt that good

men were chosen to undergo hardships and adversity initially to harden them. In using contemporary Roman similes, Seneca compared Fortune to a gladiator seeking worthy adversaries in the form of good men, or men who practised virtue. In the same way that a gladiator would gain small benefit from fighting an inferior opponent, so too would Fortune have no reason to test or seek out a 'bad man' for there would be no gain in testing such a person.

He believed that once a person had been toughened and had attained, by enduring hardships, the strength of which they were capable, then a higher moral and spiritual purpose could be obtained through their suffering. Having espoused the practical benefit of suffering, namely that it toughens the sufferer and reveals to them resources of which they were probably unaware, it is then in the final submission and acquiescence to this suffering that the moral man can become One with the divine will.

In aligning oneself with the universal plan synonymous with Fate, Providence or divine will, a person who was exposed to adversity could find true and enduring happiness. It is at this stage that the circumstances that caused such suffering could be seen to be external only. Seneca believed that it is the internal life, the tranquillity and peace that comes from within oneself, that is the supreme goal and the ultimate gift of philosophy.

Regardless of the 'misfortunes' Fate could throw at a good man, a 'good man' was good by definition, due to his practice of virtue and acquiescence to Providence. Such a man would be unmoved and no longer suffer, for regardless of the circumstances, the good, virtuous and moral man had control over his own soul, and over the tranquillity of his mind, if not the external circumstances of his life.

But how was one to acquiesce with the divine plan? Mere knowledge was not enough and Seneca acknowledged that this ultimate acquiescence was far from effortless. He felt that to achieve such a state, 'First of all, we must have a sound mind and one that is in constant possession of its sanity; second, it must be courageous and energetic, and also, capable of the noblest fortitude, ready for every emergency, careful of the body and of all that concerns it, but without anxiety', Seneca goes on to stress the most crucial point that this mind, 'lastly … must be the user, but not the slave, of the gifts of Fortune' (*De Vita Beata*, III. 3-4).

Such a mind could be achieved only by constant vigilance and effort. The use of such a mind would then obviate the suffering which occurred when people ascribed incorrect interpretations or 'masks' to circumstances. Instead, people should, by using their reason, see the 'true value of things' and realize that the erroneous labels and values that we give to circumstances lead to an anxiety and fear that cause our suffering. Seneca uses a host of illustrations for this. In writing to his friend, Lucilius, regarding the possible outcome of a lawsuit against him he argued that should Lucilius lose this court case he may become poor. However he awful prospect of losing one's wealth means that one is now in the majority and in the real event that one becomes an exile (for Seneca was himself banished from Rome) then he could console himself with the thought 'I shall think of myself as a native of the place I am sent to' (*Epistle to Lucilius*, XXIV, 17).

Seneca was one of the few philosophers who was sympathetic to the weaknesses in men's characters as they attempted to live well and virtuously. He acknowledged that the practices he advocated were difficult and needed practice. He, himself, was often accused of hypocrisy because of his vast wealth while he preached the unimportance of wealth as a means of happiness. He replied by saying that first his wealth had been acquired virtuously and honestly. Second and more importantly he acknowledged that words and deeds were often disparate and it was the attempt to meld the two that was ultimately important.

However, given the rewards of enduring happiness then it was worth the effort expended for if one had attempted to live well by enduring hardships and then acquiescing to them, then life had been lived in an exemplary way.

In one of his more notable essays, *On the Shortness of Life* (*De Brevitate Vitae*), Seneca wrote that complaining about the shortness of life was wrong for he felt that 'it is not that we have a short space of time but that we waste much of it' (*De Brevitate Vitae*, I.3). In dissipating valuable energy and time with trivial concerns such as squabbling with one's wife and rushing about the city on social duties, 'the part of life we really live is small' (*De Brevitate Vitae*, II.18).

Seneca exhorts his readers to spend time wisely, in the company of philosophers, studying their works and learning how to live wisely. 'Honours, monuments, all that ambition has commanded by decrees or reared in works of stone, quickly sink to ruin ... But the works which philosophy has consecrated cannot be harmed ... no age will destroy them' (*De Brevitate Vitae*, XV.4).

References and Suggestions for Further Reading

Costa, C.D.N. *Seneca*. London; Boston: Routledge and Kegan Paul, 1974.

De Botton, Alain. *The Consolations of Philosophy*. New York: Pantheon Books, 2000.

Hornblower, Simon and Anthony Spawforth. *The Oxford Classical Dictionary*, 3rd Edition, Oxford University Press, 2003.

Seneca. *Moral Essays*. With an English translation by John W. Basore. In 3 Vols. Vol. II. Loeb Classical Library. Cambridge, MA.: Harvard University Press, 1963.

Seneca. Ad Lucilium Epistulae Morales [Letters to Lucilius]. With an English translation by Richard M. Gummere. In 3 Vols. Vol. I. Loeb Classical Library. Cambridge, MA.: Harvard University Press, 1961.

Timothy, H.B. *The Tenets of Stoicism*. Amsterdam: Adolf M. Hakkert, 1973.

Chapter 44

Apollonius of Tyana

1–10 AD–96 or 98 AD

Gabriele Cornelli

> Such were the discourses he delivered to the public or on behalf of different communities, and in behalf of those who were dead or who were sick; and such were the harangues he delivered to wise and unwise alike, and to the sovereigns who consulted him about moral virtue. (Philostratus. *Life of Apollonius* 6.43)

There are philosophers who defy the limits of philosophy, burst open the doors of the traditional understanding of Greek *sophía* (wisdom) and pose many problems for historians of ancient philosophy. Of them all, Apollonius of Tyana, the Neopythagorean (see Glossary) philosopher is perhaps the most outstanding example.

Apollonius was born in the Greek city of Tyana, in Cappadocia, and died, almost a centenarian, between 96 and 98 AD. He is born into a rich family. He is handsome and very intelligent, and for this latter reason, at the age of fourteen he goes to study in Tarsus. From the beginning he shows a deep interest in the spirit world and occultism. He follows a strictly vegetarian diet and is sexually continent. Every morning he worships the Sun, he practises incubation (ritual sleep) in order to gain knowledge of the occult. He employs his powers to fight for justice and, sometimes, to take revenge. These are actually powers of *his own*: he would not acknowledge them as coming in any way from some divinity. So, Apollonius *learned* by himself how to develop them. Three 'study' travels are essential to shape his personality: first, he goes to Babylon, where he meets the *magi*, the most famous wise and divine men of the ancient world, then he goes to India, where he studies with the Brahmans; finally, he arrives in Egypt, where he meets the community of the 'naked wise men', an ascetic sect which claimed to have godly powers. Actually, he attends the three greatest 'universities' of the ancient world: Babylon, India and Egypt. In Rome, when he was charged with having sacrificed a young man in divinatory rites, he is miraculously transported to Asia Minor, where he stays until his death (or, according to other witnesses, until his ascension into heaven).

In Philostratus' *Life of Apollonius of Tyana* (LA), Fraotes, an Indian king, in the letter in which he recommends Apollonius and his disciples to Iarchas, head of the Brahmans, calls them philosophers and disciples of a divine man (LA 2.40). Here, two figures—that of *philosopher* and that of *divine man*—seem to coincide:

the philosopher, the *lover of wisdom*, is actually the divine man. Apollonius and his itinerant disciples are recognized everywhere by two characteristic symbols of the philosopher: the cloak and books. Actually, in Egypt, the young Timasion concluded that 'the crew consisted of wise men, because he judged them by the cloaks they wore and the books they were hard at work studying' (LA 6.3).

The Apollonians—as Apollonius's disciples were called—aroused people's admiration because of their dedication to philosophy:

> From Ionia also there came to see him the band of companions who were named in Hellas the company of Apollonius; and mixing with people of the place they formed a band of youths, remarkable for their number and for their philosophic enthusiasm. (LA 8.21)

Apollonius is imprisoned because of his criticism of the Roman emperor, Nero, and another dialogue between the philosopher and his disciple, Damis, shows an extremely interesting (and somehow very modern) understanding of philosophy as a cure for suffering:

> 'Let us talk, Damis, with the people here. For what else is there for us to do until the time comes when the despot will give me such audience as he desires?' 'Will they not think us babblers,' said Damis, 'and bores, if we interrupt them in the preparation of their defense, and moreover, it is a mistake to talk philosophy with men so broken in spirit as they.' 'Nay', said Apollonius, 'they are just the people who most want someone to talk to them and comfort them. For you may remember the verses of Homer in which he relates how Helen mingled in the bowl of wine certain drugs from Egypt in order to drown the soul-ache of the heroes; well, I think that Helen must have picked up the lore of the Egyptians, and have sung spells over the dejected heroes through their bowl of wine, so healing them by a blending of words and wine'. (LA 7.22)

Philosophy is understood, then, as an activity of dialogue and cure—Helen of Troy mixed logos (dialogue and ideas) with wine in order to wash pain away from the heroes' souls, thus curing them with the mixture of words and wine. Philosophy, then, is a cure through dialogue.

But not only that. Dreams, for example, are as important a part of philosophy as medicine. When entering Babylon, Apollonius, is visited by a dream. When he tells Damis about his vision, Damis is afraid and wants to depart, but Apollonius reprimands him: 'You have not become a philosopher yet, if you are afraid of this sort of thing' (LA 1.23).

The self-image of Apollonius as a philosopher includes what we will refer to as mystic and was, above all, definitely linked to magic practices. This *inclusive* view is deeply linked to the Pythagorean tradition.

In one of his writings, Philostratus declared that while he did not wish to prolong unduly his account of Apollonius, he also was taking pains not to skip over important details—he would choose the biographical events most worthy of note:

I think it is time to record the most important incidents and matters which will repay the remembering; for we must consider that such episodes are comparable to the visits to mankind paid by the sons of Asclepius. (LA 6.35)

The comparison of Apollonius with the Asclepiads is relevant. A popular belief was ascribed to the two physicians, Machaon and Podalirius, the sons of Asclepius: both immortality and an itinerant life on the earth as physicians of the ill. According to the myth, the Asclepiads originated with these two descendants of Asclepius whose seventeenth descendant would have been Hippoctrates himself. Hence, according to Philostratus, the most important events in Apollonius' life are exactly those which can be compared with those in the lives of the two itinerant divine physicians (or rather, *sons of a god*), linked to the Asclepiad tradition. This is another indication of the importance of cure in the philosophy of Apollonius.

In the idea of philosophy as dialogue and cure, Apollonius' capability to forgive sins is demonstrated in the case of a man who unintentionally killed an inhabitant from Memphis, in Egypt. He wandered about for seven months, begging to be forgiven but was not pardoned. Apollonius severely criticized the lack of forgiveness of the community:

Apollonius went through the rites over him which Empedocles and Pythagoras prescribe for the purification of such offences, and told him to return home, for that he was now pure of guilt. (LA 6.5)

Employing a special formula linked to the Pythagorean tradition, Apollonius accomplishes a ritual forgiveness, and thus—in a way—a cure.

The reader might now ask whether all that has been said here is actually philosophy, or something very different from what is normally acknowledged as philosophical activity. To answer the question, it is necessary to go back to the origins of the Pythagorean tradition which Apollonius followed.

The earliest sources, before Plato, present Pythagorean doctrine as a complex set of theories about numbers, its meanings and influences on men and nature, doctrines on the immortality of the soul, and rules of ascetic life spiced with oriental knowledge: Babylonian mathematics, Iranian wisdom, and the theory of Indian metempsychosis (see Glossary). The great aim of Pythagoreanism is not based on abstract ideas, but on an actual, concrete way of living within a community that was set up on the principles practised by the master, Pythagoras.

The life style included rules about diet, such as not eating beans (but not absolute vegetarianism, as was to be adopted later by Apollonius), and restraints on behaviour, including the direction not to engage in sexual intercourse outside marriage. He had many guidelines, such as: 'Don't stir the fire with a knife, ... , don't eat your heart. ... This is what they meant. Don't stir the passions or the swelling pride of the great. ... Don't waste your life in troubles and pains' (Diogenes Laertius, 8.18). There are many more such teachings, all providing practical advice for daily living.

Keeping these points in mind, how can one understand Pythagoreanism as philosophy in the rational sense of the word? And how can one consider the future development of philosophy up to the Neopythagoreanism of the time of Apollonius of Tyana, where (Pythagorean) philosophy is understood as cure?

Two ways of understanding all the ancient philosophy are implied in these questions above: on the one hand, we could think about spiritual life and philosophic activity as experiences intrinsically distinct in shape and language: in a certain way two totally different things. But, on the other, we could understand the two forms of human expression as reciprocally implicated in ancient Greek wisdom. Apparently the Pythagorean philosophy seems to lead to this second conclusion.

Much of the biography by Philostratus is an attempt to present Apollonius as a rational and metaphysical philosopher: this is contrary to the criticisms of the powerful men who considered him to be an agitator, a sorcerer, and a braggart. Committing itself to 'popular' culture and its priorities seems to be the main problem faced by the Pythagorean movement, especially of Apollonius. A new political form is proposed in the structure of Pythagorean communities, whose association was always the result of free rather than ethnic, social, tribal or gender predetermination. Persecution, which is verbal, literary and physical, political and religious, is the attempt of a certain dominant culture to defend itself against a philosophy too 'close' to popular culture, its everyday life, and its vision of the world.

It is an important to note that, right from its beginnings, Greco-Roman culture was aware of the clear link between Apollonius and Jesus of Nazareth—not a direct historical link, of course, but an interesting parallelism of time and places of miracles and cures. This parallelism must be referred to the presence of many wise and divine men in the ancient Mediterranean area, especially in the first centuries of our era: Just a sign, maybe, one more proof of the extreme dynamism and scope of the ancient wisdom, especially in the Hellenistic times.

References and Suggestions for Further Reading

Burkert, W. *Lore and science in ancient Pythagoreanism*. Cambridge, Mass.: Harvard University Press, 1972.

Diogenes Laertius. *Lives of Eminent Philosophers*. With an English translation by R.D. Hicks. London; Cambridge, Mass.: Harvard University Press, 1972.

Guthrie, K. Sylvan. *The Pythagorean Sourcebook and Library*. Grand Rapids: Phanes Press, 1988.

Kingsley, Peter. *Ancient Philosophy, Mystery and Magic: Empedocles and Pythagorean Tradition*. Oxford: Clarendon Press, 1995.

Penella, R. *The Letters of Apollonius of Tyana*. Leiden: Brill, 1979.

Philostratus. *The Life of Apollonius of Tyana*. With an English translation by F.C. Conybeare. Loeb Classical Library. London/Cambridge, Mass.: Harvard University Press, 1948-50.

PART VI
THE ROMAN PERIOD

Chapter 45

Epictetus

c. 55 AD – c. 135 AD

Keith Seddon

> What have you been studying all along but to distinguish what is yours from what is
> not yours, what is in your power from what is not in your power, what is subject to
> hindrance from what is unhindered? Why did you go to the philosophers? To be as
> unfortunate and miserable as always? No—but to be free from fear and troubles.
> (Epictetus, *Discourses*, 4.1.83–4)

Epictetus (pronounced Epic–TEE–tus) was a Stoic philosopher who taught for a
brief period in Rome and then in his own school in Nicopolis (in north-western
Greece) from the end of the first century into the early decades of the second
century. His school acquired a good reputation, attracting students from all over the
Roman Empire. One of his students was Flavius Arrian (*c.* 86–160) who composed
both the longer *Discourses* and the short *Handbook* through which we know of
Epictetus and his teaching. We are told by the early Christian writer Origen (*c.*185–
254) that Epictetus had been more popular in his day than had Plato in his (*Contra
Celsum*, 6.2).

Along with all the other philosophers of the Hellenistic period, Epictetus saw
moral philosophy as having the practical purpose of guiding people towards
leading better lives. The aim was to live well, to secure for oneself a happy and
flourishing life—what Epictetus frequently refers to as a 'good flow of life', or
simply a 'good flow'. Although his curriculum was comprehensive, and included
alongside ethics the other traditional branches of philosophy, logic and physics, the
emphasis of his teaching—if we are to accept the *Discourses* and *Handbook* as
representative of his approach—was practical ethics. His intention and his hope
was that his students would become happier and better people, striking examples of
how well one may live in a world of uncertainties with all its potential for
dissatisfaction, illness, and vexation of spirit.

> What is it to study philosophy? Is it not to prepare yourself for the things that come
> upon us? ... What, then, should each of us say as each hardship befalls us? 'It was for
> this that I was exercising, it was for this that I was training.' (*Discourses*, 3.10.6-7)

The Stoic outlook that Epictetus seeks to convey, originated by its founder
Zeno of Citium, 400 years earlier, promises immunity to all harms. The ills we

suffer, says Epictetus, result from mistaken beliefs about what is truly good and where our real advantage lies. There is very little we can do to free ourselves from the presence of bad people, and things that break down or just break. There is no way we can *guarantee* the success of our ventures and the securing of those material goods that we desire and whose possession (we think) will make our lives better or even cure our misery. And despite taking every precaution, there is nothing we can do permanently to ward off ill-health, disease and eventual death— for ourselves and for those we love. Most people ignore what on the face of it is a bleak prospect, or muddle along gaining what temporary pleasure they can from this or that until misfortune deprives them of it, and the old disappointments and frustrations return, and the whole cycle is repeated. Our ability to control these 'external' things (as Epictetus calls them) is limited, partial, and at best temporary. Instead of changing these external things to suit our desires and preferences, Epictetus teaches us to change *ourselves*—that is, to change the way we regard these things and to change what we hold to be of real value and real importance. In short, he seeks to effect a transformation of his students' inner selves.

The central claim of Stoic ethics is that only virtue (excellence of character) and actions motivated by virtue are good, and that conversely, only vice and actions motivated by vice are bad (*Discourses*, 2.9.15, 2.19.13). The sorts of things that people usually value and pursue, such as pleasure, wealth, possessions, health, status and so forth, are commonly regarded as *good* (and being deprived of these things, *bad*)—but the Stoics deny that this is so, saying that such advantages do not benefit those who possess them in all circumstances: wealth, for example, can be put to bad uses, and health does not benefit you if, because you have it, you are conscripted and marched off to war. Virtue, on the other hand, understood as the capacity to make use of such advantages wisely, can never fail to be beneficial, and is thus held to be the only good thing (this argument does not originate with the Stoics, but goes back at least as far as Plato where we find it in the *Euthydemus* 278e-281e and the *Meno* 87c-89a).

The person who leads a flourishing life and is happy—happy, not in the sense that they are having a good time, or are enjoying some temporary pleasure, but whose happiness is of a special kind, being stable and enduring, a persistent flourishing that pervades their whole life—this person is virtuous (that is, they possess an excellence of character) and everything they do results from the perfected application of virtue.

For Epictetus, the way to attain and maintain this special sort of excellence is to understand what is 'in our power' or 'up to us' (*Discourses*, 1.22.9–16; *Handbook*, 1). The 'external things' we have already mentioned—other people, our possessions, the health of our bodies, and so forth—are not in our power, that is, they are not completely and always in our power. If we let our happiness depend upon these things we will be doomed to disappointment and frustration. But our own characters, our inner selves if you like—what we think about things, our intention to act this way rather than that (and for these reasons), what we think is worth pursuing or avoiding (and why)—these are always in our power, if only we can learn how to exercise this power.

In order to develop the right sort of character, and to maintain a 'good flow of life', even when adversity strikes, free from anxieties, frustrations and emotional upsets no matter what the provocation (which to this day is referred to as 'being stoical'), we need to learn how to 'make proper use of impressions'. This is the key that opens our way to the transformation of character that will secure, if not an enduring and permanent 'good flow' (for this is reserved for the Stoic Sage whose wisdom and practice is fully perfected), at least worthwhile progress towards it.

To have an impression is to be aware of something. Suppose that on my way to the lounge as I walk past the front door I glance through the coloured glass and have an impression of someone standing on the porch. Epictetus talks about 'assenting to impressions', and to assent to this impression I must be prepared to accept the truth of the proposition *that there is someone standing on the porch*. I am not altogether sure. I look again, and decide to open the door to look properly. And what I find is my old coat hanging there where I left it to dry off after being caught in last night's storm. *Now*, of course, I assent to the proposition *that my old coat is hanging up in the porch*. This interpretative move from impression to conviction of how things stand is in most circumstances immediate and unconscious. But we also *evaluate* what we believe to be the case, and this, in any one case, also requires assenting to the proposition *that this is something good for me*, or *this is something bad for me*. Epictetus' concern is with this evaluative type of assent; his claim is that assenting to external things being good or bad is an error.

Imagine that out on the porch I look down my driveway to notice for the first time that at the height of last night's storm a tree has blown down onto my rare and expensive classic car, causing severe damage. My immediate reaction, as someone whose Stoic training is barely underway, is to think that this is terrible, and this is to assent to the impression that the tree lying across my car is something *bad* for me, and further, that it is appropriate for me to have an emotional response to what has happened. Accordingly, I am assailed by anger, disappointment, and also self-reproach (for not parking my car in a safer place). There goes my 'good flow of life'.

> It is not the things themselves that disturb people but their judgements about those things. (*Handbook*, 5)

My mistake is to assent to something's being bad when really it is 'indifferent'—it is indifferent with respect to being good or bad, being neither. The tree's falling is an 'external' event which is not up to me. To let my well-being, my 'good flow', rest on external things that are not in my power, to which I allow myself to respond with disturbing emotions, is a recipe for disaster. As we have seen, the only good thing is virtue, my own inner character or disposition of spirit. It is right for me to assent to the impression that a tree has fallen on my car, but wrong to assent to the impression that this is something bad. Epictetus teaches that I should replace the faulty impression by some 'fair and noble' one (*Discourses*, 2.18.25). Well, there are several impressions I can assent to: this is nothing bad for me, because the only harm I can suffer is to act viciously, and to be overcome by violent or disturbing emotions; this event concerns external things which are not in my power, and does not affect my 'good flow of life'; this is the sort of thing that can happen to external things, and something of the sort is bound to happen eventually. This latter observation reflects an exercise that is called 'acting with reservation', carried out by the Stoic who goes about their affairs reflecting that 'I will succeed in this action, I will continue to exercise possession of this object, and it will stay in good condition, *unless something intervenes to prevent the outcome I most prefer*'.

For if nothing but virtue and vice (excellence of character or its opposite) are really good and bad, and everything else is 'indifferent', then the Stoic, who just like everyone else has undertakings to complete and projects to further, will have preferences for some 'indifferent' things occurring, and preferences for others (the 'dispreferred indifferents') *not* occurring. Their task is to pursue them, or avoid them, virtuously.

Epictetus teaches that what actually comes about is down to Zeus, or the gods, or providence, or fate understood as an organizing principle that permeates the whole of creation, bringing about the unfolding of the universe according to a divine plan. Of course there is much to say about this, but let us conclude this chapter by noting that the Stoic trainee considers that they are in service to Zeus, and that their ultimate responsibility in striving to foster their excellence of character is to contribute through their own virtuous actions to the divine plan, and no matter what actually happens (whether their preferred indifferents come about or not) they accept in good spirits their own fate and the fate of the world.

References and Suggestions for Further Reading

Hadot, Pierre. *Philosophy as a Way of Life*. Trans. Michael Chase. Edited with an introduction by Arnold I. Davidson. Oxford: Blackwell, 1995.

Hadot, Pierre. *What is Ancient Philosophy?* Trans Michael Chase. Cambridge, MA.: Harvard University Press, 2002.

Hard, Robin. *The Discourses of Epictetus*. Edited, with introduction and notes, by Christopher Gill. London: Everyman/Dent, 1995. [Includes the complete *Discourses*, the *Handbook*, and *Fragments*.]

Long, A.A. *Epictetus: A Stoic and Socratic Guide to Life*. Oxford: Oxford University Press, 2002.

Seddon, Keith. *Epictetus'* Handbook *and the* Tablet *of Cebes: Guides to Stoic Living*. London: Routledge, forthcoming.

White, Nicholas. *Handbook of Epictetus*. Indianapolis: Hackett, 1983.

Chapter 46

Apuleius of Madauros

c. 125 AD–??

Bruce J. MacLennan

Platonic philosopher, popular orator, author of a risqué novel, accused sorcerer: what are we to make of Apuleius? He was born about 125 AD in Madauros (modern M'daurouch, in Algeria), a thriving, multicultural Roman colony. His family was prosperous and his father was the chief magistrate. Punic was probably his first language, but his family was deeply immersed in Roman culture and he became proficient in both Latin and Greek. He received a thorough education at Carthage, Rome, and Athens, and after extensive travels returned to Carthage to become a popular philosophical orator, a well-respected citizen, and high priest of the imperial cult; statues were erected in his honor. In addition to his novel, he wrote music, hymns, poetry, satire, erotica, fiction, and treatises on Platonic philosophy, mathematics, music, astronomy, medicine, history, botany, and zoology, only a few of which survive. His insatiable curiosity, especially about religion, mythology, mysticism, and magic, occasionally got him into trouble.

In particular, when Apuleius had completed his stay in Athens, about 156 AD and was on his way to visit Alexandria, he was introduced to Pudentilla, a wealthy widow somewhat older than himself, and they married. Some of her relatives, who were probably afraid of losing control of her money, brought a charge of sorcery against Apuleius, alleging that he had seduced Pudentilla by magic. This was a serious charge, for sorcery was punishable by death.

Apparently he was acquitted, and his *Defense* (*Apologia*) is a valuable source of information about ancient magical practices for, ironically, in the process of defending himself he displays considerable knowledge of magic. (Indeed, *Defense* is a comparatively recent title; all the manuscripts call it some variant of *On Magic*.) He argues that he is a philosopher, and that philosophers and magicians engage in superficially similar practices (e.g. collecting plants and animals), but for different purposes. He ridicules his accusers for their ignorance of philosophy and for their impious confusion of religious ritual with magic. Overall, it is a masterful rhetorical display (perhaps thanks to some rewriting after the trial).

He was acquitted, but was he guilty? As his *Defense* argues, he had little need of love spells, but that does not prove that he did not practise magic. In particular, it is not implausible that Apuleius practised *theurgy*: ritual techniques for union with the gods, which were popular with later Platonists and can be traced to his time. Theurgical and magical techniques are superficially similar, for they both depend on symbolic associations and make use of objects, incantations, etc. for their symbolic value.

Apuleius is most famous for his *Metamorphoses* (*Transformations*), better known as *The Golden Ass*. In a first-person account the hero Lucius tells how, by dabbling in magic, he was accidentally transformed into a jackass, and about his subsequent (often ribald) adventures and eventual salvation. The basic storyline is not original, for we have another version, but Apuleius makes two significant additions.

The first is the well-known tale of Cupid and Psyche (Love and Soul). The story begs for an allegorical interpretation, and many have read it as a Platonic allegory of the soul's redemption through love.

The second major change is in the last book of the novel, the so-called 'Isis book', in which the hero repents and appeals to the goddess Isis to 'restore me to myself' (XI.2). The narrator describes a magnificent epiphany of the goddess, in which she says:

> Behold, Lucius, I am present, moved by thy prayers, I, Nature's mother, mistress of all the elements, the first-begotten offspring of the ages, mightiest of deities ... (XI.5)

After the restoration of his humanity, Lucius decides to become an initiate in the mysteries of Isis, after which he addresses to her a beautiful prayer, which begins:

> Thou, O holy and perpetual savior of the human race, ever bountifully cherishing mortals, dost apply the sweet affection of a mother to the misfortunes of the miserable. Nor is there any day or night, or even a slender moment, which passes unattended by thy blessings. (XI.25)

Later he was initiated into the mysteries of her consort, the god Osiris.

The Isis book is suffused with a genuine piety, which contrasts with the wittier and more superficial tone of the earlier books (except 'Cupid and Psyche'). Nevertheless, the entire novel has been read as a Platonic allegory of the transformation of the soul and its salvation from the miseries of an unenlightened life. However, it is difficult to say whether Apuleius intended any such allegorical interpretation. The narrator states at the outset that his intention is to entertain, but the true purpose may be hidden under multiple layers of irony and intentional misdirection. Apuleius was a very sophisticated rhetorician and he toys with his reader.

This leads to the vexed issue of whether the *Metamorphoses* is autobiographical. There are many parallels between the hero Lucius and the author Apuleius. Indeed, until recent times they were assumed to be the same, and the author was often called 'Lucius Apuleius'. One apparent similarity is their excessive but superficial curiosity about magic. Apuleius also drops tantalizing hints, but there are also significant differences, so we cannot take the novel as a source of biographical information. Nevertheless, the real depth of feeling in the Isis book and the ritual details, which have been confirmed from other sources, have convinced most scholars that at least this part reflects Apuleius' personal experience.

References and Suggestions for Further Reading

Apuleius. *Apuleius' Golden Ass and other Philosophical Writings*. Trans. Thomas Taylor, Vol. XIV of Thomas Taylor Series. Somerset: Prometheus Trust, 1997. Includes Taylor's 1822 translations of *The God of Socrates* and *Plato's Doctrine*.

Apuleius. *The Golden Ass*. Trans. P.G. Walsh. Oxford: Clarendon Press, 1994.

Apuleius. *The Golden Ass, or Metamorphoses*. Trans. E.J. Kenney. New York: Penguin, 1998.

Apuleius. *Metamorphoses*. Ed. and trans. J. Arthur Hanson. 2 Vols. Loeb Classical Library. Cambridge: Harvard University Press, 1989. Includes Latin text.

Apuleius. *The Rhetorical Works*. Trans. and ann. S. Harrison, J. Hilton, and V. Hunink. Oxford: Oxford University Press, 2001. Includes the *Defense* and *The God of Socrates*.

Chapter 47

Marcus Aurelius

121 AD–180 AD

William O. Stephens

How putrid is the matter which underlies everything. Water, dust, bones, stench. Again, fine marbles are calluses of the earth; gold and silver, its sediments; our clothes, animal-hair; their purple, blood from a shellfish. Our very breath is something similar and changes from this to that. (*Meditations*, 9.36)

Marcus Aurelius, Roman emperor from 161 to 180 AD, was the last of the great Stoic philosophers. He was born in Rome as Marcus Annius Verus, of Spanish ancestry. His father died when he was a young boy, but Marcus soon enjoyed the favor of the emperor Hadrian. Nicknaming him Verissimus, meaning 'the most truthful', Hadrian made Marcus a priest at the tender age of eight, and betrothed him to the daughter of Lucius Ceionius Commodus when he was fifteen. When Ceionius died two years later, Hadrian arranged for the trustworthy Antoninus Pius, Hadrian's successor to the throne, to adopt both Marcus and Ceionius' son Lucius Verus.

Marcus learned rhetoric, grammar, philosophy, and law from the best teachers of his day. Frank, sincere, and sensitive in character, Marcus was frail, but also lean and athletic. He married Pius' daughter Faustina in 145 AD, and they had a daughter the next year. An ever loyal and obedient son-in-law, around 147 AD Marcus abandoned rhetoric for Stoicism, which inspired him the rest of his life. His own Stoic philosophy was deeply influenced by the great Stoic teacher and ex-slave Epictetus.

After twenty-two years of administrative experience, Marcus ascended the throne. Much of his reign was spent defending and expanding the frontiers of the empire. He battled tribes in northern Italy, Britain, Parthia, and especially Germany. During these many wars Marcus would return to his tent, under the cold gloom of a foreign sky, weary from another day of shouldering his staggering imperial duties, and take up a pen to jot down his private thoughts on the place of human beings in the universe. These personal reflections, written only for himself, in Greek, the language of philosophy, rather than Latin, range in length from a short sentence to several paragraphs. Later compiled into twelve books, Marcus' unique philosophical notebook became known as the *Meditations*.

The cosmic perspective, insistence on the plain truth, and acting for the common good characterize Marcus' thought. One of his favourite techniques is to take what many prize the most—wealth, power, luxuries, sex—strip them of their glitz and glamor, and reveal how paltry they truly are. In *Meditations* he writes:

> When you sit before delicacies and fancy foods, you will recognize their nature if you bear in mind that this is the corpse of a fish, that is the corpse of a bird or a pig; or again, that imported wine is merely grape juice, and this purple robe some sheep's wool dipped in the blood of a shellfish; and as for sexual intercourse, it is the rubbing of a piece of intestine, then a convulsion, and the spurting of some mucus. Thoughts like these go to the heart of actual facts and penetrate them, allowing us to see them as they really are. (*Meditations*, 6.13)

Such sobering reminders helped Marcus remain upright and clear-eyed amidst regal bewitchments. Surrounded daily by such enticements, Marcus was intent on not falling prey to them. He warns himself that 'pride is an arch-seducer of reason' in order to keep himself honest and humble despite his lofty position of authority.

As a Stoic, Marcus believed that the only real goods are wisdom, temperance, justice, courage, and the other virtues of a good moral character. All else he considered transient, cheap, and superfluous, as he writes:

> All that is prized in life is empty, rotten, and petty, puppies snapping at one another, little children bickering, laughing, and then soon crying ... What is one to do? ... What else than to worship and praise the gods, to do good to people, to bear with them and to show forbearance. (*Meditations*, 5.33)

Concern for communal unity and tolerance of others is a common refrain:

> Human beings are here for the sake of one another; either instruct them or put up with them. (*Meditations*, 8.59)

By concentrating on what is up to him, Marcus offers himself sound Stoic advice:

> Another does me wrong? Let him look to that; he has his own disposition, and his actions are his own. For my part, I now have what universal nature wills that I should have, and I am doing what my own nature wills that I should do. (*Meditations*, 5.25)

Dying is no big deal, Marcus thinks, since thousands upon thousands, entire cities, have perished for century after century. He often looks at things from the viewpoint of the universe:

> How small a fraction of infinite and unimaginable time has been assigned to each of us. For all too swiftly it vanishes in eternity. And what a fraction of the whole of matter, and what a fraction of the whole of universal soul. And on what a small clod of the whole earth you creep. Bearing all this in mind, imagine nothing to be great but this: to act as your own nature directs, and to love what universal nature brings (*Meditations*, 12.32).

With these somber reflections, the Stoic emperor situated himself in the world. 'All things are ever the same,' he writes (9.14), 'familiar in experience, fleeting in time, foul in their matter; all is just the same now as it was in the days of those whom we have buried.' What comforting wisdom does Marcus derive from these observations? He explains:

> Our security in life is to see each thing in itself, in its entirety, its material, its cause; and to do what is right and to speak the truth with all our heart. What remains but to enjoy life, linking one good act to another, so that not even the smallest space is ever left in between? (*Meditations*, 12.29)

In a letter to his rhetoric teacher, Marcus Cornelius Fronto, he reports that he is a lucky man because from Fronto he learns 'how to speak the truth; and that ability, to tell the truth, is a hard task indeed, for men and gods alike'. Is it any easier for us today?

References and Suggestions for Further Reading

Birley, A. *Marcus Aurelius: A Biography*. London 1966, 2nd edn 1987.

Brunt, P.A. 'Marcus Aurelius in his *Meditations*'. *Journal of Roman Studies* 64 (1974), 1-20.

Farquharson, A.S.L. Ed. with translation and commentary. *The Meditations of Marcus Aurelius Antoninus*. 2 Vols. Oxford: 1944.

Gill, Christopher. Introduction and notes. *Marcus Aurelius: Meditations*. Trans. R. Hard. Ware, Hertfordshire: 1997.

Hadot, Pierre. *The Inner Citadel: the Meditations of Marcus Aurelius*. Trans. M. Chase. Cambridge, Mass.: 2001.

Long, A.A. 'Epictetus and Marcus Aurelius' in J. Luce, Ed. *Ancient Writers: Greece and Rome*. Vol. 2. New York: 1982, 985-1002.

Rutherford, R.B. *The Meditations of Marcus Aurelius: A Study*. Oxford: 1989.

Chapter 48

Plotinus

204 AD–270 AD

David J. Yount

Good and kindly, singularly gentle and engaging: thus the oracle presents him, and so in fact we found him. Sleeplessly alert—Apollo tells—Pure of soul, ever striving towards the divine which he loved with all his being, he laboured strenuously to free himself and rise above the bitter waves of this blood-drenched life: and this is why to Plotinus— God-like and lifting himself often, by the ways of meditation and by the methods Plato teaches in the Banquet, to the first and all-transcendent God—that God appeared, the God who has neither shape nor form but sits enthroned above the Intellectual-Principle and all the Intellectual-Sphere. (Porphyry's *Life of Plotinus*, 23)

Plotinus was born in Egypt, and died aged sixty-six, in Campania, now South Central Italy. Not much is known about his life until after he reached adulthood, and what we do know we get from his pupil, editor, and friend, Porphyry. When Plotinus was twenty-eight, he became very interested in philosophy and actively searched the conference halls of Alexandria for a suitable teacher, and he became depressed, not being happy with any of them. Finally, a friend recommended that he listen to Ammonius Saccas (185–250 AD) about whom little else is known but who is said to have dressed in a sack, hence, Saccas. After hearing Ammonius, Plotinus is reported to have said, 'This was the man I was looking for', and proceeded to study with Ammonius in Alexandria for about ten years, a period during which he refused to write a single word. Besides Plotinus, his most famous student, Ammonius also taught Longinus, Origen (early Christian theologian), another Origen the Neo-Platonist, and Erennius, among others. After studying with Ammonius, Plotinus became deeply interested in learning about Persian and Indian philosophy first hand, and so, says Porphyry, he joined the Roman emperor Gordian III's expedition against Persia in 242–243 (*Life*, 3). The expedition failed, however, so Plotinus was not able to realize his intellectual goal; after managing to avoid capture, he escaped to Antioch, and soon thereafter moved to Rome, where he established a school of philosophy.

Porphyry tells us that:

Plotinus ... seemed ashamed of being in the body. So deeply rooted was this feeling that he could never be induced to tell of his ancestry, his parentage, or his birthplace. He showed too, an unconquerable reluctance to sit to a painter or a sculptor, and when Amelius persisted in urging him to allow a portrait being made he asked him, 'Is it not enough to carry about this image in which nature has enclosed us? Do you really think I must also consent to leave, as a desirable spectacle to posterity, an image of the image?' (*Life*, 1)

Plotinus was a vegetarian, who also refused any medicines made from animals, and he abstained from bathing (*Life*, 2). Porphyry also tells us that he sacrificed on the traditional birthdays of Plato and of Socrates, afterwards giving a banquet at which every member of the circle who was able was expected to deliver an address. These practices show us that Plotinus did not merely *teach* his philosophy to Romans and visitors; he lived it.

Plotinus informally taught for twenty-six years until his death, which may have been caused by leprosy. He lectured in a free-flowing manner, answering questions that his pupils and visitors put to him. His most avid pupil was Porphyry, who, upon meeting and listening to him for the first time, thought he had an ill-conceived philosophy. In the end, however, Porphyry encouraged Plotinus to write more than the twenty-one treatises he had already written, and Porphyry became the editor of Plotinus' writings.

After editing and arranging the fifty-four treatises, Porphyry entitled the work the *Enneads*, because there are six sets of nine treatises (and '*ennea*' is Greek for 'nine'). Porphyry tells us that Plotinus' eyesight was very poor in his later years, such that Plotinus could not reread his manuscript even once:

> his handwriting was slovenly; he misjoined his words; he cared nothing about spelling; his one concern was for the idea. ... He used to work out his design mentally from first to last: when he came to set down his ideas, he wrote out at one jet all he had stored in mind as though he were copying from a book. (*Life*, 8)

Plotinus is widely known as the founder of Neo-Platonism, a philosophical school that claimed to be based on the views of Plato. Plotinus claims that his philosophy adds nothing new to what Plato said, but most commentators on Plotinus and Plato disagree with him on that point. Plotinus attacked the views of the Christians and anti-Platonists in his school, and the views of the Gnostics in *Enneads* II.9. Although Plotinus was not a Christian himself, his influence on the theology of Christianity was substantial. For instance, it was through reading Plotinus' *Enneads* that Augustine learned about Plato's thought. He adapted much of Plotinus' theory to his own ends, and was clearly influenced by him in other important ways.

For Plotinus, there are three primary metaphysical entities (or 'Hypostases'): The One, Intellect, and the All-Soul. As for the first hypostasis, the One, Plotinus says it is possible for us to come to have a vision or experience of the One; in fact, he claims that having this experience is the ultimate goal of philosophy, equivalent to achieving happiness in this lifetime. Plotinus says that the One cannot be known through the use of discursive (i.e., logical) reasoning (*Enneads* VI.9.4). Indeed, the One is beyond being and not being, and is 'neither thing nor quantity nor quality nor intellect nor soul; not in motion, not at rest, not in place, not in time' (*Enneads* VI.9.3); Plotinus insists on its ineffability; namely, the inability adequately or logically to describe in words the experience or vision of the One.

The second hypostasis is Intellect (or, alternatively, Nous, the Intellectual Principle, or The All). Intellect is Being, or the intelligible realm of the Forms, which are eternal, immutable, immaterial natures, the same natures which Plato argues for and discusses in his dialogues. These are knowable beings that are in some sense an outflow, an 'emanation' of the One. According to Plotinus, the Intellect eternally contemplates itself and the One.

The third hypostasis, or All-Soul, is the Soul of the visible universe, the Soul which all individual souls are one with, and the Soul of which individuals' souls are a part. Soul both contemplates Intellect and the One by itself, and acts by being connected with material bodies. Plotinus, like Plato, holds that dialectic (or conversing by questioning one's assumptions about knowledge and reality) is the most important part of philosophy and therefore the most important activity one's soul can perform (*Enneads* I.3.5), the goal of which is to become a 'likeness to God as far as is possible' (*Enneads* I.2.1).

Besides these three entities, the last and lowest outflow from the All-Soul is matter: matter is for Plotinus ultimately imperceptible, unknowable, lacking in form and true being, and in general, the furthest entity 'away from' the One. Also, souls can get caught up in thinking that nothing immaterial exists and that only material comfort and 'happiness' count. For these reasons, matter is said by Plotinus to be evil; that is, matter is (or can be) in some sense the cause of unhappiness for humans.

According to Porphyry (*Life*, 7), Plotinus had a 'large following' which included several physicians and many Roman senators, who regularly attended his lectures. The obese Roman senator Rogatianus was so impressed with what Plotinus said that he gave away all his wealth, his position and rank, began eating only every other day, and studied with Plotinus. A number of women embraced his philosophy: Gemina, in whose house he lived, her daughter Gemina, Amphiclea, and Chione, who lived in the same house with her children (*Life*, 9). Plotinus was not only a great teacher and thinker, but seems to have been a great person as well. Further examples: First, Porphyry tells us that people of high rank left many children and much property to Plotinus, and that Plotinus, as their guardian, took great care in accounting not only for their money and property, but for their well-being (*Life*, 9). Second, he was a remarkable judge of character, and once determined, just by looking at some suspects, who, among several people, had stolen a valuable necklace (*Life*, 11). Third, Plotinus also detected that Porphyry himself was considering suicide, and encouraged him to take a vacation, so Porphyry left for Sicily, which was successful in lifting his spirits, but prevented him from being in attendance for Plotinus' death. Fourth, apparently Plotinus was so taken with Plato's thoughts about his ideal state, the *Republic*, and its laws, that he made arrangements with Emperor Gallienus and his wife Salonina (who both greatly honored and venerated Plotinus) to revive a Campanian city and call it 'Platonopolis', but the emperor's courtiers (from jealousy, spite, or for some other reason) prevented his efforts (*Life*, 12). Fifth and finally, even though he had acted as arbiter in Rome for twenty-six years, he never had made an enemy of any citizen (*Life*, 9).

Porphyry also tells us that Olympius of Alexandria adopted a superior attitude to Plotinus and used magic in an attempt to harm him, but that Plotinus' soul warded off the attacks (*Life*, 9). He was also accused of plagiarizing Numenius' writings, but his pupil, Amelius, wrote a treatise explaining the differences between the two thinkers and successfully defended him against the charge.

Unfortunately, despite Porphyry's editorial efforts, Plotinus' writings, though very profound and worthy of study, are neither systematic nor readily understandable. Porphyry says of Plotinus' writing:

> In style Plotinus is concise, dense with thought, terse, more lavish of ideas than of words, most often expressing himself with a fervid inspiration. He followed his own path rather than that of tradition, but in his writings both the Stoic and Peripatetic doctrines are sunk; Aristotle's *Metaphysics*, especially, is condensed in them, all but entire. (*Life*, 14)

If one wishes to understand the thought of Plotinus there are some points to keep in mind. First, one should read and study Plato (especially the dialogues *Republic*, *Symposium*, *Phaedrus*, *Phaedo*, and *Timaeus*). In addition, it would certainly be helpful to read Aristotle, especially *Categories*, Metaphysics, and *De Anima* (*On the Soul*), works on Pythagoras and also the Stoics [e.g., Seneca (3 – 65 AD), Epictetus, (60–138 AD), and Marcus Aurelius (121–180 AD)]. Third, of course, one must read all of the *Enneads*.

Porphyry relates that, during the time he knew Plotinus, Plotinus attained union four times with the One, and Porphyry himself claims, also, to have had this experience once. Because of these statements concerning the ineffability and uniting with the One, Plotinus is seen as a mystic. Plotinus' last words to Eustochius, his friend and physician, were a concise yet inspirational summary of his philosophy: 'Try to bring back the god in you to the divine in the All!'

References and Suggestions for Further Reading

Plotinus' works

Plotinus. *Plotinus: The Enneads*. Unabridged. Trans. Stephen MacKenna. Burdett: Larson
    Publications, 1992.
Plotinus. *Plotinus: The Enneads*. Abridged. Trans. Stephen MacKenna. Ed. John Dillon.
    London: Penguin Books, 1991.

General Books on Plotinus' thought

Moore, Edward. *Plotinus*. Entry for the *Internet Encyclopedia of Philosophy*, at
    www.utm.edu/research/iep/p/plotinus.htm.
O'Meara, Dominic J. *Plotinus: An Introduction to the Enneads*. Oxford: Clarendon Press,
    1993.
Yount, David J. *Plotinus: THE Platonist*. Forthcoming. Contact him at:
    david.yount@mcmail.maricopa.edu.

Chapter 49

Sextus Empiricus

c. 160–210 AD

Sabatino DiBernardo

When people search for something, the likely outcome is that either they find it or, not finding it, they accept that it cannot be found, or they continue to search. So also in the case of what is sought in philosophy, I think, some people have claimed to have found the truth, others have asserted that it cannot be apprehended, and others are still searching. Those who think they have found it are the Dogmatists, properly so called—for example, the followers of Aristotle and Epicurus, the Stoics, and certain others. The followers of Cleitomachus and Carneades, as well as other Academics, have asserted that it cannot be apprehended. The Skeptics continue to search. Hence it is with reason that the main types of philosophy are thought to be three in number: the Dogmatic, the Academic, and the Skeptic. Concerning the first two it will best become others to speak; but concerning the Skeptic Way we shall now give an outline account, stating in advance that as regards none of these things that we are about to say do we firmly maintain that matters are absolutely as stated, but in each instance we are simply reporting, like a chronicler, what now appears to us to be the case. (Sextus Empiricus, *Outlines of Pyrrhonism* I 1-4)

So begins Sextus Empiricus' *Outlines of Pyrrhonism* (PH)—a book that would forever challenge the dogmatic assumptions, tendencies and goals of the Western philosophical tradition. In these prefatory remarks, Sextus provides a concise summary of the various philosophical schools of thought and the issues at stake regarding absolute truth, knowledge and reality. Here we are given a key glimpse into the heart and mind of Sextus and a Pyrrhonian way of life that began with Pyrrho of Elis from whom Pyrrhonism derives its name (PH I 7).

Sextus' testimony is based on his inability to decide between competing philosophical schools of thought and their perspectives without the assistance of an available metacriterion (or absolute standard) with which to judge the Truth in its essence or reality. This led him to an acceptance of the fallibility of the self and one's perception of things, thereby engendering humility with respect to claims of absolute truth, knowledge, and certainty. In the process of suspending judgment on such matters, Sextus and other Pyrrhonists discovered a tranquility of soul that previously had eluded them during their philosophical quests (PH I 12).

It is crucial to note that the philosophical possibilities described by Sextus are not rooted in abstract theoretical debates without real-life consequence or significance. Indeed, what is at stake is the spiritual well-being of anyone concerned with achieving tranquility of soul (*ataraxia*) and happiness (*eudaimonia*)—the primary goal for most ancient philosophers. Sextus' Pyrrhonian Skepticism and its ability to bring about this desired goal (PH I 8-10; I 25-30) is a far cry from what the history of philosophy and popular opinion have maligned as a corrosive, degenerative disease that infects cultures with relativism (i.e., 'truth' is related to subjective interpretation; thus, there is no Truth), cynicism (i.e., a pessimistic, negative, antisocial outlook on life; unlike the ancient movement that offered a critique of constructed culture over and against a life in harmony with natural impulses), and nihilism (i.e., literally 'nothing-ism'; in other words, no truth, no overarching meaning, all is hopeless and lost in an abyss of meaninglessness). This historically perpetuated misunderstanding of Pyrrhonism has led to a spiritually denuded skepticism obsessed with doubt and denial rather than the vital, spiritually transformative Pyrrhonian Skepticism concerned with everyday life as taught by Sextus (PH I 17-23; II 102). Current representations continue to treat the ancient Skeptic as an odd, contentious person, one who approaches all beliefs with a negative, doubting, denying predisposition; in other words, one who is constantly saying 'no' to all of the 'yeses' possible—a denial of any affirmation without allowing for the possibility of truth. This is not the spiritual perspective that one encounters in the prophetic voice of Sextus Empiricus.

One might describe Sextus as a spiritual tour guide and physician of the soul, and the *Outlines* as a therapeutic travel guide for those on the quest for Truth and, thus, tranquility. The *Outlines* and Sextus' other writings are invaluable for the Skeptic Way that he maps out. Other extant works by Sextus include *Against the Dogmatists* (2 books against the Logicians, 2 books against the Physicists; 1 book against the Ethicists; designated: *Against the Mathematicians VII-XI* [M]) and *Against the Professors* (6 books against Grammarians, Rhetoricians, Geometers, Arithmeticians, Astrologers and Musicians; designated: *Against the Mathematicians I-VI* [M]).

Although we have a large body of Sextus' work, the details of his life remain largely obscure. His dates, geographical origins and occupation remain a matter of scholarly debate. Scholars are divided as to the central location of Sextan Pyrrhonism (e.g., Rome, Alexandria, Athens, or elsewhere) and whether he was an empirical or methodical medical doctor (distinctions that relate directly to philosophical theories), or, for some, whether he even was a physician.

Notwithstanding the scholarly debates regarding Sextus' occupation, ancient Skepticism and medicine were intimately related. His medical treatises (e.g., M 7 202; M 1 61) would lend themselves naturally to what is probably the most central and powerful analogy marshalled by Sextus with respect to the Pyrrhonian spiritually therapeutic way of life and thought; namely, the medical model (e.g., diagnosis and remedy) as its basis for purgative arguments (PH I 206).

Sextus' books represent the meticulous work of a master physician and chronicler of the various strains of philosophical disease. The philosophical quest for Truth as taught by non-Skeptics is diagnosed by Sextus as the *cause* of the malady of anxiety and *not* the remedy for it (PH III 280-281). Indeed, it is precisely this dogmatic pretense to having found Truth—a perennially tantalizing siren song that hides an insidious malignancy within a seductive melody of certain knowledge—that infects one with the very contagion it was meant to cure. In the process, it prevents rather than produces the tranquility that it promises. Sextus' unwillingness to maintain or advance any belief(s) dogmatically, including his own, reverberates throughout his writings. In his opening remarks one witnesses this Pyrrhonian qualification of statements (i.e., a Pyrrhonian meditation) put into action, thereby revealing a person of great spiritual and philosophical maturity.

Pyrrho, Sextus, and other Pyrrhonists accidentally stumbled upon this spiritual treatment during their own philosophical travels (PH I 29). Sextus testifies to his own serendipitous liberation and subsequent philanthropic desire to heal the souls of those afflicted with the malady of dogmatism and anxiety (PH III 280) and spiritual tranquility by means of an inoculation of suspension (*epoche*) of absolute judgment on matters of Truth, Knowledge and Reality. Once inoculated and sustained by the Skeptics' spiritual exercises (e.g., juxtaposing opposing arguments on any given question), one may engage in daily life shorn of desired certainties, living tranquilly by virtue of a 'wise ignorance' as to the absolute nature of things (PH I 36 ff).

Although some travel guides offer The Way to the 'definitive' travel experience, in the Pyrrhonian travel guide we are presented an alternate but, perhaps, much more fulfilling way. Sextus invites us on a journey to an exotic destination where the quest for Truth—that continues to plague philosophers and religionists alike—leads to a questioning of this quest and, instead, gently suggests that we proceed along a path exceedingly less travelled.

References and Suggestions for Further Reading

Bury, R.G. *Sextus Empiricus*. Loeb Classical Library, 4 vols. Cambridge: Harvard University Press, 1933-1949; repr., 1939-1993.

DiBernardo, Sabatino. *The Skeptic Way as a Religious Way: A Meditation on Religion and Pyrrhonian Spirituality*. (Unpublished Dissertation: Syracuse University, 2000).

Groarke, Leo. *Greek Scepticism: Anti-Realist Trends in Ancient Thought*. McGill-Queen's Studies in the History of Ideas. Montreal: McGill-Queen's University Press, 1990.

Hallie, Philip P. ed. *Scepticism, Man, and God: Selections from the Major Writings of Sextus Empiricus*. Trans. Sanford G. Etheridge. Middletown, Connecticut: Wesleyan University Press, 1964.

Mates, Benson. The Skeptic Way: Sextus Empiricus's Outlines of Pyrrhonism. Oxford: Oxford University Press, 1996.

Chapter 50

Iamblichus of Chalcis

c. 245 AD–c. 325 AD

Bruce J. MacLennan

> Further yet, we preserve the mystical, ineffable image of the gods complete in our soul and through them lead our soul up toward the gods, and when it is elevated as much as possible, we unite it with the gods. (Iamblichus (DM. vii.4)

It used to be fashionable to dismiss Iamblichus as representing the final decadence of classical Greek philosophy, but in recent decades we have come to appreciate him for his revitalization and reorientation of Platonic philosophy in the 4th century AD and as a critical link in the transmission of Platonic ideas into the Middle Ages, Renaissance, and modern world. This reassessment is partly a result of our own improved understanding of the role and function of ancient philosophy. But first, some biographical background.

Iamblichus was born in Chalcis (modern Qinnesrin) in north Syria, an intellectually lively city in a prosperous region, which had been at peace for over 200 years. He became a student of Porphyry, an important neo-Platonic philosopher, and probably studied with him in Rome or Sicily. Although they came to differ on many philosophical points, there is no reason to suppose that they did not respect each other.

Eventually, perhaps around 305, Iamblichus returned to Syria to found his own school at Apameia (near Antioch), a city already famous for its neo-Platonic philosophers. Among the philosophers he trained was Aedesius (died c. 355), himself the teacher of Maximus of Ephesus (died 370), who in turn initiated the Emperor Julian (331–363) into the mysteries of neo-Platonism and encouraged him in his unsuccessful attempt to revitalize paganism in the face of spreading Christianity.

At a time when most wealthy families chose Greek names, Iamblichus decided to retain his Semitic name, perhaps to honor his noble ancestors, who included several priest-kings of Emesa. This choice was consistent with his general view of Greek culture for, like Plato (*Laws* 657a), he felt that the Greeks changed ancient traditions too capriciously and had too little respect for the 'old nations':

> For the Greeks are naturally followers of novelty and, being volatile, are carried off everywhere, neither possessing any stability themselves, nor preserving what they

have received from others, but rapidly abandoning this, they transform everything through an unstable love of novel arguments. (Iamblichus, *DM* VII.5)

Therefore, in his philosophy, Iamblichus tried to harmonize the rational discourse of classical Greek philosophy with the ancient religious practices of Egypt, Assyria, and Chaldaea.

Iamblichus wrote a great deal, but much of it has been lost. He also established the definitive neo-Platonic curriculum, which was followed for the next two centuries. The first part was his own *Collection of Pythagorean Doctrines* in ten books, a compendium of extracts from ancient philosophers. (Only the first four books, and perhaps fragments of the fifth, survive.) The next subject was the works of Plato and Aristotle, for which Iamblichus wrote a number of commentaries (only fragments survive). In particular, he set down the order in which the Platonic dialogues should be studied, for each was supposed to effect a specific transformation in the student's soul, and he also defined principles for their allegorical interpretation.

Already in the 6th century BC Pythagoreans had devised allegorical interpretations of Homer, and by the second century AD neo-Platonic philosophers had applied them to Plato's dialogues by distinguishing three or four levels of meaning, based on correspondences between the levels of reality (the macrocosm) or of human existence (the microcosm); but it was Iamblichus who systematized these methods of interpretation and applied them consistently. Neo-Platonic theologians had also applied allegorical methods to Jewish and Christian scriptures (as early as the 1st century AD), but Iamblichus' systematic formulation laid the foundations for biblical exegesis by theologians and also influenced others, such as Dante.

With his emphasis on respect for ancient wisdom, Iamblichus treated Plato's dialogues as divinely inspired scripture. He also accorded great respect to the *Chaldean Oracles*, a collection of inspired verses dating to perhaps the 2nd century AD. He devoted at least 28 books to their interpretation and taught their doctrine of *theurgy*, explained below.

Like other neo-Platonists, Iamblichus explained reality as an inevitable, hierarchical emanation into multiplicity from an Inexpressible One. Within the Inexpressible One are two opposed principles, Limit and the Unlimited (or the One and the Many), the mixture of which generates the levels of reality. The One is the ultimate principle of Limit, whereas the multiplicity of pure, unformed, chaotic matter is the ultimate expression of the Unlimited. The emanation proceeds through the Forms, the eternal archetypal principles of all things, to the World Soul, which unites the Forms with matter and thereby imparts order to the cosmos. The individual soul is a microcosm, that is, an image in miniature of the cosmos.

Love or Desire, conceived as a cosmic force (the active power of unity) and a deity (firstborn of the One), is essential to the structure of reality, for it coordinates the Forms and draws multiplicity into a cosmic unity. The One 'inserts, by union, the indissoluble principle of love, which supports and preserves both things that exist [eternally] and those that come into being' (*DM* IV.12), 'an affection that embraces all things, producing this bond through a certain ineffable communion' (*DM* V.10).

Further, it is necessary for the One to proceed outward into matter—and for individual souls to become embodied—for otherwise desire could not manifest: there can be no desire without an 'other' to be desired. Thus, by means of embodied souls, the One loves and desires itself, and so binds the cosmos in unity.

Iamblichus' view contrasts with that of the Gnostics and of some other neo-Platonists. Gnosticism refers to a loose group of 2nd century (primarily) Christian sects, which had adopted ideas from a variety of sources and practised rites directed toward salvation by *gnôsis*, knowing God. They shared with neo-Platonists the idea that reality is an emanation from the One, which makes it a divine unity, but like some neo-Platonists their focus on ascent to the divine led them to devalue this world. Iamblichus, however, did not consider matter to be evil or the embodied soul to be 'fallen'. Rather, humans have an essential role in the creation and providential ordering of the cosmos, for 'from the first descent, divinity sent souls down here so that they might return again to him' (*DM* VIII.8). They fulfill this role best through the practice of theurgy.

'Theurgy,' which may be translated 'god-work', refers to practices (rituals) directed toward the gods, in contrast to *theology* (god-talk), which is rational discourse about the gods. It also refers to the subsequent action of the gods by which they transform the theurgist, for it aims at 'purification, liberation, and salvation of the soul' (*DM* X.7). The theoretical basis for theurgy is described in one of Iamblichus' surviving works, *The Reply of the Master Abammon to 'Porphyry's Letter to Anebo'*, better known as *On the Mysteries of the Egyptians* (*De Mysteriis*); it is a systematic reply to a number of objections raised by Porphyry against the practice of theurgy.

Theurgy is based on the idea that the Demiurge, the creator god of Plato, has organized matter in accord with the eternal Forms, and therefore material objects reveal the Forms and can be used as a means for the soul to realign itself with Providence and to unify itself with divinity. In particular, a theurgic rite makes use of certain *symbols* (signs, tokens), which the gods have imprinted with the Forms. 'For there is nothing that is in the smallest degree assimilated to the gods, to which the gods are not immediately present and conjoined' (*DM* I.15). For example, the heliotrope is a symbol for the sun because it turns toward it, as is the cock because it heralds the rising sun. Likewise, the sun, as source of light and life, governing our cosmos, points toward the Inexpressible One. Similarly, the Demiurge has placed symbols within each embodied soul, but most people are unconscious of them.

Through emanation a unified, eternal Form is scattered into multiplicity in space and time. The theurgist attempts to restore the unity of the Form by reassembling its symbols: materials, objects, images, shapes, sounds (invocations, hymns), and so forth. In this way the theurgist creates a suitable receptacle for the god. In addition, these external symbols awaken the symbols in the theurgist's soul, which bring it into alignment with the god.

Although Form proceeds from its essence into matter, by theurgy the embodied soul returns to its essence. Furthermore, the love or affinity that draws together all of a god's symbols also draws the god and theurgist closer together. Therefore love, which has proceeded outward into the world, is redirected by the theurgist back towards its source. Thus the theurgist completes the erotic circuit that binds the universe into a whole. 'And with a knowledge of the gods there comes a conversion to, and a knowledge of, ourselves' (*DM* X.1).

Iamblichus' philosophy and theurgy were very influential on later neo-Platonists, such as Proclus (c. 410–485). From Proclus, in turn, perhaps by way of Damascius (fl. c.529), these ideas passed to pseudo-Dionysius the Areopagite (6th century?), whose works laid the foundation of the Christian mystical tradition. Theurgy was rediscovered by Marsilio Ficino (1433-1499), whose Platonic Academy helped engender the Italian Renaissance. More recently, Iamblichus' ideas have influenced the psychological theories and practices of C.G. Jung (1875-1961) and his followers.

References and Suggestions for Further Reading

Clarke, Emma C. *Iamblichus' De Mysteriis: A Manifesto of the Miraculous.* Aldershot: Ashgate, 2001.
Dillon, John M., *Iamblichi Chalcidensis in Platonis Dialogos Commentariorum Fragmenta.* Leiden: E.J. Brill, 1973. The introduction (in English!) is an excellent overview of his life, works, and philosophy.
Fowden, Garth. *The Egyptian Hermes: A Historical Approach to the Late Pagan Mind.* Rev. ed. Princeton: Princeton University Press, 1993. Chapters 5 and 6 are especially relevant to Iamblichus and theurgy.
Iamblichus. *Iamblichus On the Mysteries and Life of Pythagoras.* Transl. Taylor, Vol. XVII of the Thomas Taylor Series. Somerset: Prometheus Trust, 1999. Classic 19th century translation, now outdated.
Iamblichus. *Iamblichus on the Mysteries.* Text, translation, and notes by Clarke, E.C., J.M. Dillon, and J. Hershbell. Atlanta: Society for Biblical Literature, 2003, and Leiden: Brill, 2004. The newest translation, with Greek text, introduction, and notes.
Shaw, Gregory. *Theurgy and the Soul: The Neoplatonism of Iamblichus.* University Park: Pennsylvania State University Press, 1995.

Chapter 51

Anthony of Egypt
and The Desert Fathers

Louis Groarke

In the Hellenistic period, philosophy concerned itself mostly with practical wisdom and the cultivation of equanimity. Epicureans fled to their gardens, Stoics sequestered themselves in the inner citadel of their own minds, Skeptics sought refuge in the practised suspension of belief, but a group of early Christian stoics fled with equal haste to desert caves carved out of remote Egyptian mountains.

The Desert Fathers were a loosely organized group, comprised of both men and women, committed, not so much to a systematic or overly-precise interpretation of theology or philosophy, but to a spiritual path or way of life. Saint Anthony the Hermit (c. 251–356 AD) is generally recognized as the founder and inspiration for this movement of monastic piety and other-worldly asceticism that sent thousands of men and women into scattered regions of the inhospitable deserts of Egypt during the 4th and 5th centuries AD.

The most valuable source for information on Anthony is the biography of Athanasius which was written in Greek soon after the hermit's death. Translated into Latin by Evagrius of Antioch, the *Vita Antonii* (*Life of Anthony*) enjoyed tremendous popularity. The sayings of the more experienced anchorites were also collected by their followers and eventually written down, usually in Greek. These sundry Greek anthologies (the *Apophthegmata Patrum*) were then translated into Latin and included in the influential *Vitae Patrum*. The result was a vast compendium of spiritual advice, *bon mots* and anecdotes, not unlike Diogenes Laertius' *Lives of Eminent Philosophers*. Although primary source materials on Anthony and other desert ascetics do not respect modern standards of historical accuracy, they do provide vivid and informative commentary on the charismatic saint and the way of life adopted by his brethren.

Anthony is depicted as a *sophos* (wise man), an anchorite (from the Greek *anachorein*, to withdraw or leave), a saint, a humanitarian, a peace-maker, and an athlete in heroic labours of self-renunciation. He gives all his possessions to the poor, hides in seclusion, prays, is tempted by demons, keeps to a strict diet of bread, salt, and water, wears a single garment, sleeps on a mat or on bare ground, works with his hands, heals the sick, foretells the future, distributes alms, dispenses spiritual advice, mediates public disagreements and counsels emperors.

Unlike the erudite Augustine, Anthony is not an intellectual. He cannot even read or write. He does not study rhetoric or practise dialectic. He claims, however, that book learning is unessential, for the ultimate source of wisdom is inside us. It does not exist in books but in an intelligence which is prior to books and which—when properly tended—produces the keen insight that accompanies spiritual perfection.

Anthony comments: 'The Greeks leave home and traverse the sea to gain an education, but there is no need to leave home ... or to cross the sea for virtue. For the Lord has told us ... the kingdom of God is within you' (20). Anthony posits, as the goal of education, the cultivation of a spiritual morality. Like Socrates, he insists that 'we ought to devote all our time to the soul instead of the body' (45). He also hints at the existence of a natural law:

> Virtue exists when the soul maintains its intellectual part according to nature. It holds fast according to nature when it remains as it was made—and it was made beautiful and perfectly straight. (20)

Moral wisdom might not require book-learning but it does require purity, perseverance, and the elimination of distractions. The *Vita Antonii* does not depict the life of the hermit as a pastoral idyll. The recluse must struggle against temptations, frightful demons, lewd thoughts, flights of anger, laziness, pride, self-centredness and *akedia* (or melancholy). Yet Anthony emerges from this spiritual warfare refreshed, a picture of equanimity: his body, 'neither fat, ... nor emaciated'; his soul, 'not constricted by grief, nor relaxed by pleasure'. Unperturbed by either 'laughter or dejection', he is neither 'annoyed', nor 'elated'. He maintains, instead, 'utter equilibrium' (14). It is reported that during the rest of his life his soul 'was never troubled, ... his mind being joyous' (67).

Anthony represents a decisive turning away from merely speculative or theoretical knowledge. When Greek philosophers come to test his wisdom, he chides them for their reliance on syllogisms, asserting that faith is more important than discursive reason. For the believer, 'demonstration through arguments is unnecessary, or perhaps even useless' (77). What believers have 'is not skill with words, but faith through love that works for Christ' (80). Christians do not prove the truth of the Christian message 'in [the] plausible words of Greek wisdom but ... persuade by the faith that clearly precedes argumentation' (80).

The *Sayings of the Fathers* found in the *Vita Patrum* usually relate anonymous incidents from monastic life. The message is oblique or indirect, a kernel of spiritual wisdom that calls for meditation. It is communicated, not by proofs or technical commentary, but through the simplest, down-to earth stories. A monk says something insightful, struggles with a demon, acts in an edifying manner, or reports on a miracle. As the following saying demonstrates, some stories display real depth of feeling:

> An old man said: ' ... When I happened to be living in Oxyrhynchus (in Egypt) near a priest who gave alms to many, a widow came to ask him for some wheat. He said to her, 'Bring a sack and I will measure out some for you.' She brought it, and measuring the sack with his hand, he said, 'It is a big sack.' Now the widow was filled with shame. I said to him, 'Abba [or Father], have you sold the wheat?' He said, 'No, I gave it to her in charity.' I said to him, 'If you gave it to her in alms, why did you cavil about the amount and fill her with shame?' (150)

Despite the obvious emphasis on self-mortification and seclusion, the monks recognized the importance of good works. In another saying, an older monk gives a younger brother some no-nonsense spiritual advice:

> A brother questioned an old man saying, 'Here are   brothers. One leads a solitary life for six days a week, giving himself much pain, and the other serves the sick. Whose work does God accept with the greatest favor?' The old man said, 'Even if the one who withdraws for six days were to hang himself up by the nostrils, he could not equal the one who serves the sick.' (224)

At the heart of the desert ethos is an emphasis on humility and selflessness. One of the sayings tells the story of a surprise visit by the Emperor Theodosius the Younger to an Egyptian monk living in Constantinople. The old man welcomes the royal visitor and engages in spiritual conversation. He then prepares the Emperor a frugal meal of bread, oil, salt and water. The Emperor replies:

> Happy are you, for you do not have the cares of life. I was born in a palace and yet I have never enjoyed bread and water as I have today; I have eaten very well. (176)

The saying relates that the Emperor comes to honor the old man. Seeing this, the monk, afraid he will become conceited 'arose and fled again to Egypt'.

References and Suggestions for Further Reading

Athanasius. *The Life of Anthony and the Letter to Marcellinus.* Translated and introduced by Robert C. Gregg. New York: Paulist Press, 1980.
Ward, Benedicta. *The Wisdom of the Desert Fathers.* Fairacres, Oxford: SLG Press, 1986.

Chapter 52

Eusebius, Bishop of Caesarea

260–339 AD

Linos G. Benakis

Eusebius remained at heart a philosopher of the old school who was eager to use the teaching of the ancients to justify the results of the Triumph of the Cross. (Sir Steven Runciman. *Eusebius of Caesarea and the Christian Empire*, *Deucalion* 4)

Eusebius was a native of Caesarea in Palestine. Bishop of Caesarea from 312 onwards, following the end of the persecution and the edict of the four emperors, Eusebius was probably to have a greater influence on posterity than any of the other great 4th century Fathers of the Church.

Eusebius grew up and was educated in the shadow of the teaching and writings of the successors of Origen (the Christian philosopher of Alexandria, who died in 254), whose library he inherited. He was even more greatly influenced by Pamphilus, who was a pupil of Origen. Pamphilus, who had set up a school and substantial library of biblical interpretations in Caesarea, was killed due to his Christian beliefs in 310 AD. From 324 onwards, the Roman Emperor Constantine the Great, controlled both the western and eastern territories of the Roman Empire, and founded the city of Constantinople, the previous Byzantium. Eusebius embarked on a prolific writing career. His earliest work was a Chronicle preserved for us only in an Armenian translation and a few Greek fragments. This marked his first attempt to record, in a systematic manner, the growth of the Christian world and structure.

In 308–309, in collaboration with Pamphilus who was imprisoned at the time, Eusebius wrote the *Defence of Origen* (Book Six was written exclusively by Eusebius). This work was followed by a number of books in which he set out his Divine Providence-based arguments for the coming of Christianity, the defeat of paganism and God's plan of salvation for man. The philosophical nature of the works is clear from the term 'dialexis', lecture, which Eusebius uses in order to describe the Christian sermon.

The Christian Church was foretold by Jesus Christ and became a supreme and universal institution for mankind. Besides the divine origin of Christianity through revelation, Eusebius describes the historical fact of Divine Providence as confirmed through the incarnation of the Son of God, the event that marked the end of 'heathen error' and the 'diffused power of demons'.

Eusebius had already started sketching out the structure of his great *Ecclesiastical History*, which is far more than a simple account of the development of the Christian Church. The term 'history' has a very broad meaning and covers all kinds of material relating to the origin and destination of the Christian Church in the context of human history. As a result, the *Ecclesiastical History* expressed an attitude towards history that was new to the Classical world. The old Greek writers had seen history as a sequence of cycles. Eusebius saw Christianity and the Christian Church as the last and defining appearance of the Divine Word that had ruled the world from the beginning of time. Christian monotheism (belief in a single God) is identified by Eusebius with world civilization, and it is this that releases man from the squalor of idolatry and polytheism (belief in more than one god). In his scheme of things, the universal adoption of Christianity is the strongest evidence for the divine origin of the Christian faith.

As the first great Christian historian, Eusebius saw history as guided by the hand of God towards its final fulfillment. The conversion of the Emperor, Constantine, heralded the last great act of the drama. Judaic in origin, this conception of history was alien to the old Greek philosophical tradition. The Jewish philosopher, Philo of Alexandria, had shown that Rome had brought peace and unity to the world and so was a favoured instrument of God. Origen had adapted this argument to a larger, Christian agenda. God had sent his Son into the world, and now the triumph of history had come with the acceptance of the Christian message by the Roman Emperor.

But what precisely was the role of the Christian Emperor? The early Christians were ready to be good citizens, but only up to a point. If the laws of the Emperor clashed with the laws of their God, it was the latter that they were obliged to obey, even at the price of imprisonment and death. Once the Emperor became a Christian, this problem was theoretically removed. The Emperor's laws would surely now conform to the laws of God. But who was to decide what the laws of God were? Was it the Emperor, the earthly lawgiver, or the bishops of the Church, the heirs of the Apostles and guardians of the Faith? The question was urgent because at the time of the 'Triumph of the Cross' the Christians were divided by heresy. There had always been schisms in the Church. But a Church that is not sanctioned by the State and is liable to persecution cannot afford the luxury of emphasizing its divisions. The position changes when the Church becomes part of the establishment and, within a few decades, the official faith of the Empire. The conversion of Constantine, the emperor, was absolutely genuine.

According to Runciman (see references), Eusebius' understanding of the conversion of Constantine as a triumphant turning point in history compelled him to justify the divine viceroyalty of his hero. Given his own religious outlook that tended towards a Subordinationist view of the Trinity (the doctrine that the Second and Third Persons of the Trinity are inferior to the First Person) among Eusebius' non-standard Christian views of his time was his rejection of the notion of predestination, the view that all is predetermined by God, it was not hard for him to stretch his Subordinationism to include the Emperor as a sort of earthly emanation predestination, the view that all is predetermined by God, it was not hard for him to stretch his Subordinationism to include the Emperor as a sort of earthly emanation of the Trinity. It was, however, hard for him to find justification for this in either the Old or the New Testament. He thus had to look elsewhere for his philosophical arguments.

To the ancient Greeks the two great monarchies of the world had been Egypt and Persia. Both claimed divine origin for their monarchs. Eusebius seems to have been familiar with the writings of the Athenian philosophers, Isocrates and Aristotle, in which King Philip of Macedon and other kings are described as being the descendants of the Greek gods, Heracles or Zeus. In an anthology of philosophical treatises by John Stobaeus (5th century AD), a section of which was concerned with essays on kingship, most of these fragments are attributed to Pythagorean philosophers. They seem to reflect philosophical opinion about kingship at a period when the Hellenistic kingdoms were established (2nd – 1st centuries BC). We may wonder if Eusebius was familiar with these texts. He undoubtedly knew the works of the great theologian Clement of Alexandria and those of Philo. Both Philo and Clement discuss the role of the ideal ruler. Indeed, Philo puts the king into a special relationship, or kinship, with God, Whom he must imitate, thereby inducing order from chaos.

Eusebius dedicated two important works to Constantine the Great. The first, *In Praise of Constantine* is a grand oration that he delivered on the thirteenth anniversary of Constantine's accession to the Empire, in which are given Eusebius' views on the monarchy. Behind the adulation there is here a genuine wish to work out a philosophical theory for the Christians. Eusebius avoids the problem of the Emperor's relationship with the law, feeling, presumably, that to stress his status as the living embodiment of law, was alien to Roman tradition. Indeed, the somewhat illogical notion that the Emperor was at one and the same time the source of law and also under the law persisted into Byzantine times and was never quite abandoned. Eusebius' second work devoted to Constantine is his *Life of Constantine*, the popularity of which was immense. The Eusebian notion of Christian kingship remained the fundamental theory of Byzantium for as long as the Emperors reigned at Constantinople up to 1453.

References and Suggestions for Further Reading

Barnes, T. *Constantine and Eusebius*. Harvard UP, 1981.

Baynes, N.H. 'Eusebius and the Christian Empire' (1925). In *Byzantine Studies and other Essays*. London: 1955.

Eusebius. *Life of Constantine*. Translated with Introduction and Commentary by Averil Cameron and Stuart G. Hall. Oxford: Clarendon Ancient History Series, 1999.

Grant, R.M. *Eusebius as Church Historian*. Oxford: 1980.

Runciman, S. *Eusebius of Caesarea and the Christian Empire*. Athens: 1975.

Chapter 53

Hypatia of Alexandria

355 AD–422 AD

Virginia Haddad

Reserve your right to think, for even to think wrongly is better than not to think at all.
(Hypatia of Alexandria in Ada Adler's *Suidae Lexicon* (Stuttgart: Teubner, 1971), Volume 4, p. 664)

As if being recorded history's first female astronomer and mathematician were not interesting enough, Hypatia possessed a dynamic personality that was legendary and a riveting, ultimately tragic, biography. She was the most charismatic teacher and woman ever to have graced Alexandria; an Eva Peron of antiquity.

Hypatia was born in and spent most of her life in Alexandria, the cultural centre of her time. She persuaded her father to send her to study in Athens where she was awarded a laurel wreath for her outstanding scholastic achievements. She continued to wear her cherished wreath when she returned to Alexandria and appeared in public.

Hypatia's Alexandria, population perhaps a hundred thousand, was the world's mecca of learning. It prominently featured the fabulous 135 metre (440 feet) Pharos lighthouse (completed c. 270 BC), one of the Seven Great Wonders of the World whose mirror reflected sunlight like a forerunner of a laser in daytime and in which a small fire, reflected in its mirror at night beamed some 50 kilometres (35 miles) offshore. The crown of the city, however, was the Mouseion, the spectacular Alexandrian library where Hypatia's father, Theon, a philosopher, mathematician, and scholar, was its last head.

Despite such a level of civilization, Hypatia's Alexandria was a society facing both a growing multi-ethnic unrest and an ideological transition from diverse pagan and philosophical cults to Christianity.

Unfortunately, it is not possible to compose a definitive account of Hypatia's life and thought because only fragments of few primary sources are left and other sources not only occasionally contradict each other, but sometimes even self-contradict! All of her own work is lost except for titles and references to her writings on mathematics and astronomy. At about 400 AD Hypatia became the head of the Platonist school of Alexandria where she lectured on mathematics and philosophy. Her specialization was in neo-Platonism. Neo-Platonism was inspired by classic Greek thought, particularly the philosophy of Plato, but developed in Egypt where, not surprisingly, it became infused with Oriental mysticism. Hypatia taught a more reason-oriented neo-Platonism. Platonism held that there is a division between the material and non-material world and that the latter was far superior. According to Plotinus (205–270 AD), founder of neo-Platonism, true reality is found in the Infinite, the Absolute—God. His attributes are Good and One. God transcends even thought and mind. God is good; goodness, like light, diffuses itself. Thus, there are categories of his diffusion: intellect, world-soul, and so on until the final degradation, matter. As such, matter is Darkness, the antithesis of God. Where there is darkness, there is unreality.

To a neo-Platonist, one's soul is an emanation of God that existed before birth and will return to God upon death, the ultimate release from the material world. By birth, a person is rendered part spirit, part matter, but it is his or her goal to return to God by distancing oneself from all that is material because matter is illusory and separates us from God. The first step is to shed the chains of the senses, especially to withdraw from feelings that pull us toward the material. As one matures along this path, the intervention of God's light will lead the soul to an ecstatic union with the Divine.

Data conflicts regarding Hypatia's marital status, but leans toward her remaining unmarried. It should come as no great surprise if this woman of profound neo-Platonist convictions remained romantically uninvolved and bore little interest in pursuing inclinations of the heart or flesh. An oft repeated anecdote is that Hypatia, whose beauty was said to be as great as her intelligence, once brazenly shattered a young student's infatuation with her by showing him her bloodied menstrual rags. 'This is what you really love, young man, but you do not love beauty for its own sake!' (Dzieska, 50).

The ethnic and religious diversity of Alexandria with its impact on the economic and political climate was complex and confrontational, yet by no means always at odds. Nevertheless, as Alexandria reached a critical stage and as a citizen of civic engagement, Hypatia did not step back from what amounted to a clash of ideology, greed, and ego around her. Antagonism existed between the native Egyptians of the city and the Roman and Greeks who were condescendingly regarded as Alexandrians by adoption. Jews, Greeks, Romans, Egyptians, and the embryonic Christian community each at various times became victimizers and victims who sandbagged their resentments until a provoking incident broke through and flooded the streets with another cycle of violence.

Christians gradually proliferated, but it was through the ascension of Alexandria's Bishop Cyril (c. 375–444 AD) that the score was set to be settled once and for all. Jews were expelled from the city, churches of heretic Christians were closed, and pagans were targeted in bitter denunciations.

As a philosophy, neo-Platonism posed no real threat to Christianity. In many ways it was congruent with, and was later even baptized into some articulations of Christian beliefs. A great many of Hypatia's students were in fact Christians; some became quite prominent as did her most famous student, Synesius, Bishop of Ptolemais (c. 375–414 AD) whose preserved letters to Hypatia demonstrate his great respect and admiration for his former teacher. Much of what we know of Hypatia comes to us through his letters.

Though she did not hold political office, Hypatia fell more in line with Plato's philosopher king than a proverbial ivory tower philosopher. As a civic leader, Hypatia befriended and advised Orestes, the Roman prefect of Alexandria, toward whom Cyril bore anger for torturing and executing a monk—in addition to their obvious and bitter political rivalry. Moreover, Cyril saw philosophy as a pagan remnant whose time was overspent. Lastly, the deadly sin of envy was undoubtedly astir as Hypatia drew throngs of adoring Alexandrians tossing flowers before her chariot as she travelled along the streets.

Then like gasoline on a fire, accusations of witchcraft detonated: according to Bishop John of Nikiu:

> ... she was devoted at all times to magic, astrolabes and instruments of music, and she beguiled many people through (her) Satanic wiles. And the governor of the city honored her exceedingly; for she had beguiled him through her magic. (John, Bishop of Nikiu, *Chronicle* 84.87-103)

Her life came to its unspeakably gruesome end when a sect of fanatical desert monks accosted Hypatia on the street one March day, stripped and dragged her into a church, skinned her alive with oyster shells, then dismembered and burned her body.

Although there is no evidence that Cyril ordered Hypatia's death, church historian Socrates Scholasticus (c. 380–450: no relation to the philosopher of Athens!) declared that Hypatia's murder brought great disgrace to Cyril and the church of Alexandria. He wrote of Hypatia 'Wherefore she had great spite and envy owed unto her and because she conferred and had great formality with Orestes, the people charged her ...' (Socrates Scholasticus quoted in Fideler, Book VII, 382).

Yet centuries later, the public is still tossing garlands before Hypatia: she has been featured in the writings of Gibbon, Voltaire, and Carl Sagan; titles of two feminist journals bear her name; two lunar landmarks were named after her—Crater Hypatia and Rimae Hypatia—as well as several college buildings.

And though the great Lighthouse of Pharos has for centuries lain crumbled beneath the Mediterranean, the light from this prominent fixture of ancient Alexandria has continued to illuminate through many long dark miles of human history.

References and Suggestions for Further Reading

Dzieska, Maria. *Hypatia of Alexandria*. Cambridge, Massachusetts: Harvard University Press, 1995.

Fideler, David, editor. *Alexandria 2: Cosmology, Philosophy, Myth, and Culture*. Grand Rapids, Michigan: Phanes Press, 1994.

Hass, Christopher. *Alexandria in Late Antiquity: Topography and Social Conflict*. Baltimore and London: Johns Hopkins University Press, 1997.

Marlowe, John. *The Golden Age of Alexandria*. London: Victor Gollancz Limited, 1971.

Reedy, Jeremiah (translator). *Alexandria 2*, David Fedeler (ed.) Grand Rapids, Michigan: Phanes Press, 1993. In 'The Life of Hypatia from Damascius's *Life of Isidore*, reproduced in *The Suda*', accessed January 5, 2004.
http://www.cosmopolis.com/alexandria/hypatia-bio-suda.html

Chapter 54

Proclus

411 or 412 AD–485 AD

Dirk Baltzly

My soul has come, breathing the might of fire,
And, opening the mind, to the aether in a fiery whirl
It rises, and clamours immortally for the starry orbits. (Marinus, *Life of Proclus,* Ch.
28, trans. M. Edwards)

Proclus' biographer, Marinus, tells us that in Proclus' fortieth year he awoke from
an inspired dream shouting aloud these verses. They show us one side of this
prolific writer's mind—that of the god-intoxicated enthusiast for all forms of
pagan religious belief. But Proclus is also the author of the *Elements of Theology*,
a work of 211 numbered propositions, each followed by a proof, that articulates
the metaphysical framework of late neo-Platonism. We moderns might suppose
that this combination is an odd one, but Proclus would not have. His philosophy
and life were a systematic attempt to synthesize non-Christian Greek religious
practices with his understanding of Platonic and Pythagorean philosophy. For him,
philosophy and religion were not separate activities but rather different
manifestations of the soul's quest for a return to its natural home among the divine
stars.

Proclus' father was a lawyer at the imperial court from the town of Xanthus
in Lycia. The parents, Patricius and Marcella, returned to Lycia shortly after the
birth. This may have been because they were 'Hellenes'—or 'pagans' to the
Christians—and a law had been passed in 415 expelling pagans from imperial
service and the army. Though it was intended that he should follow his father into
the law, the gods intervened. While studying rhetoric in Alexandria, Proclus had a
dream in which the goddess Athena urged him to turn all his energies to the pursuit
of philosophy. He moved from Alexandria, where he had been studying rhetoric,
to Athens and became a pupil of the neo-Platonist philosopher Syrianus. As nearly
as we can tell, this move marked a complete break with his old life and for all
intents and purposes, Syrianus became his new father as well as teacher. Indeed,
after Proclus' own death, he was buried in the same tomb with his master.

Proclus was such an exceptional student that he worked through the neo-
Platonic sequence of studies in record time. After the death of Syrianus, he became
head or *Diadochos* of the neo-Platonist school when he was twenty-five years old.
In this capacity, he lectured to students (sometimes five lectures in a day), wrote

extensively (700 lines a day Marinus tells us!), and administered the school. In addition to this, he celebrated nearly every form of religious belief available to cosmopolitan Hellenes: the rites of Cybele, Egyptian forms of worship, Chaldean or Babylonian rites, Orphic purifications, as well as the rituals of ancient Athens. He was particularly attached to the cult of the healing god Asclepius. He fasted on holy days, largely refrained from meat, and abstained from sexual contact of any kind. It seems likely that on at least one occasion his devotion to pagan religious belief may have placed him in a delicate political position. He left Athens for a year to travel to Lydia. This afforded him the opportunity of being initiated into the religious mysteries practised in that region, but his biographer hints that his only hiatus from Athens was prompted by darker forces. Some scholars speculate that it may have been his opposition to the conversion of the temple of Asclepius to a Christian place of worship.

Proclus' writings can be divided into roughly three sorts. First we have some of the commentaries that he wrote on the dialogues of Plato. These analyze the dialogues almost line by line and would have formed the basis of Proclus' lectures in the neo-Platonic school. Far from being concerned solely with Plato, the commentaries aim to show that Plato's writings hint at, or are at least consonant with, all other sources of philosophical and religious wisdom—whether it be the more philosophical works of the pre-Socratics and Aristotle or the more revelatory Orphic poems and the so-called Chaldean Oracles of the second century Julian the Chaldean or his son Julian the Theurgist. (Proclus also wrote a commentary on this very abstruse work, but it survives only in fragments.)

In addition to commentaries on Plato's works, Proclus was the author of several monographs. Perhaps the most well-known of Proclus works is the *Elements of Theology* which attempts to demonstrate the most basic principles of neo-Platonic metaphysics in the geometric style of Euclid's *Elements*. Another equally rigorous work by Proclus is his *Eighteen arguments on the eternity of the world*, sometimes known by the sub-title 'Against the Christians'. Finally, Proclus also wrote hymns or prayers to the gods, a small selection of which survive.

Proclus' philosophy is a detailed elaboration of a hierarchically ordered metaphysics like the one found in the work of Plotinus. The font of all things is an utterly simple and ultra-transcendent principle of unity called 'The One'. This much is common to Plotinus. However in the details of the One's unfolding of the rest of reality, Proclus complicates and corrects Plotinus' picture of things. No summary can do justice to the richness of Proclus' conception, but an initial metaphysical consequence of the One is Intellect or intelligible reality. This is a *bit* like Plato's realm of Forms, except that for the neo-Platonists, each Form is itself a living, thinking intellect. For Proclus—though not so clearly for Plotinus—this realm of Intellect is itself hierarchically structured. The next 'layer' in the metaphysical picture is Soul and this category encompasses both individual human souls, as well as more exalted souls like those of the heavenly bodies and, indeed, of the entire physical cosmos. Finally, there is the matter of the sensible world itself.

A problem presents itself when we consider the differences between the layers in this metaphysics. How can the One, which is utterly transcendent and simple, give rise to something which is so different?—Intellect involves a kind of duality between thinking and being thought of, for example. Proclus' general answer to this worry is to suppose that in between any two entities which seem opposed to one another in some sort of fundamental way, there is an intermediate entity which somehow incorporates both aspects of the opposition. So, for example, between the One and Intellect he supposes some intermediate entities called *henads* or 'one-lets' which are individually totally unitary but collectively more than one in number. Applying this axiom to the layered conception of reality generates a picture of this reality as a continuous and unbroken 'great chain of being' that stretches from the most supreme god, through various orders of divinities, down to the most basic of physical elements like fire or water. Each link in this chain is both a reflection of previous links and a pattern or paradigm for subsequent ones. This is true of us too, as our own souls are links in the chain. There is within each of us an image of all those gods higher than us and, if we know ourselves well enough, we can join with the gods in ordering and administering the physical cosmos that is subordinate to us.

Proclus' religious beliefs go hand in hand with his charting of the links in this chain. His massive *Platonic Theology* attempts to locate the manifestations of various Greek gods at different levels of reality. Religious practice and philosophy are not divorced: metaphysics locates the links in the chains and thus shows us to whom and in what order we pray. Prayer and religious ritual provide important clues for the articulation of and identification of the reality above us. Philosophical investigation and worship are but two sides of one and the same coin—the philosophical life.

The school of which Proclus was the head did not survive long after his death. He was succeeded by Marinus and then by Damascius in 515. In 529 the emperor Justinian purged all remaining non-Christians from imperial offices and forbade all public teaching by pagans. Damascius and the remaining members of the neo-Platonic school left Athens for somewhere in Asia Minor. The last great writer in this school was Simplicius. He may have returned to Athens and kept a low profile, or he may have remained at Harran in present-day Syria.

But if Proclus' school was suppressed his influence on western philosophy was heightened because of the way in which his works were appropriated and misidentified subsequently. In the 6th century some unknown author composed a series of works heavily indebted to Proclus' metaphysics but which substitutes for his pagan gods biblical Seraphim and Cherubim. These works were subsequently believed to be the philosophy of Dionysius the Aeropagite—the disciple of St Paul in Athens. They had a huge impact on Christian mysticism through medieval authors such as John Scotus Erigena in the Latin west and Maximus the Confessor in Byzantium. Arabic philosophy was influenced by Proclus as well. A compendium of some of Plotinus' works and Proclus' *Elements* appeared in Arabic under the title *The Book of Causes* and was attributed to *Aristotle*! This work was eventually translated into Latin and became known in the West as the *Liber de Causis*. Finally, Proclus has a long history in the occult tradition. This stems from his engagement with works such as the Chaldean Oracles, as well as his interest in forms of ritual magic as evidenced in his work *On the priestly art: sacrifice and magic*.

There are two sites in Athens with which Proclus is associated. His biographer records that he was buried with Syrianus on the hill of Lycabettus which you can see to your northeast if you are standing on the Acropolis. Near the temple of Asclepius on the southern side of the Acropolis is a large structure that some archaeologists believe to be the house used by Syrianus, Proclus and the members of the neo-Platonic school. It is a large building—32 metres across at least—and contains many items of pagan worship.

References and Suggestions for Further Reading

Dodds, E.R. *Proclus: The Elements of Theology*. Oxford: 1963.

Edwards, Mark. *Neoplatonic Saints: the live of Plotinus and Proclus by their students*. Liverpool: 2000.

Morrow, G. and J. Dillon, *Proclus' Commentary on Plato's Parmenides*. Princeton: 1987.

Siorvanes, Lucas. *Proclus: neoplatonic philosophy and science*. London: 1996.

Travlos, J. *Pictorial History of Ancient Athens*. New York: 1980. pp. 127–138.

Chapter 55

John Philoponus

c. 490–575 AD

Antonia Kakavelaki

John Philoponus was an Alexandrian polymath (a person with broad knowledge of many subjects), one of the most outstanding and original thinkers of the Neo-Platonic school of Ammonius, c. 440–520 AD, who was the student of Hermeias, and a well known theologian. Unfortunately the extant (still existing) sources concerning his biography are very poor and in order to fill in this lack of information, recent scholars propose a number of possibilities.

The literal meaning of the sobriquet *Philoponus* is 'lover of work', and it was a name given to the most industrious scholars in antiquity. Some scholars have suggested that it may also refer to the Alexandrian guilds of *philoponoi*—a community of very committed Christian lay workers.

He is also known as John *grammatikos*, the grammarian. Two grammatical works of his are still extant, and Simplicius, another student of Ammonius, informs us that John himself used the name, John grammatikos, so we may conclude that he was a professional grammarian at Alexandria.

Another question debated among researchers is whether he was born Christian or converted during his lifetime. His name, being Christian, suggests the first proposition, but his work poses a problem: His earlier texts stay close to the pagan philosophical teaching of his teacher Ammonius, whereas the later ones offer strong verbal support of the Christian beliefs, and against the neo-Platonist views he had defended in his previous works. This contradiction made some researchers distinguish distinct pagan and Christian periods in Philoponus' life. However, keeping in mind that the works written during the first period of his career are, as their titles suggest, composed from notes taken during his professor's classes, one can conclude that in these Philoponus is not expressing his personal beliefs.

The works of Philoponus available today are primarily commentaries on Aristotle's works. When Philoponus was studying and teaching, the 'commentary' was the main work undertaken by philosophers. The scholars developed and taught their philosophy by composing commentaries on the texts of Plato and Aristotle, who were considered as 'authorities of truth'. These commentaries were mainly written either as textbooks for the philosophical courses of the professor or, during the course, by students responsible for taking notes of the lessons. Philosophical training began with the study of Aristotle (first logic, then physics, then metaphysics), and then the study of the works of Plato. The commentator's goal was first, to prove that Plato and Aristotle are in agreement, and then, that the thought of all the eminent ancient philosophers—including the distinguished poets such as Homer and Hesiod—is in harmony. All great minds were said to be inspired by the divine, truth was considered as mystical revelation accorded by the divine realm—that is, the gods—to those who have purified their soul by virtuous life and their mind by intellectual exercise, and precisely, the act of commenting on 'inspired' texts, was considered a spiritual exercise.

Philoponus was the first to question this assumption of harmony of Plato and Aristotle and to reject it. In his later works he openly criticizes aspects of Aristotle's and Plato's theories. He claims that the agreement that his contemporary philosophers try to prove existed between Aristotle and Plato is quite false. He treats these two 'authorities', Plato and Aristotle, as fallible; they could be wrong. This skepticism was probably due to the fact that, being a Christian, John was ideologically detached from his pagan background.

As a pupil of Ammonius, John was responsible for recording his teachers' lectures on a number of Aristotle's works: *On Generation and Corruption; On the Soul; Prior Analytics*; and *Posterior Analytics*. These commentaries state explicitly in their titles that they are based on Ammonius' seminars. Evidence suggests that Philoponus was, himself, teaching the courses on Aristotle's *Categories*, *Physics*, and *Meteorology*, and writing commentaries, having presumably taken over as lecturer from Ammonius.

The works in which Philoponus professes his own ideas are: *the Physics commentary* (whose most important achievement is an innovative theory of impetus which is a decisive step away from an Aristotelian dynamics towards a modern theory based on the notion of inertia—a theory which ties in with criticisms of other Aristotelian principles of physics such as Space, Place and Matter); *the commentary on the Meteorology* (where he abandons the Aristotelian assumption of an immutable and divine celestial fifth element (called aether) and argues that light and heat must be rather explained as consequences of the nature of the sun, which is fire); two critical treatises *On the Eternity of the world against Proclus* (which is a detailed criticism of a work written by the Athenian neo-Platonist, Proclus (c. 411–485)—who was Ammonius' teacher—in which Proclus defended the pagan Greek belief in the eternity of the world. His work, *On the eternity of the world against Aristotle* involves a close examination of the first chapters of Aristotle's *On the Heavens*. In the eighth book on *Physics* he argues for the eternity of time and motion. John aims there to remove obstacles for the Christian doctrine of the divine 'creation' of the world, and if time and motion are eternal, any belief in creation of the world would be unwarranted. To prove this, he points to numerous inconsistencies and improbable assumptions in Aristotle's philosophy of nature.

Although Philoponus presumably took over as lecturer from Ammonius, he most probably never held the chair of philosophy. After his professor's death the Alexandrian's philosophical school's leadership seems to have passed to a mathematician, Eutochius, and then on to another philosopher, Olympiodorus (495–570).

By the end of 530 Philoponus had stopped producing philosophical works and concentrated on writing theological topics: '*On the creation of the world*', his only theological work extant (still existing) in Greek, was a commentary on the creation story told in the Bible. His inspiration came from the creation theories expressed by St. Basil the Great, who refers frequently to philosophers while discussing the Bible.

Philoponus suggests that the movement of the heavens could be explained as a force impressed on the celestial bodies by God at the time of creation, and he applies the theory of the regular and natural motions of the universe in the way he had developed in his past philosophical works.

The later theological treatises of Philoponus are essentially a mixture of Christian and Aristotelian doctrines: By the time of the fifth church Council at Constantinople (553) he was a follower of 'monophysite' Christology—a theological movement very influential in the eastern part of the Roman empire, which emphasized the divinity of Christ—that is, Jesus was considered one of the holy trinity, God incarnated. At that time, John composed a treatise called '*Arbitrator*' or Umpire (extant only in a Syrian translation), proposing a new interpretation of the traditional Christological formulas by means of philosophical ideas based on Aristotle's *Categories*.

Later, he professed a doctrine of three separate divinities, Father, Son and Holy Spirit, pointing out that, unlike the individually differentiated gods of the pagans, these three divinities are all of the same single divine nature. This last theory faced immediate and severe criticism and, in 680–681 AD, Philoponus was condemned by the council of Constantinople.

Finally, Philoponus was in the unfortunate position of being disliked both by pagan philosophers and by Christian theologians—of whom the former resented his upsetting the harmony of their philosophical system by means of his Christian convictions, the latter condemning his attempt to understand the mystery of the Holy Trinity by means of philosophical notions.

His condemnation by the council made the spread of his theological ideas impossible. On the other hand, Simplicius, in his commentaries on Aristotle's *De Caelo* (*On the Heavens*) and on the *Physics* submitted John's theories to very severe criticism which passed through the ages and made later thinkers such as Thomas Aquinas and Zarabella (1533–1589), and the Arabic scholars underestimate Philoponus' work altogether. By contrast, in Byzantium, his philosophical work was highly esteemed, and studied throughout the years, and intellectuals such as Psellos (1018–1078) claimed that in his dispute with Simplicius, Philoponus emerged as the clear winner.

Eventually, John's theories were adopted by many prominent theologians, and philosophers from Bonaventure (1217–1274) through to the scientist Galileo Galilei (1564–1642). Bonaventura was persuaded by John's arguments against the eternity of the world, and Galileo adopted John's impetus theory, after having discussed and being convinced by the criticism of Aristotelian dynamics in Philoponus' *Physics* commentary.

References and Suggestions for Further Reading

Sorabji, R.R.K., editor. *Philoponus and the rejection of Aristotelian Science*. London: Duckworth, 1987.

Sorabji, R.R.K., editor. *Aristotle transformed*. London: Duckworth, 1990.

Wildberg, C. *John Philoponus' Criticism of Aristotle's Theory of Aether*. Berlin: De Gruyter, 1988.

Chapter 56

The Closure of the Academy of Athens

George Arabatzis

Some philosophical facts surpass the sheer exposition and analysis of ideas and doctrines; Socrates' trial, for instance, or Spinoza's excommunication. Such an event of the utmost importance is the closure of the Academy of Athens in 529 AD by the Christian Byzantine emperor Justinian. In that closure, according to the words of the historian Edward Gibbon who, writing between 1776–1788, described the *Decline and Fall of the Roman Empire*, certain minds foresaw a sign of 'the triumph of religion and barbarism' over reason and philosophy. The order to cease the educational functions of the Academy, originally established by Plato himself, had been seen by some as an act from a controversial drama between faith and reason that led to a thousand years of medieval lowering of philosophy, thus becoming the 'servant of theology'; to others like Gibbon himself, the closing of the Academy was not an assassination—rather it was euthanasia since the ancient glamour of the institution had been far diminished and was continually losing ground because of the constant advances of Christianity. Today this picture is somehow less black and white and this concerns the autonomous value of medieval thinking as well as the closing of the Academy of Athens itself. While some scholars insist on the definitive character of Justinian's action and on the rupture that it provoked in the philosophical tradition, others doubt the effectiveness of the imperial measures and even the closure itself. The existing evidence is rather thin: we have direct knowledge of numerous legal actions taken by Justinian against the Pagans but only John Malalas, a Byzantine chronographer, speaks of an imperial edict against the Academy:

> During the consulship of Decius, the emperor [Justinian] issued an edict and sent it to Athens ordering that no one should teach philosophy, nor interpret the laws ... (John Malalas, *Chronographia*, 451; Jeffreys, *Chronicle,* 264)

Another Byzantine source allows us to think of both a temporary, and a definitive, closure of the Academy: the historian Agathias writes that neo-Platonic philosophers were forced to leave Athens and find refuge in the Court of the Persian king Chosroes. The seven philosophers who fled the Byzantine Empire were Damascius the Syrian, Simplicius the Cilician, Eulamius (or Eulalius) the Phrygian, Priscianus the Lydian, Hermias and Diogenes, both from Phoenicia and Isidore of Gaza. Very soon, their dreams about the Persian court, according to Agathias, were proven naïve and utopian and the philosophers tasted a bitter disappointment.

Chosroes, however, permitted them to return to their homeland and live with no fear or abjuration of their philosophical beliefs. He accomplished that by introducing a special clause in a peace treaty concluded with emperor Justinian in 532. The philosophers would live henceforth, according to the text, with no fear and '*eph'heautois*'; the interpretations of this Greek term given by the specialists are divided. Does it mean 'back to their business', that is, working as philosophical teachers? Or, does it mean 'in privacy', that is to say away from philosophical activity? The choice between these interpretations equals a different understanding of the Byzantine authorities' resolution to keep the pagan Academy closed. Doubts also exist about the locality where the philosophers were installed after returning to Byzantine lands. Was it Athens or Alexandria? Was it some other city in Asia Minor? The answers to all these questions, if we ever could obtain them, would have serious and heavy consequences on the history of philosophy in the times of the Christian Empire.

Alan Cameron, in a well-known paper, supports the view that Justinian's edict was never fully enforced and that the philosophers, mainly Simplicius, returned to Athens and resumed their teaching activities. He convincingly argues that the philosophers left for Persia only late in 531 AD since it is only then that Chosroes became king. Consequently, there was no persecution of the philosophers in 529. On the basis of a remark by Olympiodorus concerning funds of the Academy, Cameron claims that the School was still working until the 560s, and the event that really put an end to the Academy's activities was the sack of Athens by the Slavs in 579 AD. H.J. Blumenthal criticized, among other things, Cameron's interpretation of Olympiodorus' remark. I. Hadot advanced the view that Simplicius chose to stay in a city in Asia Minor, probably situated in Cilicia, his homeland, and certainly did not return to Athens and did not teach at a re-opened Academy. The fact that Simplicius' later commentaries have the style of research material rather than that of teaching notes supports the position that he never resumed his activity as professor of philosophy. R. Sorabji commented on Cameron in favour of the view that the School was finally closed and that Justinian's edict was made effective. Blumenthal, after considering all the evidence, concluded that one way or another Justinian's edict affected the School, that the philosophers for that reason had to leave and that the Academy's reopening or Simplicius' return to Athens after 532 is only hypothetical.

Some archaeological evidence is now available, but like the whole of the written testimonia, it is not conclusive. Excavations in Athens have brought to light two constructions each of which could have housed the School. The first, described by J. Miliades, and situated at the Northeast of the theatre of Herodus Atticus (which abuts the Athenian Acropolis), is said to be the house of Plutarch, later used by Syrianus and Proclus as the seat of the Academy. The second, found by the archaeologists of the American Archaeological School, is in the south of the Ancient Agora, and appears as though it was used for educational purposes. Statues were found there, placed down a well. Some other statues, not removed from their original position, were found damaged. In the whole, the picture of this second house is that of Christians taking over the place and damaging the pagan statues that were not hidden. The statues found in the well lead us to assume that the house was never recovered by its owners. Was this second construction that of the School, abruptly closed in the aftermath of Justinian's edict? Or, perhaps the School was situated in the first house that carries no sign of sudden dramatic transformation and wherein the Academy's activities could carry on well after 529? The answer is a subjective choice.

In any case, what we have here is in fact a chapter in the history of the most philosophical city ever. When Synesius visited Athens, in the beginning of the 5th century AD, he wrote that he found only the 'husk' of its former intellectual life. Yet, many centuries later, the legend of the Athenian philosophy still remains strong: we see scholars from 'barbarian' Northern Europe claiming with pride that they have studied philosophy in 'Great Athens', and that at a time when the flame of Athenian philosophy had long been extinguished.

References and Suggestions for Further Reading

Blumenthal, H.J. '529 and its Sequel: What Happened to the Academy?' *Byzantion*, 48/2 (1978), 369-385.

Cameron, Alan. 'The Last Days of the Academy of Athens'. *Proceedings of the Cambridge Philological Society*, n.s. 15 (1969), 7-29.

Frantz, Alison. 'Pagan Philosophers in Christian Athens'. *Proceedings of the American Philosophical Society*, 119 (1975), 29-38.

Hadot, Ilsetraut. *Le problème du néoplatonisme Alexandrin: Hiéroclès et Simplicius*. Paris, 1978, 33-34.

Hällström, Gunnar af. 'The Closing of the Neoplatonic School in A.D. 529: An Additional Aspect'. *Papers and Monographs of the Finnish Institute at Athens, I: Post Herulian Athens*, (1994), 141-160.

Jeffreys, E., M. Jeffreys and R. Scott, Trans. 'The Chronicle of John Malalas'. Melbourne, 1986, *Byzantina Australiensia* 4, p. 264).

Malalas, John. *Chronographia*, ed. L. Dindorf. Bonn: 1831.

Miliades, J. Ανασκαφαί νοτίως της Ακροπόλεως, *Πρακτικά της Αρχαιολογικής Εταιρείας*, 1955 (Athens 1960), 47-50.

Sorabji, Richard. *Time, Creation and the Continuum*. London: Duckworth, 1983, 199-200.

PART VII
ARCHAEOLOGICAL SITES

Chapter 57

The Athenian Acropolis

Evanthia Speliotis

... it is necessary to found the city in the center of the country as nearly as possible, choosing a place that has all the other provisions necessary for the city, which it is in no way difficult to conceive of nor to name. After this, it is necessary to divide off twelve parts—when one has first set aside a holy place for Hestia, Zeus, and Athena, calling it the 'acropolis', and enclosing it in a circle—and starting from the twelve parts, to divide up the city and the entire country ... . (Plato, *Laws* V.745b-c)

As the highest point of a city, an acropolis automatically draws the eye. When situated by nature in the middle of a plain, it provides a central point from which the city can radiate out, like spokes from a wheel (Herodotus, *Histories*, 7.140). To make this highest, central point the home of the gods is to place the gods always at the center of the city both literally and symbolically. To conclude the city's sacred festivals at the acropolis is to weave this symbolic home of the gods into the fabric of civic life. The pomp, the ceremony, the *ascent,* all serve to raise the human beings' minds above their mundane and political affairs, toward the divine. Thus it was with the Athenian acropolis.

The Athenian acropolis is a rock that stands about 156m (514ft) above sea level at its highest point, 270m (885ft) long, and 156m wide (Hurwit, p. 4). It is situated in the middle of a plain surrounded by mountains on three sides, and the sea on a fourth. Inhabited at least since Mycenaean times (1600–1065 BC) during which it most likely served as a citadel—stronghold and domicile of the royal family (Hurwit, Ch. 4)—the acropolis evolved into a centre for the worship of Athena, the patron goddess of the city. Already by Homer's day, the acropolis is referred to as the home of Erechtheus and Athena (*Iliad,* 2.546-52, *Odyssey,* 7.78.81). As Athens started to flourish politically from the 7th century BC onward, the acropolis grew increasingly in activity and importance as well. Several versions of a temple to Athena Polias (the goddess Athena, guardian of the city) housing an olive wood statue of the goddess were constructed; the processions and ceremonies of the Panathenaic Festival (an annual celebration dedicated to Athena,) were planned so that they culminated atop the acropolis; and great numbers of statues and votive offerings from the 7th and 6th centuries have been found. There was a hiatus in the building activity after the Persians burnt down the still unfinished temple to Athena built on the site of the current Parthenon in 480 BC, because the Athenians opted to keep the burnt remains as a memorial rather than to begin building anew. From the time of Pericles' rise to power (roughly 449–429 BC, see Hurwit, Ch. 8), however, building on the acropolis was resumed with new fervour, and produced the most magnificent and spectacular focal point for the city ever.

So grand was the Periclean building programme that Thucydides says of Athens: 'one would conjecture from what met the eye that the city had been twice as powerful as it in fact was' (Thucydides, *The History of the Peloponnesian War*, 1.10). While the number and size of the acropolis' monuments might overstate Athens' power, they are a testament, even in ruins as we find them today, to Athens' culture, spirit, hopes, and greatness in the 5th century BC.

The most remarkable aspect of the Periclean building project on the acropolis was neither the number of new buildings it sought to construct, nor the numbers of people it involved, nor the cost, nor even the grandeur it finally achieved. Rather, the most remarkable and novel aspect was its aim. The architecture and statuary were magnificent. The art and architecture, however, were not created for their own sake, merely to showcase the talent of the artisan, to conform to the standards of the day, nor even simply to pay homage to the goddess Athena. They were created with the goal of appearing beautiful to the spectators, and thereby eliciting an appreciation and reverence for what the art represented and glorified. Thus, for example, while the Parthenon is immediately notable for its size (it is the largest building atop the acropolis), it is more noteworthy for the innovations it embodied: The long side of columns (17 on the sides, 8 at the ends) stood taller at the middle of the row than at the ends; each column was wider in the middle than at either end; and all the columns inclined inward slightly, so that if you followed through on the inclination, they would meet and form a pyramid about 1½ miles up in the air. The purpose of all this? So that the lines of the Parthenon would appear correct and beautiful. The size and location of the temple were such that, if it were drawn 'straight', that is, true to an objective set of proportions, it would appear less beautiful to the observer. By introducing these artistic and architectural irregularities, the artists ensured that the resulting building would appear beautiful. By bringing the perspective of the viewer into the art, the Athenian craftsmen of the 5th century changed the meaning and function of their creations. All the grandeur, all the artistry, was geared toward creating an experience of the beautiful in the beholder. It was this experience of the beautiful that was the gateway to the divine, not the temples, statues, and other buildings by themselves.

One might say that by making the statue of Athena Parthenos so rich in gold and ivory and making her the principal occupant of the Parthenon the Athenians were secularizing the divine, using images of the divine for purely secular and political purposes. But the perspectival distortion built into the buildings suggests otherwise. True, it served to bring the divine and the human closer together, but not by debasing the divine. Rather, it elevated the human, precisely by allowing human beings to experience the divine: to experience beauty, and to feel the awe and reverence elicited by that experience of beauty—to feel it first in the face of that human creation—the temple, the statue, the entrance gates—but then to move beyond that to a glimpse, a sense, an inkling of the divine that the human creation is representing.

References and Suggestions for Further Reading

Herodotus. *The Histories.* Translated by David Grene. Chicago and London: University of Chicago Press, 1987.

Hurwit, Jeffrey M. *The Athenian Acropolis.* Cambridge, UK: Cambridge University Press, 1999.

Plato. *The Laws of Plato.* Translated by Thomas L. Pangle. New York: Basic Books, Inc., 1980.

Plutarch. *Life of Pericles. Plutarch's Lives*, vol. 3. Cambridge, Mass.: Harvard University Press, 1951, pp. 1-115.

Rhodes, Robin Francis. *Architecture and Meaning on the Athenian Acropolis.* Cambridge, UK: Cambridge University Press, 1995.

Thucydides. *History of the Peloponnesian War.* Translated by Rex Warner. New York: Penguin Group (USA) Inc., 1954, 1972.

The theatre at Epidaurus: ©Kevin Glowacki

The Greco-Roman theatre at Miletus, Turkey ©Thomas Hines, Professor of Theatre, Whitman College

Didyma: The last few hundred metres of the Sacred Way, the Processional Way, which connected the temples at Miletus and Didyma ©Trevor Curnow

Chapter 58

The Athenian Agora

Kevin Glowacki

> As Euboulos [a comic poet of the 4th century BC] says in his Olbia, you will find everything sold together in the same place at Athens: figs, summoners, bunches of grapes, turnips, pears, apples, witnesses, roses, medlars, haggis, honeycombs, chickpeas, lawsuits, beestings, beestings—pudding, myrtle, allotment machines, irises, lambs, water clocks, laws, indictments. (Athenaeus, *Diepnosophistai*, 14.640 b-c)

One of the most important parts of any ancient Greek city was its *agora*, the marketplace and civic centre. In addition to being a place where people gathered to buy and sell (*agorazein* in Greek) all kinds of commodities, it was also a place where people assembled to discuss (*agoreuein*) all kinds of topics: business, politics, current events, or the nature of the universe and the divine. The Agora of Athens, where ancient Greek democracy first came to life, provides a wonderful opportunity to examine the commercial, political, religious, and cultural life of one of the great cities of the ancient world.

The earliest Agora of Athens was probably to the east or northeast of the Acropolis. By the early 5th century BC, however, the Agora had been relocated to a wide, gently sloping valley northwest of the citadel. This spacious area is bordered on three sides by natural landmarks: on the north by the Eridanos River, on the west by a low hill called the Kolonos Agoraios, and on the south by the Areopagus hill. The eastern edge of the Agora is marked by the Panathenaic Way, one of the main streets of the city throughout antiquity.

Archaeological investigations by the American School of Classical Studies have revealed much about the history of this area. Excavations have shown, for example, that in the Late Bronze Age (c. 1600–1000 BC) and Iron Age (c. 1100–700 BC), parts of the area were used as a cemetery. Numerous graves from these periods have been found. At the same time, private houses probably occupied other areas, to judge by the number of wells discovered. Some of these Iron Age wells even contained debris from pottery workshops, suggesting that the area was part of the original *Kerameikos* ('Potters' Quarters') of the city. The closure of the wells during the 6th century may reflect a gradual change from private to public land. It is clear that several monuments of a distinctively public nature were constructed in the second half of the 6th century. By the early 5th century, stone markers inscribed with the words 'I am the boundary of the Agora' stood at the entrances of the area, unequivocally distinguishing the civic space from the private property surrounding it. From the 5th century on, the development of the Agora and the activities that took place there are well documented, both by archaeological evidence and written sources.

Throughout the Classical and Hellenistic periods, the centre of the Agora was kept free of any major buildings except for altars, shrines, and statues of gods and important heroes of the state. Within this open space, people gathered to buy and sell, debate politics, stand for jury selection, view dramatic performances, and meet their neighbours from all walks of life. The administrative buildings were located along the periphery and included the Royal Stoa (the office of the magistrate in charge of religious matters; it was here that Socrates was indicted in 399 BC), the Bouleuterion (Council House), Tholos (headquarters of the Executive Committee of the Council), the Metroon (sanctuary of the Mother of the Gods but also the public archives), the Monument of the Eponymous Heroes (a public bulletin board for important announcements pertaining to the ten political tribes of Athens), as well as law courts, offices of weights and measures, and the mint. The importance of religion in the lives of the ancient Athenians is reflected in other monuments throughout the Agora, such as the Altar of the Twelve Gods (the official centre of the city), the Temple of Apollo Patroos (father of the Ionian Greeks), and the Temple of Hephaistos (god of smiths and craftsmen). In fact, many of the 'state' buildings in the Agora also had religious associations, reminding us that the concept of 'separation of church and state' did not really apply in the ancient world!

An important type of public building found in Athens and throughout the Greek world is a *stoa*—a long, rectangular structure with a row of columns across the front. These were truly multi-functional buildings and could be used for several different purposes: commerce, meetings of all kinds, poetry readings, lectures, dining, jury trials, or just getting out of the hot Athenian sun! The foundations of a stoa, constructed around 470–460 BC, have recently been uncovered at the northern side of the Agora. Although only the western end of the stoa has been cleared so far, the excavators have suggested that this building is the famous Painted Stoa (*Stoa Poikile*), which took its name from a series of paintings on display there. The Painted Stoa was also a favorite meeting place and classroom for philosophers, most notably Zeno of Citium and his students, who came to be known as 'Stoics'.

We know from ancient sources that people who were guilty of certain crimes (e.g., impiety, mistreatment of parents, young men who had not fulfilled their military service) could not enter the Agora, reminding us that the boundary stones were taken seriously. In order to meet with students too young to come into the Agora, Socrates is said to have frequented the shop of a shoe-maker named Simon. In fact, excavations at the southwest corner of the Agora have uncovered a house/shop of the 5th century BC, just beyond a boundary stone, where archaeologists found iron hobnails and bone eyelets for shoes, and a cup inscribed with the name of 'Simon' (on display in the Agora museum)!

Other private houses and workshops lined the streets leading into the Agora. Of particular interest in one such neighborhood southwest of the Tholos is a large building with several rooms on either side of a narrow corridor, an enclosed courtyard, and a tower. It has been suggested that this building was the state prison (*desmoterion*) where Socrates was put to death in 399 BC. The evidence for the identification is suggestive (e.g., several small clay pots that could have been used to hold hemlock, a small marble statuette of Socrates), but not conclusive, and the building could equally have served some industrial or commercial function.

By the end of the 4th century BC, Athens had lost most of her former military strength and political independence. The city continued to be an important cultural and educational center in the Hellenistic and Roman periods, and people came from all over the Mediterranean world to study. King Attalos II of Pergamon, for example, studied in Athens as a young man with the philosopher Carneades. When Attalos became king (159–138 BC), he repaid his 'alma mater' by financing the construction of a large two-story stoa along the eastern side of the Agora. The American School of Classical Studies at Athens restored the Stoa of Attalos in 1953 – 1956, and today it serves as offices and storerooms for archaeologists as well as the Agora museum (not to be missed!). On display are many artifacts that truly bring to life the history and people of ancient Athens and the workings of Athenian democracy.

References and Suggestions for Further Reading

Athenian Agora Excavations   http://www.agathe.gr/

Camp, J. *The Athenian Agora: A Short Guide to the Excavations.* Athens: American School of Classical Studies, 2003.

Camp, J. *The Athenian Agora: Excavations in the Heart of Classical Athens.* 2nd Edition. London: Thames and Hudson, 1992.

Goette, H.R. *Athens, Attica, and the Megarid: An Archaeological Guide.* London: Routledge, 2001.

Lang, M. *Socrates in the Agora.* Princeton: American School of Classical Studies, 1978.

Chapter 59

Corinth

G.S. Bowe

I shall come to know fortunate Corinth
Poseidon's porch on the Isthmus
Glorious in its young men. (Pindar, *Olympian Ode xiii)*

Young women, hostesses to many, handmaidens
Of Attraction in wealthy Corinth
Who burn the golden tears of fresh frankincense,
Often you soar in your thoughts
To Aphrodite in the sky,
The mother of loves. (Pindar fr. 307)

The oldest settlement in the vicinity of Corinth dates to perhaps 4000 BC. This is probably closer to the place that Homer knew as Corinth, which he called Ephyra; its legendary kings were Sisyphus and Bellerophon, and it is also the place where the murderous sorceress Medea lived with her husband Jason, the Captain of the Argo, before she set about killing Corinthian nobility and family alike. Euripides wrote a tragedy about her that bears her name. Corinth was also the place where Oedipus grew up as the adopted son of King Polybus, before heading off to Thebes to fulfill the famous prophesy of the Oracle at Delphi about killing his father and wedding his mother. The later Greek and Roman Ancient Corinth is at the foot of the Acrocorinth, a high natural citadel, about 8 kilometers from Modern Corinth. It was settled by Dorian descendants of Heracles, the much-loved Greek hero, in the 8th century. The kings known as Bacchiads came from this race, and ruled Corinth until overthrown by Kypselis in c. 655 BC. Kypselis implemented the second longest tyranny in Greece, being succeeded by Periander and Kypselis II. The latter was overthrown by a popular movement. Tyrannies, as both Aristotle and the Oracle at Delphi (who predicted the overthrow of Kypselis II) observed, are always short-lived. Though not properly a philosopher, Periander is given a short chapter in Diogenes Laertius' *Lives of Eminent Philosophers.* Diogenes tells us that Aristotle considered him to be one of the Seven Sages of Ancient Greece, but that Plato did not.

At times Corinth rivalled Athens for commercial dominance in Greece, and initially sided with Sparta against Athens in the Peloponnesian War, helping to defeat her in the Sicilian Expedition. Later however, wary of Sparta's growing power, she sided with Athens, Argos, and Thebes against the Spartans. The decline of Corinth seems ultimately to be the result of being caught in the middle of political situations between Athens and Sparta, and inciting wars that she was incapable of winning. Destroyed by the Roman general Mummius in 146 BC, Corinth was re-established as a Roman Colony by Julius Caesar and became the capital of Roman Greece.

Above all, Corinth was famous for two things in the ancient world—wealth and prostitution. It is possible to overestimate Corinth's geographical position as a crossroads as the reason for her success in these areas. The expense of land carriage in ancient Greece makes it much more plausible to suggest that Corinth's access to sea trade with the west was more important, as is shown by the large amounts of Corinthian wares that were exported westward. Corinthian factories are famous for producing red figure vase pottery, metal works, textiles, woodwork, and statues. Corinthian craftsmen and architects were known to have contributed to the construction of several temples at Delphi, and many of the temple roofs there.

Periander's construction of a *diolkos*, or slipway, on which small ships could be transported across the Isthmus of Corinth on rollers may have helped with sea trade—the *diolkos* was in use until the 13th century; the canal which now allows for the passage of ships across the isthmus was first proposed by Alexander the Great and later by the Roman emperor, Caligula, and first attempted by Nero, who struck the first blow with a golden pickaxe in 67 AD. (He committed suicide three months later.) 6000 Jewish slaves were left to complete the project, but it was abandoned due to a miscalculation of water levels—the Aegean Sea was thought to be higher than the Adriatic and hence likely to cause flooding. It was not until the 19th century that the work was completed by a French firm who started exactly where Nero had left off.

Unlike many other Greek city-states, in Corinth the citizenry partook of trade and manufacture to a very large extent. For example Corinth's rival in trade and sea power, Athens, left trade and manufacture to resident alien foreigners, metics, such as the wealthy arms merchant Cephalus of Plato's *Republic*, who gave up respect and citizenry in Syracuse in order to make money living as a foreigner in the Piraeus. It is more likely that a great deal of comparative political stability in Corinth arose from the fact that more citizens were involved in trade. As citizen merchants and traders were more keenly interested in their city's trade policies, the oligarchies that ruled Corinth were intelligent enough to make decisions that coincided with the majority opinion.

Corinth was famous for the abundance of prostitutes and lust for life shared by its citizenry. Symposium (drinking party) scenes are popular on Corinthian pottery, and the Acrocorinth was a popular symposium site. Some ancient sources claim that as many as 1000 prostitutes were dedicated to the Corinthian cult of Aphrodite, the goddess of love. The fact that Aphrodite's prostitutes were 'sacred' allowed them to escape reformist edicts against secular prostitution; this did nothing to help Corinth's reputation for licentiousness. Many ancient slang words involving prostitution or sexuality are associated with Corinth, most famously the use of the phrase 'Corinthian girl' for a prostitute. The comic playwright Aristophanes seems to use the verb *korinthiazomai* (I act the Corinthian) for 'procuring sex'. The Christian St. Paul, who lived and worked in Corinth as a tent maker in the year 51 AD, duly registered his dissatisfaction with the young Christian community there in his well-known *Letters to the Corinthians*.

Every student of classics learns the three principle architectural orders of building columns—the Doric, Ionian, and Corinthian. Corinthian columns are the most ornate of the three orders. Doric columns are plain, and shorter in height in relation to their diameter. Ionic columns have 'capitals' on top that consist of a scroll-like portion above a decorative shaft. The Ionians figured out that by employing *entasis*—swelling the center of the column out a bit, you can prevent the illusion of concavity. This technique is employed most famously in the Parthenon at Athens. Corinthian Columns also employ *entasis*, and their capitals have flowering, leaf-like structures that make them the most pleasing to the eye.

While her greatest athlete, Xenophon, won a victory in the *stadion* (foot race), and the pentathlon at the 464 Olympic Games, Corinth is also important as the host of the second most important ancient Greek games, the Isthmian Games, held in honor of Poseidon. The Corinthians believed that the founder of these games was their legendary king Sisyphus, one of the tortured prisoners Odysseus sees on his trip to Hades in the 11th book of Homer's *Odyssey*. His story is revisited by the French/Algerian existentialist writer, Albert Camus in *The Myth of Sisyphus*. Sisyphus was condemned for all eternity with the task of rolling a heavy stone to the top of a hill only to have it roll back down again and be required to push it back up in perpetuity. Perhaps the Athenians had Sisyphus punished for falsely taking the credit of founding the games; according to them, their hero Theseus (son of Aegeus, namesake of the Aegean Sea) was responsible for founding them. The prize for winning the Isthmian games was often a wreath of pine, which apparently was not as popular as Olympia's olive wreaths or those of fresh celery given at Nemea, 20 kilometers SW of Corinth. Perhaps the most famous victor at the Isthmian games was the emperor Nero, who competed in musical composition in 66–67 AD—while he failed at the canal, he won at music, perhaps characteristic of the man who fiddled while Rome burned.

Corinth is the location of the legendary meeting between Alexander the Great and Diogenes the Cynic. Diogenes is from Sinope on the Black Sea Coast, but seems to have taken up residence in the Corinthian suburb of Craneium at about the time Alexander was rounding up troops in support of an invasion against Persia. Diogenes had something of a reputation in Corinth, and when he did not show at the meeting of Corinthians, Alexander sought him out, only to find him sunbathing. According to Plutarch, when asked by Alexander if he wanted anything, Diogenes replied to the great military leader 'Stand out of my sunlight'. Alexander is reported to have said that if he could not be Alexander, he would like to be Diogenes. A more historically important meeting took place at Corinth in 337 BC, when Phillip II of Macedon summoned a number of states to the city seeking their allegiance. For the purpose of this meeting, a large *stoa* or porch was constructed. Known simply as the South Stoa, it is the largest secular building in Greece.

Of the site itself much that remains are merely foundations. Ancient Greek Corinth was destroyed in the Roman invasion and subsequent earthquakes in modern times (1858, 1921, 1928) have taken their toll on the Roman remains, and indeed on Modern Corinth to the north east of the ancient city. An exception is perhaps the supposed temple of Apollo that dates to the mid 6th century BC, making it one of the oldest surviving temples in Greece.

To the Northwest of the ancient city is the Roman Odeion (theatre) a few hundred metres from the North Stoa and North Market stalls. To the south of the Odeion is a collection of temples and the Glauke Fountain. East of the Odeion is a semicircular market. The old Lechaion Road, which runs straight to the port in the Gulf of Corinth, and would have been the main trading road, separates the market from public baths thought to have been donated by Eurykles of Sparta in the 1st century AD. These were praised by Pausanias, the author of Greece's first guide book, as the finest baths in Corinth. Just below the baths is the *Peribolos* (walled enclosure) of Apollo's Temple, probably of early construction, but later reconstructed by the Romans. Adjacent to the *peribolos* is the Peirene fountain named after a woman who cried so much that the gods turned her into a fountain. Corinth is in fact rich in natural springs, and the nearby town Loutraki is the source of one of Greece's best bottled waters of the same name. Still strolling south on the Lechaion Road, one reaches the Roman Bema, a speaker's platform for public gatherings. Straight ahead of the Bema is the south Stoa, the place of the meeting called by Phillip II. Behind this is the Bouleterion or voting house. The Bema is actually in between two sets of central shops to the east and the west. To the west of the western shops is an area containing Byzantine ruins (5th–8th centuries) and Frankish ruins from the 14th century.

References and Suggestions for Further Reading

Aristotle, *Athenian Constitution*. London: Heinemann, 1981.
Diogenes Laertius. *Lives of Eminent Philosophers*. Loeb Classical Library. London: Heinemann, 1988.
Pausanius. *Guide to Greece*. Loeb Classical Library. London: Heinemann, 1984.
Plutarch. *Lives*. Loeb Classical Library. London: Heinemann, 1988.
Rhodes, P.J. *The Greek City States*. London: University of Oklahoma Press, 1986.
Salmon, J.B. *Wealthy Corinth*. Oxford: Clarendon, 1997.
Schoder, R.V. *Ancient Greece from the Air*. London: Thames and Hudson, 1974.
Thucydides. *History of the Peloponnesian War*. London: Heinemann, 1979.

Chapter 60

Delphi

Deborah Nash Peterson

Located near the modern Greek town of Arahova high in the mountains near the famed Mt. Parnassus and above the Bay of Corinth, the historic ruins of Delphi stand out starkly against the horizon. A unique calm emanates from the massive stones of the ruins of the Temple of Apollo; the winds blow quietly through the pines and olive trees. The site is strikingly quiet, yet, in ancient times, it was a centre of great spiritual activity and political power. Why was it of such interest to so many? And what did ancient visitors learn when they came here?

An oracle is, by definition, a person through whom a deity is believed to speak, or it is a shrine, in or from which that deity reveals hidden knowledge or divine purpose. Archeological excavations suggest that worship and divination took place in the area of Mt. Parnassus from Neolithic times onward. Ancient legend claims that, when the great god Zeus wanted to find the centre of the earth, he released two eagles, one to fly East and the other West, and when the sacred birds met in Delphi, he threw down a holy stone (a 'navel stone') in order to mark the area. It was also held that there was there a chasm in the earth from which a foul smelling vapor emanated—but one which, ironically, had a cleansing effect on the spirits of humans and animals and gave them powers of both clairvoyance and foreknowledge. In the Mycenean Period (14th–11th centuries BC), Delphi became the centre of worship of the female deity, Gaia, the goddess Earth.

The sanctuary of the oracle was guarded by Python, a great and voracious serpent, the son of the Earth goddess. Apollo, the son of Zeus, slew the serpent using his torch and golden arrows and himself became master of the oracle (approx. 800 BC). In honour of this victory, a festival of music and poetry known as the Pythian Games was established and held every eight years (later more frequently as athletic events were also introduced) at Delphi. This competition was second in importance only to the Olympic Games, and involved singing and instrumental music as well as recitation of verse and prose in honor of 'Phoebus' Apollo, the bringer of light (the 'bright one').

An event such as the conquest of the Python was of great symbolic significance to the Ancient Greeks. Apollo, a youthful deity often portrayed naked with bow and lyre and reputed for his masculine beauty, was worshipped throughout Greece as the god of music, archery, prophecy and medicine. He was therefore also an ideal of rationality, spiritual purity and proper human moral development in keeping with religious and philosophical principle. With this victory, therefore, the higher order, rational capacities of man, had overcome the dark forces of primitive religion and the instability associated with rural existence. Chaos and uncertainty had given way to orderly civic life, and what followed was an age of stability, prosperity and untold advances in politics, science, the arts and philosophy. Apollo came to be regarded as the chief deity not only of Delphi, but of all the Greek oracles. The 'Pythian Oracle divine', as it is referred to by Sophocles, came to be the centre of Greek religious life—a centre of spiritual authority and activity roughly equivalent to the Christian institution of the Vatican. Greek faith in the god's prophetic power was absolute and unquestioned. As Tiresius, the blind seer of Sophocles' *Oedipus Rex* stated in response to doubts expressed by Oedipus about the veracity, or accuracy of the oracle's predictions: 'Apollo is sufficient. He will bring all to pass.'

Greek reverence for, and dedication to, the god Apollo is shown by the fact that his temple at Delphi, originally built in 7th century BC was destroyed and rebuilt several times with the aid of contributions from all over Greece, including colonies as far away as Egypt, and eventually also by Alexander the Great and the Macedonians. King Croesus of Lydia is known to have dedicated to the sanctuary a solid gold lion standing on a pedestal of 117 blocks, some of gold and some of silver.

Under the administration of a union of neighbouring towns, known as the Amphyctonia (4th century BC), the shrine at Delphi reached the peak of its flourishing. This association was a mutual protective union, a sort of prototype of the United Nations. By common agreement, it institutionalized and oversaw the process of divination to ensure that it was not subject to undue political influence.

Anyone who inquired of the oracle (usually a king or wealthy individual, since doing so would have been costly) would have come to Delphi because he was facing a major decision or unresolved life problem. To benefit from the consultation, the visitor had, in essence, to be willing to hold a mirror up to himself—to be prepared to face the irrational or darker element of his own character. Two distinct sides of human nature were therefore brought into contact with each other in this experience: The irrationality, uncontrollability and incoherence of the passions, and the calm, collected, self-possessed and sublimely ordered powers of the rational mind. And, the sort of self-possession and harmonious reconciliation of higher and lower order powers which Apollo represented can only be achieved through such a confrontation, hence the inscriptions on the temple: 'Know Thyself' and 'Moderation in all Things.' As the Pre-Socratic philosopher, Heraclitus, is known to have said, 'The lord of Delphi neither speaks not hides, but reveals signs'.

Among the many leading figures in Greek society who journeyed to Delphi was King Croesus of Lydia. When he asked if he would be victorious in war, the god foretold that he would 'destroy a great power'. History proved the oracle to have been right—but the great power he eventually destroyed was his own.

During the following centuries Delphi suffered under a series of invaders and was stripped of its wealth and robbed of the great works of art with which its devotees had adorned it. When Theodosius the Great closed and had the temple complex burned in 394 AD, the oracle of Apollo officially became defunct.

The sanctuary at Delphi did not, however, disappear totally from the mind of man. European archeologists frequently journeyed there to carry out excavations in the 19th century. Their work made accessible startlingly well preserved, brilliant and hitherto unknown works of art associated with the site (e.g. the 'Charioteer'). It also gave to the world a clearer sense of the overall design of the temple complex, its functioning, and its unmatched historic stature as a place sacred to all humanity—a place where the god's utterances were regarded as of paramount importance in guiding the affairs of men.

Today, relatively little remains of the sanctuary. Archeologists' analysis of it and their retrospectives suggest that, at the height of its activity, it consisted of the various treasuries of the Greek cities (Athens, Corinth, Megara, Rhodos, etc.), a gymnasium (for exercise and sports spectacles—also built in the 4th century BC, the Stoa of the Athenians, a sort of porch which provided a façade for the building in which Athenian naval victories trophies were housed, a stone theatre (constructed in the 4th century BC for festivals), and, finally, several temples (two to Athena including the famous 'tholos' or circular temple made of pristine white marble, several to minor gods, and the great Temple of Apollo). Of the latter, there remains only the rectangular foundation and a half-dozen massive stone columns.

Delphi is now the site of international conferences and meetings organized by the European Cultural Center—called 'European' (as opposed to Greek) because of its link to the concept of a united Europe. Visitors and conference attendees come there to deliberate and discuss major problems faced by the modern world. The oracle may have long fallen silent, and little of its ancient energy may be perceptible except in the faint rustling of the winds, but Greek wisdom is still a sort of Castilian spring from which the world can drink—and Delphi a testament to the unique cultural insight on which that wisdom was grounded: The power of rationality is only truly at our disposal when we can also acknowledge and grapple with the irrational forces at work within ourselves—and, for this, courage is required.

References and Suggestions for Further Reading

Andronikos, Manolis. *Delphi,* Ekdotike Athenon, S.A., Athens, 1975.

Crane, Gregory, ed., *Perseus,* a CD-Rom interactive multi-media guide to ancient Greek history and culture (Windows & Macintosh). Yale Univ. Press, New Haven, CT.: 2000.

Fontenrose, J.E. *The Delphic Oracle: Its Responses and Operations.* Berkeley , CA: USA, 1978.

Krontira, Leda. *Getting to Know Apollo's Sanctuary at Delphi.* Ekdotike Athenon, S.A., Athens, 1996.

Lipsey, Roger. *Have you been to Delphi? Tales of the Ancient Oracles for Modern Minds.* Albany State Univ. NY Press, 2001.

Parke, H.W. *Greek Oracles.* London: Hutchinson, 1967.

Pentreath, Guy. *The Hellenic Traveller, A Guide to Ancient Sites of Greece.* N.Y., N.Y.: Crowell Press, 1964.

Chapter 61

Didyma

Peter Sommer

The memory of the pleasure which this spot afforded me will not be … easily erased. The columns … are so exquisitely fine, the marble mass so vast and noble, that it is impossible perhaps to conceive greater beauty and majesty in ruin. (Richard Chandler, *Travels in Asia Minor*, 1764)

A monument of enormous proportions and grandeur, the temple of Didyma vies for the most impressive site on Turkey's west coast. This is no gentle, graceful shrine, quietly echoing former glories, instead it shouts loud its power and prestige. Here as you walk beneath soaring columns, or down dark vaulted corridors to the innermost holy of holies, you can still feel the might and influence wielded by the old gods.

As famous in its heyday as the oracle at Delphi, Apollo's prophetess at Didyma was visited by pilgrims from across the Greek world. The oldest oracular responses date back 2,600 years. One inscription answers a question whether it was right to engage in piracy—the god's response, 'it is right to do as your fathers did'. The site itself is older still, and like the name, Anatolian. Even before the Greeks settled here, the location with its laurel trees and holy spring was sacred.

I first visited Didyma when walking across Turkey retracing the footsteps of Alexander the Great. Setting out from ancient Miletus, I headed into the hills searching for the Sacred Way, connecting city and temple, repaved by the Emperor Trajan c. AD 100. It's not for the faint hearted, but if you have time, fitness, and water, ask a villager in Akkoy if he'll take you on the old way (eski patika) to Didyma. The statues and monuments that once lined the route are gone (some are stored in the British Museum), but you can still pick out the processional path, and the waystations where pilgrims rested.

If you can't face an endurance test, the greatest section of the Sacred Way is easier to hand, unearthed in recent times by German archaeologists immediately north of the temple. Beside antique baths and shops, lies a grand boulevard laid out in giant white slabs that dazzle in the Mediterranean light. Here you can tread the very footsteps of the ancients, the pilgrims coming to seek Apollo's guidance, or the tourists en route to the Great Didymeia festival held every four years.

The modern road is lined with souvenir shops and tourist touts, but don't turn your head in dismay. Little has changed. 2,000 years ago, travellers would have run the gauntlet of local guides, the exegetai 'explainers' who took them around for a fee, and the trinket sellers, with their Apollo pots, or miniature temples—silver for the wealthy, terracotta for the masses.

The mighty ruins lie as they originally fell, piled up like shattered icebergs. (Sir Charles Newton, 1863)

A few centuries back, the temple was almost hidden from view, covered in a mound of detritus following an earthquake. Now the temple stands completely exposed. Great Ionic capitals with swirling volutes lie scattered about. Enormous Medusa heads that decorated an architrave atop the columns sit prone on the ground.

Walk around to the west where a collapsed column lies, its segments like giant fallen dominoes. Imagine it re-erected into the sky along with the other 119 columns that surrounded the temple—a vast sacred grove turned to stone. Strolling back along the south side, picture the festival in full swing, the songs of poets in the air, and the steps beside you crammed with spectators watching athletes race in the stadium.

Quite how the oracle functioned remains obscure:

The ... singer of prophecies, is filled with divine radiance, either when holding a rod ... originally handed over by some god, or sitting on an axon (tripod ?) she foretells the future, or dampening her feet ... or breathing from the water, she receives the god. (Iamblichus, *De Mysteriis*, 3.11)

Her prophecies were written down, there was even a place for them to be transcribed, the 'chresmographeion', but where this was, and where supplicants waited eagerly for answers is unclear. We do know that Apollo's mouthpiece fell silent at times. 2,500 years ago Didyma was sacked and looted, either by the Persian king Darius following the area's revolt in 494 BC, or by Xerxes after the invasion of Greece in 479. The priests who administered the temple, the Branchidae (named after Branchus, a shepherd seduced by Apollo and given the power of divination) willingly handed over the treasures, including Apollo's bronze statue. Their sacrilege was infamous in antiquity. They were resettled by the Persian king in Central Asia, and their descendants extraordinarily discovered by Alexander the Great north of Afghanistan in 329 BC. For their ancestors' act of treason he killed all the men and sold the rest into slavery.

Next, walk through the porch, and single out the column bases carved in the most stunning designs, a feature almost unique in the Greek world. Down one of the dark passages, you'll come into the temple's heart, its cella, so large, Strabo reports that to roof it proved impossible. Instead it was left open, a court planted with laurel, Apollo's hallowed tree, with a shrine housing the god's image and sacred spring.

After 150 years' silence, the spring magically gushed again and the oracle spoke forth when Alexander the Great liberated the region from Persian control. The prophetess declared Alexander 'born of Zeus' and forecast his triumph over

One of his successors, Seleucus, returned the stolen Apollo statue from Persia c. 300 BC, and set to work rebuilding the temple you see today.

For nearly 700 years it remained a building site, with up to eight architects and 20 construction companies working simultaneously. But this vast wonder was never finished. Alongside knife-edge masonry remain protruding nodules inscribed with Greek letters, referring to the workmen who worked on a block, but never dressed it smooth. Even unfinished, it was considered in antiquity one of the greatest of all Greek temples. It is without doubt one of the biggest.

Didyma's end came in 385 AD with the edict of Theodosius:

> No mortal man shall have the effrontery to encourage vain hopes by the inspection of entrails, or (which is worse) attempt to learn the future by the detestable consultation of oracles.

Apollo's oracle was silenced forever, and a Christian church erected in the temple's cella.

References and Suggestions for Further Reading

Bean, George E. *Aegean Turkey: An Archaeological Guide*. London: Ernest Benn Ltd, 1966.
Fontenrose J. *Didyma: Apollo's Oracle, Cult, and Companions*. Berkeley: University of California Press, 1988.
Lloyd, Seton. *Ancient Turkey: A Traveller's History of Anatolia*. London: Guild Publishing, 1989.
Parke, H.W. *The Oracles of Apollo in Asia Minor*. London: Croom Helm, 1985.
Stoneman, Richard. *Across the Hellespont*. London: Hutchinson, 1987.

Chapter 62

Eleusis

Anne Farrell

Into these things of love, Socrates, perhaps even you may be initiated, but I do not know whether you are able [to be initiated] into the rites and revelations for the sake of which these exist if one pursues them correctly. (Plato's *Symposium* (209e-210a). Translation after R.E. Allen)

Eleusis, modern day Elefsina, is located about fourteen miles west of Athens. The site is renowned as the location of the rites of the Eleusinian Mysteries, religious rituals that honored the earth goddess Demeter. The sanctuary functioned for more than 1,700 years, during which period it was rebuilt several times after being damaged or destroyed. The remains from several different archaeological periods can be discerned today. The site was of great religious significance to the Greeks and Romans, and references to the Eleusinian Mysteries feature prominently in the works of Plato.

Mystery rites are not as well known today as other Greek rituals. Most people are familiar with temples and religious practices dedicated to Olympian gods, such as Zeus, Hera, and Apollo. However, almost all Athenians—men and women, slave and free—also worshiped chthonic gods, gods of the earth, including Demeter, Persephone, and Dionysus. Unlike the jealous and vengeful Olympian gods, the sympathetic earth gods were purported to work to benefit human beings, and individuals sought initiation into the Eleusinian Mysteries in order to receive Demeter's promises of bountiful crops and a blessed afterlife.

The site at Eleusis has been occupied for millennia. We find a mythical account of the origins of the cult in the *Homeric Hymn to Demeter*, which was written around the 7th or 6th century BC. In this account, the rites of the Mysteries were an expression of gratitude by Demeter to the people of Eleusis, who had been kind to her. According to the *Hymn*, when Hades abducted Demeter's daughter, Persephone, and took her to the underworld, Demeter, the goddess of agriculture, grieving the loss of her daughter, withdrew from the gods. She wandered the earth in disguise, and stopping by a well, met the daughters of Keleos, the king of Eleusis, as they came to draw water. The girls were compassionate toward her, and she was brought into Keleos' house to serve as a nurse to his infant son, Demophoon. Demeter took steps to make the boy immortal, but his mother, Metaneira, fearing for the well being of her son, interfered. After the intervention by Metaneira, Demeter revealed herself as a goddess, instructed the people of

Eleusis to build a temple to her, and promised to instruct them in the rites of the Mysteries:

> I am the goddess Demeter, holder of honor, who is
> For immortals and mortals alike the greatest boon and joy.
> But come now, let all the people build me a great temple,
> And an altar to stand beneath it, under the citadel and its sheer fortification wall
> Upon a rising hill above the Kallichoron well;
> And I myself will lay down for your instruction my rites,
> So then, by performing them piously, you might appease my mind.
> (Verses, 268-72) Translation after Michael Crudden

While Persephone was in the underworld and Demeter was grieving, crops stopped growing, and famine was imminent. But after Zeus arranged the return of Persephone to the upper world for two thirds of the year, Demeter made the earth fertile once more, and instructed the people of Eleusis in her rites. Those who were initiated were promised material prosperity on earth in the form of bountiful crops as well as a blessed afterlife. According to the *Hymn*,

> The goddess Demeter then went and [showed] to...
> Kelos leader of people— the way to perform her rites,
> And disclosed sacred actions to all that can in no way be [transgressed,]
> Learned, or divulged, for the tongue is curbed by the gods' great awe.
> Blessed is he who has seen them of humans who walk on the earth;
> But he who has not been enrolled in the rites, who is lacking in a share,
> In death has no matching portion down in the mouldy gloom.
> (Verses, 475-82) Translation after Crudden

Initiation into the Eleusinian Mysteries involved several stages, including rites of purification, disorientation, and the visual revelation of the secrets of the Mysteries. We know little about what occurred during much of the Mysteries, because the initiates themselves were sworn to secrecy about the final stages of initiation. However, we do know the rites involved two degrees of initiation, the Small or Lesser (*smikra*) Mysteries, and the Great (*megala*) Mysteries. We have evidence indicating that later the purificatory rites of the Small Mysteries were conducted in the Ilissos River (a river near Ancient Athens), and several sources record that the rites were held in honor of Persephone.

The Great Mysteries took place in sanctuaries in Athens and Eleusis and along the processional route between the two cities. The Great Mysteries began with the transport of the *hiera*, the holy objects of Demeter, from their storage place in Eleusis to the Eleusinion in Athens. Mystery priests later processed from Athens to Eleusis carrying these sacred objects. A day later, the Mystery initiates also made the fourteen mile trip from Athens to Eleusis along the Sacred Way (*Iera Odos*). Before making the trip, initiates participated in additional purificatory rites, including bathing in the sea with piglets, which they later sacrificed. Soon after arriving at Eleusis, individuals were initiated into the secret rites of the Mysteries, the high point being the *epopteia*, the revelation to the initiates of the secrets of the Mysteries. During the *epopteia* the Mystery priest burst upon the initiates in a blaze of bright light to reveal the secret. Because of the proscription against revealing the secret of the Mysteries, we know little about the sacred object that was revealed. Hippolytus proposes that it was an ear of corn, which was sacred to Demeter.

Due to wars and the fortunes of different rulers, the sanctuary at Eleusis underwent many incarnations as it was destroyed, rebuilt and expanded. The first major expansion appears to have occurred during 760 BC, the year of the 5th Olympiad. At this time famine ravaged Greece, and a festival and sacrifice were dedicated at Eleusis to propitiate Demeter. About this time the sanctuary was enclosed by a precinct wall and the cult began to receive pan-Hellenic recognition.

During the reign of Solon in 600 BC, a special law established the Eleusinian Mysteries among the Athenian sacred festivals. The fame of the Sanctuary grew, and, over the following centuries, further building was carried out to cater to the larger crowds that came to the Sanctuary. Unfortunately, the Sanctuary was destroyed during the Persian Wars, around 479 BC. Redevelopment was undertaken during the reign of Cimon, (479 and 461) and the Sanctuary was enlarged. In the second half of the 5th century BC Pericles continued building and enlarged the area of the temple. This sanctuary escaped harm during the Peloponnesian War (431–404 BC).

Under Roman rule the privilege of initiation was extended to all Roman citizens, and Roman rulers further developed the Sanctuary. The emperors Hadrian (117–138), Antoninus Pius (138–161) and Marcus Aurelius (161–180) added the Triumphal Arches and the Greater and Lesser Propylaea, which were modelled after the Propylaea or gateway to the Acropolis at Athens.

Initiation continued at the site until late into the 4th century AD, but with the rise of Christianity ancient cults were forbidden. A decree of Theodosius I in 379 AD outlawed the cult at Eleusis, and the Sanctuary was destroyed during the invasion of Alaric's Visigoths in 395 AD. The walls of the Sanctuary were repaired in the time of Justinian in order to provide protection against invasion by barbarians from the north, but the site was mistreated in modern times. During the 1821 War of Greek Independence it was used as a military camp by the troops of Karaiskakis. And after the Greeks were liberated from the Turks, the Greeks built a settlement on the east hill with material taken from the sanctuary. Excavations to uncover the site began at the beginning of the 19th century and continue today. A visitor to Greece can still identify many of the routes, geographical landmarks, and remains of buildings associated with the Eleusinian Mysteries.

Writers, especially those writing during the Classical period, frequently incorporated motifs from the Eleusinian Mysteries in their writing. Because of the proscription against revealing the secrets of the Mysteries most literary references to the Eleusinian Mysteries are to public aspects of the earlier stages or are very oblique references to the later stages. For example Aristophanes, in the *Frogs,* gives details of the public procession from Athens to Eleusis. However, according to Aristotle, Aeschylus endangered his life by being too specific in the Mystery allusions in works such as *Iphigeneia*, and *Sisyphos*. At one point Aeschylus was attacked by an angry crowd in the theater because of this and had to flee.

He escaped death only because members of the Aeropagus of Athens begged the crowd not to kill him.

Both Socrates and Plato appear to have been very familiar with the rites of the Eleusinian Mysteries. When mocking Socrates as a natural philosopher and sophist in *The Clouds*, Aristophanes paints a portrait of Socrates initiating Strepsiedes into a school, which Aristophanes calls the Phronesterion or Thinkery. The Mysteries here are in honor of the Clouds, goddesses from whom lazy men get their thoughts. However, this initiation includes several elements from the Eleusinian Mysteries, including the crowning of the initiate with a wreath (250ff). In addition a student in the Thinkery mockingly refers to the exalted questions they study there, such as the distance a flea can jump, as 'secrets of our holy mysteries' (145ff).

In middle period dialogues, such as the *Republic*, *Symposium* and *Phaedrus*, Plato finds the metaphor of the revelation of the secrets of the Mysteries useful to express his view that knowledge of the forms, or ideal paradigm, is a sort of visual revelation. In the *Symposium*, when describing coming to know the form of Beauty, Diotima says that she thinks Socrates is capable of being initiated into the preparatory mysteries of love, but not into the *epoptika*, or final revelation, designed to follow (209e-210a). And in the *Phaedrus* Plato describes the soul's pre-birth vision of the form of Beauty in terms of an *epoptic* revelation (250b-c).

Elefsina, the industrial town on the Saronic Gulf in which the sanctuary is located, is easily reached from Athens by bus. Today it is a small beach town that draws local people, but it is a far from idyllic setting, given the surrounding ship yards and tankers. The archaeological site of Eleusis occupies several square blocks and stands in stark contrast to the rest of the industrial area.

The sanctuary is several blocks up from the bay at the intersection of Iera Odos and Gioka near Nikolaidou. The hours for the museum are 8:30-3:00. The sanctuary is closed on Mondays.

References and Suggestions for Further Reading

K. Clinton, *Myth and Cult: Iconography of the Eleusinian Mysteries*. Stockholm: Svenska Institute in Athens, 1992.

G.E. Mylonas, *Eleusis and the Eleusinian Mysteries*. Princeton: Princeton University Press, 1961.

K. Preka-Alexandri, *Eleusis*, 3rd ed. Athens: Ministry of Culture, 2000.

The Homeric Hymns, translated with an introduction and notes by M. Crudden. New York: Oxford University Press, 2001.

Chapter 63

Epidaurus

Glenn Rawson

Ancient Epidaurus lies just south of modern Epidaurus (Nea Epidavros), across the Saronic Gulf from Athens. This otherwise unimpressive town became famous in the 5th century BC for its sanctuary of the healing god Asclepius, whom pilgrims visited from all over Greece, seeking healing dreams and miraculous cures. Eventually this sanctuary hosted a pan-Hellenic festival with athletic and literary competitions. In the 4th century it received an ambitious architectural development, which included what is now one of the best preserved and most familiar monuments of ancient Greece, the grand and elegant Theatre of Epidaurus. Our best ancient guidebook wrote of this open-air structure and its supposed architect:

> The Epidaurians have a theatre in the sanctuary I think very well worth seeing. For while Roman theatres are in a way much superior to those anywhere in the world ... what architect is worthy to compete with Polycleitus in the composition and beauty of his work? (Pausanias, *Guide to Greece*, 2.27.5)

Thousands still enjoy it each summer at the Epidaurus Theatre Festival, repeating something of its ancient pan-Hellenic function.

The origins of the cult of Asclepius are obscure. Homer portrays two sons of Asclepius as doctors from Thessaly in northern Greece, and refers to Asclepius as an extraordinary medical man (*Iliad* 4, 190-219). But somehow in Archaic times this hero was promoted to the status of a god, and somehow during the 5th century he became the featured deity in a sanctuary that had belonged to his father Apollo (who was also a god of medicine). The resulting sanctuary of Asclepius at Epidaurus became the most famous healing sanctuary in Greece. From Epidaurus the cult of Asclepius was brought to many other communities, including Athens in 420 BC and Rome in 293 BC.

At its height, the sanctuary of Asclepius at Epidaurus included a ceremonial entryway, at least three temples, sacrificial altars, a banquet hall, baths, hostel, gymnasium, and stadium. The central Temple of Asclepius was in the style of the famous ones at Athens and Olympia, but smaller; it housed a gold and ivory statue of the god. The most distinctive buildings were next to this temple, in the most important part of the sanctuary. They are the Abaton, where patients received healing dreams in the 'incubation' (ritual sleep), and the elaborate Thymele, whose name means 'hearth' or 'altar,' but whose function remains mysterious. (These and some other buildings are being at least partially rebuilt.)

The Thymyle was a rotunda, circled by twenty-six columns supporting a conical roof. It was larger and more lavishly decorated than the main temple, and took more than twenty-five years to complete. Among the richly carved ornamentation, deep ceiling coffers framed large, robust flowers, and an especially intricate finial sprouted from the center of the roof. The center of the inner chamber must have led down to the strange basement where concentric walls with doorways and barriers formed a simple underground maze. This curious arrangement indicates some ritual function, but no ancient source tells us what that was. Perhaps it was kept a holy secret. But as the adjacent temple glorified Asclepius the god, the Thymele probably related to Asclepius the man, who lived and died before being deified. Pindar's third Pythian ode tells that Zeus had punished him with death for using his art to raise the dead. The concentric basement walls are visible on site, and much of the impressive architectural decoration is displayed in the museum.

Official inscriptions on stone slabs discovered in the sanctuary report many miraculous cures; some are effected by the sanctuary's priests, snakes, or dogs, but mostly they come about through the ritual of *enkoimesis* or 'incubation', being visited by the god in a dream while sleeping in the Abaton. (The name of this building means 'unapproachable' to those who have not sacrificed and ritually purified themselves.) The Abaton was a long, narrow stoa open towards the temple. Here people were allegedly cured of blindness, paralysis, chronic pains, stones, worms, infertility—even delivered of pregnancies that had lasted years.

> Antikrates of Knidos, eyes. This man had been stuck with a spear through both his eyes in some battle, and he became blind and carried around the spearhead with him, inside his face. Sleeping here, he saw a vision. It seemed to him the god pulled out the dart and fitted the [pupils] back into his eyelids. When day came he left well. (Inscription B12, trans. LiDonnici)

> Ephanes, a boy of Epidauros. Suffering from stone, he slept here. It seemed to him the god came to him and said, 'What will you give me if I should make you well? The boy replied, 'Ten dice'. The god, laughing, said that he would make it stop. When day came he left well. (A8, trans. LiDonnici)

The official display of reported miracles probably served to prepare new visitors for similar experiences, and as propaganda. They sometimes mention unbelievers being converted by being cured.

The cult of Asclepius had grown during the 5th century, and received special impetus from the plague of the 430s, during the Peloponnesian Wars. That is about when some Greeks were trying to develop medicine on a rudimentary scientific basis, as we see in the so-called Hippocratic body of medical writings, some of which openly repudiate supernatural remedies. We do not know how much of the more methodical developments in diet, drugs, bloodletting or surgery might have been practised at Epidaurus. More traditional prescriptions of diet and exercise, rest and prayers, herbs and bloodletting, must have been practised; there were baths and a gymnasium here. But throughout ancient Greece the best of medicine had very limited success, leaving ample yearning for the snakes and dogs and dreams of Asclepius. Even the notoriously logical Socrates could use Asclepius rather than Hippocrates to represent the spiritual healing he hoped to receive in death. In Plato's *Phaedo*, Socrates' last words after drinking the poison hemlock are 'Crito, we owe a cock to Asclepius. Do make the offering, and don't neglect it.'

The theatre was one of the last large projects in the great 4th century BC development of the sanctuary. It is generally thought that it was originally designed and built for about 6000, and that the upper section was conceived and added later, increasing the capacity to the 14,000 still available today. But there is architectural evidence that it was designed for that larger size from the start (Tomlinson p. 90). The acoustics are excellent for such a large outdoor space; every day tourists smile from the back row as they hear coins being dropped in the orchestra. The theatre is so well preserved because it was covered in earth for centuries before being excavated in the late 19th century. Modern interpreters consider it the perfection of the Classical style in theatre construction (Bieber, p. 73). It is a grand and living testament to the power of ancient Greek drama, to its immense popularity in the centuries after its invention in Athens, and to the resources gladly devoted to theatre in communities throughout ancient Greece.

References and Suggestions for Further Reading

Bieber, Margarete. *The History of the Greek and Roman Theater*. 2nd ed. Princeton: University Press, 1961.

LiDonnici, Lynn R. *The Epidaurian Miracle Inscriptions*. Atlanta: Scholar's Press, 1995.

Lloyd, G.E.R., editor. *Hippocratic Writings*. Viking Press, 1984.

Pausanias. *Guide to Greece*. Vol. 1: Central Greece. Translated by Peter Levi. Harmondsworth: Penguin Books, 1971.

Tomlinson, R.A. *Epidaurus*. Austin: University of Texas Press, 1983.

Chapter 64

Marathon

Trevor Curnow

> Here, in the public burial-place which is in the most beautiful quarter outside the city walls, the Athenians always bury those who have fallen in war. The only exception is those who died at Marathon, who, because their achievement was considered absolutely outstanding, were buried on the battlefield itself. (Thucydides, *The Histories* (slightly adapted))

One day in the August or September of 490 BC, a man arrived exhausted in the centre of Athens. He just managed to tell those who gathered around him that the Athenians and their allies, the Plataians, had defeated the armies of the mighty Persian king before he collapsed and died. He had run all the way from Marathon.

This story is the stuff of legend, and legend is what it almost certainly is. But the battle of Marathon was real enough, as was the Persian defeat there. And the burial mounds raised to cover the remains of the dead can still be seen. The battle did not end the Persian threat (they were to return), but it was a defining moment in the history of the age. When the great dramatist Aeschylus died in 456 BC, his epitaph (which he is thought to have composed himself) recorded not his literary achievements but the fact that he had fought at Marathon. The men of Marathon were authentic heroes.

Marathon today is a rather less heroic place, but it is also far more than just an ancient battlefield. It lies, as one might suppose, about 40 km from the centre of ancient Athens, in a north-easterly direction. However, modern Athens has advanced to within less than a quarter of that distance. The small town known as Marathon (or Marathonas) today stands to the north of the site of its illustrious ancient predecessor, which was probably located near what is now the village of Vrána. It was in the vicinity of the village's church of Agios Dimitrios that what is thought to be the burial mound of the Plataians was rediscovered as recently as 1970. Excavations have unearthed the bones of mostly young men and the grave goods that were interred with them.

But the real glory of Marathon is the burial mound of the 192 Athenians who fell there. Standing to a height of nearly 10 metres (three times as high as that of the Plataians), it stands in massive and silent dignity in its own park not far from the shore, to the north of the village of Néa Mákri. Unlike the Plataians, the Athenians were cremated and only their ashes lie within. Neither city took its dead home, which would have been the usual custom. This serves as further evidence of the special status attached to the *Marathonomachai* ('the men who fought at Marathon'), and recalls the real or supposed burial places of Achilles and Protesilaus at Thymbra and Elaius respectively (both in modern Turkey) who died in the Trojan War. In both of these places, and perhaps at Marathon too, the tombs of heroes became cult centres.

Remains of the Persian dead, said to have been numbered in their thousands, have been found on the edge of what is now a marshy area about 3 kilometres to the north of the mound of the Athenians. Since they were presumably buried near where they fell, this may have been the place where the fiercest fighting took place. A monument commemorating the famous victory was erected near the spot. The ruins of a medieval watch tower contain fragments of a far older structure, possibly the monument itself. The Greeks called it a *tropaion*, from which the modern word 'trophy' derives. However, the literal meaning of *tropaion* suggests a turning-point, and it may therefore have marked the place where the decisive shift in fortunes in the battle took place.

The indelible memory left by the battle makes it easy to forget that there is much more to the history of Marathon than a single day in 490 BC. The mound of the Plataians stands near other tombs, some of which are at least 1,000 years older. One, which has been restored, is of the *tholos* ('beehive') type found at Mycenae, and dates to the period between 1500 and 1100 BC. In its entrance were found the skeletons of two horses. Their exact significance is unclear. One possibility is that they were placed there to guard the tomb. To the south, on the conspicuous hill of Mount Agríliki, the ruins of an acropolis have been found, also dating to Mycenean times.

Older still are the remains of a Neolithic settlement that were found near Néa Mákri. It is also thought that the so-called Cave of Pan at Inói, three kilometres to the west of modern Marathon, may have been a cult centre in Neolithic times. An inscription dated to 60 BC found at the site when it was excavated in 1957 seems to confirm its connection with Pan. It appears that the cult enjoyed a significant revival in this area at around the time of the battle. According to Herodotus (book VI), the Athenians sent a runner named Pheidippides to Sparta to appeal for help, and the god appeared to him on his journey. He berated the Athenians for neglecting him despite all he had done and would do for them. The Athenians duly dedicated a shrine under the acropolis to him in gratitude after they had emerged victorious.

Between the cave and Vrána lay the estate of Herodes Atticus, a second century AD personage of wealth and power who was a native of this area. He was also a philosopher and philanthropist. One of his best known public works can still be seen in Athens where the Odeion of Herodes Atticus can be found just to the south of the entrance to the acropolis. Finds from his estate, and from elsewhere around Marathon, are displayed in the Archaeological Museum in Vrána.

Although much of Marathon's past can still be seen in its scattered ruins, other elements of it have disappeared altogether. For example, it once had its own oracle, attached to the cult of Aristomachus. Unfortunately, as with many cults that were essentially local in nature, next to nothing is known about that of Aristomachus, not even who he was. His cult was associated with healing, and appears to have been based in or near a temple of Dionysus which has hitherto escaped detection. One possibility is that it lay in the vicinity of the church of Panagia Mesosporitissa, near the site of the ancient *tropaion*. Churches are often to be found on the sites of earlier religious foundations. The cult of Aristomachus itself, which also had a centre at nearby Rhamnous, appears to have faded from history no later than the end of the 2nd century BC. At least one of the reasons was the great popularity of another healing cult, that of Amphiarus at Oropos, which lay only 20 kilometres away to the north east.

While it is possible to visit all of the remains of ancient Marathon on foot (signposting is generally accurate and adequate), they are substantially scattered over a wide area and private transport offers a considerable advantage. It also furnishes the opportunity to visit other sites of interest in the vicinity such as Rhamnous and Oropos.

It is one of the quirks of fate that the name of Marathon is now best known for being attached to a long-distance run. When it comes to a contest between history and legend, the smart money is usually on legend.

References and Suggestions for Further Reading

Burn, A.R. and Mary Burn. *The Living Past of Greece*. New York: HarperCollins, 1980.

Curnow, Trevor. *The Oracles of the Ancient World*. London: Duckworth, 2004.

Herodotus. *The Histories*. Trans. de Sélincourt. Harmondsworth: Penguin, 1965.

Mee, Christopher and Antony Spawforth. *Greece: an Oxford archaeological guide*. Oxford: Oxford University Press, 2001.

Mehling, Marianne. Ed. *Athens and Attica: a Phaidon cultural guide*. New York: Prentice Hall Press, 1986.

Chapter 65

Miletus

Patricia F. O'Grady

> Maeander's flood deep-rolling swept thereby
> Which from the Phrygian uplands, pastured o'er
> By myriad flocks, around a thousand forelands
> Curls, swirls, and drives his hurrying ripples on
> Down to the vine-clad land of Carian men. (Quintus Smyrnaeus, *Fall of Troy*, 1.284-7)

In Miletus, perhaps more than at any other ancient site, one becomes conscious of the past and its impermanence, for here lie the ruins of a city which was the greatest and most powerful of the Greek ports. An atmosphere of sadness, almost of eeriness, seems to hang in the air. Miletus, in Ionia, was once a vigorous Greek city-port on the banks of the Latmian Gulf through which the Maeander River emptied its waters into the Aegean Sea. During its most prosperous period, the four centuries from about 700 BC, its citizens numbered between twenty and thirty thousand. It boasted four ports which protected the ships which engaged in a thriving trade throughout the Mediterranean Sea. By the 7th century BC, Miletus had founded colonies throughout the Mediterranean, including forty-five colonies in the Black Sea from where they traded a wide range of goods and produce. Through a concession granted by King Amasis of Egypt, the Milesians established a trading city at Naucratis on the Nile.

Miletus was famous for the fine wool shorn from the sheep farmed in the hinterland, the wool being manufactured into blankets and quilts. We may, perhaps, picture magnificent quilts in vibrant colours, for we learn from Homer's *Iliad* (3.125-8) of Helen of Troy, weaving a tapestry, and 'working into it the numerous struggles of Trojans, breakers of horses, and bronze-armoured Achaians'. Colour-fast vegetable dyes were probably available, already being in use in the country around Phasis, a Milesian colony on the eastern shore of the Black sea, and Xenophanes complained about the 'vainglorious Greeks' attending the Assembly in scarlet robes. The merchants of Miletus quickly adopted the use of coinage that had been invented in Lydia, further inland. They struck their own coins which further advantaged their trading ventures over the cumbersome and inefficient system of bartering.

Here in Miletus, amongst the great names we know (mentioned below), all kinds of people—ordinary and extraordinary, famous and infamous, politicians and theologians, farmers and philosophers, concubines and wives, criminals and honest men, disenfranchised slaves, agrarian workers and land owners—all lived their lives, surviving the many sackings and levellings of the city. The final Miletus was rebuilt on the grid system of town planning which was devised by the Milesian architect, Hippodamus, who provided the archetype for modern city-planning.

If you avoid the glitz of the many souvenir stalls to which guides and hawkers will direct you, as they always have, and envisage the Miletus of 2,500 years ago, you will be rewarded with a truly memorable experience.

The most imposing of the ruins is the massive theatre which seated an audience of 15,000. Wander around its base and examine the reliefs, still sharp and breathtaking after the passage of more than 2,000 years. Climb the heights of the theatre and enjoy the panorama. Marvel at the patient power of the Maeander River which, over the centuries, meandering from its source in the highlands, has dropped its rich silt into the Gulf of Latmus. The once Island of Lade is now part of the fertile river plain, and the flourishing ports of Miletus and Priene are now isolated, about ten kilometres inland from the Aegean coast. Observe those moving dots far below, men and women working in their fertile fields, and orient yourself to the ancient sites. Although little of the original buildings remain, apart from the foundations, stroll through them to understand the extent of the ancient Miletus. Perform some mental reconstruction.

To the north-east, at your back, is the Lion Port, guarded at its mouth by two statuary lions. To the west is the Delphinium, the main sanctuary, dedicated to Apollo Delphinus, the god of the revered dolphin. To the south-west, past the Theatre Port, are the gymnasium, the stadium, the Temple to Athena, and the West Agora, the latter being one of three such market places in the once bustling city, as well as the baths of Faustina, the only building not in alignment with Hippodamus' grid plan.

Take the path which leads eastwards and up a slight rise to some fine remains, which are not visible until you reach the top of the gentle hill. Visit the beautiful Ionic stoa with its four remaining pillars, and the ruins of the bouleuterion (the boule or meeting place of the senate).

Don't miss the pleasant little museum and a 15th century mosque, which is significant because of the size of the dome: it is no longer in use because there is no longer a town at Miletus.

Take time to dream a little. Conceive of a flourishing city, and its four bustling ports crowded with cargo ships from all over the known world. Listen carefully! In the quiet you may hear the water lapping against the hulls of the ships, and the shouted orders of the overseers as they direct the unloading and loading of the cargo. Can you catch the banter of the sailors as they toil with their loads? And can you overhear the hushed negotiations of those two wealthy merchants making their deals? All so long ago—but fresh to an imaginative, pensive mind.

This dynamic city was highly regarded throughout Greece, and the Greek world mourned its loss in 494 BC, when the Persian fleet of 600 warships defeated the 353 Milesian triremes. A play written by Phyrynichus, *The Capture of Miletus*, so distressed its Athenian audience that they burst into tears. As Herodotus tells us in *The Histories* (6.21), the playwright was fined a thousand drachmas for reminding them of the disaster and future productions of the play were banned.

Still in your state of contemplation, try to envisage old Miletus for here lived remarkable men and women. Let your thoughts turn to the 6th century before Christ, and to Thales, and his pupils, Anaximander and Anaximenes, attending the theatre, listening to the travelling bards reciting Homer, and perhaps sounding out their bold conjectures with their fellow citizens in the market place. These three Milesians, the first philosophers, were astronomers, mathematicians, statesmen, and engineers, and they were also men of practical ability. In addition to Hippodamus, the city was home to Hecateus, an historian, and the poets Timotheus, and Phocylides. Also born in Miletus was Aspasia, a remarkable woman who, in about 450 BC associated with and later married Pericles of Athens. The women of Miletus appear to have made quite an impact: Hippias of Elis, a contemporary of Socrates, wrote that one of many Milesian women known for her beauty was 'Thargelia of Miletus, who has been married fourteen times, and who was very beautiful in looks as well as clever'.

When you leave Miletus you will pass through the site of the Sacred Gate. The ancient people would make their religious processions through the Sacred Gate and along the Sacred Way, once lined by statues, lions and sphinxes, to the Temple of Apollo at Didyma. The modern road, via a new route, is a pleasant drive of about twenty kilometres. It crosses the now gentle Maeander River, and through lush checkered fields where dolphins once played in the Gulf as they escorted the ships to and from the harbours of Miletus.

References and Suggestions for Further Reading

Dunham, Adelaide Glynn. *The History of Miletus down to the Anabasis of Alexander*. London: University of London Press, 1915.

Freely, John. *Classical Turkey*. London: Penguin Books, 1990.

Freely, John. *The Western Shores of Turkey*. London: John Murray, 1988.

Freeman, Kathleen. *Greek City States*. London: Macdonald, 1950.

O'Grady, Patricia F. *Thales of Miletus: The Beginnings of Western Science and Philosophy*. Aldershot, England: Ashgate, 2002.

Chapter 66

Ancient Olympia:
Athletic Games and Intellectual Contests

Glenn Rawson

The home of the original Olympic Games occupied a special place in Greek thought for over a thousand years, from its obscure prehistoric origins until the breaking of the Roman empire. The games were performed as a national religious festival at a sanctuary of Zeus, leader of the Olympian gods. It was the first of the great pan-Hellenic sanctuaries, and the history of its contests illustrate deep currents in Greek culture. Our greatest resource for ancient Olympia, the travel writer Pausanias, wrote in the second century AD: 'There are many wonders to see in Greece, and many wonders to hear. But divine care is enjoyed most of all in the sacred rites of Eleusis and the contests at Olympia' (*Guide to Greece* I.x.1). In addition to the great Games, those wonderful sights and sounds include many artistic and intellectual triumphs.

The unifying influence of Olympia grew along with Greek identity, as scattered, rival, city-states continually forged a roughly common culture. In the Archaic period (8th to 6th centuries BC), established cities founded colonies in many foreign lands, and the enhanced sense of Greekness among 'barbarians' found a corresponding centre in Olympia's all-Greek, only-Greek worship of Zeus through competitive sport.

Olympia's creative energy flourished, especially early in the Classical period (5th and 4th centuries BC), when the cooperative Greek defeat of the immense Persian empire fuelled the classic art, architecture, and literature that were richly displayed at this national sanctuary. Even during the disastrously divisive Peloponnesian Wars, which drew all of Greece into the conflicts between Athens and Sparta, the quadrennial Sacred Truce of Olympia demanded safe passage for all who travelled to the festival. This Olympic ideal of peaceful common culture was not always realized. The games were manipulated politically, and battles were fought for the right to control them (as early as 665). Some festivals were interrupted by armed assault (as in 364) or conducted under armed guard (as in 420). And quarrels about athletic professionalism and the place of sports in culture attended those Olympics as they do ours. Yet the unifying and civilizing influence of Olympia was often real and important. For a time treaties throughout the land were ratified or recorded at Olympia, symbolically adding the protection of Zeus at his greatest sanctuary.

The artistic and literary exhibitions became regular events, as ambitious teachers and practitioners engaged in their own kind of competition for patronage and influence through the great national audience. Philosophers and other educators were attracted to Olympia's outstanding displays of Greek philotimia, or love of honour. From celebrations of the champions to critiques of their celebrity status, artists and intellectuals used the Olympic festivals as occasions and examples for promoting peace and Greek culture.

The remains at Olympia today are extensive, impressive, and easy to reach by major roads in the northwest Peloponnese. The early sanctuary's altars and modest racetrack had grown into a vast complex with grand temples and numerous treasuries, stadium, hippodrome, gymnasium, pool, hotels and administrative buildings, together with hundreds of monuments to divinities, athletes, military victories, and eventually Roman emperors. After centuries of Roman occupation and patronage, destruction of the sanctuary began with barbarian raids and anti-pagan decrees from Constantinople (now Istanbul). Then, 6th century earthquakes, floods and landslides buried the site—not to be rediscovered until AD 1766. Generations of archaeologists (first French, but German since 1876) have uncovered, studied, and partly restored much of the ancient complex.

Visitors to Olympia today experience acres of ancient foundations and colonnades, once again within an altis or grove of wild olives and other trees and flowering shrubs. For the 2004 Olympics, Greece reconstructed new portions of the Temple of Zeus and the Philippeion (where Philip (382–336 BC) and his son Alexander the Great (356–323) installed divine images of themselves). Today we can race in the ancient stadium, where the ancient starting blocks still remain to mark the starting line. We can wander the double colonnades of the palaestra or wrestling hall. We can visit the remains of the Prytaneion or city hall, which kept the sacred fire for ritual sacrifices, and feasted the winners on the meat of the sacrificial animals. We can stand at the ancient Bouleuterion or council-house, where athletes and judges opened the games with oaths of fair play before the statue of Zeus of Oaths.

There does seem to have been an effective reverence for honourable competition here: few cases of cheating or corruption are recorded before Roman times, and the heavy fines funded series of admonitory statues of Zeus (the Zanes) near the entrance to the stadium. Visitors to the museum can recall the more respectable cheating of legend. According to one tradition, Pelops (hence Peloponnese) established the games after winning the local princess in a race with her father, by bribing his servant to sabotage his chariot. Another tradition credits Heracles with founding the games. On the Temple of Zeus, the east pediment sculptures represented the story of Pelops, and twelve relief sculptures over the front and back porches celebrated the Labours of Heracles. (The pediments are reconstructed here in the Olympia museum, but the best of the Heracles sculptures are in the Louvre Museum in Paris.)

The two central temples were architecturally quite special, and so are their remains. The Heraion was originally a temple of Zeus and Hera, but when Zeus received a new house in Classical times, Hera got to keep the old. It is one of the earliest large temples in Greece (c. 650 or 600). Unlike later temples, much of the

Heraion was originally wood: the columns were replaced in stone over centuries, in the various Doric styles of different periods. Pausanias reported one wooden column still in place when the temple was about 800 years old. The base of the temple walls and most of the lower drums of the stone columns were uncovered in position; some are restored to their full height of over sixteen feet. This temple was central to the quadrennial Festival of Hera and its games for women. Women were forbidden to compete in the main Olympic festival, and married women were forbidden even to watch events. But unmarried women could attend the men's competitions, and they competed in their own footraces at the much smaller Festival of Hera. Winners received olive crowns and erected statues in the sanctuary, just like the men.

The much larger Temple of Zeus, completed in 456 BC, became a paradigm of the elegant Doric style, like the slightly later Parthenon at Athens. The original grandeur is evident in what remains: a massive platform with massive columns splayed in rows of drums like fallen dominoes for giants. It was built of local limestone coated with stucco, with imported marble for the roof. This temple housed one of the great artistic achievements of antiquity: the 40 foot gold and ivory cult statue of Zeus, seated on a throne with a sceptre in his left hand and the winged figure of victory in his right. The pioneering artist and architect Phidias created it in the 430s, after completing a similar statue of Athena for the Parthenon. Both were famously impressive, but the Zeus was the greater success, universally admired for its representation of divine power. Allegedly, Phidias was inspired by Homer's *Iliad,* where Zeus shakes Mount Olympus with just the nod of his head (*Iliad*, I.560-2). It was considered one of the seven wonders of the world, and a late work in that tradition reports that while all seven call for admiration, the Zeus at Olympia also evokes reverence (pseudo-Philo of Byzantium, *On the Seven Wonders*). Some ancient writers claimed it advanced religious thought with an unprecedented portrayal of a god's serene majesty. It is fitting that this would occur at the greatest common sanctuary of Greece.

Phidias had created his marvel next door, in a workshop built for the purpose, with the same dimensions and arrangement as the part of the temple where the statue would be installed. It was later converted to a Byzantine church, which is why its walls are still so well preserved. The hard proof that the church was Phidias' workshop came in the 1950's, when materials and tools were discovered underground—along with a cup inscribed 'I belong to Phidias'. The statue was probably burned in a fire at Constantinople, where it had been moved by the Church that destroyed its sanctuary in 426.

It is easy to feel at Olympia today the national prestige it must have enjoyed to achieve such a wealth of great art. Indeed, the quadrennial festival became the basis of common Greek chronology. Hippias, the 5th-century sophist who was born near Olympia and became famous throughout Greece, provided the foundation by producing the first thorough register of Olympic victors, with the eventual result that Greeks counted years from the first recorded Olympic festival (in what we now call 776 BC). Even Thucydides identifies certain years with the winners at Olympia, and later historians, starting with Timaeus, made it a systematic tool, coordinating local devices like the lists of officeholders at Athens and Sparta. The first historian, Herodotus of Halicarnassus, had another special relationship with Olympia: it is said that after his travels, he published his groundbreaking inquiries into east-west conflicts (his *historiai*) by reading them in 444 BC on the back porch of the Temple of Zeus, which often served this sort of literary function.

The most famous literary displays at Olympia took up the theme of Greek unity in common struggle against 'barbarians'. In 404, towards the end of the long Peloponnesian Wars, the esteemed orator and ambassador Gorgias of Leontini 'advised the Greeks on concord' in an Olympic Oration; he proclaimed that 'victories over foreigners demand festive songs; those over Greeks, lamentations'. Lysias of Syracuse, who lost family and estate in Athens when Sparta conquered her, addressed a yet strife-ridden Greece in 384 with his own Olympikos (oration), which bade the city-states unite against the king of Persia and the tyrant of Sicily. He even urged the audience to plunder that tyrant's ostentatious embassy on the spot, as a warning that impious tyranny was not welcome at the sacred games. At the following Olympic festival, another such panegyric was delivered by the Athenian educator Isocrates. His shyness required him to distribute copies instead of speaking it himself, yet in this speech he openly competes with his predecessors:

> For I believe that philosophy, oratory and the other arts will advance best if we admire and honour not those who practise a craft first, but those who finish it best; and not those who seek to speak about what no one has spoken before, but those who know how to speak as no one else was able. (*Panegyricus*, 10)

These public speeches highlight a growing intellectual trend. Plato's contemporary work, the *Republic*, argues that Greeks should avoid fighting, enslaving, and ravaging other Greeks, and that the custom of dedicating memorials of such conquests at temples is actually impious. In the same period, authorities began to discourage or disallow such dedications at Olympia. Isocrates went so far as to write that 'the name "Greek" suggests no longer a race but a way of thinking, and we call "Greek" those who share our culture rather than those who share a common descent'. Posterity judged this Panegyric the winner on the pan-Hellenic theme; but it was his teacher, the sophist, Gorgias who received a monument at Olympia, inscribed in part: 'No man yet has found a fairer art than Gorgias: to train the soul for virtue's contests.'

The literature that best expresses the spirit of the festivals are the epinikian odes, the non-sacred choral songs that celebrated winners in the games. The master of the genre was Pindar, whose works were commissioned throughout Greece for victories at all the pan-Hellenic festivals. Local festivals at Delphi, Corinth and Nemea had nationalized their games in imitation of Olympia, but the original kept pride of place, as is made clear in the ode which Pindar wrote for Hieron of Syracuse, winner of the horse race in 476 BC:

> Best of all is water, and gold like gleaming fire at night
> outshines all other glorifying wealth.
> And if you desire, dear heart,

to sing of contests, seek not beyond the sun
another star that shines by day more brightly in the lonely sky:
nor shall we sing of a festival more noble than Olympia. (*First Olympian Ode*)

Like almost all Greek poets, Pindar warns us against the hubris or arrogance
that often comes with success, insisting that we owe all success to the gods. But he
does so as a partisan of waning aristocratic traditions of athletic competition as the
domain of great families with wealth, leisure and god-given greatness in their
blood. Well-trained winners from humbler backgrounds do not really deserve to
win:

What comes by nature is always best. Many men
strive to win fame with virtues trained.
But anything acquired apart from god is better left unsung.
(*Ninth Olympian Ode*, written for Epharmostos of Opous, champion wrestler in 466)

The most obvious feature of his poems, which are related to religious hymns,
is their glorification of the champions through association with legendary heroes
and gods:

My hymns, lords of the lyre,
what god, what hero, and what man should we celebrate?
Truly Pisa belongs to Zeus, and the Olympiad was founded with Heracles' spoils of
war.
And Theron too we must proclaim, for his triumph with the four-horse chariot.
(*Second Olympian Ode*, written for Theron of Akragus, winner of the chariot race in
476)

These poems are the greatest surviving monuments to the extraordinary
honours received by the Olympic champions. We know that statues
commemorating their victories were erected at Olympia and in their hometowns,
and that the coveted olive crown at Olympia was often matched with hefty cash
prizes at home—or even free meals for life in city hall, as at Athens. Others
criticized these extravagant honours for athletes. Xenophanes, Euripides and
Isocrates complained that prizes for athletes' personal achievements outstripped
honours for public service through mental accomplishments. Socrates made the
point unforgettable when, convicted of impiety and required to propose an
alternative penalty to the prosecution's proposal of death, he suggested free meals
in city hall for his philosophical services, for 'your winners at Olympia make you
think you are happy; I make you be happy' (Plato, *Apology*, 36 D-E).

Other philosophers complimented Olympia's spirit of philotimia, or love of
honour, in their very attempts to transcend it. Pythagoras contrasted honour-
seeking athletes with the dignity of the wisdom-loving philosophos—a term he
may have coined in the process. The ancient biographer Diogenes Laertius reports
that Pythagoras 'compared life to the great festival, saying that some go to compete
and others to sell things, but the best go to be spectators; so also in life some grow
up servile, chasing fame and gain, but philosophers seek the truth' (D.L. VIII.8).

Plato's *Republic* more subtly argues that since natural honour-lovers are indeed better than most people, who seek money and physical comfort instead, ideally they renounce material wealth in a life of athletic and martial excellence in service to the whole community. But natural wisdom-lovers are even better, the source of the knowledge that guides others to genuinely honourable lives; such philosophers should get no wealth, but all the power—and the highest honours. In this tradition, the Stoic teacher Epictetus, a near contemporary of Pausanias, trains student minds for moral strength with frequent analogies to the Olympic games: 'those engaged in the greatest contest should not flinch, but take their blows; for the contest before us is not in wrestling or the all-out boxing ... but in good fortune and happiness itself' (*Discourses* III.25). Olympic victories require opportunities and regimens we cannot control, but success in morality is even more honourable and always within our reach. We can always win at choosing to be good and renouncing other desires, because 'you can be invincible if you enter no contest whose victory is not up to you' (*Handbook* 19). Epictetus, like centuries of philosophers before him, makes the glory of Olympia a motivating figure for all noble struggles.

References and Suggestions for Further Reading

Gardiner, E.N. *Olympia: Its History and Remains*. Oxford: Clarendon Press, 1925.
Hall, Edith. 'Literature and Performance.' In Paul Cartledge, editor, *The Cambridge Illustrated History of Ancient Greece*. Cambridge: Cambridge University Press, 1998.
Nisetich, F.J. *Pindar's Victory Odes*. Baltimore: The Johns Hopkins University Press, 1980.
Pausanias. *Guide to Greece*. Vol. 2: *Southern Greece*. Harmondsworth: Penguin Books, 1971.
Raschke, Wendy J. editor. *The Archaeology of the Olympics: The Olympics and Other Festivals in Antiquity*. Madison: The University of Wisconsin Press, 1988.
Saunders, A.N.W. *Greek Political Oratory*. Harmondsworth: Penguin Books, 1970.

Chapter 67

Piraeus

Daniel Silvermintz

Wretched ones, why sit you here? Flee and be gone to remotest
Ends of earth, leaving your homes, high places in circular city;
For neither the head abides sound, no more than the feet or the body;
Fire pulls all down, and sharp Ares, driving his Syrian-bred horses.
Many a fortress besides, and not yours alone shall he ruin.
Many the temples of God to devouring flames he shall give them.
There they stand now, the sweat of terror streaming down from them.
They shake with fear; from the rooftops black blood in deluging torrents.
They have seen the forthcoming destruction, and evil sheerly constraining.
Get you gone out of the shrine! Blanket your soul with your sorrows.
(Herodotus, *The Histories* 7.140)

Nothing could have been less assuring to the Athenians readying for the impending invasion of Persian marauders in 480 BC than the command issued by the Delphic Oracle to 'flee to the ends of the earth'. In spite of this foreboding counsel, the Athenians were not prepared to relinquish their freedom and accept subjugation under the lash of eastern despotism without a valiant struggle. Having already won far-reaching fame for routing the Persians at Marathon, the Athenians supplicated themselves before the god, Apollo, and refused to leave his temple until the oracle issued them a better fate. Their pleadings were successful in swaying the will of the gods insofar as the priestess now promised that the city's 'wooden walls' would be its stronghold against complete and utter destruction. While most Athenians believed that the cryptic prophesy referred to the fortress built around the Acropolis, the military commander, Themistocles, argued that the oracle was referring to the wooden walls of Athens' tall ships. The great tactician's interpretation won the day and Athens marshalled its fleet to engage the Persians in a sea battle off the coast of Salamis.

Athens defeated its foe, but (as the Oracle had predicted) not before the eastern invaders had sacked and burned the city to the ground. The city's monuments were rebuilt with greater grandeur in the years following the Persian Wars; the culture that engendered the Marathon fighters could not be resuscitated. Rather than prowess on the battlefield, the new Athenian identity would be shaped by its emerging naval supremacy. As the dominant power of the Delian League, Athens grew into an empire extracting tribute from smaller city-states in return for protection against future eastern attacks. The transformation of Athens into a maritime power brought its harbour town in Piraeus into increasing military, political, and cultural significance. Plutarch notes how the fortification of Athens by means of the connecting Long Walls with the harbour inverted the city's power dynamics:

> But Themistocles did not, as Aristophanes the comic poet says, 'knead the Piraeus on to the city', nay, he fastened the city to the Piraeus, and the land to the sea. And so it was that he increased the privileges of the common people as against the nobles, and filled them with boldness, since the controlling power came now in the hands of skippers and boatswains and pilots. (Plutarch, _Themistocles_ 19.2)

While protecting Athens' security from enemy attack, Piraeus was radically undermining the identity of Athens from within. Sailors and salesmen, foreigners and hucksters, prostitutes and philosophers equally found the harbour town an inviting place to call home. This receptivity to alien ideas made Piraeus a particularly ideal setting for the unconstrained inquiry into the nature of justice presented in Plato's _Republic_. With echoes of Themistocles' charge for the people to descend to the port in defense of their city, Socrates journeys to Piraeus in order to instigate a quite different sort of war. In telling us of his excursion to Piraeus, Socrates reveals its character as a place of religious and cultural innovation:

> I went down to the Piraeus yesterday with Glaucon, son of Ariston, to pray to the goddess; and, at the same time, I wanted to observe how they would put on the festival, since they were now holding it for the first time. (Plato, _Republic_ 327a)

Thwarted in his attempt to return to his home in Athens, Socrates is cajoled into staying the night in Piraeus by a group of young men eager to satisfy their appetites at the evening's festival. These men will, under the influence of the philosophic gadfly, soon forget their sensual desires as they are increasingly drawn by the vision of a world beyond beautiful spectacles. The all-night inquiry in pursuit of justice and the good life will herald a new epoch, challenging men to fight a war within one's soul rather than on the battlefield.

References and Suggestions for Further Reading

Garland, Robert. _The Piraeus_. Bristol: Bristol Classical Press, 2002.

Herodotus. _The Histories_. Trans. David Greene. University of Chicago Press, 1987.

Pausanias. _Description of Greece_. Loeb Classical Library. London: Heinemann, 1960.

Plato. _The Republic of Plato_. Trans. Allan Bloom. New York: Basic Books, 1968.

Plutarch. _Plutarch's Lives_. Trans. Bernadotte Perrin. Cambridge, MA.: Harvard University Press, 1968.

Von Reden, Sitta. 'The Piraeus: A World Apart', _Greece & Rome_. Vol. 42, No. 1. (1995), pp. 24-37.

Wycherley, R.E. _'Peiraeus'_. In Stillwell, Richard. MacDonald, William L. McAlister, Marian Holland, eds. _Princeton Encyclopedia of Classical Sites_. Princeton: Princeton University Press, 1976. p. 684.

Chapter 68

Samos

Tim O'Keefe and Patricia F. O'Grady

Samos is a blest country that is praised in the proverb that 'it produces even birds' milk'. (Strabo, *Geography*, 14. I.15)

Samos is the birthplace of two of ancient Greece's most prominent philosophers, Pythagoras (fl. c. 530 BC) and Epicurus (c. 341–271 BC). Both departed from Samos, however, and left their most enduring philosophical marks elsewhere. According to some ancient sources, Pythagoras fled Samos in order in escape from the rule of the tyrant Polycrates. After leaving Samos, he founded a religious and philosophical community (the Pythagorean Order) in Croton, in southeastern Italy. Members of this community had to follow strict laws regarding diet and cleanliness in order to maintain the purity of their souls, and the Pythagoreans made important advances in mathematics, as they tried to discover the numerical order they thought structured the universe. Epicurus set up the Garden, a combination of philosophical school and community, in Athens; its members tried to attain tranquillity by ridding themselves of vain desires and withdrawing from entanglement in politics and public life.

There are no ancient sites in Samos directly related to either Pythagoras or Epicurus, but Samos has more recent monuments to Pythagoras. The town of Pythagorio, on the southeastern coast, is named after him, and the town boasts a recent statue of the philosopher, on the jetty at the eastern end of the harbour. It plays with the achievement almost all schoolchildren know Pythagoras for—the 'Pythagorean theorem'. The statue features the figure of Pythagoras, with one hand pointing up, forming one side of a right triangle, while the base is inscribed with Pythagorean phrases about the harmony of the *cosmos*.

One street back from the water-front of Pythagorio, on tree-lined Plateia Irinis, is an imposing bust of Pythagoras. Behind this is a small but very interesting museum which should not be missed—and entry is free. Apart from the life size statue of the Roman Emperor Trajan (2nd century AD) and an impressive statue of the seated Aeces, who was the father of Polycrates, the tyrant of Samos, there is a fine collection of tiny funerary or oil vases. But the most beautiful and outstanding exhibit is a magnificent amphora, about two feet high, and with a geometric pattern. Its beauty, and the realization that it dates from the time of Pythagoras, are awe-inspiring.

Samos attained its greatest military and political prominence under the tyrant Polycrates, who ruled the island during the second half of the 6th century BC. His motto apparently was 'bigger is better', as he was famous for the scale of his building projects. Eight kilometres west of Pythagorio are the ruins of the Hereon, the Sanctuary of Hera. The Temple to Hera on this site was four times the size of the Parthenon in Athens, but all that remains standing is a single pillar, evoking Percy Bysshe Shelley's 'Ozymandias': Shelley's reflections on the futility of striving for fame and power would have been quite congenial to Epicurus.

Poylycrates, who was tyrant when Pythagoras lived in the town later named Pythagorio, built Samos into a great sea power. It was at this time that the Eupalinos tunnel was built, and the temple to Hera and the long walls which protected Pythagorion were constructed. Ruins of an ancient theatre, and short sections of the long walls which remain, can be seen as one walks to view the tunnel, which was named after the engineer who accomplished the remarkable building feat. The tunnel was constructed to bring spring water to Pythagorion, and is about 900 metres long. It was cut through a hill, with workers commencing at each end and meeting almost exactly in the middle.

Herodotus, who is known as the Father of History, was extremely impressed by these remarkable engineering accomplishments. This is how he described them:

> I have gone on about the Samians at some length because three of their achievements are unsurpassed in the Greek world. The first is a tunnel which was dug right through the bottom of a hill 150 fathoms high, so that there is an opening at either end; the tunnel is seven stades long and eight feet in both height and width. Along the whole of its length another channel has been dug, which is 20 cubits deep and three feet wide, and which carries water from a great spring through pipes to the town. The master builder of this tunnel was a Megarian called Eupalinus the son of Naustrophus. The second of the three achievements is a mole in the sea, over two stades long, enclosing the harbour in water which is as much as twenty fathoms deep. The third thing they built is the largest temple ever seen; its original design was drawn up by Phoecus the son of Phileas, who was a native of Samos. These achievements of theirs are my justification for going on about them at some length. (Herodotus, *The Histories*, 3.60)

Vathy is the capital of Samos, but it is almost always called Samos Town. Plateia Pythagora (Pythagoras Square), located along the waterfront of Samos Town, is ringed with low walls or benches that have triangular cross sections, reminiscent of the triangle for which Pythagoras is commonly known.

Samos features no ancient or modern monuments to its son Epicurus, who would have derided such things as foolishness anyway. However, those who wish to reflect on Epicurus' doctrine that tranquillity is the goal of life could do much worse than visit the village of Manolates, west of Samos Town, a few kilometers inland from the northern coast. This peaceful place is nestled among the pine trees, on a mountain-side overlooking the ocean. Enjoy some of the simple but satisfying fare at Lucas Taverna, located at the back and top of the village, look down at the water, and think of the notorious sentiment of the Epicurean poet, Lucretius:

> It's pleasant to be able to look down from tranquil heights, view the turbulent sea, and think of troubles other people have that you don't share. (*On the Nature of Things* II.1-13)

References and Suggestions for Further Reading

Herodotus. *The Histories*. Translated by Robin Waterfield. New York: Oxford
    University Press, 1998.
Lucretius. *The Way Things Are. The De Rerum Natura of Titus Lucretius Carus*. Trans.
    Rolfe Humphries. Bloomington: Indiana University Press, 1968.
Shelley, Percy, Bysshe. *Selected Poems*. Dover Thrift Editions. Dover Publications.
Strabo. *The Geography of Strabo*. With an English translation by Horace Leonard Jones.
    Vol VI. Loeb Classical Library. London: Heinemann, 1929.

Chapter 69

Syracuse

Phillip Meade

> I have many arrows in my quiver; they have a voice that speaks to men who can
> understand, but for the crowd they need interpreters. The wise is he who knows much
> by inborn genius; those who have learnt from others are like ravens chattering in vain
> against the divine bird of Zeus. (*The Second Olympian Ode*, lines 83-86. Written by
> Pindar for Theron of Acragus (a city in central Sicily), the winner of the Chariot Race
> in the Olympic Games in 476 BC)

Located at the crossroads of the Mediterranean Sea's north-south axis, Syracuse
became a prosperous city second only to Athens in the Classical age. It plays a
pivotal role in the development and full flowering of Greek culture, philosophy and
science. The founding men and women of Syracuse were a hardy and industrious lot.
They came from farm and merchant stock in and around the city of Corinth with a
hope for a new life and a sense of adventure. These were Greek pioneers in the late
8th century BC. The colonists picked the site of a former Mycenaean trading post on
the offshore island of Ortygia for the original colony. This choice location created
two excellent natural ports, one, the large Great Harbour, is the finest on the east
coast of Sicily to this day. The city grew rapidly and soon had four colonies of its
own. As a city it has been in continuous existence since 733 BC.

Arethusa, a water nymph, is said to have fled to Sicily from mainland Greece
in order to evade the amorous advances of the river god Alpheus. The island of
Ortygia has a fresh water spring likewise named Arethusa whose image is also
seen on early coin designs of Syracuse. The city soon expands to the mainland and
farming and trade flourishes. Syracuse received luxury goods from Corinth and
sent back wheat, fruit, timber and vegetables. Cult centres of Persephone and
Demeter arise in Syracuse. According to one tradition Persephone left her mother's
house to pick flowers with a group of girls, the glorious Oceanides, daughters of
Oceanus and Tethys. As Persephone bends to collect a particularly beautiful
narcissus bloom, the earth suddenly opens up and the god of the underworld rides
out of the cavern in a chariot drawn by black horses to seize her and take her to
Hades, where she is to reign as its queen. The flower meadow is traditionally
believed to lie on the island of Sicily near Syracuse although another site the Lago
di Pergus at Enna, contests the claim.

Aristocratic landowning families ruled Syracuse in its early days and, around
575 BC, built a large temple to Apollo on Ortygia. Trade now includes imports and
exports with Carthage and other neighbors.

Sicily and especially the area around Syracuse became safe havens for Pythagorean communities after the destruction of the city of Sybaris and the political unrest in the city of Croton which are both less than a day's travel by boat. Pythagorean groups flourished, and arts, mathematics, science and philosophy all are encouraged with the increasing agricultural and mercantile prosperity.

The oligarchic and democratic government of Syracuse was suppressed by Gelon, tryant of the neighboring city of Gela, who took possession of the city in 485 BC. Gelon's successor, Hiero I, made Syracuse into one of the great centres of Greek culture: the poet Pindar and the dramatist Aeschylus lived there for a time and composed at the court.

The dramatist and comic poet Epicharmus was a resident and perhaps a native of Syracuse as well. Plato refers to him as the prince of comedy and Plutarch records that he became a Pythagorean. Thirty seven titles of his works have come down to us, and were perhaps performed at the local festivals of Artemis and Demeter in Syracuse. Soon after Hiero's death a democracy was established, which lasted for sixty years. Syracuse extended its control over eastern Sicily and, in 414 BC, even defeated an Athenian expedition led by Alcibiades. Democracy had run its course and by 406BC, the strong man Dionysis the Elder became tryant (see Glossary) and pushed Syracuse to its high point of power and territorial expansion.

The philosopher Plato visited Syracuse a number of times with great hopes. One of his students, Dion, was an advisor to Dionysis. Dion continued to urge Plato to put his teachings concerning the Philosopher King (the ideal of the king being a philosopher, and a philosopher being king) to practical use by tutoring Dionysis' son, Dionysis the younger, in the ways of philosophy. Plato's *Seventh Letter* details the tragic results and Plato's close encounter with an almost untimely end on one of his visits to the city.

Pythagorean friendship was put to the test by this same Dionysis the younger, now tyrant of Syracuse. Later, when he was in exile in Corinth, he related the following story of Phintias and Damon to Aristoxenus (fragment 31):

This is how it was: certain intimates of his had often mentioned the Pythagoreans, defaming and reviling them, calling them arrogant, and asserting that their gravity, their pretended fidelity, and discipline would disappear on falling into some calamity. Others contradicted this; and as contention arose on the subject, it was decided to settle the matter by an experiment. One man accused Phintias, before Dionysis, of having conspired with others against his life. Others corroborated the charges, which looked probable, though Phintias was astonished at the accusation. When Dionysis had unequivocally said he had verified the charges, and that Phintias must die, the latter replied that if Dionysis thought that this was necessary, he requested the delay of the remainder of the day, to settle the affairs of himself and Damon, as the two men lived together and had all things in common; but as Phintias was the elder, he mostly undertook the management of the household affairs. He therefore requested that Dionysis allow him to depart for this purpose, and that he would appoint Damon as his surety. Dionysis claimed surprise at such a request, and asked him if any man existed who would stand surety for the death of another. Phintias asserted that there was, and Damon was sent for; and on hearing what had happened, agreed to become the sponsor, and that he would remain there until Phintias' return. Dionysis declared astonishment at these circumstances, and they who had proposed the experiment derided Damon as the one who would be caught, sneering at him as the 'vicarious stag'. When however, sunset approached, Phintias came to die, at which all present were astonished and subdued. Dionysis, having embraced and kissed the men, requested that they would receive him as a third into their friendship. They however would by no means consent to anything of the kind, though he entreated them to comply with his request.

Timoleon (411–337 BC), a noble aristocrat from Corinth, restored democracy to Syracuse and for a generation made it so peaceful and prosperous that new settlers were drawn from all over the Hellenic world.

Pyrrhus, the great warrior king of Epirus, married Lanassa, daughter of Agathocles the Syracusan and for a time fought and defeated both the Romans and Carthaginians on Sicily and around Syracuse.

Less than a generation later Hieron, a distinguished military commander who fought defeated both the Carthaginians and Romans, was proclaimed king Hieron II, of Syracuse about 270 BC. He ruled the city for 54 years and all, according to the historian Polybius 'without killing, exiling, or injuring a single citizen, which indeed is the most remarkable of all things.' (Polybius vii, 8). Hieron skilfully made a treaty with the Romans to supply troops and grain, and despite the many battles between Carthage and Rome he never broke his treaty with the Romans. He built a 'supership', the *Syrakosia* (Lady of Syracuse) half a stadium (407 feet) in length. It had a sports deck with a gymnasium, a marble bath and a garden deck. The ship could carry three hundred passengers and was manned by a crew of six hundred seamen. It would rival our modern passenger liners with its elegant cabins inlaid with ivory carvings and mosaic tiles along with precious woods. The ship weighed a thousand tons and could carry three thousand nine hundred tons of cargo. The plan was to use the supership for regular service between Syracuse and Alexandria. Hieron however found the ship very expensive to maintain and too large for his own docks, so he filled it with fish and corn from Sicily's abundant sea and fields and sent the vessel and contents as a gift to Ptolemy Philopator, the ruler of Egypt. Many civic projects to benefit the citizens were started under Hieron's rule. Hieron led a modest and temperate life even though he was surrounded by all the means of luxury. He died at the age of 90. Polybius tells us that on several occasions he wished to resign his authority, but the people begged him to retain it (Polybius vii, 8). While visiting Hieron's court, the poet Theocritas, a native of Sicily, wrote a poem singing the praises of Hieron and the loveliness of Sicily. At this time Syracuse had become the most prosperous and populous city in all Hellas. One of Syracuse's most famous sons was the multi-talented mathematician, scientist and inventor, Archimedes (see the essay, Archimedes).

In the second Punic War, soon after Hieron's death, Syracuse made the mistake of siding with Carthage against Rome. Rome sent two legions under Marcus Claudius Marcellus who, after a long siege, captured and sacked the city. It was during the sacking that Archimedes, then 75, lost his life. The historian, Livy, says Marcellus 'removed to Rome the ornaments of Syracuse—the statues and pictures in which it abounded ... the spoils were almost greater than if Carthage itself had been taken'.

Syracuse's early Christian remains are poorly preserved but extensive, with more catacombs than any other city save Rome. In 491 AD, Syracuse and all of Sicily were occupied by the Ostrogoths. Syracuse returns to the Byzantine empire in the next century and in 663 Constans II moved the imperial court from Constantinople to the Ortygia of Syracuse. The Arabs invaded Sicily and after a long siege captured Syracuse in 878. The Normans defeated the Muslim fleet in 1085 and restored Syracuse to papal jurisdiction. Syracuse has always been one of the jewels of the Mediterranean.

References and Suggestions for Further Reading

Grant, Michael. *The Rise of the Greeks.* New York: Macmillan, 1987.

Konstan, David. *Friendship in the Classical World.* Cambridge: Cambridge University Press, 1997.

Plato. *The Epistles: Epistle VII. (The Seventh Letter).* Translated by R.G. Bury. Loeb Classical Library. London: Heinemann, 1961.

Plutarch's Lives: Dion; Timoleon. Translated by Bernadotte Perrin. Loeb Classical Library. London: Heinemann, 1961.

Randall-MacIver, David. *Greek Cities in Italy and Sicily.* Oxford: Clarendon Press, 1931.

Chapter 70

Troy and Heinrich Schliemann

Patricia F. O'Grady

> So tribe on tribe, pouring out of the ships and shelters
> Marched across the Scamander plain and the earth shook,
> tremendous thunder from under the feet of trampling men and horses.
> They took their position in the blossoming meadow of Scamander,
> numberless as the leaves and spears that flower forth in spring. (Homer, *Iliad*, 2.464-68)

Christmas, 1829. Heinrich joyfully opened his Christmas present, Ludwig Jerrer's *Illustrated History of the World*. When the excited seven year old, who already knew Homer's *Iliad* from his father, saw the illustration of Troy in flames he was captivated. From that time, his faith in the existence of Troy never wavered, and he set himself the goal of discovering Troy.

Driven by an almost fanatical passion, Schliemann devoted himself to work and study. He amassed a considerable fortune and learnt to speak and write seven languages. Almost fifty years after receiving *The Illustrated History,* Schliemann was financially able to pursue his intense ambition to reveal Troy.

With a large number of local workmen, with his Greek wife, Sophia, and assisted by Frank Calvert and Professor Wilhelm Dörpfeld, he commenced digging at Hissarlik, the Turkish name for the hill. Schliemann was an amateur archaeologist, and his methods were rough and destructive, but it could be said that the criticism of Schliemann has been excessive. Opinion remains widely divided, but he was probably no worse than other diggers of the time, and it should be remembered that it was through his total conviction that Troy really existed that the ancient cities were discovered and excavated.

It was a deplorable act when, counter to his agreement with the Turkish government, Schliemann stole, and smuggled out from Turkey, many valuable artefacts, including Priam's treasure of golden jewellery which, in a photograph taken by her husband, adorns the neck of Sophia. At the end of World War II, the Russians removed the treasure from Berlin to the Pushkin Museum in Moscow, where it is likely to remain.

Troy—the word itself invokes the presence of gods, goddesses, and heroes in an almost legendary place. We are familiar with Troy because of the story of the *Iliad* which Homer retold in about 750 BC perhaps five hundred years after the Trojan War. The *Iliad* records the ninth year of the Trojan War between the Achaeans, as the Greeks were then called, and the Trojans in their city of Troy (or Ilium) on the north-west corner of Asia Minor, modern Capadoccia.

The war began because the Trojan prince, Paris, son of Hecuba and Priam, the King of Troy, had stolen, or enticed, Helen, the most beautiful woman in the world, from her husband, Prince Menelaos of Lacedaemon (Sparta) in the Peloponnese. (In his *Histories,* Herodotus who is known as the Father of History, explains the ultimate cause of the war as the abduction of Helen but the real cause was probably commercial, the Hellespont, the narrow strait dividing Europe from Asia being vitally important for trade. Hellespont is not named after Helen of Troy as one might expect, but after Helle, a mythical princess who, legend tells us, drowned in the dangerous waters.) The treacherous abduction of Helen had to be avenged, and the Greeks, led by the Great King Agamemnon, who was the brother of Menelaos, gathered together the mightiest army the world had ever seen. The catalogue of ships, and the numbers of men gathered from all over Greece to form this immense army, are described in Book II of the *Iliad.* They sailed to the Hellespont on the Troad, the land of the Trojans, where they beached their "black ships" (*Iliad*, 2. 630) at Kum Kale to the north-west of the high city.

Windy Troy, as it is aptly described, has "the wine-dark sea" (*Iliad*, 2.613) as a backdrop. Closer, just down the slope from the windy city, are the lush green fields where the armies fought, the feet of horses and men trampling the blossoms on the Plain of the Scamander River, as Homer wrote.

Visiting Troy may be likened to a pilgrimage. It is a mystical place for one is conscious of the spirit of the Greeks and the Trojans: their kings, Agamemnon and Priam, the princes Menelaos and Paris, the princesses Cassandra and Helen, and the heroes, Achilles, Odysseus, Hector and Patroclus. And over it all, hovers the spirit of the lovers, Paris and Helen, and the tragedy which was the consequence of their love, for here the leaders of the mighty armies led their men into battles, guided (and misguided), as they thought, by the capricious, deceitful Olympian gods.

To the Ancient Greeks Troy was very real. They relished the story of the War and accepted Homer's version of the event. Later, belief in Troy waned and the tale of Troy assumed a legendary nature. It was the result of Schliemann's single-minded devotion to his belief in Troy that the firm archaeological evidence was revealed, confirming the existence of the Windy City and the fact of a Trojan War, although perhaps not just as the *Iliad* portrays it.

The entrance to the ruins is dominated by an immense replica of the wooden horse which calls for a photograph of oneself peeping out of a high tiny window. The story is that the Achaeans built a hollow wooden horse, large enough to conceal a number of their warriors. They dragged it to the gates of Troy and 'sailed away'. The Trojans dragged the 'gift' into the city and, believing themselves to be the victors, proceeded to celebrate. Pausanias tells us that the wooden horse contained the most valiant of the Greeks (Pausanias, *Description of Greece*, I, xxiii. 8). During the night, when the Trojans were either drunk or asleep, these 'valiant Greeks' crept from the belly of the horse and opened the gates to the Achaeans who had returned, unseen. By morning, the victorious Achaeans had slaughtered the Trojan men and boys, while the women and girls were enslaved.

To the right of the replica of the wooden horse is a small but well organized museum which contains artefacts from the site, as well as useful plans and models.

The city of Troy consists of nine layers, and many levels of accumulated debris which represent the cities built one atop the other as, over the millennia, the Trojans rebuilt their cities on the same site. Using the word 'debris' belittles the fact that the levels relate the day to day personal lives of flesh and blood people, the Trojan men, women and children, and their homes.

At first sight Troy may be a disappointment, for little remains above ground-level, but the atmosphere is permeated by the past. We may be certain that Homer's characters are based upon real people and so one may easily identify and empathise with them. Reconstruct the cities in your mind's eye, and meet the characters. Feel the anguish of the men who left their wives and children back in lovely Greece to pursue a long war. Rejoice in the joy of the lovers, endure the pain of the suffering, the courage and treachery of the foes, and grieve for the dead. Suffer with them when they witness the death of their friends, and when they, themselves, are cut down in agony. Endure the grief of the Trojans and their dreadful fate. Hear their cries, for this is real. Homer did not romanticize the war: He describes battle in all its frightful detail:

> There the screaming and the shouts of triumph rose up together of men killing and men killed, and the ground ran blood. (*Iliad*, 8.65)

> Peiros stabbed with his spear next the navel, and all his guts poured out on the ground, and a mist of darkness closed over both eyes. (*Iliad*, 4. 520-526)

> For on that day, many men of the Achaeans and Trojans lay sprawled in the dust face downward beside one another (*Iliad*, 4. 543-44)

Turn to breathe the sea air, as the ever-present wind ruffles the blood-red poppies, just as the Achaeans and the Trojans might have done; ponder and link with Achaeans and Trojans alike who recognized the futility of it all. Such is the writing in the *Iliad*! It is easy to fall in love with Homer—that is why the *Iliad* has lasted for nearly three thousand years.

The Troy which Homer, and the Homeridae (later Homeric writers and commentators) who followed him, describe in the *Iliad* is now identified as Troy VIIb. Schliemann, and the archaeologists who have continued the excavations since that time, reveal much of the plan of Troy VIIb. They identify a number of particular sites: the Temple to Athena, the city walls which are dated to various periods, the bouleterion or senate house, and the Scaean Gate, mentioned by Homer a number of times.

In the locality of Kum Kale where the great army of the Achaeans first landed, the supposed Heroic Tumuli, or burial mounds, of the Greek heroes, Achilles and Patroclus have been identified and, further to the east, is the Heroic Tumulus of Aias (Ajax), who, after Achilles, was the greatest of the heroes. To the south-east is Mt. Ida, from where, according to Homer, the gods and goddesses, the mighty Zeus and his wife, Hera, the beautiful Apollo, the war-like Athena, Aphrodite, the goddess of love, Iris, the messenger of the gods, and others, watched the war, and debated their tactics.

To get the most from the experience, visitors should seek the expertise of an experienced guide, one who is equally captivated by Troy and Homer's *Iliad*, and eager to discuss the ancient city with interested tourists. Try to plan a leisurely pace to ponder on the ages of inhabited Troy, to reconstruct the idea of the primitive bronze age, Troy I of 3,000 BC, and to observe the many levels of Trojan life up to Homer's city, Troy VIIb.

Tourists with a passion for literature and history will be well rewarded if they make the time to read the history of Troy, and to learn something of the story that Homer so skilfully and dramatically relates in the *Iliad*. Best of all, of course, is to read the *Iliad*, for it is clear that Homer visited Troy. Homer is still the best guide to Troy (Freely, 1988, 28). No one relates the story as well as he does, or displays a deeper understanding of man's humanity and inhumanity, his courage, treachery, and folly.

References and Suggestions for Further Reading

Blegen, Carl W. *Troy and the Trojans.* London: Thames and Hudson, 1963.

Freely, John. *The Western Shores of Turkey.* London: John Murray, 1988.

The Iliad of Homer. Trans. with an introduction by Richard Lattimore. Chicago: The University of Chicago Press, 1976.

Page, Denys L. *History of the Homeric Iliad.* Berkeley: University of California Press, 1959.

Payne, Robert. *The Gold of Troy.* London: Robert Hale Limited, 1958.

Pausanias. *Description of Greece.* Loeb Classical Library. London: Heinemann, 1960

Glossary

Glenn Rawson

Academy: school founded by Plato at the Athenian gymnasium of that name, and the first stable centre of higher education. After Plato and his near successors, it became a skeptical school under leaders like Arcesilaus and Carneades, then again a school of more positive theories. It was a centre of neo-Platonism under Proclus, and finally closed by Emperor Justinian in 529 AD.

aether: in Hesiod's *Theogony*, a daughter of Night and sister of Day. In Aristotle's science, the 'fifth element' in addition to earth, air, fire, and water; the matter of the moon, sun and stars, which naturally moves eternally in circles.

altar: the essential element of any Greek sanctuary, where the burnt sacrifice was made to the god. There was an altar in the centre of the theatre at Athens, where plays were performed in a festival to Dionysus (compare temple).

Archaic: of the period from the rise of the Greek *polis* to the defeat of the Persian invasions (early 8th century to 479 BC). This period includes the establishment of pan-Hellenic sanctuaries like Olympia, the beginnings of philosophy and science, the invention of Greek writing and theatre, and authors from Homer to Aeschylus (compare Classical and Hellenistic).

Areopagite: a member of the Areopagus.

Areopagus: the 'Hill of Ares' near the Athenian Acropolis; also the ancient aristocratic council that met there, which was incorporated in the Classical democracy, then served various functions in various forms of government through the centuries.

astronomy: scientific study of the motions of heavenly bodies, including attempts to reconcile their apparently disorderly motions with the belief that they always move in perfect circles around the earth (not to be confused with astrology, which includes nonscientific predictions according to the mythologically based zodiac).

Byzantine: relating to the city called Byzantium in ancient times, which later became Constantinople, then Istanbul. The Byzantine Empire was centered in Constantinople.

chorus: in Greek drama, a group of twelve or fifteen actors who sing and dance, interact with the main actors and comment upon the action.

Classical: of the period from the defeat of the Persian invasion to the conquests of Alexander the Great (479 to 323 BC). This period includes the great wars between Athens and Sparta, and a flourishing of artistic and intellectual achievements, including authors from Aeschylus to Plato and Aristotle (compare Archaic and Hellenistic).

cosmogony: study of the origins of the universe (compare cosmology).

cosmology: study of the universe (*kosmos*) as a natural and well-ordered whole (compare cosmogony).

cult: worship of a god or dead hero, including sacrifice and related rituals (used here without the sense of sinister or unusual).

cynicism: a philosophical tradition inaugurated by Diogenes of Sinope, advocating an extreme, anti-conventional form of living according to nature. They were called *kynikos* or 'doglike' for allegedly shameless behavior.

Demiurge: Plato's metaphorical maker of the whole physical universe (Greek *dêmiourgos*, 'skilled craftsman').

dialectic: the art of conducting philosophical conversation by exploring logical consequences of agreed premises. Some engaged competitively with the goal of refutation, others cooperatively in hopes of discovering truth. Aristotle contrasted it with both scientific demonstration and rhetoric (compare rhetoric).

dogmatism: in its philosophical sense, any position that claims to be justified in affirming or denying something. It is the opposite of skepticism, and need not imply uncritical or closed-minded (compare skepticism).

ellipse: a shape like an oval that has two foci instead of one centre. Technically, the sum of the distances to the two foci must be the same from any point on the curve.

empiricism: the view that all knowledge must be acquired and justified at least in part through sense-perception. Epicureans and Stoics are early empiricists (compare rationalism).

epistemology: traditionally the study of the nature of knowledge (*epistêmê*), what sorts of things can be known, and how we can come to know them; together with related matters like the nature and formation of belief (compare empiricism and rationalism).

ethics: as the study of human nature and how we should live (from *ethos*, 'character'), this was a focus of philosophy since at least Heraclitus. Beginning with early Stoics, it became one of three basic divisions of philosophy (compare logic and physics).

etymology: the study of words and their meanings through their origins (from *etymos*, 'true,' and *logos*, 'word').

fragments: portions of original writings that survive in incomplete form, sometimes because they are found now only in broken scrolls or books, but usually because the original survives only in quotations by other authors.

gloss: an explanation of unfamiliar language. Often these were inserted in the margins of ancient texts by scribes or commentators, but they were also collected in 'glossaries'.

Hellene: a Greek person; from *Hellên*, which Greeks have called themselves since ancient times.

Hellenic: Greek (compare Hellene).

Hellenistic: of the period from the rule of Macedonian Alexander the Great to that of Roman emperor Augustus (323–331BC). This period saw the loss of autonomy in the Greek city-states and a great diffusion of Greek culture abroad. It includes authors from Epicurus to Lucretius (compare Achaic and Classical).

Ionia: the west coast of Asia Minor, now part of Turkey, with many ancient Greek cities such as Miletus and Ephesus. The earliest recorded philosophers are the Ionian 'school' of Thales, Anaximander and Anaximenes. (The Ionian Sea, between Greece and Magna Graecia, probably got its name by colonizers from Ionia.)

irrational number: a number not expressible in whole numbers or finite fractions, such as the square root of two.

logic: the science of good reasoning (from Greek *logos*), which was unsystematic in ancient philosophy until forms of valid argument were studied by Aristotle. Beginning with early Stoics, it became one of three basic divisions of philosophy, and included what we call epistemology and grammar (compare ethics and physics).

logos: this general Greek word for things said is used by philosophers both for various kinds of explanation or reason, and for the mental faculty by which we reason and explain things.

Lyceum: Aristotle's school in Athens, established at the gymnasium of that name. It also became known as Peripatetic, from the *peripatos* or colonnade there. The site of the Lyceum was rediscovered in Athens in 1997.

Magna Graecia: Latin for 'Great Greece', referring to southern Italy and sometimes also to Sicily, which were colonized by Greeks in Archaic times.

metaphysics: the study of certain questions which go beyond what natural science can explain, such as the nature of God, space, time, causality and freedom. In the study of ancient philosophy the term often refers to theories of basic elements of reality or kinds of being, as in Aristotle's *Metaphysics* (whose title, added centuries later, is the first recorded occurrence of the word).

neo-Platonism: a philosophical and spiritual tradition begun by Plotinus, claiming especially inspiration by Plato but also attempting to reconcile Plato and Aristotle. It includes Porphyry, Iamblichus, Proclus, Hypatia and Philoponus, and it influenced many early fathers of the Christian church.

nihilism: arguments, theories or behavior implying that nothing has genuine meaning or value (from Latin *nihil*, 'nothing').

orchestra: the round, flat central part of an ancient theatre where the chorus sings and dances (compare *theatron* and *skene*).

pan-Hellenism: the spirit of common Greekness, usually with the feeling of superiority to all non-Greeks or 'barbarians'. Pan-Hellenic sanctuaries, such as Delphi and Epidaurus, served all Greeks; some, such as Olympia, even excluded all non-Greeks.

physics: from Greek *physis* or 'nature' this term embraced a broad range of ancient studies, including cosmology, physiology, and the 'nature' of basic reality (before the term 'metaphysics' existed). Aristotle's *Physics* is his theory of natural changes. Beginning with early Stoics, physics became one of three basic divisions of philosophy (compare ethics and logic).

polis: the 'city-state' or typical community from Archaic until Hellenistic times. These were usually politically autonomous with an urban administrative, religious and market centre.

polymath: one who knows or studies many kinds of things (from *poly*, 'much', and *mathein*, 'to learn').

pre-Socratics: a modern conventional term grouping philosophers and scientists up to the time of Socrates (from Thales to Democritus), but not the contemporary poets, playwrights and sophists.

Pythagoreans: followers of Pythagoras either in a philosophical tradition (which includes mathematical and musical studies) or a religious-political tradition (which includes vegetarianism, reincarnation, and a communitarian lifestyle).

Pythian: a term referring to Apollo and his sanctuary at Delphi, derived from the mythical serpent Python who preceded him there. The Pythia was the priestess of the oracle there, the pan-Hellenic Pythian Games were held there, and Pindar's Pythian Odes honored winners there.

rationalism: the view that at least some genuine knowledge cannot be achieved or justified by empirical evidence. Parmenides and Plato are considered stellar examples of rationalists (compare empiricism).

rhetoric: the art of persuasive speaking. It was developed by sophists and other teachers in Classical times as a staple of higher education and of practical politics in democratic assemblies and lawcourts. Plato famously disparaged rhetoric as causing persuasion without knowledge or even truth, but Aristotle's sympathetic study influenced all later theories (compare dialectic).

skene: the scene building behind the actors in an ancient theatre (compare *orchestra* and *theatron*).

skepticism: a philosophical position whose goal is to suspend judgement (neither affirm nor deny), perhaps even about everything. The main ancient schools of skepticism were the followers of Pyrrho and the Academy in its skeptical period (compare dogmatism).

stoa: a common type of building that basically consisted of an open colonnade opposite a wall with a roof over the space between. Zeno of Citium founded Stoicism (sometimes called 'The Stoa') while teaching at the Painted Stoa in Athens.

Stoicism: the philosophical tradition founded by Zeno, Cleanthes, and Chrysippus. It thrived for centuries into Roman times, including Seneca, Epictetus, and the emperor Marcus Aurelius.

teleology: explanation in terms of ends or goals. Plato and Aristotle famously pursued teleological explanations in science, as opposed to mechanistic theories like the atomism of Democritus and Epicurus.

temple: a typical but not universal feature of Greek sanctuaries, it is the god's house, containing the cult statue of the god and the most valuable offerings to the god (compare altar).

theatron: the part of an ancient theatre where spectators sat, typically semicircular and built on a natural slope (compare *orchestra* and *skene*).

theogony: an account of the origins and generations of gods (*theoi*), as in Hesiod's *Theogony*.

Time Line of ancient authors

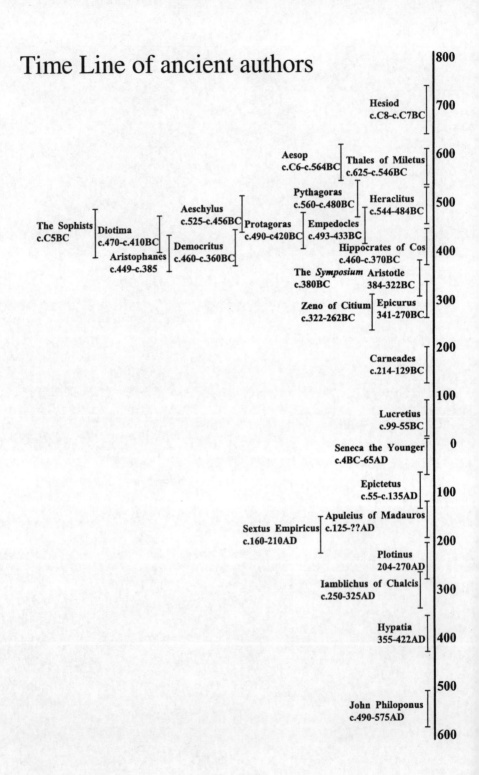

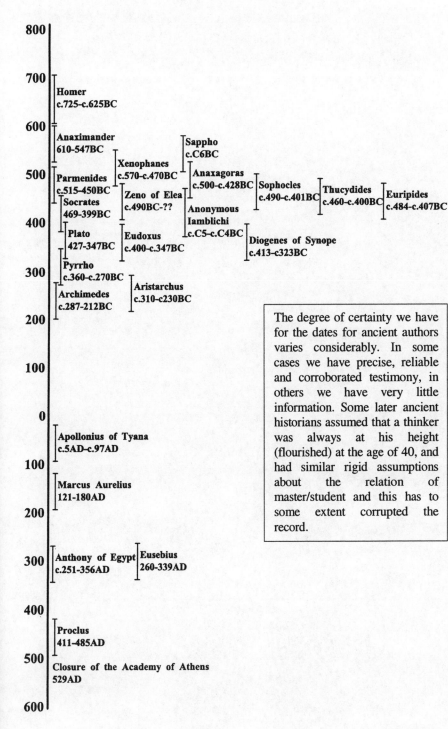

800

700 ⊤ Homer
c.725–c.625BC

600 ⊤
Anaximander
610–547BC   Sappho
                                         c.C6BC
500   Xenophanes
Parmenides   c.570–c.470BC   Anaxagoras
c.515–450BC   c.500–c.428BC   Sophocles   Thucydides   Euripides
    Socrates   Zeno of Elea   c.490–c.401BC   c.460–c.400BC   c.484–c.407BC
    469–399BC   c.490BC–??   Anonymous
400   Iamblichi
     Plato   Eudoxus   c.C5–c.C4BC
     427–347BC   c.400–c.347BC   Diogenes of Synope
                                                         c.413–c323BC
Pyrrho
300 c.360–c.270BC
                     Aristarchus
Archimedes   c.310–c230BC
c.287–212BC
200

100

0

       Apollonius of Tyana
       c.5AD–c.97AD
100

       Marcus Aurelius
       121–180AD
200

The degree of certainty we have
for the dates for ancient authors
varies considerably. In some
cases we have precise, reliable
and corroborated testimony, in
others we have very little
information. Some later ancient
historians assumed that a thinker
was always at his height
(flourished) at the age of 40, and
had similar rigid assumptions
about the relation of
master/student and this has to
some extent corrupted the
record.

300   Anthony of Egypt   Eusebius
      c.251–356AD   260–339AD

400

       Proclus
       411–485AD
500
       Closure of the Academy of Athens
       529AD
600

© Andrew Gregory